Your Reading

NCTE Editorial Board: Pat Cordeiro; Hazel Davis; Brenda Greene; Richard Luckert; Alleen Pace Nilsen; Karen Smith, Chair, *ex officio*, Dawn Boyer, NCTE Staff Liaison

Committee on the Middle School and Junior High Booklist

Barbara G. Samuels, Chair
G. Kylene Beers, Associate Chair
Richard F. Abrahamson
Steven D. Bauer
Lois Buckman
Betty Carter
Claudia H. DeShay
Margaret H. Hill
Mary Beth Hines
Marvin Hoffman
Be Be Hood
Rosemary Oliphant Ingham
Lee Kobayashi
Karen S. Kutiper
Teri S. Lesesne
Hollis Lowery-Moore
Karen Ferris Morgan
Steven J. Rakow
Judith Romo
Rosemary Smith
Mary Snyder
Marti Turner
Eleanore S. Tyson
Judy Mayne Wallis
Maureen White
Patricia Potter Wilson

 Bibliography Series

Your Reading

An Annotated Booklist for Middle School and Junior High

1995-96 Edition

Barbara G. Samuels and G. Kylene Beers, Editors,
and the Committee on the Middle School and Junior High Booklist of the National Council of Teachers of English

With a Foreword by
Joan Lowery Nixon

National Council of Teachers of English
1111 W. Kenyon Road, Urbana, IL 61801-1096

Grateful acknowledgment is made for permission to reprint the quotation from Poem #1263 by Emily Dickinson on page 267: Reprinted by permission of the publishers and the Trustees of Amherst College from *The Poems of Emily Dickinson,* Thomas H. Johnson, ed., Cambridge, Mass.: The Belknap Press of Harvard University Press, Copyright © 1951, 1955, 1979, 1983 by the President and Fellows of Harvard College.

Manuscript Editor: Anne McCrary Sullivan

Production Editor: Rona S. Smith

Interior Design: Doug Burnett

Series Cover Design: R. Maul

Cover Illustration: Victoria Martin Pohlmann

NCTE Stock Number: 59435-3050

© 1996 by the National Council of Teachers of English. All rights reserved. Printed in the United States of America.

It is the policy of NCTE in its journals and other publications to provide a forum for the open discussion of ideas concerning the content and the teaching of English and the language arts. Publicity accorded to any particular point of view does not imply endorsement by the Executive Committee, the Board of Directors, or the membership at large, except in announcements of policy, where such endorsement is clearly specified.

ISSN 1051-4740

ISBN 0-8141-5943-5

About the NCTE Bibliography Series

The National Council of Teachers of English is proud to be part of a process that we feel is important. It begins when an educator who knows literature and its value to students and teachers is chosen by the NCTE Executive Committee to be a booklist editor. That editor then works with teachers and librarians who review, select, and annotate hundreds of new trade books sent to them by publishers. It's a complicated process, one that can last three or four years. But because of their dedication and strong belief in the need to let others know about the good literature that's available, these professionals volunteer their time in a way that serves as an inspiration to all of us. The members of the committee that compiled this volume are listed on one of the first pages, and we are grateful for their hard work.

In our bibliography series are five different booklists, each focused on a particular audience, each updated regularly. These are *Adventuring with Books* (pre-K through grade 6), *Kaleidoscope* (multicultural literature, grades K through 8), *Your Reading* (middle school/junior high), *Books for You* (senior high), and *High Interest—Easy Reading* (middle school, junior/senior high reluctant readers). Together, these volumes list thousands of the most recent children's and young adult trade books. Although the works included cover a wide range of topics, they all have one thing in common: they're good books that students and teachers alike enjoy.

Of course, no single book is right for everyone or every purpose, so inclusion in this booklist is not necessarily an endorsement from NCTE. However, it does indicate that the professionals who make up the booklist committee feel that the work in question is worthy of teachers' and students' attention, whether for its informative or aesthetic qualities. On the other hand, exclusion from an NCTE booklist is not necessarily a judgment on the quality of a given book or publisher. Many factors—space, time, availability of certain books, publisher participation—may influence the final shape of the list.

We hope that you will find this booklist a useful resource in discovering new titles and authors, and we hope that you will collect the other booklists in the NCTE series. Our mission is to help improve the teaching and learning of English and the language arts, and we feel the quality of our booklists contributes substantially toward that goal. We think you will agree.

Dawn Boyer
Director of Acquisitions
and Development in Publications

Contents

Acknowledgments   ix

Foreword: We Have the Power   xi

Introduction   xiii

I. Growing Up

1. Family and Home   3
2. Friendship and Romance   31
3. Problems and Challenges   49
4. Playing the Game: Stories about Sports   69

II. Imagined Lands

5. Myths, Legends, and Folklore   75
6. The Fantastic World of Fantasy   87
7. Science with a Twist: Science Fiction   103

III. Shudder and Shake!

8. Whodunnit? Mysteries   115
9. Occult, Horror, Ghosts, and Unexplained Phenomena   121
10. Staying Alive! Adventure and Survival   135

IV. People, Problems, and Places: Yesterday and Today

11. Looking Back: Historical Fiction   147
12. Understanding the Past: History   167
13. People to Know: Autobiography and Biography   192
14. Customs, Cultures, and Lands   210
15. Analyzing Issues of Today   215

V. Science All around You

   16. Physical Science   231
   17. Nature, Ecology, and the Environment   239
   18. The Animal Kingdom   248
   19. Mental and Physical Health   257

VI. Words to Remember

   20. Poetry   269
   21. Short Stories   278

VII. Facts, Figures, and Fun

   22. The Arts! Music, Dance, Drama, Painting, and Crafts   289
   23. More about Sports   300
   24. How, Why, and What: Fun, Facts, and Trivia   306

Appendix A: 100 Books from 25 Years of Young Adult Literature (1967–1992)   317

Appendix B: Award-Winning Books in Your Reading   321

Directory of Publishers   329

Author Index   335

Title Index   345

Subject Index   360

Editors   377

About the Committee   379

Acknowledgments

This edition of *Your Reading* represents the hard work of a group of dedicated colleagues and professionals. Our committee responded enthusiastically to the challenge of reviewing hundreds of books and creating well-written annotations that will stimulate reading by junior high and middle school students. For two years, they received the boxes of books we sent them, searched for additional titles, and contributed their energy and expertise to the project. Each member of our committee took responsibility for a chapter of the book. They answered our cries for help and responded with extra annotations and advice whenever we called upon them. We cannot thank them enough! These teachers, librarians, and university professors are a unique and special group.

In addition to the members of the committee, a few other people contributed their time and talent. Catherine Bush Partridge read many of the books in the sports chapters. Dawn Bradford and Cathy Moore also reviewed books and wrote annotations.

Also, we must offer a special thanks to the publishers whose generosity provided the books that are the heart and life of this project. We appreciate their commitment to the promotion of a population of readers. Without their support, this booklist would not exist.

The NCTE staff, while experiencing changes during our tenure as editors, supported us by answering our relentless questions about format, editing, and organization.

Finally, we could not have done this project without the continuing support and encouragement from our husbands, Vic Samuels and Brad Beers. They lugged boxes of books, made trips to the post office, provided advice on word-processing problems, lived with piles of books and papers cluttering every room of our houses, prepared dinners, tended to children and other family obligations, and generally made it possible for us to complete the book.

Barbara G. Samuels and G. Kylene Beers

Foreword: We Have the Power

Aladdin had a genie at his command.

"Take me wherever I wish, Genie. Bring me whatever I want. Give me the world, the moon, the stars."

Powerful stuff . . . for those days before books.

Today we don't need to rub a lamp to get our wishes. All we have to do is open a book of our choice and travel wherever our mood takes us. That's *real* power.

Want to have fun being scared? We can join Agatha Christie, pairing up with private eyes or amateur detectives to cleverly solve crimes; or we can use our wits to escape from danger.

Have a yen for fantasy? Search for unicorns, wizards, and magic stardust. Slip into the enchanted worlds created by C. S. Lewis and J. R. R. Tolkien.

Looking for excitement? Turn a book cover and jump into adventure to rival anything an enchanted genie could dream up. Walk on the moon with Neil Armstrong. Pilot a spacecraft and outwit evil forces from another planet. Save a civilization.

Delve into history with the courageous Anne Frank and Rosa Parks. Leave our friends and family to join a wagon train heading for Oregon. Fight beside Jim Bowie and Davy Crockett at the Alamo. Search for a brother missing after the Battle of Gettysburg.

Dream of love through the sonnets of Elizabeth Barrett Browning and William Shakespeare. Slip with the fog and Carl Sandburg into the rhythm of Chicago. Let our minds play with the magic of e. e. cummings and T. S. Eliot.

Learn of the world around us. Learn of the worlds within us. Read to understand our love, our pain, and our eagerness to find ourselves so we can grow.

Step into science. March into math. Explore. Invent. Create new dreams.

Books, books, books. Enjoy them to their fullest. Reading is as important to our quality of life as breathing, sleeping, and eating.

Read the old books and read the new ones. Gulp them down like popcorn or savor them, tasting with tiny bites. Delight in familiar favorites, but investigate different flavors. Gobble them down or spit them out and reach for another.

Relish the freedom to explore and expand the world we live in. Read to run through the gamut of joy, laughter, excitement, indignation, anger, and even tears.

Read *about* books in the pages that follow. Make choices, then find those books and enjoy!

Read! We have the power.

Joan Lowery Nixon

Joan Lowery Nixon is the only four-time winner of the Edgar Allan Poe Best Juvenile Mystery Award for The Kidnapping of Christina Lattimore, The Seance, The Name of the Game Was Murder, *and* The Other Side of Dark. *In addition to her reputation as "the grande dame of mysteries for young readers," she is also known for her historical books, such as the Orphan Train and Ellis Island series. Her books, over a hundred titles, combine suspense, drama, and appealing characters.*

Introduction

My task which I am trying to achieve is, by the power of the written word to make you hear, to make you feel—it is, before all, to make you see.

Joseph Conrad

Like Joseph Conrad, the NCTE Committee on the Middle School and Junior High Booklist wants to help you feel, hear, and see—through the power of books. Because we believe in the power of words, we, the writers of *Your Reading,* spent over two years reading, rereading, discussing, sharing, and writing about books we think you will enjoy and find meaningful. The purpose of our book is to connect you with titles that will enhance *your reading.* Whether you are looking for a book because you need to complete an assignment or project, because you want to learn more about a topic that interests you, or because you are browsing to find something good to read, *Your Reading* can help you find the right book. Published by the National Council of Teachers of English, the various editions of *Your Reading* provide an ongoing annotated list for junior high and middle school students, teachers, librarians, and parents.

What books are listed in this edition of *Your Reading*?

Thousands of books are published every year. It's impossible to read all of them. To help you find the best books, a committee of teachers and librarians screened books that were published in 1993 and 1994. We also included reissues of older books, so a book that was originally published prior to 1993 but reissued during 1993 or 1994 may be annotated in this edition of *Your Reading.* Although we can't say we read everything published in those two years, we tried to identify as many books as possible that junior high and middle school students would find useful, interesting, and meaningful.

How is the listing of books organized in *Your Reading*?

As we read the books, we found that they seemed to group themselves in a variety of ways. A quick look at the Table of Contents will show you that *Your Reading* is organized into seven sections and twenty-four chapters. Within each chapter, the annotations are arranged alphabetically by the author's last name.

The first section, Growing Up, has four chapters about teens maturing into adulthood. Novels in the chapter called "Family and Home" are focused on family issues such as sibling rivalries, divorce, relationships with parents and stepparents, or coping with aging grandparents. The other chapters in this section involve friends, romance, school, sports, or tough life situations.

Perhaps you prefer to let your imagination wander in the Imagined Lands section. "Myths, Legends, and Folklore" includes versions of stories handed down to us through the generations. Many wonderful new editions of familiar stories are listed in this chapter, as well as tales from cultures around the world. Books of fantasy and science fiction to stimulate your creative thinking are also a part of this section.

Do you like books with suspense, adventure, or unexplained phenomena? Shudder and Shake is the section for you. Mysteries and survival stories, ghosts and horror stories will stir your blood and keep you reading to the last page.

The books annotated in People, Problems, and Places: Yesterday and Today can help you with your social studies projects. The books are grouped together in five chapters: "Looking Back: Historical Fiction," "Understanding the Past: History," "People to Know: Autobiography and Biography," "Customs, Cultures, and Lands," and "Analyzing Issues of Today." In these books, you can get to know fascinating people, places, and events that have shaped history, as well as issues, people, and problems that are creating history today.

How do you feel about science? Whether you want to know more about the environment and how to save our planet, wonder about the way things work, enjoy studying the stars and planets, find fascinating the habits of animals, or want to know more about your own body, the section titled Science All around You offers many choices. (It might also provide ideas for a science-fair project.)

Obviously, some categories overlap. In the section Words to Remember we grouped all the short stories in one chapter and the poems in another. Short stories include some ghost stories that could also be listed in Chapter 9, "Occult, Horror, Ghosts, and Unexplained Phenomena," and other stories about families or growing up. But we chose to list them by genre. One way you can find books about a subject that might be listed in another category is to look up the topic in the subject index. If you look under "ghosts" in the subject index, for example, you will find a listing of all the books about ghosts, not just those in Chapter 9.

We ended this volume of *Your Reading* with Facts, Figures, and Fun. This is the section where you'll find books about how to build or make things, books about your favorite sports or entertainment, books of jokes, and trivia. Browse through this section. Something is sure to catch your attention.

How can I use the different indexes at the end of the book?

At the end of *Your Reading,* you will find three different indexes. Each index directs you to a chapter and annotation number (i.e., 2.22 directs you to Chapter 2, the twenty-second annotation). One index lists the authors of the books alphabetically. Another index lists the titles. The index you may use the most often is the subject index. If you are looking for a book on a particular topic, check here. For example, suppose you want to learn more about Native Americans. If you look under Native Americans in the subject index, you will be directed to *Fly Like an Eagle,* a novel in Chapter 1, *The Choctaw Code,* historical fiction in Chapter 11, and *Wounded Knee,* a history book in Chapter 12. Though each of these books is annotated in a different chapter, the index will lead you directly to them.

Can *Your Reading* help me with a school assignment?

Absolutely! We hope you will use *Your Reading* regularly to help you find books about the topics you are studying in school. Suppose your class is about to begin a thematic unit on the environment. An entire chapter of *Your Reading* is devoted to books that focus on saving the planet. Browsing through that chapter should lead you to several helpful books. In addition, the subject index might lead you to fictional works about teens who worked on environmental issues.

Perhaps your assignment is to write a paper about some aspect of World War II. The subject index will point you to specific novels in the "Looking Back: Historical Fiction" chapter; to biographies and autobiographies in "People to Know"; and to historical accounts in "Understanding the Past: History." The subject index will save you the trouble of reading every annotation in those three chapters to find the specific books that will help you collect information for your paper.

Does *Your Reading* include series books?

Of course. Many of the books published today are organized into series by the book publishers. We annotated at least one book in any series we selected, and we included the titles or subjects of other books in the series that were published during 1993 and 1994. To help answer your questions and guide your research, the subject index will lead you to some of these other series books. We could not include the names of all the books in some of the series because new books continue to be published. For nonfiction series, our subject index at the end of the book includes information about other titles in the series. For example, an ecology series that has separate books on endangered animals would be listed in the subject index under each of the endangered animals included.

How can we find out about titles published before 1993?

To find annotations of books published prior to 1993, we recommend that you look in previous editions of *Your Reading*. The National Council of Teachers of English has published nine prior editions, and one of them may help you find the book you want.

To help you identify some outstanding titles published prior to 1993, we have included an appendix titled "100 Books from 25 Years of Young Adult Literature." This is a list of one hundred of the best books published during the past twenty-five years. Obviously, our list does not have every important book published since 1967, but we have tried to include the best-known, touchstone books for junior high and middle school students. If you haven't read many of these, you might want to try a few.

How can we identify books that have won awards or other recognition in 1993 and 1994?

Some journals, groups of teachers and librarians, and even young people themselves publish lists of what they consider the best books for each year. To help you identify those titles which others have recognized, we have included a list of noted books in the appendix "Award-Winning Books in *Your Reading*." Because we didn't want to limit your reading to only those books which had been recognized as "best" by others, we have placed this information at the end of the book rather than within the chapters. That way, you can select the books that meet your own particular needs, not necessarily those that others have chosen for you.

The quotation from Joseph Conrad at the beginning of this introduction refers to his goal as a writer, using the power of words to make you see. All the authors in this book have used words in powerful ways. As you wind your way through *Your Reading*, we hope you'll enjoy reading their words. We did! Reading helps us see ourselves and the world around us in new ways. Enjoy!

I Growing Up

He was always reading. At his meals an open book lay by his side on the table. His mutton and potatoes might grow cold, but his interest in a work never cooled. He invariably sallied forth, book in hand, reading to himself if alone, or aloud if he had a companion. He took a volume to bed with him and read as long as his candle lasted; then he slept—impatiently, no doubt—until it was light, and he recommenced reading at the early dawn.

> Thomas Jefferson Hogg, English biographer, describing
> Percy Bysshe Shelley, English poet

1 Family and Home

1.1 Ackerman, Karen. **The Leaves in October.** Dell/Yearling, 1993. 117 pp. ISBN 0-440-40868-7.

Livvy and her brother Younger live in a homeless shelter while their father searches for a job. Livvy counts the days until they will leave. To earn money, she makes and sells tissue-paper carnations. After earning $200, she believes they will be able to join their father. But he has gotten a job in road construction and believes it best for the children to live in a foster home for a while. Livvy is hurt and angry over broken promises.

1.2 Adler, C. S. **Daddy's Climbing Trees.** Clarion Books, 1993. 134 pp. ISBN 0-395-63032-0.

Although her father never returns with that ice cream cone he just *had* to have, Jessica convinces herself that he isn't really the victim of a hit-and-run accident. She believes that he is alive and well at their former house in Oldminesville. So she and her brother Tycho sneak out, trekking across the state park, determined to find him. The adventure offers more challenges than anticipated, leading Jessica to learn some important lessons about life and love.

1.3 Angell, Judie. **Yours Truly.** Orchard Books, 1993. 184 pp. ISBN 0-531-05472-1.

Nicki Stine is thirteen years old and growing up in a hurry. She, her mother, and her younger brother have moved to escape her father's ruinous drug habit. Resentful of the new man in her mother's life, Nicki drinks, takes drugs, and joyrides with older friends; she is always on the edge of serious trouble. When her unsteady father reappears, she is forced to make some important decisions about her future.

1.4 Avi. **Blue Heron.** Avon/Camelot, 1993. 186 pp. ISBN 0-380-72043-4.

Maggie Lavcheck believes in magic. When Maggie's father leaves her and her mother, he promises that he will magically solve all of Maggie's problems. Six years later, Maggie's father becomes her problem during her visit with him and his new family at a lakeside cottage. Maggie questions her father's erratic behavior and wonders how she can help him and his family. She looks to a mysterious bird for the answers her father can no longer provide.

1.5 Banks, Jacqueline Turner. **The New One.** Houghton Mifflin, 1994. 107 pp. ISBN 0-395-66610-4.

Judge, his twin brother Jury, and their friends try to make the new African American student feel a part of their group from the first day. But Ayreal doesn't seem to appreciate the offer of friendship. Judge and Jury have some other worries, however. Their mom's new boyfriend Frank may soon become their new father. They have to convince their mom that Frank is not Mr. Right. Surprisingly, Ayreal may be the one who can help.

1.6 Banks, Lynne Reid. **One More River.** Avon/Camelot, 1993. 248 pp. ISBN 0-380-71563-5.

Lesley Shelby is a fourteen-year-old Canadian Jewish girl whose store-owner father decides to emigrate to Israel following his son's conversion to Catholicism. A resistant Lesley suffers through adjustment to kibbutz life, as do her parents, now workers in the dairy barn and the laundry. Life becomes more complicated as Lesley enters a long-distance relationship with an Arab boy. The family lives through the exhilaration and the losses the entire country experiences during the 1967 war.

1.7 Barrett, Elizabeth. **Free Fall.** HarperCollins, 1994. 249 pp. ISBN 0-06-024465-8.

Ginnie Ryan spends her seventeenth summer sorting out both anger and confusion. Ginnie's anger comes from learning that her parents sent her to stay with her grandmother because they were considering divorce while she was gone. Her confusion comes from her involvement with new friends and a new romance that seems out of hand. All in all, Ginnie feels as if her whole life is hurtling out of control, and she is not sure what to do about it.

1.8 Bauer, Marion Dane. **A Question of Trust.** Scholastic, 1994. 130 pp. ISBN 0-590-47915-6.

Brad and his younger brother Charlie are so angry and hurt by their mother's decision to leave and live on her own that they refuse to even return her phone calls. To console themselves, they secretly take in a pregnant cat, against their father's prohibitions. They mistakenly assume that the mother has killed one of her kittens and desperately try to protect the survivor.

1.9 Bawden, Nina. **The Real Plato Jones.** Clarion Books, 1993. 166 pp. ISBN 0-395-66972-3.

Plato's half-Greek and half-Welsh ancestry makes him uncomfortable. He wants to be one whole, himself. When Plato's Greek grandfather dies, he flies to Greece to confront the mystery of his grandfather's life. Searching for answers about his grandfather adds to Plato's self-doubt and confusion. Finally, however, a village tragedy helps Plato find himself.

1.10 Blacker, Terence. **Homebird.** Bradbury Press, 1993. 139 pp. ISBN 0-02-710685-3.

Life has been pretty normal until now for thirteen-year-old Nicky Morrison, but things are changing quickly. His parents' marriage is in trouble, and he has run away from his new boarding school. Nicky tries to buy some time to sort things out and ends up living in an abandoned building known as St. Mark's Road Squat. When his housemates recruit him for criminal capers, Nicky discovers how tough life can be on the streets of London.

1.11 Blume, Judy. **Here's to You, Rachel Robinson.** Orchard Books, 1993. 196 pp. ISBN 0-531-06801-3.

In this sequel to *Just as Long as We're Together,* Rachel faces upheaval in her life when her brother Charles returns home after being expelled from boarding school. Charles knows just how to needle her, teasing her about her status as a "gifted" intellect. Her friends like him and can't understand why she is upset. As Rachel struggles to live with Charles, she learns more about her own identity and becomes closer to others, particularly some very handsome members of the opposite sex.

1.12 Bond, Nancy. **Truth to Tell.** Macmillan, 1994. 325 pp. ISBN 0-689-50601-5.

Leaving Cambridge, England, and her stepfather makes no sense to fourteen-year-old Alice, but her mother is determined to take an opportunity to assist Miss Fairchild in writing the history of her estate, Florestan, in New Zealand. When Alice and her mother arrive at Florestan, however, they find themselves tending to the elderly Miss Fairchild and her enormous, neglected house instead of writing the book.

1.13 Boyd, Candy Dawson. **Chevrolet Saturdays.** Macmillan, 1993. 176 pp. ISBN 0-02-711765-0.

The divorce of Joey's parents, and his mother's subsequent remarriage to a man he can only bring himself to call Mr. Johnson, have thrown Joey into a tailspin. He is in constant trouble with his fifth-grade teacher, who fails to recognize Joey's scientific gifts. When, through an act of negligence, Joey is responsible for the near-death of Mr. Johnson's beloved dog, he gains a new understanding of responsibility.

1.14   Buchanan, Dawna Lisa. **The Falcon's Wing.** Avon/Camelot, 1993. 116 pp. ISBN 0-380-72102-3.

After her mother's death, Bryn and her father move to Canada to live with Aunt Pearl and Cousin Winnie on their farm. Bryn is miserable among these strangers. Her grief for her mother colors everything that happens, pushing her into a near tragedy. The only thing that can mend Bryn's broken heart is for her to become part of a family again, if she can allow those who love her to reach her.

1.15   Buehler, Stephanie Jona. **There's No Surf in Cleveland.** Clarion Books, 1993. 136 pp. ISBN 0-395-62162-3.

Sixth-grader Phillip wants his old home in Ohio back, complete with snow at Christmas and Dad. But since his parents' divorce, Phillip has lived with Los Angeles sunshine and sweat. His mom and best friend, Washington, tell him to "adjust." Phillip hates that word. Finally, a starfish, a tofu burrito, and the school bully help him learn how not to be miserable forever.

1.16   Bunting, Eve. **Sharing Susan.** HarperTrophy, 1994. 122 pp. ISBN 0-06-440430-7.

Twelve-year-old Susan knows something is wrong at home. Her parents are engaging in secret conversations, and they seem upset. Susan learns that they have spoken with an attorney and suspects her parents must be getting a divorce. Even though Susan tries to imagine the worst, she is unprepared for the news that she and another baby were switched at birth. Now, twelve years later, her mom and dad break the news that her biological parents want her back.

1.17   Bunting, Eve. **The In-Between Days.** HarperCollins, 1994. 119 pp. ISBN 0-06-023609-4.

George Bowser is quite content with the life he, his father, and younger brother James have on the island. During the summer, George spends time with his friends fishing and riding bikes. After school in the winter he helps his father work on the bikes for the rental shop he owns. The pattern of his life is completely upset, however, when Caroline Best and his father become more than just friends. George's plan to keep Caroline away from his family works, but during the in-between days of winter, George learns about how love and sacrifice can keep a family together.

1.18 Cannon, A. E. **Amazing Gracie.** Dell Publishing, 1993. 214 pp. ISBN 0-440-21570-6.

In troubled families, super-kids like Gracie often emerge to keep things together. Gracie's father died young, and her mother, Cynthia, suffers from severe depression; when she collapses, there's only Gracie to take care of things. When Gracie is fifteen years old, Cynthia marries a good-hearted but inept man with an endearing but emotionally needy six-year-old son from a previous marriage. The family tries to make a new start, but Gracie's mother attempts suicide, putting Gracie through a series of emotional crises.

1.19 Carris, Joan. **Just a Little Ham.** Minstrel Books, 1993. 135 pp. ISBN 0-671-74783-5.

Cory is used to her psychologist-mother bringing home animals to observe, so she isn't too surprised to see a week-old orphaned mini-pig sitting on the kitchen table. Pandora soon becomes part of the family, jogging, swimming, and raiding the refrigerator. Cory thinks it's fun being a pig's mom until Pandora unlocks the door, escapes, and Cory finds out that there are laws against keeping farm animals in town. How can she convince everyone that Pandora's really just a pet?

1.20 Casey, Maude. **Over the Water.** Henry Holt and Company, 1994. 241 pp. ISBN 0-8050-3276-2.

Isolated by her strict Catholic mother, Mary is forced to live friendless on her grandmother's farm in Ireland. Working alongside her relatives, Mary learns about her heritage. She begins to see her mother in a new way as she starts to understand the prejudice and sorrow that surrounded her mother's life.

1.21 Cooney, Caroline B. **Whatever Happened to Janie?** Delacorte Press, 1993. 199 pp. ISBN 0-385-31035-8.

In this sequel to *The Face on the Milk Carton*, fifteen-year-old Janie Johnson discovers she is actually Jennie Spring, kidnapped at the age of three and now presumed dead. Learning she is alive, Jennie's birth family insists she live with them. But she can neither relinquish her former life nor cultivate a new one, despite pleas from both sets of parents to do so. Confused, Janie attempts to transform herself into Jennie, causing upheaval while inspiring love and pain in both "real" families.

1.22 Cooper, Melrose. **Life Riddles.** Henry Holt and Company, 1993. 90 pp. ISBN 0-8050-2613-4.

At twelve, Janelle's life is difficult. With her dad gone, the family struggles with almost no money, disconnected electricity, and little hope of things getting better. When Aunt Barbara encourages her to follow her dream and become a writer, Janelle finds that she indeed has something to say. Her writing becomes not only a way to help the family but also a way to cope with the hardships of life.

1.23 Creech, Sharon. **Walk Two Moons.** HarperCollins, 1994. 280 pp. ISBN 0-06-023334-6.

Thirteen-year-old Sal journeys with her grandparents from her new home in Ohio, where her father's new "friend" Margaret lives, to Idaho, where her mother has recently moved. Sal hopes to reach Idaho before her mother's birthday. Anxious to pass the time, Sal tells the story of Phoebe, a friend whose mother has disappeared. But as Phoebe's story unfolds, so too does Sal's, and Sal renders a powerful account of her struggles to understand her mother's departure.

1.24 Crew, Linda. **Nekomah Creek Christmas.** Delacorte Press, 1994. 147 pp. ISBN 0-385-32047-7.

This companion to *Nekomah Creek* treats readers to more lively living with the untraditional Hummer family. Along with the typical chaos of Christmas preparation, the Hummers haphazardly prepare for an income tax audit and for Robby Hummer's costume for the school play. The humiliated Robby finds himself wearing green tights and pointed ears just to please his mother!

1.25 Cuneo, Mary Louise. **Anne Is Elegant.** HarperCollins, 1993. 167 pp. ISBN 0-06-022992-6.

It is a cold, snowy Christmas season in 1936 when Anna's adopted grandmother dies, an occasion Anna marks by noting its parallels with the recent death of her infant brother Johnny. Anna chronicles her own responses to both events as she stands witness to the curious grieving processes of adults, many of whom seem to lack effective strategies for coping with death. Fortunately, her kinship with Aunt Maria strengthens Anna, enabling her to confront anger, pain, and some unresolved issues related to her brother's death.

1.26 Davis, Deborah. **My Brother Has AIDS.** Atheneum, 1994. 199 pp. ISBN 0-689-31922-3.

For Lacy Mullins, being thirteen is about friendships, school, and swimming. She spends her days practicing and planning how she can become a better and more competitive swimmer; that is, until she learns about Jack, her brother. Twelve years older than Lacy and a lawyer in Denver, Josh shocks everyone when he says he wants to come home. Then they find out why: he has AIDS and is dying.

1.27 Derby, Pat. **Grams, Her Boyfriend, My Family, and Me.** Farrar, Straus, and Giroux, 1994. 195 pp. ISBN 0-374-38131-3.

To survive living with four sisters, Andy keeps a low profile, but that works only until his mother gets a job. Now he has to share chores and babysitting responsibilities, which cut into his soccer practice. How can he make the team if he has to miss practice all of the time? Adding to his woes, his grandmother moves in with them, and Andy finds himself being advisor to her love life and helping her elope.

1.28 DeVito, Cara. **Where I Want to Be.** Houghton Mifflin, 1993. 187 pp. ISBN 0-395-64592-1.

Whether hitchhiking to Lake Havasu or teasing her guardians, older half-brothers Darren and Kyle, Kristie enjoys mischief. Darren and Kyle learn to live with Kristie's antics as Kristie adjusts to life without her father. Then her mother, who abandoned her years ago, re-appears, threatening the fragile stability of Kristie's life. Kristie realizes that coping with change is not her strong suit.

1.29 Dickinson, Peter. **A Bone from a Dry Sea.** Delacorte Press, 1993. 199 pp. ISBN 0-385-30821-3.

Vinny, an archeologist's daughter, goes on a dig with her father in hopes of sorting out family problems while uncovering secrets of the past. While participating in the dig, she comes across a find that changes thoughts on human history. That find comes to life as you are taken to prehistoric time to watch another young girl, Li, and see how her intelligence changes the course of her clan. Told through the alternating points of view of Vinny and Li, the story allows you to see the conflicts and confusion that come with growing up, whether now or long ago.

1.30 Duffey, Betsy. **Coaster.** Viking, 1994. 114 pp. ISBN 0-670-85480-8.

Roller coasters are all that twelve-year-old Hart is interested in. They are the connection to his father now that his parents are divorced. He spends his spare time secretly building one in the woods with his friend Frankie. His life would be perfect if only his mother weren't getting serious about Dub, the goofy TV weatherman. An afternoon spent with Dub to ride "the Jaguar," a letter from his father, and a midnight coaster ride on the "Termite" help Hart realize that maybe his life is close to perfect now.

1.31 Dyjak, Elisabeth. **I Should Have Listened to Moon.** Minstrel Books, 1993. 136 pp. ISBN 0-671-73830-5.

Twelve-year-old Nadine does not want her Grandmother Lyon moving in and sharing her bedroom. She thinks other things in her life are already changing too fast. Even her best friend Moon is wearing nail polish and talking about boys. Then Lyon gets lost for one day, and Nadine realizes that Lyon has problems, too. She decides to help her grandmother, and finds out that growing up can be fun.

1.32 Fakih, Kimberly Olson. **High on the Hog.** Farrar, Straus, and Giroux, 1994. 166 pp. ISBN 0-374-33209-6.

The family may be moving from Iowa to New York City to live high on the hog, but twelve-year-old Trapp has no intention of joining them. She convinces her parents to let her visit her great-grandparents' farm for the summer with the secret intentions of staying at the farm permanently. Trapp, however, uncovers a long-kept family secret while staying with her great-grandparents and has to reconsider what "home" and "family" really mean.

1.33 Ferris, Jean. **Relative Strangers.** Farrar, Straus, and Giroux, 1993. 229 pp. ISBN 0-374-36243-2.

It's quite a surprise when Berkeley's father invites her to go with him on a trip to England and France as a graduation present. It's an even bigger surprise when his new wife and stepdaughter come along. The best parts of the trip are the occasional meetings with Spike Sullivan, a boy from home who is also touring Europe. Developing a relationship with a father she barely knows is difficult, and Berkeley wonders if they were better off as strangers.

1.34 Fine, Anne. **Alias Madame Doubtfire.** Bantam Books, 1993. 199 pp. ISBN 0-553-55615-6.

Though divorced from his wife, Daniel refuses to be separated from his three children. They also want to be near their dad, but they find themselves angry at him for continually fighting with their mother and never keeping a job. Daniel sees a solution when he hears his ex-wife needs a housekeeper. He dons a disguise, applies for and gets the job. The children soon recognize him, but keep the secret, do the housework themselves, and hope a reconciliation is in sight.

1.35 Fox, Paula. **Western Wind.** Orchard Books, 1993. 201 pp. ISBN 0-531-06802-1.

Twelve-year-old Elizabeth Benedict doesn't want to spend the month of August with her grandmother. Her artistic grandmother lives in a rustic cottage without plumbing on Pring Island off the coast of Maine. Her only neighbors are a strange family with a troubled son. Elizabeth feels that she was sent away because of her new baby brother. Why else would her parents force her to endure the eccentric lifestyle of her grandmother?

1.36 Garland, Sherry. **Shadow of the Dragon.** Harcourt Brace & Company, 1993. 313 pp. ISBN 0-15-273530-5.

Danny Vo and his family arrived in Houston, Texas, when he was young. Although the family is ruled over by Danny's traditional Vietnamese grandmother, he is well on his way to becoming altogether American. Trouble for Danny begins when Sang Le, a relative from a Vietnamese prison camp, joins a Vietnamese gang. Danny's desire to fit in clashes with his strong family values, and his choices affect his family, his friends, and maybe his life.

1.37 Gleitzman, Morris. **Misery Guts.** Harcourt Brace Jovanovich, 1993. 122 pp. ISBN 0-15-254768-1.

In this companion to *Worry Warts,* Keith tries to bring laughter into his parents' gloomy lives. But when Keith paints his father's shop Tropical Mango Hi-Gloss, for instance, no one is amused. His attempts typically backfire, resulting in more misery; consequently, he convinces them that a move to idyllic Paradise, Australia, will cure their blues. Once there, Keith discovers misery looms over its horizon, too. He thinks that if he keeps his parents from discovering the problems with Paradise, he can prevent their unhappiness.

1.38 Goodman, Joan Elizabeth. **Songs from Home.** Illustrated by Joan Elizabeth Goodman. Harcourt Brace & Company, 1994. 213 pp. ISBN 0-15-203590-7.

Anna and her father live a life that other people might find romantic. They travel all over Europe, literally singing for their suppers. At the moment, they are in Rome, far from her father's Missouri birthplace. But Anna is tired of moving; she wants a home and a family. Her father, however, is not ready to settle down. He is still fleeing from his wife's death and from the people who might take Anna from him.

1.39   Grant, Cynthia. **Uncle Vampire**. Atheneum, 1993. 151 pp. ISBN 0-689-31852-9.

Carolyn believes that her Uncle Toddy is really a vampire. He is secretly sucking her blood, but her parents won't believe her, and her twin sister, Honey, a pretty cheerleader, denies anything is wrong. Their older sister, Maggie, has fled to college 3,000 miles away; Carolyn dreams of joining her. Brother Richie has escaped into drugs. The awful reality hiding behind the vampire story is this book's secret.

1.40   Greene, Constance C. **Nora: Maybe a Ghost Story.** Harcourt Brace & Company, 1993. 202 pp. ISBN 0-15-277696-6.

When thirteen-year-old Nora and her younger sister Patsy learn that their father is planning to marry "the Tooth," they are upset and try to think of ways to discourage him. Nora is further upset when her younger, but prettier, sister shows interest in Nora's boyfriend. Too much is happening at once, and Nora, more than ever, misses her deceased mother. When she begins feeling her mother's presence, she wonders why no one else does and wonders what it all means.

1.41   Grove, Vicki. **Rimwalkers.** G. P. Putnam's Sons, 1993. 227 pp. ISBN 0-399-22430-0.

Victoria has always been overshadowed by her popular younger sister, Sara. All that changes the summer they spend on their grandparents' farm with their cousins Ethan and mysterious Rennie. Victoria is always with the boys, and for the first time, Sara is left alone. The more outgoing Victoria becomes, the more withdrawn Sara is, until she recklessly tries for attention with an act that changes all of their lives forever.

1.42   Hafen, Lyman. **Over the Joshua Slope.** Bradbury Press, 1994. 172 pp. ISBN 0-02-741100-1.

Instead of hanging out with his friends, as he would like, twelve-year-old Brian must spend the summer helping his father and two of his friends drive their cattle over Joshua Slope to the summer pasture. Herding cattle is tough work, but Brian must also endure the attitude his father has shown since being injured in an accident for which Brian was partly responsible.

1.43 Hamilton, Virginia. **Plain City**. Scholastic, 1993. 194 pp. ISBN 0-590-47364-6.

Buhlaire Sims does not live the life of most twelve-year-olds. While her blues-singing mother is on the road, she is cared for by her Aunt Digna and a community of relatives. Buhlaire has been told that her father died in Vietnam, but then she learns not only that he is alive but also that he lives in town, homeless and emotionally unstable. Angry over having been robbed of her "back time," Buhlaire wrestles with whether she should live with him.

1.44 Haynes, Betsy. **The Great Dad Disaster.** Skylark Books, 1994. 168 pp. ISBN 0-553-48169-X.

Readers who enjoyed *The Great Mom Swap* will delight in the return of eighth graders Scotti Wheeler and Lorna Markham. This time, however, the girls' fathers become the problem! Scotti's father refuses to let her go out when Cary Calheim, a ninth grader, asks for a date. Lorna's father is just the opposite. He is too accommodating when the popular cheerleader, Mike Kilpatrick, asks Lorna out. The girls, once again, team up to help each other with their dads.

1.45 Hendry, Diana. **Double Vision.** Candlewick Press, 1993. 271 pp. ISBN 1-56402-125-4.

Fifteen-year-old Eliza knows she has double vision. She sees with her head and her heart. Trying to cope with traditional English parents in the 1950s, peer pressure to sneak out with undesirable boys, and adjusting to two sisters confuses Eliza. Can she see clearly enough to sort out her own feelings and live her own life?

1.46 Hermes, Patricia. **Nothing but Trouble, Trouble, Trouble.** Scholastic, 1994. 182 pp. ISBN 0-590-43499-3.

Although Alex is never far from trouble, she makes a deal with her parents to stay out of trouble for two weeks to prove that she is responsible enough to babysit. This deal gets complicated, however, when Alex's science assignment involves caring for a pet over the weekend. Since her younger sister is allergic to animals, Alex "borrows" two cats without the owner or her parents knowing about it. Staying out of trouble for two weeks may be two weeks too long for Alex!

1.47 Hermes, Patricia. **Someone to Count On.** Little, Brown and Company, 1994. 184 pp. ISBN 0-316-35925-4.

Sam longs for a real home. Her mother is a free spirit who stays out all night and checks Sam in and out of schools whenever she decides it's time for them to move on. Sam dreams of finding a home and staying put in one place. When her mother announces they are going to visit her grandfather's ranch, she hopes she will have such permanence. Sam loves it there and wonders what she will do when her mother says, "Pack up, we're leaving now."

1.48 Hermes, Patricia. **The Cousins' Club: I'll Pulverize You, William.** Pocket Books, 1994. 147 pp. ISBN 0-671-87966-9.

The first title in The Cousins' Club series finds cousins Meghann and Marcie disappointed with the discovery that their weird cousin William is coming for the summer. They plan to dodge William, who is plagued with allergies, by starting a pet sitting business. They fail to consider, however, the possibility of snake sitting. The cousins find themselves contending not only with William but also with an escaped boa constrictor.

1.49 Hest, Amy. **Pete and Lily.** Beech Tree Books, 1993. 112 pp. ISBN 0-688-12490-9.

"Pete" (Patricia) is convinced that her mother, a widow, isn't ready to date anyone, especially Henry, the divorced father of her friend Lily. After all, Pete's mother needs more quality time with her daughter, not with a male neighbor. So when Pete's mother and Henry start jogging together, Pete and Lily become wary. As they conspire to end their parents' budding romance, Lily finds a boyfriend. Pete then feels abandoned by both her mother and her best friend.

1.50 Hickman, Janet. **Jericho.** Greenwillow Books, 1994. 135 pp. ISBN 0-688-13398-3.

Twelve-year-old Angela dreads the summer away from familiar surroundings and friends. She is stuck with her parents and obnoxious brother at her great-grandmother's, where she gets the job of watching over frail and cranky Grand-Mim. As Grand-Mim relates family history through four generations of women, Angela grows to recognize much of her great-grandmother in herself.

Family and Home 15

1.51 Hobbs, Will. **Changes in Latitudes.** Avon/Flare, 1993. 162 pp. ISBN 0-380-71619-4.

"Changes in latitudes/Changes in attitudes." These lyrics from a Jimmy Buffett song frame the action of this novel about an ill-fated family trip to Mexico. Leaving his teacher father behind, Travis, an angry, alienated teenager travels to a seacoast town with his mother, his fourteen-year-old sister, and his nine-year-old brother, whose precocious interest in preserving endangered sea turtles brings the family to a tragedy for which both Travis and his mother must share an unusual degree of guilt.

1.52 Hodge, Merle. **For the Life of Laetitia.** Farrar, Straus, and Giroux, 1993. 214 pp. ISBN 0-374-32447-6.

Lacey Johnson is the first in her family to pass the exam for secondary school. Now her father, whom she has seen only a few times in her twelve years, wants to help her with school expenses. Accepting his help means living in *his* house with his wife and their messy nine-year-old son. Things in Lacey's new school and new home do not go according to plan, and something dark and sinister is troubling her only friend.

1.53 Honeycutt, Natalie. **Ask Me Something Easy.** Avon/Flare, 1993. 152 pp. ISBN 0-380-71723-9.

Addie's dad left one day when she was seven years old; he never came back. At seventeen, she is still trying to untangle the events of the past ten years: how Dinah became the "good sister," how her younger twin sisters became so troubled, and how she became the one who could do nothing right. Her search for answers only brings more questions about her family.

1.54 James, Mary (also known as M. E. Kerr). **Frankenlouse.** Scholastic, 1994. 184 pp. ISBN 0-590-46528-7.

Fourteen-year-old Nick Reber's future is already set. He will go to West Point like his father and grandfather. Now he is a cadet at Blister Military Academy, where his father is the commanding officer. But what Nick really wants to do is draw. He has even created a cartoon about book lice who live in the library and fear the monster Frankenlouse. Nick is not the only malcontent at Blister. The strict General Reber begins to understand his son better while helping the other cadets work through their personal and family problems.

1.55 Johnson, Angela. **Toning the Sweep.** Orchard Books, 1993. 103 pp. ISBN 0-531-05476-4.

Fourteen-year-old Emmie's beloved grandmother Ola is dying. For as long as Emmie remembers she has visited Ola in the California desert, where she has lived since her husband's awful, violent death. In the course of interviewing friends and neighbors for a videotape she is making about her grandmother, Emmie learns the full story of her grandfather's death and why her own mother never shared Emmie's love for the desert, fleeing from it as soon as she could.

1.56 Johnston, Julie. **Adam and Eve and Pinch-Me.** Little, Brown and Company, 1994. 180 pp. ISBN 0-316-46990-4.

Having lived in numerous foster homes, fifteen-year-old Sara Moone prides herself on her ability to wall in her feelings and wall out people. She humorously records her relationships on her computer, deleting and canceling people out of her life. This works until she joins the Huddleston family with their other foster children. The Huddlestons' acceptance, along with the appearance of a woman searching for her lost daughter, throw Sara so much that even her escape command won't work.

1.57 Johnston, Julie. **Hero of Lesser Causes.** Little, Brown and Company, 1993. 194 pp. ISBN 0-316-46988-2.

In 1946 when Keely's brother Patrick develops polio, she experiences his disease as a loss, too. Patrick has always been her favorite companion in swimming, horseback riding, and other adventures. When he returns home paralyzed, he alternately vents silence and rage upon Keely, disdainful of her efforts to make him feel better. Nonetheless, Keely musters hope for the both of them, intent on convincing Patrick that he can lead a productive and meaningful life.

1.58 Kimmell, Eric A. **One Good Tern Deserves Another.** Holiday House, 1994. 188 pp. ISBN 0-8234-1138-9.

Peebee Floyd and his banjo-playing mother set out from Oklahoma on a cross-country journey after his stepfather dies in Operation Desert Storm. They come to rest along the Oregon coast, where they meet Lani Kealoha and her widower father, Kimo. Two romances blossom in this beautiful natural setting, rich in opportunities for bird-watching and octopus training. During their time together, Lani and Peebee encounter long-lost treasure, though the discovery almost costs them their lives.

Family and Home 17

1.59 Klass, Sheila Solomon. **Rhino.** Scholastic, 1993. 161 pp. ISBN 0-590-44250-3.

Annie Trevor has a great family, a talented boyfriend, and the Trevor family nose! Though her dad and grandpa wear the nose well, she wishes she'd gotten her mom's nose as her sister Kate did. At twelve, Fats Russell makes Annie aware of the funny bump. Now she wants to convince the family that rhinoplasty is the answer. In the end, the lessons she learns about life are more than skin-deep.

1.60 Koertge, Ron. **Mariposa Blues.** Avon/Flare, 1993. 171 pp. ISBN 0-380-71761-1.

Graham needs his sense of humor. This summer he's going to prove he can make his own decisions about his life and about a special race horse. Unfortunately, Graham's dad, a horse trainer, disagrees. Graham decides to race the young horse against his father's wishes. Sweating through confrontations with his dad, Graham awaits the day of the race. What if Graham is wrong and his dad is right?

1.61 Koertge, Ron. **Tiger, Tiger, Burning Bright.** Orchard Books, 1994. 179 pp. ISBN 0-531-06840-4.

As Jesse's grandfather, Pap, becomes more forgetful everyday, Jesse worries more that his mother will put Pap into a nursing home. Jesse's worries mount when on a camping trip, Pap insists he saw a tiger paw print—even though everyone assures him there are no tigers in California. To prove Pap's assertion, Jesse and several of his friends accompany Pap into the mountains to search for the tiger; instead, they end up searching for Pap, who becomes lost in the mountains.

1.62 Koertge, Ron. **The Harmony Arms.** Avon, 1994. 177 pp. ISBN 0-380-72188-0.

Gabriel balks at spending the summer with Dad and his puppet, Timmy the Otter. Dad does not talk; the puppet speaks for Dad. Timmy the Otter, not Dad, tells Gabriel the facts of life. As Gabriel discovers in his California apartment complex a geriatric nude swimmer, a rollerblading psychic, other eccentrics, and a girl, summer with Dad and Timmy the Otter begins to seem quite normal.

1.63 Lance, Kathryn. **Going to See Grassy Ella.** Lothrop, Lee & Shepard, 1993. 134 pp. ISBN 0-688-12163-2.

Can New York City faith healer Graciella Bujold cure twelve-year-old Peggy Jean "Peej" West of cancer? Knowing that her parents will consider faith healing a hoax, Peej convinces her older sister to slip off with her to find "Grassy Ella" in New York. Peej plans the trip to the last detail—except for what to do with the thieves, kidnappers, and hoodlums they stumble upon. In the style of *Home Alone 2*, these two sisters prove that faith is needed for more than healing cancer!

1.64 Lasky, Kathryn. **Memoirs of a Bookbat.** Harcourt Brace & Company, 1994. 215 pp. ISBN 0-15-215727-1.

Harper Jessup refers to herself as a "bookbat," rather than a bookworm. Unfortunately, just as fourteen-year-old Harper is into books, her parents are into religion and book censoring. As migrants of God, missionaries of Family Action for Christian Education, Harper's parents travel in their motor home on a quest across America to promote book banning: the very books that Harper has always loved. Harper's tragic story begins on a bus. Harper is miles from her parents and her only friend, explaining how she got there.

1.65 Lawlor, Laurie. **Little Women: A Novel Based on the Motion Picture Screen Play by Robin Swicord from the Novel by Louisa May Alcott.** Minstrel/Pocket Books, 1994. 133 pp. ISBN 0-671-51902-6.

Do you want to get to know the March sisters better but find the 500+ page, original 1868 classic hard to understand? Try this contemporary rewrite of the story, aimed at teens of the 1990s. Lawlor has simplified the language and condensed the story as a companion to the new movie of *Little Women*. Read about the plays the sisters put on in their New England home, their struggle with poverty, their quarrels, their friendship with Laurie, and the coming-of-age of Meg, Jo, Beth, and Amy.

1.66 Levinson, Marilyn. **No Boys Allowed.** BridgeWater Books, 1993. 124 pp. ISBN 0-8167-3135-7.

After her parents' unfriendly divorce, eleven-year-old Cassie is determined never to be hurt again. All males, even her best friend Bobby, will be out of her life. Then Great-Uncle Harry (who is rich and interesting) comes to stay. As the two of them share memories of her father, Cassie begins to deal with the changes in her life and decides that "No boys allowed" may not be a good policy after all.

1.67 Levinson, Nancy Smiler. **Sweet Notes, Sour Notes.** Lodestar Books, 1993. 54 pp. ISBN 0-525-67379-2.

When David's grandfather, Zayde, takes him to a concert by the famous violinist Mischa Elman, David falls in love with the instrument. He dreams of making it sing with the sweet notes he heard in the concert hall. David's parents agree to rent him a violin. He begins lessons and soon discovers all that stands between him and those sweet notes, including long practice hours and an unsympathetic younger sister.

1.68 Levitin, Sonia. **The Golem & the Dragon Girl.** Dial Books, 1993. 187 pp. ISBN 0-8037-1280-4.

Laurel, a Chinese American girl and Jonathan, a Jewish American boy, meet when Jonathan, his mother, and a newly acquired and resented stepfather move into a house being vacated by Laurel's family. Laurel hates to leave the house in which she feels protected by the spirit of her great-grandfather, now displaced by a golem, a spirit rooted in Jewish culture. The golem causes problems so Jonathan and Laurel pool their Chinese and Jewish traditions to drive it away.

1.69 Lynch, Chris. **Gypsy Davey.** HarperCollins, 1994. 179 pp. ISBN 0-06-023586-1.

Joanne's mother, Lois, likes to slip out for a good time, leaving the five-year-old Joanne to care for her two-year-old brother Davey. Sneaky Pete, the absent man of the house, has fled to Florida where he lives off his earnings at the race track. At seventeen, Joanne herself becomes a mother and, following in the family tradition, leaves her child to be cared for by Davey, whose only escape is to ride endlessly on the bicycle his father has left behind on one of his hit-and-run visits.

1.70 Maguire, Gregory. **Missing Sisters.** Margaret K. McElderry Books, 1994. 152 pp. ISBN 0-689-50590-6.

Alice Colossus makes an amazing discovery when she goes to summer camp: she has a twin sister living in the same city. Alice is an orphan at a girls' school run by nuns. Because of speech and hearing problems, Alice has never been adopted. Life suddenly becomes very complicated for Alice as she searches for answers about her past and copes with a new sister and the possibility of a new family.

1.71 Marino, Jan. **For the Love of Pete.** Little, Brown and Company, 1993. 197 pp. ISBN 0-316-54627-5.

Her mother dead and her guardian grandmother in a nursing home, Phoebe must go to live with a father who abandoned her at birth. Bishop, Bertie, and Billy, practically part of the family, close up Grandmother's house and travel with the heartbroken Phoebe to her father's. A series of setbacks occur, making the trip eventful. Nevertheless, Phoebe feels a deep loss as she says good-bye to her grandmother's house, a past life, and those she will always love.

1.72 Marsden, John. **Letters from the Inside.** Houghton Mifflin, 1994. 146 pp. ISBN 0-395-68985-6.

How could Mandy have known what she would learn when she answered Tracey's ad for a pen pal? Mandy has a dog with no name, a family with one seventeen-year-old problem brother, and a super boyfriend. Tracey has a horse, two dogs, a cat, an older sister, and a boyfriend. And each has problems they think they can never share with anyone. Yet as their letters grow more candid, each of the girls reveals her problems and secrets to the other.

1.73 Mazer, Harry. **Who Is Eddie Leonard?** Delacorte Press, 1993. 188 pp. ISBN 0-385-31136-2.

Eddie Leonard lives a miserable life with his ill-tempered grandmother. He can't remember ever having seen either of his parents. When his grandmother dies, he is alone, until he discovers a poster in the post office about Jason Diaz, missing since age three. Suddenly his own shadowy past seems to match Jason's and he presents himself to his long lost family. But is he or isn't he the missing Jason?

1.74 McLean, Susan. **Pennies for the Piper.** Farrar, Straus, and Giroux, 1993. 150 pp. ISBN 0-374-45754-9.

Bicks and her mother had an agreement; immediately after her mother's death, she should go straight to Aunt Millicent in Iowa. However, she can't leave without saying a proper good-bye, and the purchase of casket flowers means that part of her bus money is gone. Now she must walk part of the way to Iowa.

1.75 Merrick, Monte. **Shelter.** Hyperion Books, 1993. 360 pp. ISBN 1-56282-862-2.

The summer of 1962 tests the limits of fourteen-year-old Nelson Jaqua. He gets pushed into spying on an elderly couple against

Family and Home

his wishes, is plagued with the constant care of his four-year-old sister, endures his parents' announcement of plans for a divorce, and discovers that his two friends are going out behind his back. When it all proves to be too much, Nelson takes a stand.

1.76 Mori, Kyoko. **Shizuko's Daughter.** Henry Holt and Company, 1993. 223 pp. ISBN 0-8050-2557-X.

Yuki's mother commits suicide and her father soon marries the woman who has been his mistress for some time. An independent spirit, Yuki despises her hypocritical stepmother, whose behavior is dictated entirely by appearances. But she is forced to live with them until she leaves for art school. She then re-establishes the ties to her mother's family that the stepmother forced her to break.

1.77 Mulford, Phillipa Greene. **Making Room for Katherine.** Macmillan, 1994. 191 pp. ISBN 0-02-767652-8.

Sixteen-year-old twins Abbey and Sheldon spend time helping their thirteen-year-old cousin from Paris adjust to life in the United States. Katherine, sophisticated and mature for thirteen, doesn't want to be in America and doesn't want to be a part of her new family. But Sheldon and Abbey plan to make Katherine a part of their family—with or without her consent.

1.78 Murphy, Barbara Beasley. **Fly Like an Eagle.** Delacorte Press, 1994. 178 pp. ISBN 0-385-32035-3.

Seventeen-year-old Ace goes on a quest with his father, Barney, in a beat-up 1960 Volkswagen. Barney, who is adopted, is looking for his natural father. Ace, who did not know his father was an orphan, learns many things about family as they travel from New York to New Mexico. From finding a long-lost grandparent to discovering his true Native American heritage, Ace's quest with his father brings them closer to the truth of many things.

1.79 Myers, Christopher A., and Lynne Born Myers. **Forest of the Clouded Leopard.** Houghton Mifflin, 1994. 112 pp. ISBN 0-395-67408-5.

Kenchendai is torn between the life he has at boarding school and the tribal life he finds at home. During summer break he goes boar hunting with his father and grandfather. His grandfather is gored by a wounded boar and Kenchendai wants to rush him to a clinic for treatment, but his father insists that the old ways are the best. When his grandfather dies, Kenchendai's father goes into the jungle after a dream, and Kenchendai must go and rescue him from the land of the dead.

1.80 Namioka, Lensey. **April and the Dragon Lady.** Browndeer Press/Harcourt Brace & Company, 1994. 214 pp. ISBN 0-15-276644-8.

April's grandmother is a Dragon Lady, tyrannical and manipulative. She has been living in the home of April's widowed father for ten years now, intent on protecting her traditional Chinese right to comfortable old age, even if it means sabotaging her eldest son's remarriage and April's college plans. Neither white people nor girls count for much in Grandma's world view. April's brother Harry is the favored child, and her "white devil boyfriend," Steve, is unwelcome in Grandma's house.

1.81 Paulsen, Gary. **Harris and Me.** Harcourt Brace & Company, 1993. 157 pp. ISBN 0-15-292877-4.

"You don't know nuthin," Harris tells the foster kid, Gooner. By the time Gooner's first hour on the farm is over, he has a concussion and is bruised by a violent cow and a sneaky attack chicken. Gooner has wanted a home for a long time, and the farm might be that home. All Gooner has to do is survive Harris's war with the animals.

1.82 Paulsen, Gary. **The Haymeadow.** Dell Publishing, 1994. 195 pp. ISBN 0-440-40923-3.

Spending the summer alone in the haymeadow with six thousand sheep scares John. He agrees to do it only because he hopes this might be what finally pleases his father. But John is not prepared for flooding rivers, attacking coyotes, and dying sheep. Scared, alone, and overwhelmed, John wonders why he so desperately wants to please a father who seemingly cares so little.

1.83 Peck, Richard. **Unfinished Portrait of Jessica.** Dell Publishing, 1993. 162 pp. ISBN 0-440-21886-1.

Teenager Jessica shuns her mother in favor of her father. After her father leaves, Jessica treats her mother as the enemy. Surely, Jessica believes, her father has finally sent for her to join him in Mexico. Jessica ends up disillusioned and betrayed by her father. Heartbroken, Jessica plans to return to her mother with newfound maturity and understanding.

1.84 Perkins, Mitali. **The Sunita Experiment.** Little, Brown and Company, 1993. 179 pp. ISBN 0-316-69943-8.

Family and Home 23

Sunita Sen's life is out of control. Just because her grandparents are coming to visit from India, her mother gives up teaching and starts wearing sarees and a red dot on her forehead. As if things aren't bad enough at home, the craziness starts to invade the rest of Sunita's life. Her best friend Liz is spending a lot of time with a certain male track star and a certain LeeAnn Schaeffer has her eye on Sunita's special friend Michael.

1.85 Pevsner, Stella. **I'm Emma: I'm a Quint.** Clarion Books, 1993. 186 pp. ISBN 0-395-64166-7.

Emma is one of the Wentworth Quints. From their birth to this year of their eighth-grade graduation, their father has shielded them from publicity and exploitation. Some of the quints are tired and would enjoy a little fame; but Emma just wants to be herself, not a freak. A wedding in the family, sibling problems, and an identity crisis give Emma more than she thinks she can handle.

1.86 Reaver, Chap. **Bill.** Delacorte Press, 1994. 216 pp. ISBN 0-385-31175-3.

Thirteen-year-old Jessica Gates knows the Kentucky backwoods like she knows her own name. She and Bill, a mixed-breed dog, spend time alone there because of her father's frequent trips to distill, drink, and sell bootleg liquor. When he is arrested and needs bail, Jess remembers stories of treasure buried on their property. As she searches for the treasure, Jess's life becomes tougher as she is pursued by her father's devious friends.

1.87 Roberts, Willo Davis. **What Are We Going to Do about David?** Atheneum, 1993. 164 pp. ISBN 0-689-31793-X.

David is shuttled to Grandma Ruthie's to live with her, almost a total stranger, for a whole month while his career-oriented parents attend to matters more important than their son. David recognizes and resents his lack of status in the family, just as he notices that the fights between his parents have increased. Homesick, angry, and hurt, David nonetheless finds solace in a secure and loving home with Ruthie, developing self-esteem and learning to care for those who are challenged by other problems.

1.88 Robinson, Barbara. **The Best School Year Ever.** HarperCollins, 1994. 117 pp. ISBN 0-06-023039-8.

The Herdmans are back, and wild as ever. In this zany sequel to *The Best Christmas Pageant Ever*, the Herdman family takes over the school. "Compliments for Classmates" is the school project, and when Beth draws Imogene Herdman's name, she knows she is sunk. Why, Imogene's hobby is collecting belly-button lint! Imogene even has the teachers locked in the teachers' lounge. Finding compliments for Imogene is a challenge that adds joy to this truly funny book.

1.89 Rodowsky, Colby. **Hannah in Between.** Farrar, Straus, and Giroux, 1994. 152 pp. ISBN 0-374-32837-4.

Hannah Brant describes her twelve-year-old world as "precomfordictable"—comfortable because it is so predictable. She and her parents spend every summer vacation at the beach with the same relatives and friends. During the other months, Hannah's life is as routine as the pizza her family orders every Friday night. Hannah's precomfordictable life begins changing, however, as she notices her mother's dependence on alcohol. Hannah gets caught between wanting to help her mom and the family's denial of the problem.

1.90 Roybal, Laura. **Billy.** Houghton Mifflin, 1994. 236 pp. ISBN 0-395-67649-5.

One too many fights lands sixteen-year-old Billy at the police station. There Billy has his fingerprints taken, and discovers that they match those of William James Campbell, a boy who was reported missing six years ago. Now Billy must come to terms with returning to his "real" family and dealing with the man he has called dad for the past six years.

1.91 Rumbaut, Hendle. **Dove Dream.** Houghton Mifflin, 1994. 119 pp. ISBN 0-395-68393-9.

Dove is sent to live with her aunt for the summer in hopes that her parents can work things out with their marriage. Aunt Anna leads an exciting life and shares it willingly with her thirteen-year-old niece. When Dove discovers the old letters of her grandmother, she decides to set off on a vision quest and learn more about her Chickasaw heritage. As the summer draws too quickly to a close, Dove also discovers love for the first time.

1.92 Sachs, Marilyn. **Thirteen Going On Seven.** E. P. Dutton, 1993. 133 pp. ISBN 0-525-45096-3.

Turning thirteen proves difficult enough without doubling the problem by being a twin to the smart, popular star of the school play. Unlike the sophisticated Dee, who appears to grow up easily, Deezy struggles in school, prefers things she did as a child,

Family and Home

and works hard at discovering her own identity. With the help of a new friend and her grumpy grandfather, Deezy develops new interests and realizes that growing up means more than just boys and makeup.

1.93   Salat, Christina. **Living in Secret.** Bantam/Skylark, 1993. 183 pp. ISBN 0-553-08670-7.

Since her parents' divorce, Amelia lives with her father. That's because her mother is a lesbian, and her father refuses to let Amelia live with her mom, despite Amelia's pleas to do so. So her mother's scheme has got to work. Moving to San Francisco in the dark of night, Amelia, her mother, and her mother's partner assume aliases and start over. But this new life offers challenges as well as rewards: Will Amelia's father buy the story that Amelia has run away? Can they withhold their true identities so that they aren't discovered?

1.94   Seabrooke, Brenda. **The Bridges of Summer.** Puffin, 1994. 143 pp. ISBN 0-525-65094-6.

Gifted teenage ballerina Zarah is dumped for the summer on a South Carolina island with her backwoods grandmother, Quanamina. Quanamina, the daughter of slaves, has no electricity or running water, but proudly owns most of the island. Zarah is stunned by the role her grandmother expects her to play as a serving girl to the rich white family on the island. Working through her anger and feelings of shame and her conflicts with Quanamina, Zarah finds unexpected riches in the heritage from her family.

1.95   Sharmat, Mitchell. **Hello . . . This Is My Father Speaking.** HarperCollins, 1994. 124 pp. ISBN 0-06-024469-0.

Embarrassed by his father's office-cleaning business, Jeff decides to make his father rich enough to retire. Impersonating his father, Jeff opens an investment club and buys stocks. He lives happily in the world of high finance until forty thousands pounds of wheat are dumped in his driveway.

1.96   Shreve, Susan. **Amy Dunn Quits School.** Tambourine Books, 1993. 96 pp. ISBN 0-688-10320-0.

Nicole is the perfect mother. She makes certain that sixth-grader Amy has every opportunity: lessons in ballet, drama, and piano, plus the perfect costume for the Halloween parade at Barton School. An honor student and a perfect daughter, Amy hasn't the heart to tell her mother that no other sixth graders will be in costume. She devises a scheme to quit school for the day and do things her way for a change.

1.97 Shusterman, Neal. **What Daddy Did.** HarperKeypoint, 1993. 231 pp. ISBN 0-06-447094-6.

When Preston's parents separate, he thinks nothing can be more devastating. But he is wrong. Soon, his father murders his mother and attempts suicide. We learn from Preston's first-hand account how these events affect him, his brother, and the grandparents who raise them. But we also gain glimpses of a father who wants his children back after his release from prison.

1.98 Smith, Doris Buchanan. **Best Girl.** Viking, 1993. 144 pp. ISBN 0-670-83752-0.

When an arsonist's fire guts Mrs. Dee's house, Nealy feels the loss, for under it is her secret sanctuary. There she stores her special insect drawings and finds refuge from an angry, demanding mother, an aloof sister exiled from the house, and a father who rarely visits. In helping Mrs. Dee reclaim her property, Neal gains new friends, strengthens family bonds, and comes to deeper understandings of her own capabilities.

1.99 Smith, Doris Buchanan. **Remember the Red-Shouldered Hawk.** G. P. Putnam's Sons, 1994. 160 pp. ISBN 0-399-22443-2.

Twelve-year-old John-too was thrilled about his grandmother Nanna moving in, but wasn't ready for it: Why did Nanna forget those special times they shared? Why did she always misplace her purse? Then there's best friend Brod, picking fights with Molo and making racist slurs. As John-too witnesses intolerance—from icy stares at Nanna to acts of violence aimed at friends and family—he struggles to understand prejudice, risking some friendships and gaining others.

1.100 Smith, Jane Denitz. **Mary by Myself.** HarperCollins, 1994. 152 pp. ISBN 0-06-024517-4.

Hurting since the sudden death of her baby sister, ten-year-old Mary attaches herself to Laura at summer camp. Laura, who is an odd, unfriendly girl, first allows, then forces Mary into casting spells to hurt the other girls. Then Laura betrays Mary. Stunned, Mary begins to realize how relieved she is to be free of Laura and to just be herself.

Family and Home

1.101 Staples, Donna. **Arena Beach.** Houghton Mifflin, 1993. 236 pp. ISBN 0-395-65366-5.

Seventeen-year-old Terra's world is rocking under her feet. Her long-lost father shows up. Her mother is losing her grip on reality. And her boss and friend suffers a serious heart attack. At the same time, Terra's boyfriend wants a relationship she isn't ready for. A California earthquake helps Terra understand that she is responsible for following her own dreams.

1.102 Staples, Suzanne Fisher. **Haveli.** Alfred A. Knopf, 1993. 259 pp. ISBN 0-679-84157-1.

In this sequel to *Shabanu, Daughter of the Wind*, Shabanu has become the youngest wife of Rahim, a wealthy Pakistani landowner whom she was forced to marry. She is a free spirit, and the other wives resent this quality. These scheming women work to humiliate her and to make Rahim suspicious of her. Shabanu's life becomes more miserable and unsafe as she attempts to save her friend from an arranged marriage to Rahim's retarded son and discovers an evil plot to steal all of Rahim's land.

1.103 Stolz, Mary. **What Time of Night Is It?** HarperKeypoint, 1993. 209 pp. ISBN 0-06-447093-8.

When Taylor's mother walks out, Taylor and her two brothers are left reeling, shattered by their mother's actions. When the children's grandmother comes to stay, household tensions increase. Taylor and her brothers cope with their mother's absence and their father's increasing emotional problems as they struggle with their grandmother's often intrusive presence in their lives.

1.104 Talbert, Marc. **The Purple Heart.** Avon/Camelot, 1993. 120 pp. ISBN 0-380-71985-1.

When Luke's wounded father comes home from Vietnam with a Purple Heart, he is a hero to Luke and his best friend Mike. But his father becomes almost a stranger, fearful and moody. Luke prefers to play his own war games with Mike and make up stories about his father's war experience rather than hear the truth. Both father and son have to accept the realities of the war if they are to build a new and lasting relationship.

1.105 Thesman, Jean. **When the Road Ends.** Avon/Camelot, 1993. 184 pp. ISBN 0-380-72011-6.

At Father Matt's, Mary Jack momentarily gains a stable family life for both herself and silent, abused Jane, whom she considers her sister. Then Mary Jack, with elderly, mentally and physically challenged Aunt Cecile, Jane, and the other foster children, must relocate to a cabin, where their caretaker immediately robs and abandons them. Convincing the others that life together is preferable to foster care apart, Mary Jack musters courage and faces hardship, determined to create family bonds against all odds.

1.106 Thomas, Joyce Carol. **When the Nightingale Sings.** HarperTrophy, 1994. 148 pp. ISBN 0-06-440524-9.

Queen Mother Rhythm calls a convention to find a new singer to lead her church's gospel choir. When her agents travel deep into the swamp to audition Ruby and her twin daughters, they hear the glorious voice of Marigold but cannot find her. "Cousin" Ruby and her daughters are determined to keep Marigold from the convention, but it will take more than this mean-spirited threesome to keep Marigold from her real family, true love, and the Rose of Sharon choir.

1.107 Tomey, Ingrid. **Savage Carrot.** Macmillan, 1993. 181 pp. ISBN 0-684-19633-6.

Dreading this day, the embarrassed Carrot sinks into a seat in the unfamiliar English classroom as the teacher introduces her, the new student. "So tell us about your father," Mrs. Smoznak urges, hoping to invite Carrot into the conversation. "No!" she yells, tears streaming down her face. Angry, confused, and full of grief, thirteen-year-old Carrot must cope with her father's recent death and with the events that follow.

1.108 Wardlaw, Lee. **Don't Look Back.** Avon/Flare, 1993. 152 pp. ISBN 0-380-76419-9.

Drew is on her way to what should be a fun-filled vacation in Hawaii, but she cannot forgive her father for abruptly leaving the family two years ago and taking her younger brother with him. Her anger increases when she learns her father has a live-in girlfriend. In Hawaii, she meets a boy, but discovers she cannot have a relationship with him until she understands what happened in her family and sorts out her feelings toward her father.

1.109 Westwood, Chris. **Brother of Mine.** Clarion Books, 1994. 186 pp. ISBN 0-395-66137-4.

Tony has trouble understanding why his identical twin brother Nick is so hostile toward him. There has always been a certain amount of jealousy between the two, but the tension really escalates when Nick's girlfriend, Alex, mistakes Tony for him. After stalking Tony and Alex, Nick decides he has to get his brother out of the way no matter what it takes.

1.110   Whelan, Gloria. **A Time to Keep Silent.** William B. Eerdman's Publishing Company, 1993. 124 pp. ISBN 0-8028-0118-8.

When thirteen-year-old Clair stops talking, her father, a pastor, blames himself. He has been shut up in his study since the death of Clair's mother. Clair's father resigns his position as pastor of a large church to be a missionary in the remote woods of Michigan. Clair is furious. Then Clair meets Dorrie who is living alone to escape her alcoholic father. Dorrie will need Clair's courage and her voice when Dorrie's father comes for her.

1.111   Williams, Carol Lynch. **Kelly and Me.** Delacorte Press, 1993. 123 pp. ISBN 0-385-30897-3.

Leah Orton's love for fun and trouble turns her eleventh summer into one hilarious adventure after another. She always includes her ten-year-old sister Kelly and frequently involves her seventy-two-year-old grandfather who acts like a kid himself. As the summer draws to a close, the trio's fun ends with a tragedy that changes the lives of the Orton family forever.

1.112   Williams, Michael. **The Genuine Half-Moon Kid.** Lodestar, 1994. 199 pp. ISBN 0-525-67470-5.

When Jay discovers that his grandfather, almost a stranger, has left a legacy to him, he embarks on a journey across his homeland of South Africa to retrieve it, a yellow box. Embarking on this adventure with acquaintances, Jay comes to care for them, particularly young, taciturn Levi, as he learns about his country and his kin. Returning home, Jay assumes responsibility for the trip and for the contents of the box, facing questions about Levi's family as well as his own.

1.113   Williams, Vera B. **Scooter.** Greenwillow Books, 1993. 147 pp. ISBN 0-688-09376-0.

Elana Rose Rosen and her mother move into a tiny apartment when her father's departure leaves them unable to afford their house. While riding her favorite scooter one day, Elana has an accident and goes to the hospital emergency room. This scary event brings unexpected happiness as it allows her to meet some of her neighbors, including little Petey whom everyone but Elana thinks is mute.

1.114 Wolff, Virginia Euwer. **Make Lemonade.** Henry Holt and Company, 1993. 200 pp. ISBN 0-8050-2228-7.

LeVaughn is a mature fourteen-year-old who knows that education is her ticket from the difficult life she's lived since her father's death. To earn college money, LeVaughn babysits the children of seventeen-year-old Jolly. Jolly is poorly equipped to handle herself, much less two youngsters. LeVaughn begins the job working strictly for the money, but soon becomes involved in all three lives, caring too much to leave, even after Jolly loses her factory job.

1.115 Wood, June Rae. **A Share of Freedom.** G. P. Putnam's Sons, 1994. 255 pp. ISBN 0-399-22767-9.

After another drunken binge, her mother lands in the emergency room, leaving thirteen-year-old Freedom to wonder who her real father is as she cares for younger brother Jackie. When a meddling social worker announces that she and Jackie must go to separate foster homes while her mother completes a treatment program, Freedom revolts. She embarks on a series of adventures with Jackie, learning lessons about life and filling in missing details about her family history.

1.116 Wood, Marcia. **Always, Julia.** Atheneum, 1993. 119 pp. ISBN 0-689-31728-X.

Julia leaves home to seek her fortune as a writer in New York. Jane stays in close contact with her older sister through letters that provide descriptions of lunches with famous authors, cocktail parties with publishers, and writing successes. However, when Jane writes to Julia about the details of her scheduled class visit to New York, it brings an abrupt halt to the stream of letters. The trip leads to some unexpected discoveries.

1.117 Young, Ronder Thomas. **Learning by Heart.** Houghton Mifflin, 1993. 172 pp. ISBN 0-395-65369-X.

Ten-year-old Rachel is growing up in a small southern town where race relations are changing. Her black classmate, Callie, and black maid, Isabelle, are very real, dignified, and independent people. Her teenage neighbor, Pamela Tucker, refers to herself as "white trash" but is, in fact, a valiant and musically talented young woman. Rachel comes of age in a tight-knit family which includes her shopkeeper parents, her newborn brother, and her unreasonable, domineering grandmother, all of whom have important lessons to teach.

2 Friendship and Romance

2.1 Arter, Jim. **Gruel and Unusual Punishment.** Dell/Yearling, 1993. 103 pp. ISBN 0-440-40891-1.

Arnold Dinklighter escapes his miserable life at home by making jokes and planning pranks at school. As a result, Arnold spends most of his second time around in seventh-grade in Mr. Applin's detention room, known by all as "The Gulag." When a new classmate, Edward Straight, arrives, the two boys become fast friends, but their mischievous plans to make Mr. Applin's life miserable take a sudden scary turn when Edward shares his plan to kill their teacher.

2.2 Avery, Gillian. **Maria's Italian Spring.** Illustrated by Scott Snow. Simon & Schuster Books for Young Readers, 1993. 265 pp. ISBN 0-671-79582-1.

Because the choices a twelve-year-old girl has are limited, especially in late nineteenth-century England, Maria finds herself at the mercy of family lawyers when her uncle dies. Impressed by her skill with Latin and Greek, a cousin takes her to Italy to continue her education. Maria is sickly and lonely until Lady Cordelia, a young neighbor, devises bold schemes for exploring the Italian neighborhood. Cordelia brings Maria a new happiness and the promise of a friendship.

2.3 Bechard, Margaret. **Really No Big Deal.** Viking, 1994. 151 pp. ISBN 0-670-85444-1.

Life is tough enough for seventh grader Jonah Truman. He is one of the shortest kids in school, painfully shy around girls, and afraid of the class bully. If all of this isn't enough, his mother confesses that she is dating his principal. As he tries to keep their dating a secret, Jonah's life takes some hilarious twists and turns.

2.4 Bridgers, Sue Ellen. **Keeping Christina.** HarperCollins, 1993. 281 pp. ISBN 0-06-021505-4.

When Annie meets new student Christina Moore, she is intrigued by her shy, waif-like appearance. Annie gradually absorbs Christina into her family and circle of friends as both girls take part in a school production of *Kiss Me Kate*. But Christina is not what she appears to be. She disrupts Annie's relationships with her boyfriend Peter and with her best friend Jill. Christina is not the friend

Annie expected, but now their lives are too intertwined to part easily.

2.5 Brooks, Caryl. **The Empty Summer.** Scholastic, 1993. 182 pp. ISBN 0-590-45863-9.

Insecure Maggie ignores her father's advice to stop comparing herself to others. During a summer at Martha's Vineyard, Maggie, feeling plain and unattractive, becomes fascinated by Kimberly, a beautiful teenage model. Maggie envies everything about Kimberly, including her boyfriend Zach. But Kimberly has a dangerous secret. If Maggie tells, she loses Kimberly's friendship. If she doesn't tell, she may lose something even more important.

2.6 Busselle, Rebecca. **A Frog's Eye View.** Dell Publishing, 1993. 191 pp. ISBN 0-440-21567-6.

Neely is furious. Her boyfriend Nick takes a summer job and is starting a rock band. Neely's only plans this summer are to be with Nick, and now he has other interests than her. When Nick asks a girl to sing with the band, Neely finds herself seething with jealousy. Soon she begins stalking Nick with a camera. Her obsession with Nick leads to consequences Neely had not anticipated.

2.7 Catt, Hastings. **Sweet Dreams: Romance on the Run.** Bantam Books, 1993. 135 pp. ISBN 0-553-29987-5.

In this Sweet Dreams book, Eric, the school jock, gives Monica advice on strategies for running track. After a superb track meet, Eric walks Monica home and ends up asking her for a date. Monica knows everything is going her way when, the next day, she gets a position on the school newspaper staff. But then, for some reason, Eric decides Monica must choose between him and the paper. Caught between a new beau and a new interest, Monica wonders how far you go for love. Some of the other books in this series include, *P.S. I Love You, Fair-Weather Love, Lessons in Love, Moonlight Melody*, and *My Secret Heart*.

2.8 Clarke, Judith. **Al Capsella Takes a Vacation.** Henry Holt and Company, 1993. 140 pp. ISBN 0-8050-2685-1.

Friends Al and Lou decide that, at sixteen, they've had enough of vacationing with their parents. Dazzled by a pal's description of Scutchthrope's beaches, discos, and fabulous night-life, they book a room at Kooka Kabins. When they arrive, they realize they won't need their resort clothing and surfboards. Though they are determined to stay the week, Al and Lou experience an unforgettable vacation—unforgettable for all the wrong reasons! Set in Australia, this novel is one of several in the Al Capsella series.

2.9 Clements, Bruce. **Coming About.** Farrar, Straus, and Giroux, 1993. 185 pp. ISBN 0-374-41339-8.

Bob Royle planned to just blend in at his new school, but Carl Riemer has different ideas. He thinks Bob is smart, different, going places. Bob can't decide whether Carl is crazy or just weird. In spite of himself, Bob gets caught up in Carl's schemes and becomes involved in Carl's family problems. Carl's effect on Bob surprises everyone—even Bob.

2.10 Cooper, Ilene. **Hollywood Wars: Seeing Red.** Puffin Books, 1993. 113 pp. ISBN 0-14-036157-X.

This book in the Hollywood Wars series takes the four teenagers of the cast of the hit television show "Sticks and Stones" to New York City on a publicity tour. Alison's lack of live television experience throws her into a complete panic which results in stage fright. While Alison sits, unable to respond to the interviewers, Jamie steals the show. Alison may be seeing more than just red; she may be looking at a very short career. Other books in this series that focus on two teens' rise in show business include *Trouble in Paradise*.

2.11 Cooper, Ilene. **Holiday Five: Trick or Trouble?** Viking, 1994. 153 pp. ISBN 0-670-85057-8.

In this Holiday Five book, Lia has been voted "all-around camper," but she dreads leaving Camp Wildwood and going to seventh grade where she will be a nobody again. She's glad the girls in bunk three have promised to stay in touch. They call themselves "The Holiday Five," and their first reunion will be Halloween. Meanwhile Lia gets into a real predicament at school. The Halloween party she's been anticipating for weeks may be more trick than treat.

2.12 Cullen, Lynn. **The Backyard Ghost.** Clarion Books, 1993. 149 pp. ISBN 0-395-64527-1.

Eleanor's campaign for popularity belly flops when she finds egghead Charlie Ormsby in her backyard ghost watching. At lunch Charlie sits next to her to discuss his latest ghost theories. Eleanor wants to concentrate on being popular, but all she can think about is Charlie and the ghost in her backyard.

2.13 Danziger, Paula. **Not for a Billion Gazillion Dollars.** Dell/Yearling, 1994. 121 pp. ISBN 0-440-40919-5.

Matthew Martin sees a forgettable summer stretching before him: the computer program he wants to buy isn't in his parents' budget and his girlfriend's plans have her spending the summer at the lake. With time on his hands, Matthew turns his attention to earning money for the program. A business is born with help from Jill and Matthew's best friend, but what a challenge it is for friends to remain friends when money is involved!

2.14 Davis, Terry. **If Rock and Roll Were a Machine.** Dell/Laurel Leaf, 1994. 209 pp. ISBN 0-440-21908-6.

Bert Bowden knows he's damaged goods. Bert also knows who took away his self-esteem. It was his fifth-grade teacher, Paul Lawler. Now, Bert is fifteen and in high school. His English teacher and a Harley-riding biker want to help him find that missing part of himself. Bert realizes he needs to find a way to earn his own self-respect.

2.15 Deaver, Julie Reece. **First Wedding, Once Removed.** HarperTrophy, 1993. 216 pp. ISBN 0-06-440402-1.

When Pokie's older brother Gib left for college during her high school freshman year, life was bad enough. But now he's marrying Nell and leaving, it seems, forever. Gib has been a perfect older brother, sharing with Pokie a love for airplanes and a dream of becoming pilots. After Nell becomes a part of her family, Pokie begins to rebuild her old friendships and to adjust to growing up.

2.16 DeClements, Barthe. **Seventeen and In-Between.** Puffin Books, 1993. 162 pp. ISBN 0-14-036475-7.

When she was a chubby fifth-grader and an insecure freshman, Elsie would have given anything to have her current problem: two men in her life. Now that she's a high school senior, she finds herself torn between her longtime steady Craddoc and her best friend Jack. Knowing that both have always been loyal to her, Elsie struggles with making a choice.

2.17 Ferguson, Alane. **Stardust.** Bradbury Press, 1993. 155 pp. ISBN 0-02-734527-0.

Welcome to the real world, Haley Loring, alias Samantha Love, former star of a popular television sit-com. In her new school

Haley copes by continuing to play the role of Samantha Love: cool, witty, full of sarcastic one-liners. But Andy Valdez, the one friend she really values, isn't impressed by her act. It takes a Halloween dance and a classroom battle featuring Gummy Worms and plastic insects for Haley to discover, "This is who I really am."

2.18 Gifaldi, David. **Toby Scudder, Ultimate Warrior.** Clarion Books, 1993. 201 pp. ISBN 0-395-66400-4.

This sixth-grade year is going to belong to Toby Scudder! With life a mess at home, he is determined to rule the school along with his best pal Leo. Toby is bigger than classmates and committed to get laughs by doing whatever it takes. Unfortunately, sixth grade holds some unexpected surprises for him that derail his plans and leave him less sure of himself.

2.19 Gilmore, Kate. **Jason and the Bard.** Houghton Mifflin, 1993. 236 pp. ISBN 0-395-62472-X.

A summer spent at the Avon Shakespeare Festival brings Jason new experiences in theater, personal relationships, and love. Sharing a small hut with five other apprentices, Jason experiences not only the drama of the stage, but that of real life. An unexpected opportunity to be actor Joe Hammond's understudy illuminates the magic of Shakespeare's plays acted on a stage lit by stars.

2.20 Godfrey, Martyn. **Please Remove Your Elbow from My Ear.** Avon/Flare, 1993. 122 pp. ISBN 0-380-76580-2.

Seventh-grader Stormy knows he and the other "dregs of detention dungeon" need a better image. Seeking school glory, they form a floor hockey team for the all-school competition and call themselves the "Detention Dregs." Enlisting hope-to-be girlfriends, a non-English-speaking Asian student, and a meditating ex-bully, the Dregs hope for the best. Their game plan is to play like their "creatively strange-like" selves.

2.21 Gorman, Carol. **The Miraculous Makeover of Lizard Flanagan.** HarperCollins, 1994. 185 pp. ISBN 0-06-024463-1.

Can middle school change ordinary, fun-loving sixth-grade kids into girl- and boy-crazy weirdos? Athletic Elizabeth "Lizard" Flanagan thinks so and is disgusted when her twin brother, his friends, and her own best friend seem more interested in clothes and dances than in sports. Lizard finally decides if she can't beat them, she'll join them—but how?

2.22 Grover, Wayne. **Ali and the Golden Eagle**. Greenwillow Books, 1993. 150 pp. ISBN 0-688-11385-0.

To Ali, a young shepherd boy living in a remote Arabian village, meeting an American is almost like meeting someone from outer space. Then Wayne becomes Ali's friend, capturing a baby gold eagle for Ali. When Ali trains his eagle well enough to win a royal falconry contest, he attracts the attention of the king himself, who then takes a special interest in Ali and his people, changing their lives forever.

2.23 Guthrie, Donna. **Kiss List.** Simon and Schuster Books for Young Readers, 1993. 134 pp. ISBN 0-671-75624-9.

Sixth-grader Travis is just sick. He knows he doesn't really want to win the bet to kiss all the sixth-grade girls. Why did he ever let that sneaky, bragging Frankie get to him? When the sixth-grade girls hear about the contest, they find humorous ways to get even.

2.24 Hahn, Mary Downing. **The Wind Blows Backward.** Clarion Books, 1993. 263 pp. ISBN 0-395-62975-6.

Lauren, always shy and quiet, is surprised and pleased whenever popular Spencer shows an interest in her. Quickly, Lauren falls in love with Spencer, his good looks and easy smile. Then slowly she discovers that loving him is scary. His easy-going nature, she discovers, is nothing but a mask of his true unhappiness and depression. When she finally realizes the depth of his despair, he has already taken some steps that changes them both forever.

2.25 Hayes, Daniel. **Eye of the Beholder.** Avon/Flare, 1994. 171 pp. ISBN 0-380-72285-2.

When Tyler gets the chicken pox and Lymie visits him, the two boys put their heads together to come up with an outrageous prank. Rumor has it that a famous but temperamental artist tossed two of his sculptured heads into the river. The boys create two fake heads and throw them into the river during the town's centennial celebration honoring the artist. However, when the fakes are found and declared authentic the boys know that they have chiseled off more than they intended!

2.26 Hill, David. **See Ya, Simon.** Dutton Children's Books, 1994. 153 pp. ISBN 0-525-45247-8.

In a New Zealand setting, fourteen-year-old Nathan narrates the story of his best friend Simon's battle with muscular dystrophy.

Friendship and Romance 37

According to Nathan, what Simon lacks in strength, he makes up in humor—frequently at Nathan's expense. Nathan shares the poignant moments of the rapid decline of his close friend, the meaning of true friendship, and the value of humor in dealing with circumstances over which we have no control.

2.27 Hosie-Bounar, Jane. **Life Belts.** Delacorte Press, 1993. 117 pp. ISBN 0-385-31074-9.

Tragic events create a bond for an unlikely threesome during their thirteenth summer, which they spend at the beach. Bold Nita convinces her best friend Molly to shed her cautions as well as her life belt for the thrill of adventure in their beat-up sailboat. Eddie, an outsider, watches in awe of Nita's beauty and mystery. One of the teens watches her mother die; another sees a small child drown; the third one watches the other two struggle to understand the tragedies of life.

2.28 Johnson, Scott. **Overnight Sensation.** Atheneum, 1994. 232 pp. ISBN 0-689-31831-6.

Kerry never meant to hurt Madeline, but Kerry had to throw aside her frumpy friend to enter the in-group at school. As for the fire that destroyed Madeline's garage, Kerry knew her new friends didn't mean any harm. The anti-Jewish graffiti on the walls was just kids having fun. Why then is Kerry consumed with guilt and fear, and what did she pick up after the fire and hide in her bedroom?

2.29 Kingman, Lee. **Break a Leg, Betsy Maybe!** Houghton Mifflin, 1993. 245 pp. ISBN 0-688-11789-9.

Betsy Maybe tells the story of her senior year as if it were a play with acts, scenes, cast, and dialogue. Orphaned and lonely, she finds a place with the Spotlight Club, a talented group of students passionate about the theater. During this eventful year, Betsy discovers her own talent, falls in love, and gains the confidence to make choices that will shape her future.

2.30 Kline, Suzy. **Who's Orp's Girlfriend?** G. P. Putnam's Sons, 1993. 94 pp. ISBN 0-399-22431-9.

Orp has girl troubles. Ellen, a classmate, and his pen pal, Jenny Lee, both make Orp's toes curl up right in his shoes. On Saturday, Jenny Lee will be in town and Orp has a date with Ellen. Juggling two girls is more than Orp can handle.

2.31 Lee, Marie G. **If It Hadn't Been for Yoon Jun.** Houghton Mifflin, 1993. 134 pp. ISBN 0-395-62941-1.

Alice faces the perfect seventh-grade year. She is on the cheerleading squad, and Troy, the cutest guy on the football team, seems to be interested in her. Alice's parents dare to disturb her universe by pressuring her to befriend the strange, new Korean student at school, Yoon Jun. Adopted as a baby, Alice feels American; she wants no part of her Korean heritage or Yoon Jun. But as the friendship grows, so does Alice's curiosity about her own past.

2.32 Levoy, Myron. **A Shadow Like a Leopard.** HarperCollins, 1994 (Originally published in 1981). 184 pp. ISBN 0-06-440458-7.

With his mother in the hospital and his father in jail, fourteen-year-old Ramon Santiago depends on his knife and his pen to survive the streets of Hell's Kitchen. Ramon uses his knife to look macho in front of the gang he wants to impress, but he is more comfortable with his pen. A foiled robbery of a wheelchair-bound artist leads to a friendship that gives Ramon hope of becoming a writer, if he can shake the gang.

2.33 Levoy, Myron. **Pictures of Adam.** Beech Tree Books, 1993 (Originally published in 1986). 218 pp. ISBN 0-688-11941-7.

From the minute amateur photographer Lisa Daniels encounters Adam Bates in science class, she becomes intrigued with capturing his shy, lost look. Lisa realizes the risks of becoming involved with Adam, who claims to be an alien from the planet Vega-X, but nonetheless falls in love with him. A visit to Adam's ramshackled cabin up in the hills gives Lisa not only the perfect subject for a photo essay contest, but also insight into the pain on Adam's face.

2.34 Levy, Elizabeth. **Cheater, Cheater.** Scholastic, 1993. 164 pp. ISBN 0-590-45865-5.

Lucy's middle school career begins with an invitation to her friend Melanie's birthday/bowling party and a date with Joey Rich, son of the owner of the local professional basketball team. He and his father are both fiercely competitive, and Lucy makes the mistake of trying to please Joey by cheating to gain a team bowling victory for them. Instead she succeeds in alienating him. Furthermore, Joey and a classmate are involved in a more serious form of school cheating against which Lucy must take a stand.

2.35 Lowell, Melissa. **Silver Blades: In the Spotlight.** Bantam/Skylark, 1993. 131 pp. ISBN 0-553-48135-5.

In this book from the Silver Blades series, Nikki, Danielle, Tori, and Jill, all Silver Blade Skating club members, share the dream of one day competing in the Olympics. When hard work and hours of practice begin to pay off for Danielle, she struggles with the pressure of being in the spotlight. Her friends notice the difference and wonder about her strange behavior. Other titles in this series about competition and friendships include *Breaking the Ice, Going for the Gold, Skating Camp,* and *The Competition.*

2.36 Makris, Kathryn. **Crosstown.** Avon/Flare, 1993. 167 pp. ISBN 0-380-76226-9.

Moving from suburban Covington to inner-city Easton seems like a nightmare to pretty, popular April Morgan. Money problems force April, her mother, and brother to the run-down Easton Arms, where there are roaches and worse. As her mother learns to handle family finances, April joins the Langley High Speech and Drama League and makes friends with Yoko and Mason. When she meets Devon Riddley, April decides it might turn out to be "the best year of her life."

2.37 Mango, Karin N. **Portrait of Miranda.** HarperCollins, 1993. 232 pp. ISBN 0-06-021777-4.

To her classmates, Miranda Hay appears confident almost to the point of being dramatic, but she can't fool herself. She feels insecure and ordinary, particularly compared to her namesake, her adventurous grandmother Miranda. Her grandmother's glamorous portrait inspires Miranda to create a more exciting life for herself and to turn that creation into a novel. Unfortunately, Miranda quickly entangles her made-up characters with real friends, such as Noel. Miranda risks losing Noel if she continues to play roles instead of being herself.

2.38 McCann, Helen. **What's French for HELP, George?** Simon & Schuster, 1993. 200 pp. ISBN 0-671-74689-8.

Fans of *What Do We Do Now, George?* will enjoy this companion novel where thirteen-year-old George and his friends take France by storm. Since George can't afford to join his friends on the school trip, he involves them in a computer scheme to help him win the one free ticket to France. With ticket in hand, George is on his way, and France is not the same!

2.39 McFann, Jane. **Nothing More, Nothing Less.** Avon/Flare, 1993. 167 pp. ISBN 0-380-76636-1.

Mackenzie Cameron is in love with her best friend and next-door neighbor, Madison. She and Madison have been friends since they were four. Now Mackenzie believes that if she changes her hair, her makeup, and her clothes, Madison will fall in love with her. She and her friend Devon make her over again and again—each time trying to produce a copy of Madison's latest girlfriend. Mackenzie learns that falling in love can drive you crazy.

2.40 McFann, Jane. **Free the Conroy Seven.** Avon/Flare, 1993. 152 pp. ISBN 0-380-76401-6.

Mr. Waldo, the assistant principal of Conroy High School, frantically interrupts classes to summon seven astonished students. Two of the top brains, a shy poet, a wheelchair-wheeling rebel, a cool skateboarder, and others report to the office to learn that they will remain there until someone confesses. To what? Solving the comic crime requires this unlikely group to put their differences aside and reveal their true selves to each other.

2.41 Mills, Claudia. **Dinah in Love.** Macmillan, 1993. 143 pp. ISBN 0-02-766998-X.

Boys are disgusting! That's what Dinah decides in this third book of her adventures. First, new boy Nick Tribble throws a pink exercise bra over her head in her father's sporting goods store. Then he embarrasses her when they're both auditioning for the school's play, and she is horrified to learn that they will be opponents at a school debate. But Dinah's feelings may be changing soon. She's in for a surprise where Nick is concerned.

2.42 Naylor, Phyllis Reynolds. **All but Alice.** Dell/Yearling, 1994. 151 pp. ISBN 0-440-40918-7.

The fourth book in the Alice series finds motherless Alice very concerned with sisterhood. At school Alice wants to be a part of the seventh-grade "in group" of girls, so she joins the All-Stars Fan Club, the earring club, and becomes one of the Famous Eight. At home, she attempts being a sister to each of her brother Lester's three girlfriends. Alice deals with each situation she gets herself into with typical humor and frankness. Other titles in the series include *Alice in April*, *The Agony of Alice*, *Alice in Rapture, Sort Of*, *Reluctantly Alice*, and *Alice In-Between*.

2.43 Naylor, Phyllis Reynolds. **Boys against Girls.** Delacorte Press, 1994. 147 pp. ISBN 0-385-32081-7.

Readers who enjoyed Naylor's *The Boys Start the War/The Girls Get Even* will delight in the continued can-you-top-this antics of the Hartford boys and the Malloy girls. In this sequel, the boys try to frighten off the girls by telling them that a strange animal known as the abaguchie has been spotted in their area. Instead of being frightened, the girls become curious, and the fun begins.

2.44 Naylor, Phyllis Reynolds. **The Boys Start the War/The Girls Get Even.** Dell Publishing, 1994. 262 pp. ISBN 0-440-40971-3.

It's war! When the three Malloy girls move next door to the four Hartford brothers, the boys are determined to make life so miserable that the Malloys will move away. The trading of tricks and insults escalates until Caroline, the youngest Malloy, is taken prisoner in the Hartford's shed while on a spy mission. The girls vow revenge. There will be a showdown at Halloween, and both sides are confident of victory.

2.45 Nelson, Peter. **Sylvia Smith-Smith.** Archway, 1993. 180 pp. ISBN 0-671-70586-5.

Smart, savvy, supercool Sylvia Smith-Smith appears capable of handling any situation in this sixth book of the Sylvia Smith-Smith series. Sylvia finds herself acting as a go-between for her separated parents, as she deals with her own romantic woes. Yet, she still makes time to take on, first, the school board, and then, a computer hacker who's wrecking her life at computer camp. Other books about Sylvia include *Dangerous Waters* and *Deadly Games*.

2.46 Neumann, Peter. **Playing a Virginia Moon.** Houghton Mifflin, 1994. 248 pp. ISBN 0-395-66562-0.

Chet Tralek is a runner. This year he expects to win the county's race and break the school record held by the legendary Johnny Fiske. However, Johnny's brother, Jimmy, comes out for track late in the season and throws a monkey wrench into Chet's nicely laid plans. Just when he thinks things could not possibly be more complicated, he meets Maggie, a flirtatious hockey player.

2.47 Paterson, Katherine. **Flip-Flop Girl.** Lodestar Books, 1994. 120 pp. ISBN 0-525-67480-2.

When she tries to cope with her dad's death, a move, and a little brother who has grown suddenly silent from grief, nine-year-old

Vinnie finds that she needs help. The family's move to Grandma's presents additional challenges. Registered in a school where the girls wear pretty clothes and make fun of five-year-old Mason, mute since his father's death, Vinnie needs a friend. However, she almost destroys the friendship offered by Lupe, the strange girl in orange flip-flops.

2.48 Paulsen, Gary. **The Car.** Harcourt Brace & Company, 1994. 180 pp. ISBN 0-15-292878-2.

When both of his parents leave home, fourteen-year-old Terry Anders suddenly realizes that he is on his own. He turns his attention to assembling a kit car, a Blakely Bearcat, in his garage. As "the Cat" comes together, Terry decides to head west to visit an uncle in Portland. On the way to Portland, Terry picks up two Vietnam veterans who take Terry "trucking" to see and experience America as an adventure in learning.

2.49 Pearson, Gayle. **The Fog Doggies and Me.** Macmillan, 1993. 121 pp. ISBN 0-689-31845-6.

Spring vacation goes awry when best friends Starr and Ivy find that a boy changes everything. As Ivy's new boyfriend crowds the girls' friendship, Starr feels betrayed and lonely. To make matters worse, her adoring little sister hounds her like the imaginary "fog doggies" that roll over San Francisco. When Ivy doesn't attend her own thirteenth birthday party planned by Starr, it becomes one more complication in Starr's changing adolescent world.

2.50 Peck, Richard. **Bel-Air Bambi and the Mall Rats.** Delacorte Press, 1993. 181 pp. ISBN 0-385-30823-X.

Last week it was credit cards and designer pasta in Los Angeles; today it's clothes from Grandmother's attic. Bankruptcy is rough, Bambi discovers after her family leaves L.A. and moves to Hickory Fork. There, in what appears to be a wholesome small town, Bambi discovers that the local mall has been taken over by a gang, the Mall Rats. She decides to clean up the town with the help of her TV-producer dad.

2.51 Pfeffer, Susan Beth. **Make Believe.** Henry Holt and Company, 1993. 135 pp. ISBN 0-8050-1754-2.

Best friends for as long as they can remember, Jill and Carrie have collected dolls, shared secrets, and played make-believe. Things change suddenly when Jill's father announces he wants a divorce.

Friendship and Romance

For the girls' parents, this marks a change in the couples' long-standing friendship and drives a wedge between Jill and Carrie. The families struggle with redefining relationships.

2.52 Philbrick, Rodman. **Freak the Mighty.** Scholastic, 1993. 169 pp. ISBN 0-590-47412-X.

Kevin is tiny, physically disabled, and brilliant. Max is huge and not so smart. Max's family fears that he is potentially dangerous like his convict father. Kevin longs for a bionic body to replace his damaged one. The two boys meet the summer before eighth grade, and for one splendid year, they are an unbeatable combination. They take on insensitive classmates, the local gang, even Max's terrifying, recently paroled, father. Together they are "Freak the Mighty!"

2.53 Sirof, Harriet. **Because She's My Friend.** Atheneum, 1993. 184 pp. ISBN 0-689-31844-8.

Shy, well-behaved fourteen-year-old Teri D'Angelo meets spoiled, sophisticated Valerie Ross while volunteering at a hospital where Valerie is a patient. Teri admires Valerie's ability to say and do whatever she pleases, but is secretly jealous of the attention Valerie gets. Valerie respects Teri's warmth and caring, but frequently takes advantage of it. Their relationship creates problems and difficulties while providing the girls with a friend that each needs.

2.54 Spinelli, Jerry. **Jason and Marceline.** Little, Brown, 1986. 228 pp. ISBN 0-316-80702-8.

Jason and Marceline are in ninth grade and their friendship is taking on a new meaning. After a couple of really bad starts, Jason convinces Marceline that they can be romantically linked and still stay friends. But he seems to be wrong, because when the kissing stops, the fighting starts. Seeing Marceline with another guy is all that it takes for Jason to use his creativity to come up with a solution for their romantic problems.

2.55 Springer, Nancy. **The Boy on a Black Horse.** Atheneum, 1994. 166 pp. ISBN 0-689-31840-5.

When thirteen-year-old Gray finds that she shares her love of horses with a mysterious and angry Gypsy boy, she also learns that he holds a dark secret. Chav, who cares for his younger brother and sister, tells people that he is searching for his father. Tormented by painful memories and self-hate, Chav rides away on his black stallion, leaving Gray to decide if she should—or even could—stop him.

2.56 Strauch, Eileen Walsh. **Hey You, Sister Rose.** Tambourine Books, 1993. 159 pp. ISBN 0-688-11829-1.

Arlene's worst nightmare becomes reality when Sister Rose becomes her sixth-grade teacher. Arlene sees Sister Rose watching her as she befriends a dirty, unloved classmate. Disaster after disaster follows Arlene through her sixth-grade year. Can she survive a year with Sister Rose?

2.57 Thompson, Joan. **The Mudpack and Me.** Minstrel Books, 1993. 148 pp. ISBN 0-671-72862-8.

A getaway health spa seems the perfect place for Susan Hubbard to lose ten pounds before beginning eighth grade, and her parents reluctantly agree. Her roommate is Tessa, the overweight and unhappy daughter of a soap opera star. Between mudpacks and yoga, the girls join forces to uncover the truth about the mysterious behavior of the handsome assistant Lorenzo. Soon, Susan is much more realistic about the importance of physical appearance.

2.58 Thompson, Julian F. **The Fling.** Henry Holt and Company, 1994. 201 pp. ISBN 0-0850-2881-1.

Felicia Gordon is baffled when the story she is writing for her high school English class begins to resemble real life. The plot of her make-believe story involves a mansion that becomes a sanctuary for teens. When Felicia and her friends step into that very scene, their lives are forever changed by their acquaintance with a troubled young man.

2.59 Vail, Rachel. **Ever After.** Orchard Books, 1994. 166 pp. ISBN 0-531-06838-2.

Molly's friends, Vicky and Grace, use and abuse her. Fourteen-year-old Molly trusts only her diary where she confides her confusion, scary shoplifting, and her secret love. When Vicky taunts her with details from her secret diary, Molly must decide what is important: her own self-esteem or her friends.

2.60 Vail, Rachel. **Wonder.** Puffin Books, 1993. 122 pp. ISBN 0-14-036167-7.

The girls in SCANTA, the popular seventh-grade clique, humiliate Jessica her first day in junior high. She is stuck with the hated name "Wonderbread." Losing her best friend Sheila to SCANTA and maybe losing her first boyfriend to Sheila leaves Jessica totally confused. Jessica isn't sure if SCANTA is ruining her life or if she's ruining her life herself.

Friendship and Romance

2.61 Vail, Rachel. **Do-Over.** Avon Books, 1994. 121 pp. ISBN 0-380-72180-5.

Whit Levy wishes he could call "do-over" in real life just as he can when he makes a mistake playing basketball. Instead, he must suffer all of the embarrassments that go along with growing up, first loves, and first heartaches. To make Whit's life worse, his parents are splitting up and his best friend's prejudice is disappointing. Only Whit's humor can get him through this difficult time.

2.62 Vornholt, John. **How to Sneak into the Girls' Locker Room.** Avon/Camelot, 1993. 90 pp. ISBN 0-380-76859-3.

The first day of junior high finds pals Brad, Vinnie, and Sean in trouble with hall monitor Clay Morris. He doesn't buy their story about being lost in the seventh-grade confusion and promises to make the school year miserable for them. The boys decide to avenge Clay's heavy-handedness by planning a brilliant scheme that will make them famous and teach Clay a lesson.

2.63 Walker, Kate. **Peter.** Houghton Mifflin, 1993. 170 pp. ISBN 0-395-64722-3.

Riding his dirt bike and practicing his photography skills are Peter's world until he meets his older brother's gay friend, David. When he realizes that he is attracted to David, Peter is horrified and scared. Rejecting the advances of a girl he does not like, fifteen-year-old Peter questions his own sexuality, and takes drastic action to find out who he is.

2.64 Werlin, Nancy. **Are You Alone on Purpose?** Houghton Mifflin, 1994. 204 pp. ISBN 0-395-67350-X.

Alison's autistic twin brother Adam is of Bar Mitzvah age, so their parents join a synagogue to introduce them both to their Jewish heritage. But Rabbi Roth refuses to admit Adam to the school at the synagogue, claiming that it isn't equipped for his special needs. Alison's mother is furious and wishes an evil fate on the rabbi's obnoxious son Harry. Then, to everyone's horror, Harry becomes paralyzed in a diving accident. This tragedy leads to a surprising romance and new understandings of differences.

2.65 Wilkinson, Brenda. **Definitely Cool.** Scholastic, 1993. 167 pp. ISBN 0-590-46186-9.

Roxanne feels "definitely cool" as she leaves the projects where she lives to attend the junior high in a fancy new neighborhood. Though making new friends proves harder than Roxanne expected, she finally settles in with a group of friends and a new boyfriend. When Roxanne begins feeling pressured by this faster-moving crowd to break rules, she has to decide what really is cool. Roxanne also gives serious thought to prejudice, friendships, and kids who are less fortunate.

2.66 Williams, Karen Lynn. **Applebaum's Garage.** Clarion Books, 1993. 168 pp. ISBN 0-395-65227-8.

Jeremy loves the clutter of his neighbor's garage and workshop. Mr. Applebaum can fix or build anything. Now that his best friend Robby is hanging around an older, tougher bunch of boys, Jeremy finds the garage a refuge. The neighbors, however, think the garage is an eyesore and insist that it be cleaned up. Jeremy has to find a way to give his old friend Mr. Applebaum a new interest in life, and he also needs to rebuild his friendship with Robby.

2.67 Wilson, Nancy Hope. **The Reason for Janey.** Macmillan, 1994. 160 pp. ISBN 0-02-793127-7.

Philly lives with her mother, brother, and since her parents' divorce, Janey, a retarded adult. For years Janey has lived in a state institution where her father abandoned her as a child. Now placed with Philly's family by a home-care program, Janey brings special needs, feelings, and confusion to Philly's family. Surprisingly, Philly discovers that she shares some of Janey's same feelings and frustrations.

2.68 Wittlinger, Ellen. **Lombardo's Law.** Houghton Mifflin, 1993. 135 pp. ISBN 0-395-65969-8.

There is a sort of an unwritten law that a fifteen-year-old girl can't be attracted to a thirteen-year-old boy, especially one who is three inches shorter. At first Justine Trainor finds Mike Lombardo a very good friend who shares her love for movies and reading. But, as they work together making their own movie, Justine finds herself with some very strong, but confusing, feelings.

2.69 Wolitzer, Meg. **Operation: Save the Teacher: Wednesday Night Match.** Avon/Camelot, 1993. 122 pp. ISBN 0-380-76461-X.

Sixth graders Julie, Trina, Allison, and Susan secretly place an ad in the personal section of the town newspaper. The girls hope to find the perfect woman to marry their widower teacher, Mr. Graham, but what they create is a humorous mix-up and embarrassment for all. Other funny books in the Operation: Save the Teacher series include *Tuesday Night Pie* and *Saturday Night Toast*.

2.70 Woodson, Jacqueline. **I Hadn't Meant to Tell You This.** Delacorte Press, 1994. 115 pp. ISBN 0-385-32031-0.

Lena lives on the poor white side of Chauncey, Ohio. When she is befriended by Marie, a leader among the popular black girls, Lena must decide whether or not to tell her terrible secret. Once Marie knows the truth about Lena's father, she urges Lena to tell authorities. The friendship the two girls share ignores unwritten rules about race and provides Lena with the support to face her problem and protect her younger sister.

2.71 Woodson, Jacqueline. **Maizon at Blue Hill.** Dell, 1994. 144 pp. ISBN 0-440-40899-7.

Maizon, the smartest girl in her Brooklyn neighborhood, leaves her grandmother and her best friend to attend Blue Hill, a predominantly white boarding school in Connecticut that has wooed her with a scholarship. Maizon's grandmother hopes the school will open new possibilities for her gifted granddaughter. Three months into the school year, Maizon must decide if her new academic success is worth the sadness she feels in being separated from her family, friends, and community.

2.72 Woodson, Jacqueline. **Between Madison and Palmetto.** Delacorte Press, 1993. 112 pp. ISBN 0-385-30906-6.

Margaret and Maizon, both black, both eighth graders, and best friends, face a hard year. Margaret's dad has died, Maizon had to change schools, and now a new girl, a white girl, is threatening their friendship. Pressures get harder when Maizon discovers Margaret's problem with bulimia. Can three girls of two races, each with problems of their own, be friends in a neighborhood where each person looks out just for herself?

2.73 Wyeth, Sharon Dennis. **The World of Daughter McGuire.** Delacorte Press, 1994. 167 pp. ISBN 0-385-31174-5.

Anna, Connie, and Daughter are best friends. Anna and Connie find out that Joey, a member of the Avengers, called Daughter a zebra and explain that zebras are the most different people and are a kind of "nothing." The truth is, Daughter is African Italian Irish Jewish Russian American. The journey to find out the mysteries of her heritage would be easier if her dad's plan to reunite the family is successful, and if ol' Jim Signet would stop coming around.

2.74 Zindel, Paul. **David & Della.** HarperCollins, 1993. 167 pp. ISBN 0-06-023353-2.

Young playwright David Mahooley's life hasn't been the same since he and girlfriend Kim parted company. Suffering from writer's block, David takes a classmate's advice and seeks help from a flamboyant but troubled young actress. Della convinces David to write again, but also tangles him in her troubled world of dishonesty, alcoholism, and her own shattered dreams.

3 Problems and Challenges

3.1 Arrick, Fran. **What You Don't Know Can Kill You.** Dell/Laurel Leaf, 1994. 154 pp. ISBN 0-440-21894-2.

Debra is jealous of her perfect sister. Then a school blood drive shatters thirteen-year-old Debra's illusions about life. Her beautiful sister is HIV-positive. Debra feels powerless against the disease and against the hostile reaction from the community. She tries to make sense out of her family's struggle to survive an uncertain future.

3.2 Barre, Shelley A. **Chive.** Simon & Schuster Books for Young Readers, 1993. 194 pp. ISBN 0-671-75641-9.

Homeless and living in a shelter because his parents have lost everything, Chive meets Terry's mom in a parking lot. He becomes friends with her eleven-year-old son. Embarrassed by his homelessness, Chive lies about his situation. After Terry helps Chive learn how to skateboard, the boys enter a competition. It isn't until after he disappears following the contest that Terry and his friends learn who Chive really is.

3.3 Barrie, Barbara. **Adam Zigzag.** Delacorte Press, 1994. 192 pp. ISBN 0-385-31172-9.

Teenager Adam Brody knows he has a good life and that he should be thankful. Instead, Adam is angry and afraid. What will happen to him if he never learns to read? Words zigzag all over the page. High school means drugs and skipping school. He keeps hoping to feel normal in spite of his dyslexia. Adam will try anything to hide his frustration.

3.4 Beake, Lesley. **Song of Be.** Henry Holt and Company, 1993. 94 pp. ISBN 0-8050-2905-2.

The old way of life for the Ju/'hoan people of Africa is gone; Be, a young Bushman woman, is caught up in the changes. She has run away from the Afrikaner farm where she has worked for the past year into the desert. She is deeply troubled by her people's suffering and longs to find the peaceful world of her childhood. For Be, love and hope lie with Khu, a young political organizer who represents the new Namibia.

3.5 Bennett, James. **Dakota Dream.** Scholastic, 1994. 182 pp. ISBN 0-590-46680-1.

Fifteen-year-old Floyd, a long-time foster child, flees from the mental institution where he had most recently been placed. Going to a Sioux Indian reservation, he asks the tribal leaders to let him attempt the task he thinks he must to become Charlie Black Crow. The leaders consider it too dangerous and, instead, send him on a hanblecheya, or vision quest. Completing this quest means more to Floyd than changing his name; it means finding a home and family to call his own.

3.6 Betancourt, Jeanne. **My Name Is ~~Brain~~ Brian.** Scholastic, 1993. 128 pp. ISBN 0-590-44921-4.

Brian decides to start sixth grade right, but he doesn't share that with his friends who have formed the Jokers Club to keep score on who can make the most jokes in class. Tired of looking lazy and dumb, Brian wants to trust his new teacher when he suggests having Brian tested for learning difficulties. Diagnosed as having dyslexia, Brian has to choose between his friends' approval and accepting his teacher's help in learning successfully.

3.7 Block, Francesca Lia. **Missing Angel Juan.** HarperCollins, 1993. 138 pp. ISBN 0-06-023004-5.

Witch Baby follows her boyfriend, Angel Juan, to New York out of concern for his safety. Her journey in search of Angel Juan will also lead Witch Baby to friends of her grandfather and a new understanding of the importance of family. She learns that, although letting go is difficult, it is the best way to show love.

3.8 Botchway, Christine. **The Jasmine Candle.** Chelsea House, 1993. 132 pp. ISBN 0-7910-2932-8.

Zenobia lives between the boundaries of the powerful Dagabusi and the weaker Brusumi tribes. Both disown her, with neither knowing the truth of her royal blood. She is determined to convince both tribes to stop the practice of ancient rites before something terrible happens. With a death threat against her, and a king who believes she is his dead daughter resurrected, Zenobia fights for life.

3.9 Broome, Errol. **Dear Mr. Sprouts.** Alfred A. Knopf, 1993. 121 pp. ISBN 0-679-83714-0.

When a balloon carrying a letter and a seed packet lands on Freddie's Australian farm, it marks the beginning of a pen-pal

Problems and Challenges 51

relationship with Anke, a schoolgirl living in the city. Though Anke and Freddie appear to have little in common, both are isolated. Freddie lives on a remote farm with his dad. Anke, who has a stuttering problem, is an immigrant to Australia. The letters they write to each other chronicle the growth of their relationship. The book comes full circle with a peek into Anke's and Freddie's future.

3.10 Cadnum, Michael. **Calling Home.** Penguin Books, 1993. 138 pp. ISBN 0-14-034569-8.

Only Peter knows the truth about his missing friend Mead. Peter killed him. Alcohol sustains Peter as he lies to his family and friends about Mead. Peter's life is a nonstop nightmare.

3.11 Carter, Alden R. **Dancing on Dark Water.** Scholastic, 1994. 144 pp. ISBN 0-590-45600-8.

Shar wants her old daddy back, not this new stranger who hates her. Shar and her brothers live with their brain-damaged and increasingly violent father. Together, they do the best they can under frightening and unusual circumstances. Fear, pain, anger, and frustration become everyday feelings for Shar as she wonders how to cope with a daddy who is more a stranger than anything else.

3.12 Carter, Alden R. **Dogwolf.** Scholastic, 1994. 231 pp. ISBN 0-590-46741-7.

Fifteen-year-old Peter LaSavage, a mix of Chippewa Indian, Metis, and Swedish, feels confused about his identity. As a summer of fighting forest fires and confronting personal problems unfolds for Pete, he is faced with even more confusion. The disappearance of his father still haunts him. And now the appearance of his grandfather—his dad's dad—stirs up more questions than answers. The fierce animal—part wolf and part dog—that is caged near home reminds him of himself: confused, wild, and looking for freedom.

3.13 Coman, Carolyn. **Tell Me Everything.** Farrar, Straus, and Giroux, 1993. 156 pp. ISBN 0-374-37390-6.

Twelve-year-old Roz Jacoby struggles with questions surrounding her mother's death. She only knows that her mother died trying to rescue a hiker lost in the mountains near their home. For almost a year, Roz calls the rescued boy just to hear his voice, knowing that he can answer her questions when she is ready. Then one day, instead of hearing his voice, she hears a recording stating that the number has changed and is now unlisted. This forces Roz to seek both the boy and the answer before she loses access to both.

3.14 Conly, Jane Leslie. **Crazy Lady!** HarperCollins, 1993. 180 pp. ISBN 0-06-021357-4.

Like all the other kids, Vernon Dibbs taunts Maxine Flooter, calling her the "Crazy Lady." When fear of failing seventh grade makes Vernon feel like a misfit too, he finds himself not only talking to Maxine, but accepting her help in finding him a tutor. In appreciation for her help, Vernon begins assisting Maxine with her disabled son, Ronald. Vernon's growing concern for Ronald leads him to a better understanding of his own capabilities.

3.15 Cooney, Caroline B. **Driver's Ed.** Delacorte Press, 1994. 184 pp. ISBN 0-385-32087-6.

Remy and Morgan love their driver's ed class. Driver's ed means that the driver's license is just around the corner, and a driver's license means independence. Life is great until Remy, Morgan, and a friend steal a stop sign from an intersection one night. That stolen stop sign meant Denise Thompson didn't know to stop at that intersection and not stopping meant she got broadsided—and killed. Now, Remy and Morgan know who took the sign and know who's responsible; they just don't know what to do.

3.16 Corcoran, Barbara. **Wolf at the Door.** Atheneum, 1993. 194 pp. ISBN 0-689-31870-7.

Lee and her biologist mother rescue a mistreated wolf from a roadside zoo and take the wolf to their Montana farm. Word gets around that this is a safe place for wolves, and four more are dropped off at the home. The sheep farmer next door, however, doesn't take kindly to wolves being so near and begins shooting at both Lee and her wolves. When one of the wolves is poisoned, Lee knows she must take action.

3.17 Cormier, Robert. **Tunes for Bears to Dance To.** Dell, 1992. 101 pp. ISBN 0-440-21903-5.

Henry and his parents move to a new community after his brother dies in a hit-and-run accident. By working at Mr. Hairston's grocery store, Henry hopes to earn money for a monument for Eddie's grave. One day Henry follows an eccentric neighbor, Mr.

Levine, to a local craft center where he is building a wooden model of his village, which was destroyed in the Holocaust. Henry's bigoted employer pressures him to destroy Mr. Levine's work, and he is forced to make a difficult moral decision.

3.18   Crutcher, Chris. **Staying Fat for Sarah Byrnes.** Greenwillow Books, 1993. 216 pp. ISBN 0-688-11552-7.

Sarah Byrnes, terribly scarred in a mysterious accident, and Eric Calhoune, overweight and outcast, base their friendship on their "terminal uglies." Then Eric joins the school swimming team and begins to trim down. Fearful he will lose his relationship with Sarah, he gorges to stay fat. As Sarah's tragic past catches up with her, she retreats from life. Eric struggles to reach the near catatonic Sarah before it's too late.

3.19   Deaver, Julie Reece. **You Bet Your Life.** HarperCollins, 1993. 209 pp. ISBN 0-06-021516-X.

After her mom commits suicide, seventeen-year-old Bess feels betrayed and alone. Then she lands a job as an intern on television's comedy hit "The Les Komack Show." Years of watching favorite movies with her mom have fostered Bess's love of comedy. Only after she and fellow intern Eliot form their comedy team and solidify their friendship is Bess able to resume life.

3.20   DeClements, Barthe. **Breaking Out.** Dell/Yearling, 1993. 130 pp. ISBN 0-440-40802-4.

Seventh grade is hard enough without having a father in prison ... again! Jerry Johnson and his good friend Grace find each day a challenge. Grace, the preacher's kid, hates the frumpy clothes her mom makes her wear, and she makes big mistakes in the way she handles classmates' taunts. Jerry struggles with a difficult stepfather while trying to untangle who he is.

3.21   Disher, Garry. **The Bamboo Flute.** Ticknor & Fields Books for Young Readers, 1993. 82 pp. ISBN 0-395-66595-7.

Times are hard in Australia in 1932. Homeless swagmen travel the roads looking for food and work. Twelve-year-old Paul has been warned to stay away from these dangerous men, but he is irresistibly drawn to one of them. Eric the Red is a cunning old sheep-stealer who makes beautiful music, the kind Paul's mother played in the old days before they became so poor. Maybe with Eric's help, Paul can bring the music back to his family's life.

3.22 Disher, Garry. **Ratface.** Ticknor & Fields Books for Young Readers, 1994. 185 pp. ISBN 0-395-69451-5.

Max and Christina live with their adoptive family, members of the cult called White League. Max, "adopted" as an infant doesn't remember anything about the outside world, but Christina does. Every day they are indoctrinated with the cult's beliefs. After a reporter infiltrates the farm and shares with Max and Christina facts about the cult's leader and their real parents, the children understand that all they have been told is lies. Together, they attempt an escape to search for their real parents.

3.23 Doherty, Berlie. **Dear Nobody.** Beech Tree Books, 1994. 232 pp. ISBN 0-688-12764-9.

Helen is pregnant. Chris, Helen's boyfriend, wants to take care of her, but she sends him away. Chris's anger and confusion grow as Helen's family enforces her decision. His feelings are compounded when his mother, who abandoned him when he was ten years old, re-enters his life. Separately, the two teenagers face their uncertain futures and the birth of their child.

3.24 Draper, Sharon M. **Tears of a Tiger.** Atheneum, 1994. 162 pp. ISBN 0-689-31878-2.

Four best friends cruise around with some cold brew to celebrate their victory after the Hazelwood Tigers basketball game. The celebration ends when Andy Jackson's car crashes into a retaining wall, bursts into flame, and kills Robert Washington. Unlike his friends, Andy isn't able to work through his grief and guilt. Instead, he becomes obsessed with death. This obsession is shared through a series of letters, articles, homework assignments, and conversations that take place in the months following the accident.

3.25 Dunlop, Eileen. **Finn's Search.** Holiday House, 1994. 155 pp. ISBN 0-8234-1099-4.

If finding an ancient Roman fort will save his town from an ugly gravel pit, then Finn will find the fort. Finn needs an alliance between Andrew, the town bully, and Chris, his fearful undersized friend. Vigilante groups opposing the gravel pit threaten Andrew's life. When Andrew is severely beaten, Chris is forced to consider his own fears and his actions toward Andrew.

3.26 Ferris, Jean. **Across the Grain.** Farrar, Straus, and Giroux, 1993. 184 pp. ISBN 0-374-40057-1.

Will isn't happy about moving to the California desert with his sister Paige. Fortunately, he finds two very special friends. Mike is a prickly classmate who is passionate about filmmaking. Sam is a middle-aged man whose passion is the adobe house he builds with Will and Mike's help. Will is offered a full scholarship to U.C.L.A., but Paige wants to pursue another of her schemes. Now Will must choose between his dreams and his sister's desires.

3.27 Fine, Anne. **Flour Babies.** Little, Brown and Company, 1994. 178 pp. ISBN 0-316-28319-3.

Each of the boys in Room 8 is given a six-pound sack of flour to look after for three weeks so that he can experience the pain and pleasure of parenthood. Most of the boys soon want to drop their "babies" in the river—except for Simon. As he struggles to protect "her" from mud, fire, and dog drool, Simon begins to understand why his own father left when Simon was a baby.

3.28 Fox, Paula. **A Place Apart.** Farrar, Straus, and Giroux, 1993. 184 pp. ISBN 0-374-45868-5.

For thirteen-year-old Victoria Finch the months after her father's death are so miserable that "all the minutes hurt." She and her mother move from Boston to the village of New Oxford, where she meets wealthy, enigmatic Hugh Todd. Hugh seems to offer the perfect friendship, and Victoria falls further and further under his spell. But Hugh has serious problems of his own, and his friendship may cost more than Victoria is willing to pay.

3.29 Fromm, Pete. **Monkey Tag.** Scholastic, 1994. 336 pp. ISBN 0-590-46525-2.

Thad is at the top of the rafters under the high bleachers when Eli tries for the tag. Suddenly Thad is no longer there. He has fallen, and the nightmare begins for the twin brothers and best friends. Thad is paralyzed from the waist down. Eli believes it is all his fault because they should not have played monkey tag, and he shouldn't have moved Thad after the fall. Eli must deal with his guilt while Thad must confront the possibility that he may never walk again.

3.30 Gabhart, Ann. **Bridge to Courage.** Avon/Flare, 1993. 147 pp. ISBN 0-380-76051-7.

"Chicken!" That's the word Luke hears when he fails the initiation into the Truelanders because he cannot cross the high railroad trestle. Shunned by the club and harassed by the school bully, fourteen-year-old Luke finally finds a friend in Shea Ashburn. She is determined to cure him of his fear of heights. What begins with a seeming act of cowardice builds to a tension-filled climax in which Luke must face his fears.

3.31 Greene, Patricia Baird. **The Sabbath Garden.** Dutton/Lodestar, 1993. 214 pp. ISBN 0-525-67430-6.

The lower East Side of New York was once all-Jewish. Now Solomon Leschko is the last remaining Jew. He forms an unlikely bond with Opal Tyler, a black teenager who dreams both of being a writer and of restoring dignity to a neighborhood which has fallen into despair. Opal's violent, angry brother Frank represents the depths to which the community has sunk. Old and young, Jew and African American team up to create a neighborhood garden, a symbol of renewed hope.

3.32 Greenwald, Sheila. **My Fabulous New Life.** Browndeer Press/Harcourt Brace & Company, 1993. 172 pp. ISBN 0-15-277693-1.

Alison Fox, founder and president of the A-Ones, must leave her A-One friends in Greenhill for a scaled-down life in New York City. She moves to a high-rise apartment surrounded by begging, homeless people and leaves behind her suburban home that was down the road from the country club. Beyond the typical difficulty of making friends in a new surrounding, Alison questions homelessness and what an eleven-year-old can do about it.

3.33 Heneghan, James. **Torn Away.** Viking, 1994. 185 pp. ISBN 0-670-85180-9.

Declan, drugged and handcuffed, is deported from Northern Ireland to Canada to live with his Uncle Matthew. At thirteen Declan is already a terrorist, living for revenge against the British for the deaths of his parents and sister. Even though Matthew and his family offer Declan a new life far from the endless fighting, he is bitter and withdrawn. Only Declan can make the final choice: the affection of his new family or a lifetime of killing.

3.34 Hicyilmaz, Gaye. **Against the Storm.** Dell/Yearling, 1993. 200 pp. ISBN 0-440-40892-X.

Eleven-year-old Mehmet tries to convince his family not to leave his beloved Turkish village for the bustling city of Ankara. The family, caught up in Mehmet's uncle's success in Ankara, moves anyway. Once in the city, they seem to lose all sense of caring for each other. Mehmet seeks solace in the friendships of Hayri, an old friend who had moved to Ankara earlier, and Muhlis, a streetwise young orphan.

3.35 Kaye, Marilyn. **Real Heroes.** Harcourt Brace Jovanovich, 1993. 144 pp. ISBN 0-15-200563-3.

What is a hero? Sixth grader Kevin Delaney always considered his father a hero, both as a police officer and as a father who was there when Kevin's mom left. But then his father joins other parents in a battle to have Kevin's HIV-positive P.E. teacher, Mr. Logan, dismissed from teaching. Torn between loyalty to his father and Mr. Logan, the only adult Kevin can really talk to, Kevin questions what it is his father fears.

3.36 Kehret, Peg. **Cages.** Minstrel Books, 1993. 150 pp. ISBN 0-671-75879-9.

Frustrated by a disappointment at school and an alcoholic stepfather at home, ninth grader Kit Hathaway impulsively shoplifts an expensive gold bracelet. Her arrest results in a sentence of twenty hours of volunteer work at the humane society. Kit feels as trapped as the animals at the shelter; she faces the possible losses of a terrier she grows to love and Tracy's friendship if Tracy learns of Kit's crime.

3.37 Kennedy, Barbara. **The Boy Who Loved Alligators.** Atheneum, 1994. 137 pp. ISBN 0-689-31876-6.

Jim feels ugly and unwanted, especially after his grandfather dies and none of the remaining relatives want to take him in. But distant relative Billie invites him to stay with her for the summer in Orlando. There, Jim spends long hours alone by a lake where he begins noticing and talking to a large alligator. Then, though warned not to, Jim begins feeding the gator, and things really get out of control.

3.38 Kerr, M. E. **Linger.** HarperCollins, 1993. 213 pp. ISBN 0-06-022882-2.

The restaurant called Linger is the biggest and best thing about small town Berryville, Pennsylvania. Why then did Bobby Peel suddenly quit his job there and join the army? Now Bobby is fighting in the Persian Gulf War and writing letters to Lynn Dunlinger, the restaurant owner's beautiful daughter. Only Gary, Bobby's younger brother, understands why Bobby left Linger and Berryville so abruptly. A tragedy in the Gulf and a near tragedy in Berryville change Bobby, Gary, and those they think they love.

3.39 Kherdian, David. **Asking the River.** Illustrated by Nonny Hogrogian. Orchard Books, 1993. 106 pp. ISBN 0-531-05483-7.

Stephan Bakaian, an Armenian American, feels trapped in the life his immigrant parents have created in Racine, Wisconsin. Still in the fifth grade at age thirteen, Stephan seems destined to a future on an assembly line in his blue-collar hometown. He knows he doesn't want that kind of life, but he is uncertain about what he does want. Stephan seeks answers and peace at the local river, where he sketches, writes, dreams, and struggles to understand life.

3.40 Killingsworth, Monte. **Circle within a Circle.** Macmillan/Margaret K. McElderry Books, 1994. 139 pp. ISBN 0-689-50598-1.

Chris no sooner puts out his thumb than he is picked up by Coyote, a Chinook Indian. Coyote is going to his tribal home, where he will try to stop resort developers from destroying sacred ground. During their journey, Chris, who is running away from his current foster home, decides to help Coyote. As they travel together, a bond forms between them, even though each has painful secrets they are not ready to share.

3.41 Kincaid, Beth. **Silver Creek Riders: Back in the Saddle.** Jove Books, 1994. 184 pp. ISBN 0-515-11480-4.

In this first book in the Silver Creek Riders series, best friends Jenna and Katie are thrilled to be spending the summer at Silver Creek riding camp and can't wait to meet their other two tentmates, who they've heard are champion jumpers. Melissa fits in easily, but all three are shocked when Sharon limps in wearing heavy leg braces and acting angry and bitter. What's happened to Sharon, and how can they help her? Looks as if it could be a long summer!

3.42 Klass, David. **California Blue.** Scholastic, 1994. 199 pp. ISBN 0-590-46688-7.

John Rodgers has never seen eye-to-eye with his father, and now his dad is dying of leukemia. To make matters worse, John discovers a new subspecies of butterfly at the mill site where his father works. Rumors spread that the discovery may close the mill if the government decides the butterfly should be protected. John risks becoming the town's worst enemy as he decides how to balance his loyalties to both his family and his amazing butterfly, the California Blue.

Problems and Challenges

3.43 Konigsburg, E. L. **T-Backs, T-Shirts, Coat, and Suit.** Atheneum, 1993. 165 pp. ISBN 0-689-31855-3.

Chloe is spending the summer with unusual Aunt Bernadette. Bernadette is being pressured by her boss to wear a revealing swimsuit on the job to increase sales. Her refusal sparks a media war on public morals. Thirteen-year-old Chloe is confused and scared by the mounting pressure and personal attacks suffered by her aunt, but Aunt Bernadette helps Chloe to understand the nature of personal choices.

3.44 LeMieux, A. C. **The TV Guidance Counselor.** Tambourine Books, 1993. 239 pp. ISBN 0-688-12402-X.

Sixteen-year-old Michael Madden's life begins to fall apart after his parents divorce and his father leaves to photograph a round-the-world yacht race. He gives Michael a camera as a parting gift. Becoming obsessed with photography, Michael uses the camera to distance himself from friends and family. Finally, an "accident" that looks to many like an attempted suicide sends Michael to a turning point.

3.45 Lipsyte, Robert. **The Chemo Kid.** HarperKeypoint, 1993. 167 pp. ISBN 0-06-447101-2.

Fred Bauer's chemotherapy treatments have weird side effects, such as turning him bright green, puffy, and bald. The experimental drug also gives Fred superpowers. Fred, alias the Chemo Kid, takes on the bad guys in the town, the ones dumping toxic waste into the water supply. As his new superpowers help fight bad guys, can they also help him fight his battle with cancer?

3.46 Marino, Jan. **Like Some Kind of Hero.** Avon/Flare, 1993. 216 pp. ISBN 0-380-72010-8.

Ted Bradford is fourteen, and he doesn't want to be different. He wants to be popular. He wants to be a lifeguard. He's willing to do whatever it takes: shave his head, lie to his mother, even turn against old friends. Soon Ted's in way over his head in more ways than one, and passing the lifeguard survival test is the least of his worries.

3.47 Mazer, Norma Fox, and Harry Mazer. **Bright Days and Stupid Nights.** Dell/Laurel Leaf, 1993. 194 pp. ISBN 0-440-21594-3.

A summer internship on a Pulitzer Prize–winning newspaper offers more than journalism experience to four teenagers: Chris escapes his Greek father's expectations; Vicki grabs an opportunity to get ahead and not end up like her mother; Elizabeth gets away from a suffocating relationship with her boyfriend; Faith leaves her past behind to establish a new life. Competition with each other, unexpected love interests, and problems from home that won't go away keep the foursome working, worrying, and sometimes laughing.

3.48 Mazer, Norma Fox. **Out of Control.** Morrow Junior Books, 1993. 218 pp. ISBN 0-688-10208-5.

Sixteen-year-old Rollo Wingate finds himself going along with buddies, Brig and Candy, when they leave a school assembly to follow Valerie Michon. Within moments, they attack Valerie. She reports the sexual offense; but the boys, their parents, and the school administration conspire to conceal the truth. Rollo and his friends go unpunished. Knowing she was violated, Valerie "goes public" with a letter to the editor of the local newspaper. Rollo then realizes those few moments of being out of control changed not only Valerie's life, but his, too.

3.49 McDaniel, Lurlene. **Baby Alicia Is Dying.** Bantam Books, 1993. 185 pp. ISBN 0-0553-29605-1.

Desi's distant mother is hostile to Desi's work at Child Care, a facility for HIV-positive babies. Desi's mother refuses to understand that Desi needs to love baby Alicia in order to feel loved herself. As baby Alicia lies dying with Desi by her bed, Desi's mother begins to confront the death, years earlier, of her own child. Slowly, Desi and her mother begin the long process of healing their fractured relationship.

3.50 McDaniel, Lurlene. **The Legacy: Making Wishes Come True.** Bantam Books, 1993. 186 pp. ISBN 0-553-56134-0.

Sixteen-year-old Jenny Crawford's fierce battle against leukemia is bearable only because of her friendship with other cancer patients and her love for her childhood friend Richard. She is determined to use her vast wealth to leave a legacy of hope for others fighting impossible odds. Fighting for her life, Jenny also fights to establish the One Last Wish Foundation that she hopes will bring other sick teenagers a bit of happiness.

3.51 McEwan, Ian. **The Daydreamer.** HarperCollins, 1994. 192 pp. ISBN 0-06-0244266-7.

Ten-year-old Peter Fortune is the last word in daydreaming. At home or at school, he is capable of disappearing into worlds where he battles his younger sister Kate's dolls, or zips himself inside his cat's skin and experiences the pleasures and problems of a feline existence! Peter's unusual powers of imagination lead him into encounters with school bullies and burglars.

3.52 Murphy, Catherine Frey. **Alice Dodd and the Spirit of Truth.** Macmillan, 1993. 176 pp. ISBN 0-02-767702-8.

Alice's summer is sure to be wonderful. She, Aunt Kate, and her three-year-old cousin are vacationing at the family's cabin. All that is expected of Alice is caring for little Amy while Aunt Kate paints. When Alice tells her first lie, she only means it to spice up her image. Unfortunately, one lie leads to another, and she soon wishes she could undo all she has done.

3.53 Murrow, Liza Ketchum. **Twelve Days in August.** Holiday House, 1993. 202 pp. ISBN 0-8234-1012-9.

The twelve days preceding the first varsity soccer game of the season are memorable for Todd O'Connor. Todd's teammate Randy begins a smear campaign against Alex, the newest member of the team. He tells everyone Alex is gay and tries to keep him from playing. Randy's harassment almost ruins the team, but the ballplayers learn that fair play is more than just following the rules of the game.

3.54 Myers, Walter Dean. **Darnell Rock Reporting.** Delacorte Press, 1994. 135 pp. ISBN 0-385-32096-5.

Thirteen-year-old Darnell Rock joins the school newspaper to prove to his principal that he is going to straighten out. Instead of hanging out with the Corner Crew gang, Darnell gets involved with the newspaper and becomes intrigued with the power of the printed word—particularly, his own. Darnell's first story leads to unexpected changes for himself and the homeless man he interviews.

3.55 Naidoo, Beverle. **Chain of Fire.** HarperTrophy, 1993. 256 pp. ISBN 0-06-440468-4.

Fifteen-year-old Naledi and her classmates are faced with the greatest challenge of their young lives. Bulldozers, backed by an army of bloodthirsty police, are about to destroy their South African community. Will protest marches, petitions, and appeals to the local arm of the South African government be enough to save their homes and their dignity? How can anyone stand against all that power? The children and their families discover what they are willing to risk as they become part of a greater struggle.

3.56 Nasaw, Jonathan. **Shakedown Street.** Delacorte, 1993. 197 pp. ISBN 0-385-31071-4.

Caro never expected to spend her fourteenth birthday living in a gully under a freeway ramp. The homeless who gather there call it "Shakedown Street," and they form a kind of family, helping and protecting each other. Caro panhandles and picks up trash. The group moves into an abandoned house, but the police aren't far behind. Caro has a dream—to sleep in a bed of her own. But dreams need money and luck, and both are in short supply.

3.57 Naylor, Phyllis Reynolds. **The Fear Place.** Atheneum, 1994. 118 pp. ISBN 0-689-31866-9.

Doug and Gordon Grillo accompany their parents every summer on a research trip in a remote area of the Rocky Mountains. For twelve-year-old Doug, a narrow, crumbling path six hundred feet above a canyon has become the "Fear Place." He froze there in a climb two years earlier, and not even his older brother's teasing can make Doug return. Only when Doug's parents are called away from the research trip on an emergency and Gordon disappears near the "Fear Place" does Doug consider facing his fear.

3.58 Nelson, Theresa. **The Beggars' Ride.** Dell/Laurel Leaf, 1994. 242 pp. ISBN 0-440-21887-X.

Their names come from Monopoly: Cowboy, Racer, Thimble, Shoe, and Little Dog. They're a street gang of homeless kids who rescue runaway Clare. Clare wants to reach her mother's ex-boyfriend Joey in Atlantic City. But Joey's gone, and the gang offers a refuge from the dangers of the street, including the sinister social worker Griffey. The gang's protection is short-lived. Soon Clare needs help, but there is nowhere to turn and no one to trust.

3.59 Nelson, Vaunda Micheaux. **Mayfield Crossing.** Illustrated by Leonard Jenkins. G. P. Putnam's Sons, 1993. 88 pp. ISBN 0-399-22331-2.

After small town Mayfield Crossing closes its only school, the kids there are bussed to the larger school in Parkview. This new school ought to be great. At least, that's what the kids from Mayfield Crossing think. More kids, a bigger school, and a chance for better sports, especially baseball. The problem is, the kids at Parkview, *white* kids, don't want the kids from Mayfield, *black* kids, at their school. This type of racial prejudice is new for the kids from Mayfield.

Problems and Challenges 63

3.60 Paulsen, Gary. **The Monument.** Dell/Yearling, 1993. 151 pp. ISBN 0-440-40782-6.

When artist Mick Strum arrives in Bolton, Kansas, to design a war monument for the city park, Rocky follows him around town, watching him capture the spirit of Bolton through sketches of people, places, and animals. Rocky comes to respect Mick as he leads Rocky to develop her own artistic talent. In an unorthodox way, Mick shows the townspeople who they are in order to help them select a meaningful monument.

3.61 Pfeffer, Susan Beth. **The Ring of Truth.** Bantam Books, 1993. 180 pp. ISBN 0-553-09224-3.

An encounter with a drunken elected official at a party pulls orphaned sixteen-year-old Sloan Fredericks into a full-blown political scandal after she tells classmates that the official made a pass at her. Her best friend Justine confesses her own involvement with the same man. Sleazy tabloids pursue Sloan as her wealthy grandmother attempts a cover-up. A painful family secret is also revealed, and Sloan knows her sheltered, privileged way of life may be coming to an end.

3.62 Pitts, Paul. **Crossroads.** Avon Books, 1994. 152 pp. ISBN 0-380-77606-5.

Fatherless and friendless, Navajo-born Hobart Sim faces life the way he faces the school bully—only dreaming of changes. It is not until Lettie Mendoza arrives that Hobart learns to believe in himself and make changes. Lettie's homeless family becomes stranded when their station wagon breaks down in front of the shabby hotel run by Hobart's mother and uncle. When the Mendozas decide to stay on, Lettie joins Hobart in the sixth grade and Hobart's life changes directions.

3.63 Polese, Carolyn. **Promise Not to Tell.** Beech Tree Books, 1993. 56 pp. ISBN 0-688-12026-1.

If Megan can pass the Trials Test at the riding stable near the campground, her father promises to take her on a cross-country ride. An offer for private lessons by her instructor, Walt, ends up in attempted molestation. Walt's threats, "You've got to promise not to tell," weigh heavily on eleven-year-old Megan. Are there promises that don't have to be kept?

3.64 Rana, Indi. **The Roller Birds of Rampur.** Henry Holt and Company, 1993. 298 pp. ISBN 0-8050-26703-3.

Angry at her English boyfriend Jimmy for rejecting her, and at her parents for taking her to a country that looks down on brown-skinned people, seventeen-year-old Sheila Mehta returns from England to India. Instead of the peace she hopes to find, Sheila discovers an India filled with poverty, ancient ways, and people resigned to both. Sheila sets out to understand her Indian heritage in order to determine who she is and where she will live.

3.65   Rhodes, Judy Carole. **The Hunter's Heart.** Bradbury Press, 1993. 184 pp. ISBN 0-02-775935-0.

In this sequel to *The King Boy*, the inheritance of his grandfather's farm at the age of eighteen challenges Benjy King to grow up quickly. Along with the responsibilities of the farm, Benjy finds himself faced with decisions that risk the friendship of Coot Hunter, someone who has always been there for Benjy. As Coot's mysterious past starts unraveling with the arrival of the attractive Sara, Benjy begins searching for answers to make his new life work.

3.66   Ross, Ramon Royal. **Harper & Moon.** Atheneum, 1993. 181 pp. ISBN 0-689-31803-0.

Moon has always been a part of twelve-year-old Harper's life. Older than Harper and orphaned as a young child, he can transform bits of lumber and scraps into magnificent creations. A summertime week spent at the mountain cabin of aging storekeeper Olinger strengthens the pair's friendship. However, when Moon enlists as a soldier in World War II, Harper makes a discovery that leads him to some serious questions about his good friend.

3.67   Rubin, Susan Goldman. **Emily Good as Gold.** Harcourt Brace & Company, 1993. 180 pp. ISBN 0-15-276633-2.

Though developmentally delayed, Emily Gold, thirteen, longs to be like other girls her age. Fearful as their daughter matures, the family's over-protectiveness causes Emily embarrassment. When she is faced with a life-changing decision, she wonders if "her head will work right" this time.

3.68   Ruby, Lois. **Skin Deep.** Scholastic, 1994. 280 pp. ISBN 0-590-47699-8.

Things changed for Dan Penner when he moved to Boulder, Colorado, in his senior year. Feeling rejected by the swim-team coach, prospective employers, and his father, Dan becomes attracted to

Problems and Challenges 65

a group of skinheads who profess the same despair and hate that he is feeling. For the first time in his life, Dan begins to feel powerful and ignores Laurel, the girl who cares for him and fears the changes she sees when Dan becomes a skinhead.

3.69 Ruby, Lois. **Miriam's Well.** Scholastic, 1993. 263 pp. ISBN 0-590-44937-0.

Fun-loving Adam thinks of Miriam as a "no" girl—no makeup, no jeans, no jewelry, no personality, no fun. Then, Miriam collapses in class. The doctors diagnose cancer. Adam is horrified by her church's refusal to allow medical treatment for her. The state takes custody of Miriam, and Adam begins spending time with her during her treatments. Wanting Miriam well, Adam tries to understand her faith even though he believes she's wrong.

3.70 Say, Allen. **The Ink-Keeper's Apprentice.** Houghton Mifflin, 1994. 199 pp. ISBN 0-395-70562-2.

Famous cartoonist Noro Shinpei presents his young student the nickname of Kiyoi when he arrives to study with the master. Thirteen-year-old Kiyoi learns not only about art but also about the world and following one's goals. A letter from Kiyoi's estranged father beckons the young artist across the world to America in pursuit of new dreams.

3.71 Sebestyen, Ouida. **Out of Nowhere.** Orchard Books, 1994. 183 pp. ISBN 0-531-06839-0.

Abandoned in the desert by his mother, thirteen-year-old Harley makes friends with a pit bull and May, a gray-haired woman running away from her former life. May takes in Harley and his dog. They are surprised to find her inherited house still occupied by a salty old man who collects everything from ladders to fast-food cartons. Singer, a caring and sensitive girl, joins this strange group of people scrubbing floors, painting walls, seeking love and a home.

3.72 Sharpe, Susan. **Real Friends.** Bradbury Press, 1994. 167 pp. ISBN 0-02-782352-0.

Fourteen-year-old Cassie has never had a friend until she meets Helen. Helen encourages Cassie to listen only to her as she isolates Helen from her classmates. Skipping school, Cassie follows Helen into a dangerous situation. Cassie realizes she must decide how to make her life her own.

3.73 Shreve, Susan. **The Gift of the Girl Who Couldn't Hear.** Beech Tree Books, 1993. 79 pp. ISBN 0-688-11694-9.

Being deaf does not keep thirteen-year-old Lucy from wanting to sing in the school musical. Eliza, Lucy's only friend, promises to teach her to sing; however, Eliza expects that neither she nor Lucy has a chance. Lucy is deaf and Eliza is very overweight. But Lucy refuses to give up her dream. Lucy's determination is strong, but is it strong enough to make a deaf girl sing?

3.74 Springer, Nancy. **Toughing It.** Harcourt Brace & Company, 1994. 119 pp. ISBN 0-15-2000011-9.

Sixteen-year-old Tuff staggers down the trail to find help for his brother, Dillon, murdered right in front of him. There is no help for Tuff's anguish over the death of the only person who ever loved him. Thoughts of violence and revenge streak through Tuff's mind as he searches for his brother's murderer.

3.75 Strommen, Judith Bernie. **Champ Hobarth.** Henry Holt and Company, 1993. 178 pp. ISBN 0-8050-2414-X.

Marty, who can't even make the swim team, is doomed to forever disappoint his achievement-oriented family. Then he befriends a stray dog Champ and works diligently at Champ's animal shelter. As his passion for animals grows, he discovers the fate that awaits some of his four-legged friends at the shelter. Outraged, he embarks on a pet adoption campaign, finding homes for many animals. As a result, Marty earns the respect of others and recognizes his own special talents.

3.76 Tolan, Stephanie S. **Save Halloween.** Morrow Junior Books, 1993. 168 pp. ISBN 0-688-12168-3.

Everyone at school looks forward to Mrs. Teator's sixth-grade Halloween projects. Johanna is no different. She and classmate Brian are asked to research and write this year's project, a Halloween pageant. All goes well until Uncle T. T. hits town with his message: Banish Halloween! When Johanna's parents support his anti-Halloween views on the basis that it is un-Christian, Johanna is furious and confused. Johanna struggles to reconcile her own beliefs with those of her family.

3.77 Tomlinson, Theresa. **Riding the Waves.** Macmillan, 1993 (American edition). 144 pp. ISBN 0-02-789207-7.

Matt learns more than local history when he visits elderly "Aunt" Florrie for a school project. Matt longs to be accepted by the surfers in his seaside town, but they ignore him. Partly out of loneliness, he continues his visits to Florrie. As she tells about her life and the exciting days before World War II, Matt sees his own adopted family with new eyes. Then it's Matt's turn to help Florrie find the courage to fight for her life.

3.78 Valasquez, Gloria. **Juanita Fights the School Board.** Arte Público Press, 1994. 149 pp. ISBN 1-55885-115-1.

Juanita's spirits plummet when she learns that she has been expelled from high school. Her proud, but poor, Mexican American family is counting on her being the first in the family to earn a high school diploma. In order to reverse the school's decision, Juanita must confront the district's school board and face their discriminatory treatment.

3.79 Wallace, Bill. **True Friends.** Holiday House, 1994. 169 pp. ISBN 0-8234-1141-9.

Courtney can't believe her good fortune. Lacy, the most popular girl in sixth grade, has become her best friend, and she and Lacy are on the cheerleading team. Then her brother, Ben, is arrested for selling drugs. Without waiting to find out if Ben is guilty, Lacy and the others drop Courtney from their group. Only Judy Baird, the girl in a wheelchair, is willing to be her friend. With the help of Judy and Judy's mom, Courtney learns what true friendship means.

3.80 Warkski, Maureen. **Dark Silence.** Fawcett Juniper, 1994. 186 pp. ISBN 0-449-70418-1.

Everything is changing for Randy—her mother has been killed in a terrible accident, her father has remarried, and the house she loved has been traded for a new one. To make matters worse, her longtime boyfriend shows interest in the new girl at school. Randy becomes friends with her next-door neighbor Delia, but then the relationship is suddenly cut off. Randy wonders why. Then she sees the purple bruise and witnesses the anger of Delia's father.

3.81 Wesley, Valerie Wilson. **Where Do I Go from Here?** Scholastic, 1993. 138 pp. ISBN 0-590-45606-7.

Nia doesn't always feel that it is such a privilege to be one of about ten African Americans at a fancy prep school. Marcus says that you get used to it, but his word doesn't count for much since his disappearance. What could be so important that he would just take off in the middle of the night with Nia's fifty dollars and without one word of explanation? Nia learns that there is always a price to pay for something you really want.

3.82 Willey, Margaret. **The Melinda Zone.** Dell, 1993. 135 pp. ISBN 0-440-21902-7.

"Some things I changed. Some things I can't change." That's how Melinda, age fifteen, describes her first summer away from her divorced parents. She is tired of shuttling between them and tired of the conflicting demands they impose on her mind and heart. On the secure turf of her aunt and uncle's home, with the help of Paul and a young neighbor, she is able to create her own "zone" of independence and to learn that there are worse things than being loved too much.

3.83 Williams, Michael. **Into the Valley.** Philomel Books, 1993. 194 pp. ISBN 0-399-22516-1.

Leaving home was something seventeen-year-old Walter Hudson believed he had to do after his brother Boetie was killed while serving in the South African Defense Force. In his struggle to find himself, Walter reads about a young black rebel leader in Zululand's war-torn "Valley of Death." Walter travels to join him and becomes involved in interracial fighting. His involvement leaves him with more questions than answers about the troubles in South Africa.

3.84 Wright, Richard. **Rite of Passage.** HarperCollins, 1994. 142 pp. ISBN 0-06-023419-9.

Johnny Gibbs is a Harlem teenager in the 1940s. He is successful in school and is supported by a strong, loving family. However, when he discovers that he is a foster child about to be reclaimed by a city agency, his world crumbles. Rather than being re-placed, he runs away and falls in with a gang of street kids who steal for a living. Although they fill a void in his life, they can never fill the void left by the loss of his family.

4 Playing the Game: Stories about Sports

4.1 Christopher, Matt. **Return of the Home Run Kid.** Little, Brown and Company, 1992. 168 pp. ISBN 0-316-14080-5.

When Sylvester experiences a slump in his batting, a mysterious stranger named Cheeko helps him to improve. Although Cheeko's aggressive style works, the suggestions are very different from the advice of Mr. Baruth, who coached Sylvester the previous year. Then Sylvester discovers a bizarre coincidence which forces him to question the true identity of both men.

4.2 Christopher, Matt. **Tackle without a Team.** Little, Brown and Company, 1989. 145 pp. ISBN 0-316-14268-9.

When fourteen-year-old Scott Kramer returns to the locker room after winning a football game, he is shocked to discover marijuana in his duffel bag. Since his brother was arrested two years earlier on a drug charge, everyone readily assumes his guilt. Even worse than being kicked off the team is his father's bitterness about the situation. Desperate to clear his name and get back on the team, Scott plays detective to find out who framed him and why.

4.3 Deuker, Carl. **Heart of a Champion.** Little, Brown and Company, 1993. 199 pp. ISBN 0-316-18166-8.

Jimmy Winter has the heart and skill of a champion, which inspires everyone on the baseball team to give his best. But, Jimmy has a drinking problem. Seth, Jimmy's best friend, who lost his dad when he was seven, knows winning in life is more complicated than a baseball game. It requires the strength to keep promises to yourself and the ability to find an inner peace. Then Jimmy breaks a vow to himself and Seth. Can his friendship and his heart survive?

4.4 Dygard, Thomas J. **Game Plan.** Morrow Junior Books, 1993. 220 pp. ISBN 0-688-12007-5.

When the Barton High School football coach is hospitalized after an accident, Beano Hatton, the student manager, is asked to coach the final game of the season. The problem is that the team lacks confidence in his ability, and Beano must learn in one hectic week how a coach can create a winning team.

4.5   Hoffius, Stephen. **Winners and Losers.** Simon & Schuster, 1993. 164 pp. ISBN 0-671-79194-X.

Curt's best friend, Daryl, seems to have it all: good looks, good grades, and athletic success. But, after Daryl collapses during a track meet, doctors discover he has a bad heart. With Daryl sidelined from competition, Curt becomes the number-one track star and enjoys the personal attention of Daryl's dad, who begins training him to win at the conference meet. When Daryl realizes he must win the conference race to win back his father, the competitive rivalry alters their friendship forever.

4.6   Hughes, Dean. **End of the Race.** Atheneum, 1993. 152pp. ISBN 0-689-31779-4.

Seventh graders Jared Olsen and Davin Carter are hesitant to run the 400-meter race on the track team, but each of their fathers forces them to try. Despite Davin's constant reminders of their racial differences, the two develop a friendship during track season. But Mr. Carter's distrust of Jared and his father leads Jared to discover how complex racial tensions can be.

4.7   Kingman, Lee. **The Luck of the Miss L.** Beech Tree Books, 1993. 153 pp. ISBN 0-688-11779-1.

Eleven-year-old Alec teams up with the dignified older woman, Miss Longley, to enter the Rowbery Junior Rowers Race. Alec supplies the brawn and Miss Longley the boat. Although Alec survives winning a doll at the town's annual raffle, his best friend avoiding him, and the town heckling him, a near-fatal wreck of his dinghy destroys his confidence. By understanding how his father is struggling to overcome his fear of water, Alec gains the courage to enter the race.

4.8   Lipsyte, Robert. **The Chief.** HarperCollins, 1993. 226 pp. ISBN 0-06-021064-8.

Boxing is Sonny Bear's life. His roots are on the reservation, but he travels from one dead-end town to another in hopes of making it to the big match and a shot at the title. Martin, his friend and a wanna-be writer, joins Sonny on the road for two years. Through Martin's determination and big mouth, Sonny lands a match in Vegas that puts him in the spotlight. Trouble on the reservation causes Sonny to examine what is truly important to him. Sequel to *The Brave*.

4.9 Lynch, Chris. **Iceman.** HarperCollins, 1994. 181 pp. ISBN 0-06-023340-0.

Fourteen-year-old Eric plays a rough hockey game. Eric is dangerous to his opponents and teammates alike. Eric's bizarre older brother, Duane, is Eric's only comfort in his friendless existence. Duane realizes Eric needs help, and in big-brother fashion he teaches Eric how to play hockey as a sport, not as a blood bath, and to face other disappointments in life as well.

4.10 Lynch, Chris. **Shadow Boxer.** HarperCollins, 1993. 215 pp. ISBN 0-06-023027-4.

When George's father dies from boxing injuries, George becomes the man of the family. He promises to look after his younger brother, Monty. Together they befriend an unusual assortment of underdog characters while working odd jobs for spending money. But Monty's growing desire to become a boxer forces George to realize he can't protect Monty forever.

4.11 Slote, Alfred. **Find Buck McHenry.** HarperTrophy, 1993. 250 pp. ISBN 0-06-440469-2.

After eleven-year-old Jason Ross is cut from his baseball team and sent to an expansion team, he discovers Mr. Mack Henry, a school janitor full of knowledge and experience about the sport. Then Jason discovers a set of baseball cards from the old Negro leagues, which includes a photo of Buck McHenry. When Mr. Henry admits he is Buck McHenry, Jason recruits him to coach for the new team with surprising results.

4.12 Walker, Paul Robert. **The Sluggers Club: A Sports Mystery.** Harcourt Brace Jovanovich, 1993. 153 pp. ISBN 0-15-276163-2.

Someone is stealing Granada's Little League baseball equipment—one piece at a time. When they take cleanup hitter Medgar Washington's favorite bat, something must be done. The Sluggers Club, a select group of team members, is determined to solve the crime. Could the thief be a rival team, or perhaps the Black Scorpions, a Cambodian gang who continues to heckle the team's lead-off batter, Nong Den?

4.13 Wallace, Bill. **Never Say Quit.** Holiday House, 1993. 184 pp. ISBN 0-8234-1013-7.

When sixth grader Justine Smith doesn't make the soccer team because she isn't part of the popular crowd, she decides to form a new group called the "Misfits." Begrudgingly, Mr. Reiner, their former elementary school principal, agrees to coach the inexperienced team. But their only hope for success is rule number five: never say quit.

4.14 Weaver, Will. **Striking Out.** HarperCollins, 1993. 272 pp. ISBN 0-06-023346-X.

Billy Baggs's life of hard work on the family farm leaves little time for rest or fun. But the twelve-year-old has a natural flair for baseball and yearns to play with the local team. When his father resists Billy's requests to let him play ball, Billy must reconcile his parents' needs and his personal wishes. While coming to grips with a past tragedy, Billy's family learns that there is a time for everything, even baseball.

II Imagined Lands

If the reader finds pleasure . . . continue; if not, . . . throw the book away. The only criterion in the end is pleasure; all the other arguments are worthless.

Claude Simon, French novelist

5 Myths, Legends, and Folklore

5.1 Avila, Alfred. **Mexican Ghost Tales of the Southwest.** Pinata Books, 1994. 172 pp. ISBN 1-55885-107-0.

If you're a reader from the southwestern United States, some of these tales and characters may be familiar to you, especially La Llorona, the wailing woman, who haunts the darkness of riverbanks. Many of these ghost stories have religious roots in Mexican folklore.

5.2 Bellingham, David. **Goddesses, Heroes, and Shamans: The Young People's Guide to World Mythology.** Kingfisher, 1994. 160 pp. ISBN 1-85697-999-7.

Whether in the Arctic, Africa, Japan, or the Amazon, people have always created stories to explain the mysteries of nature and life. This book offers an overview of characters and stories from the myths and legends of various cultures. Read about Napi, the creator god of the Blackfoot Indians, or Fafnir, a man turned into a dragon in Norse mythology, or Nyame, the supreme god of the Ashanti people of Ghana, in this illustrated book.

5.3 Brooke, William J. **A Telling of the Tales.** HarperTrophy, 1993. 132 pp. ISBN 0-06-440467-6.

"Do you have any form of identification with you?" The startled prince can't believe his ears. He has fought dragons and thorns to awaken Sleeping Beauty from her long sleep, and she insults him. Prince Charming finds his Cinderella, but she is not at all what he expects. Five old tales echo the voices of all who have ever told them, but each Brooke retelling includes puzzling and humorous twists and turns.

5.4 Brooke, William J. **Teller of Tales.** HarperCollins, 1994. 170 pp. ISBN 0-06-023399-0.

Here are some favorite stories from our childhood told as never before. What would happen if Goldilocks decided to move in with the Three Bears? If Little Red Riding Hood knew that the wolf did not eat grannies or little girls? Suddenly those old familiar stories take on new meaning, not to mention a great deal of humor.

As he has in his two previous retellings of classic tales, Brooke delights and surprises readers who think they know the true story.

5.5 Bruchac, Joseph. **The Great Ball Game: A Muskogee Story.** Illustrated by Susan Roth. Dial Books, 1994. 32 pp. ISBN 0-8037-1540-4.

The bat cannot find his place with either birds or animals until he chooses sides and makes a heroic goal in an important game. This *pourquoi* tale, which answers the question *why*, comes from an Oklahoma elder of the Muskogee (Creek) Indian Nation. The tale is enhanced with beautiful collage illustrations.

5.6 Chase, Richard, editor. **The Jack Tales.** Illustrated by Berkeley Williams, Jr. Houghton Mifflin, 1993. 202 pp. ISBN 0-395-66951-0.

This is not the Jack of beanstalk fame. This collection tells of Jack as a young man going out "to seek his fortune." He doesn't let multi-headed giants stand in his way; rather, he cuts off their heads. Jack also captures a massive wild hog and rides an enormous people-eating lion.

5.7 Cohn, Amy, compiler. **From Sea to Shining Sea: A Treasury of American Folklore and Folk Songs.** Illustrated by various Caldecott Medal Winners. Scholastic, 1993. 400 pp. ISBN 0-590-42868-3.

Here is a huge book containing, well, almost everything, such as stories from Native American mythology; tales of tricksters, fools, and sages; music and lyrics to many of our most popular American traditional songs; and ghost stories from all over the United States. There are legendary heroes like John Henry and Pecos Bill, and real-life heroes like Harriet Tubman and Martin Luther King. Many of America's finest writers and illustrators contributed to this important book that traces American history.

5.8 Czernecki, Stefan. **The Hummingbirds' Gift.** Illustrated by Timothy Rhodes. Hyperion Books for Children, 1994. 32 pp. ISBN 1-56282-605-0.

Named as the place of the hummingbirds, Tzintzuntzan was once the capital of the Tarascan empire and is now a village in Mexico. In picture-book format, this book tells the legend of how hummingbirds helped humans in a time of drought by giving them a gift: the *panicuas*, tiny figures woven from straw. Because a peas-

Myths, Legends, and Folklore 77

ant family is able to sell *panicuas* on the Day of the Dead, they keep from starving.

5.9 Gatti, Anne. **Tales from the African Plains.** Illustrated by Gregory Alexander. Dutton Children's Books, 1994. 83 pp. ISBN 0-525-45282-6.

Celestial rulers, talking animals, and ordinary people spin tales rooted in the oral tradition of African folk literature. Twelve well-loved stories retold by Gatti are enhanced by vibrant paintings which portray dusty plains, jungle landscapes, exotic wildlife, and joyous village gatherings. These African tales are punctuated with humor and vivid images of tribal customs. They're a great resource for storytelling.

5.10 Goode, Diane. **Diane Goode's Book of Scary Stories and Songs.** Illustrated by Diane Goode. Dutton Children's Books, 1994. 64 pp. ISBN 0-525-4517-7.

Do you want to learn to tell some good ghost stories? These short, not-too-scary tales are fun to tell and might make your audience jump and groan. There's one about a man who refuses with a "tain't so" when everyone tells him he truly is dead. Other tales include the one about the girl with a ribbon around her neck (Know what happens when the ribbon comes off?), and one about the giant's missing toe (Guess what is served for dinner?).

5.11 Grimm, Jacob, and Wilhelm K. Grimm. **Iron Hans.** Illustrated by Marilee Heyer. Viking, 1993. 32 pp. ISBN 0-670-81741-4.

Using a picture-book format, illustrator Marilee Heyer retells this old tale about a prince, a princess, and a wild creature. When the prince's golden ball disappears into the cage of a monstrous wild man, the wild man gives it back in return for his release. Prince and wild man leave the castle together to escape the King's rage. As the prince grows to manhood, far from home and disguised as a commoner, he proves his heroism, aided by "the creature."

5.12 Isaacs, Anne. **Swamp Angel.** Illustrated by Paul Zelinsky. Dutton Children's Books, 1994. 40 pp. ISBN 0-525-45271-0.

This is a tall tale about a larger-than-life, incredibly strong, love-her-for-a-friend type, red-headed heroine. Called Swamp Angel after age twelve by the grateful folks she saved in Dejection Swamp, Angelica Longrider regularly performs "eyepopping" acts of bravery. The author's use of colorful language and

Zelinsky's rich, good-humored illustrations make this book special.

5.13 Jaffe, Nina. **Patakin: World Tales of Drums and Drummers.** Illustrated by Ellen Eagle. Henry Holt and Company, 1994. 145 pp. ISBN 0-8050-3005-0.

Imagine hearing the story of an Inuit skeleton woman, the drama intensifying as drums beat in the background. Better yet, imagine telling another tale, for instance, that of the Biblical Miriam and the Red Sea, your solo enhanced by drum music. The book not only contains ten folktales, it also describes the types of drums and drumming patterns appropriate for each story.

5.14 Jaffe, Nina, and Steve Zeitlin. **While Standing on One Foot: Puzzle Stories and Wisdom Tales from the Jewish Traditions.** Illustrated by John Segal. Henry Holt and Company, 1993. 120 pp. ISBN 0-8050-2594-4.

In his wise custody ruling, King Solomon decreed that an infant be given to the woman who preferred that her child be given away rather than split in half. Jewish tradition includes numerous stories like this in which wise people think up ingenious solutions to horrible predicaments. Test your problem-solving skills on situations from Jewish folklore. Be the entrepreneur who chooses between death by hanging or death by losing one's head, or imagine yourself as Hershel, the starving cook, who ate a goose leg and now has to prove to the nobleman, his employer, that some geese really have just one leg.

5.15 Knutson, Barbara, reteller. **Sungura and Leopard: A Swahili Trickster Tale.** Illustrated by Barbara Knutson. Little, Brown and Company, 1993. 32 pp. ISBN 0-316-50010-0.

Hare and leopard, two mortal enemies, find themselves sharing the same house. How they come to terms with each other and how Sungura, which means hare in Swahili, comes to scare the leopard away makes this story a good choice for oral storytelling. The hare in this African tale is a trickster and could be contrasted to the Cherokee rabbit in Gayle Ross's *How Rabbit Tricked Otter* or Brer Rabbit in *The Last Tales of Uncle Remus* by Julius Lester.

5.16 Lester, Julius, reteller. **The Last Tales of Uncle Remus.** Illustrated by Jerry Pinkney. Dial Books, 1994. 156 pp. ISBN 0-8037-1303-7.

They may be little, but they're powerful, so don't ever "cross swords with a mad crawfish," Julius Lester warns in "Why the

Myths, Legends, and Folklore

Earth Is Mostly Water." All thirty-nine African American folktales in this collection are short, powerful, and full of great wit, great fights, and lots of roaring and hollering. The tales, filled with familiar characters like Brer Rabbit, Bear, and Fox, also include newcomers like Linktum Lidy Lody Tinktum Tidy.

5.17 Lester, Julius. **John Henry.** Illustrated by Jerry Pinkney. Dial Books, 1994. 40 pp. ISBN 0-8037-1607-9.

John Henry is a folk hero often told about in song, and this story renders a version full of rich details about his life, from his birth to his incredible battle of human might against the machine. John Henry's early race against Ferret-Faced Freddy and his later burial on the White House lawn may surprise some readers. The beautiful illustrations and powerful language make this book enjoyable.

5.18 Lewis, J. Patrick. **The Frog Prince.** Illustrated by Gennady Spirin. Dial Books, 1994. 32 pp. ISBN 0-8037-1624-9.

This famous Russian folktale includes the transformation of a prince into a frog and involves the traditional Russian royalty (tsar and sons), as well as beautiful Vasilisa the Wise, gruesome Baba Yaga, and evil Koskchei, the Invincible. The sumptuous illustrations of embroidered textiles and period costumes add to the pleasure of this tale.

5.19 Mayo, Margaret. **Magical Tales from Many Lands.** Illustrated by Jane Ray. Dutton Children's Books, 1993. 128 pp. ISBN 0-525-45017-3.

These fourteen short tales with international roots (Caribbean, French, Zulu, Japanese, Native American) are as interesting to read as they are fun to tell. There are stories about looking for acceptance, needing a place to belong, and finding someone to love.

5.20 McKinley, Robin, reteller. **Beauty: A Retelling of the Story of Beauty and the Beast.** HarperTrophy, 1993. 247 pp. ISBN 0-06-440477-3.

Like the traditional version, this tale focuses on Beauty, the youngest of three daughters, the one who, because she agrees to live in the Beast's castle, saves her father from death. But the modern Beauty is more complicated than her fairy-tale counterpart, and she must summon courage, acting quickly as her father loses the family fortune and home.

5.21 Minters, Frances. **Cinder-Elly.** Illustrated by G. Brian Karas. Viking, 1994. 32 pp. ISBN 0-670-84417-9.

This funny rap version of the Cinderella story begins, "Once upon a time/ Or so they tell me,/ There was a girl/ Called Cinder-Elly." In this version, Prince Charming plays basketball and the "slipper" is a sneaker, but even in this jazzed-up tale, true love prevails so that in the end they look "pretty snappy" and live "forever happy."

5.22 Napoli, Donna Jo. **Magic Circle.** Dutton Children's Books, 1993. 118 pp. ISBN 0-525-45127-7.

A version of "Hansel and Gretel," this tale features a mysterious woman whom the townspeople call "Ugly One." Afraid and suspicious of her, they don't understand her powers but remain quite willing to accept her gifts of healing. As she attempts to improve her abilities to help others, Ugly One inadvertently creates and uses the "magic circle," tempting the devils and becoming a sorcerer who eats children.

5.23 Onyefulu, Obi, reteller. **Chinye: A West African Folk Tale.** Illustrated by Evie Safarewicz. Viking, 1994. 32 pp. ISBN 0-670-85115-9.

Orphaned, with a mean stepmother and a lazy stepsister, Chinye obediently does all family work. Because of her own good qualities, Chinye finds her fortune, aided by compassionate animals and a kindly old woman. Sound familiar?

5.24 Oodgeroo. **Dreamtime: Aboriginal Stories.** Illustrated by Bronwyn Bancroft. Lothrop, Lee & Shepard, 1994. 96 pp. ISBN 0-688-13296-0.

Both author and illustrator of this attractive book come from Australian Aboriginal roots. Together, they've created a book of the Aboriginal myths of how Rainbow Serpent created life, why bones and shells must be gathered and piled together after meals, who accompanies the dead to the shadow land, and much more.

5.25 Orgel, Doris. **Ariadne, Awake!** Illustrated by Barry Moser. Viking, 1994. 74 pp. ISBN 0-670-85158-2.

Ariadne, daughter of Minos, wonders if her half-brother, whose birth killed their mother, is the indisputably cruel monster everyone says he is. Maybe this creature, half-human, half-bull, is evil because he never knew kindness. Ariadne may not be able to change her half-brother, but she does transform herself as she finds love and faces great danger.

5.26 Perham, Molly. **King Arthur & the Legends of Camelot.** Illustrated by Julek Heller. Viking, 1993. 174 pp. ISBN 0-670-84990-1.

Step back in time and meet Arthur, Guinevere, Merlin, Sir Lancelot, Sir Gawain, and Morgan Le Fay in this rewrite of the legends. Visit the well-known sword Excalibur and go on a search for the Holy Grail, or follow Gareth, the Knight of the Kitchen, as he rises from a mysterious past to defeat the Black Knight, the Green Knight, and the Red Knight. Illustrations of menacing animals, stark skulls of defeated warriors, and dramatic battle scenes enhance these stories.

5.27 Picard, Barbara Leonie, reteller. **Tales of Ancient Persia: Retold from the Shah-Nama of Fidausi.** Illustrated by Victor Ambrus. Oxford University Press, 1993. 173 pp. ISBN 0-19-274154-3.

The legends of ancient Persia (now Iran) are full of adventure, adversity, heroism, and courage. And then there's the infamous Zohak, the ruler with a giant, brain-eating serpent growing from each shoulder. Ruthless and evil, obsessed with power, the man kills his own father. And that's just the beginning of his career! Zohak's story is one of the many exciting Persian folktales contained in this volume.

5.28 Rollins, Charlemae Hill, compiler. **Christmas Gif': An Anthology of Christmas Poems, Songs, and Stories.** Illustrated by Ashley Bryan. Morrow Junior Books, 1993. 106 pp. ISBN 0-688-11667-1.

This spirited collection of songs, stories, poems, recipes, and remembrances takes its title from a Christmas tradition that originated among slaves on plantations in the American South. Voices from the past rise again as a testimony to the strength of a people who found joy and hope in spiritual freedom.

5.29 Ross, Gayle, reteller. **How Rabbit Tricked Otter and Other Cherokee Trickster Stories.** Illustrated by Murv Jacob. HarperCollins, 1994. 79 pp. ISBN 0-06-021285-3.

Dramatic illustrations by Cherokee artist Murv Jacob enhance the text by Cherokee storyteller Gayle Ross in this collection of fifteen trickster tales. These tales follow the adventures of Rabbit, who uses trickery to work his way free from situations like Brer

Rabbit in *The Last Tales of Uncle Remus* and like Hare in *Sungura and Leopard: A Swahili Trickster Tale*.

5.30   Sanfield, Steve, collector. **The Feather Merchants and Other Tales of the Fools of Chelm.** Beech Tree Books, 1993. 114 pp. ISBN 0-688-12568-9.

Are they the world's wisest people or the biggest fools? Reach your own conclusion about the people of Chelm after reading these funny and wise tales from Eastern European Jewish folklore. Can you answer their riddles? (What do you have that other people use more than you? Your name.) These thirteen folktales feature the mythical village of Chelm, but you might know people like them in your town.

5.31   San Souci, Robert. **Song of Sedna.** Illustrated by Daniel San Souci. Dell/Yearling, 1994. 32 pp. ISBN 0-440-40948-9.

A result of the collaboration of the San Souci brothers, this picture book tells the haunting, ancient Eskimo legend of a young woman who discovers that the lies her new husband tells her put her life at risk. Even her father may not be able to save her. In fact, Sedna discovers that her own inner strength and courage are all she has in the struggle to survive.

5.32   San Souci, Robert. **The Snow Wife.** Illustrated by Stephen Johnson. Dial Books, 1993. 32 pp. ISBN 0-8037-1409-2.

In this Japanese folktale, eighteen-year-old Minokicki is saved from an icy death by a snow spirit. Keeping and breaking promises to a loved one and suffering in order to preserve true love are themes in this story.

5.33   Schwartz, Alvin, collector. **Cross Your Fingers, Spit in Your Hat: Superstitions and Other Beliefs.** Illustrated by Glen Rounds. HarperTrophy, 1993 (Originally published in 1974). 160 pp. ISBN 0-06-446138-6.

This collection of American superstitions is fun, whether or not you actually believe in them. Browse the book and find beliefs about passing tests (carry lucky rocks, don't shave, or wear your underwear inside out), getting married (yes, you will if you eat the point of a pie piece first), or how many children you may someday have (slap the seeds in one apple on your forehead and count how many stick). Concluding reference notes indicate regional differences about superstitions.

Myths, Legends, and Folklore

5.34 Schwartz, Alvin, collector. **Gold and Silver, Silver and Gold: Tales of Hidden Treasure.** Illustrated by David Christiana. Farrar, Straus, and Giroux, 1993 (Originally published in 1988). 128 pp. ISBN 0-374-42583-3.

Have you dreamed of finding hidden treasure? If so, you need this book! Blending fact and fiction, Schwartz tells of treasures of the past that have been discovered, those that remain lost today, and recently hidden treasures waiting to be found. Solve one puzzle and find sixteen million dollars buried somewhere in Virginia! Maps, clues, puzzles, and legends make these tales of hidden treasure a treasure of their own.

5.35 Schwartz, Alvin, collector. **Witcracks: Jokes and Jests from Folklore, American.** Illustrated by Glen Rounds. HarperTrophy, 1993 (Originally published in 1973). 160 pp. ISBN 0-06-446146-7.

Many know Schwartz from his collections of scary stories, but in *Witcracks* this versatile author goes for laughs. There are riddles, "What did one eye say to the other? There's something between us that smells," and incredible exaggerations, "Last winter a cow nearly caught such a cold she gave nothing but ice cream." Schwartz divides all this fun into categories and discusses the background of each. If you get caught reading this book, just say you're doing social studies research!

5.36 Scieszka, Jon. **The Book That Jack Wrote.** Illustrated by Daniel Adel. Viking, 1994. 32 pp. ISBN 0-670-84330-X.

From the author of *The True Story of the Three Little Pigs* and *The Stinky Cheese Man* comes this zany retelling of an old cumulative nursery rhyme—"The House That Jack Built." The adventure begins when Jack writes a book and ends with a squashed man, a stomped bug, a flying pie that hits a baby, and a cow sailing over the moon. Adel's strange, detailed paintings offer clues and additional humor to this funny tale told in verse.

5.37 Small, Terry. **The Legend of John Henry.** Illustrated by Terry Small. Doubleday Books for Young Readers, 1994. 32 pp. ISBN 0-385-31168-0.

The steam drill reportedly could do the work of ten men. Shakers, water boys, cooks, and hammer men were being put out of work by this new invention. Then John Henry, born a slave and now the strongest of the steel drivin' men, challenged the new machine with his brawn, his heart, and his hammer. Told in rhyme, this book offers a look at the legendary hero John Henry.

5.38 Sutcliff, Rosemary. **Black Ships before Troy: The Story of the Iliad.** Illustrated by Alan Lee. Delacorte Press, 1993. 128 pp. ISBN 0-385-31069-2.

Adapted from the epic poem, *The Iliad*, this book tells the story of Agamemnon, Achilles, Odysseus, and Amazon warriors, with just enough detail about the Trojan War to keep you spellbound. This story recounts the tremendous battles of that war, the twisted conspiracies, the deceptions, the romance, and the Greek gods' involvements with humankind. Lee's illustrations add extra emotion and insight.

5.39 Sutcliff, Rosemary. **The Light beyond the Forest.** Puffin Books, 1994 (Originally issued in 1979). 144 pp. ISBN 0-14-037150-8.

In this retelling of the legend of King Arthur and his knights, Sir Galahad assumes his place with the Knights of the Round Table. Now that he has filled the long empty Perilous Seat, Sir Galahad, Sir Lancelot, Sir Percival, and the others may begin their quest for the Holy Grail. This long-awaited quest means death and adventure to these famous Knights of the Round Table.

5.40 Sutcliff, Rosemary. **The Road to Camlann.** Puffin Books, 1994 (Originally issued in 1979). 143 pp. ISBN 0-14-037147-8.

Mordred, King Arthur's evil and illegitimate son, wants the throne for himself at any cost. In order to capture the throne, he implicates Sir Lancelot and the Queen in wrongdoings and works to defeat King Arthur. Mordred's maneuverings may mean the end of Camelot and the Knights of the Round Table.

5.41 Sutcliff, Rosemary. **The Sword and the Circle.** Puffin Books, 1994. 261 pp. ISBN 0-14-037149-4.

This first volume of the Arthurian trilogy chronicles the birth and rise to fame of Arthur. From the time he pulled the sword from the stone, Arthur was destined for greatness. With his magical Excalibur, Arthur was able to restore order to England and create a kingdom where peace reigned. Arthur courts and wins the hand of Lady Guinevere, who joins him at Camelot. As Arthur faces the challenges of leading England, he is joined by the brave Knights of the Round Table.

5.42 Thomas, Roy Edwin. **Come Go with Me: Old-Timer Stories from the Southern Mountains.** Illustrated by Laslo Kubinyi. Farrar, Straus, and Giroux, 1994. 188 pp. ISBN 0-374-37089-3.

Myths, Legends, and Folklore

Enjoy oral history and folk humor from recollections by older residents of Appalachian, Ozark, and Ouachita Mountains. These old-timers tell of a style of life long since past for most Americans. Because most of these stories have their details in actual history, this book provides a true feel of rural life from the time of the Civil War.

5.43   Ude, Wayne. **Maybe I Will Do Something.** Illustrated by Abigail Rorer. Houghton Mifflin, 1993. 75 pp. ISBN 0-395-65233-2.

These seven tales stress the confusion, humor, and outrageousness of Coyote, a well-known trickster of Native American folktales. Coyote does act the fool, but he also accomplishes a lot. Read to find out how, despite his laziness, coyote frees the imprisoned buffaloes and brings dancing to the world.

5.44   Vuong, Lynette Dyer. **The Golden Carp and Other Tales from Vietnam.** Illustrated by Manabu Saito. Lothrop, Lee & Shepard, 1993. 128 pp. ISBN 0-688-12514-X.

This is a collection of six stories from Vietnamese folklore about keeping love and losing it, about being brave in battle and in life, and about being a friend and taking advantage of friends. Folk art of Southeast Asia accompanies each tale and adds authenticity to the book.

5.45   Vuong, Lynette Dyer. **Sky Legends of Vietnam.** Illustrated by Vo-Dinh Mai. HarperCollins, 1993. 103 pp. ISBN 0-06-023000-2.

Vietnamese folklore explains why the rooster crows at dawn, why day is separate and distinct from night, and who lives on the moon. These are but three of the six stories in this book, all focusing on the stars and sky.

5.46   Waldherr, Kris, reteller. **Persephone and the Pomegranate: A Myth from Greece.** Illustrated by Kris Waldherr. Dial Books, 1993. 32 pp. ISBN 0-8037-1191-3.

When Persephone is kidnapped by a mysterious chariot driver, her mother hears only the echoes of her last cry and searches vainly for her. In Waldherr's dramatic illustrations of this ancient myth, fierce, fire-breathing, dark horses rise to the earth's surface as Pluto forces the young woman to accompany him to the underworld to become his bride and queen of the dead. Later the planet's surface is frozen in a first winter, which might never be followed by spring.

5.47 Yep, Laurence, reteller. **The Shell Woman and the King.** Illustrated by Yang Ming-Yi. Dial Books for Young Readers, 1993. 32 pp. ISBN 0-8037-1395-9.

Shell, a mysterious, beautiful young bride, has three seemingly impossible tasks to perform or her husband's head will be cut off and hung from the evil king's tower. At one point, she finds herself cutting off the grisly arm of a ghost. Unlike Yep's novels *Dragonwings* or *Dragon of the Lost Sea*, this book is done in picture-book style.

6 The Fantastic World of Fantasy

6.1 Alcock, Vivien. **Singer to the Sea God.** Delacorte Press, 1993. 200 pp. ISBN 0-385-30866-3.

When the king's court is turned to stone by Medusa, only a few, including Phaidon, nephew of Perseus, escape the stony curse. Phaidon's sister is one of Medusa's victims, but he cannot leave her behind when he flees the castle. He begins his perilous journey carrying her lifeless marble form. However, he is soon parted from her and stranded on a deserted island. He must find a means of leaving the island and rescuing his sister.

6.2 Alexander, Lloyd. **The Remarkable Journey of Prince Jen.** Dell/Yearling, 1993. 273 pp. ISBN 0-440-40890-3.

Prince Jen sets off in search of a faraway kingdom ruled by the wisest of emperors in hope of learning more about being a good ruler. He carries with him six gifts which he believes will endear him to this wise monarch. On his journey, Jen bequeaths these same gifts to people who come to his aid when bandits attack him. These gifts are destined to be returned to him if he can survive the perils of his journey.

6.3 Amoss, Berthe. **Lost Magic.** Hyperion Books, 1993. 184 pp. ISBN 1-56282-573-9.

By the age of fourteen, Ceridwen has been named as the Royal Healer to Lord Robert and his daughter, Elinor. When the plague infects the inhabitants of the castle, Ceridwen is accused by a jealous rival of being a witch. Matters become more complicated when Ceridwen decides she must flee the castle and take little Elinor so that the child might survive the epidemic. Now Ceridwen must escape two enemies: her jealous rival and the deadly disease running rampant through the countryside. It will take all her healing powers to survive.

6.4 Avi. **City of Light, City of Dark: A Comic Book Novel.** Illustrated by Brian Floca. Orchard Books, 1993. 192 pp. ISBN 0-531-06800-5.

In a quite distant future, Carlos and Sarah find themselves key players in a race to save their city. If they are unable to locate a special transit token, the city will freeze solid. Carlos and Sarah must battle against Mr. Underton, a blind man whose neon creations light a world he can no longer see. Embittered, Underton longs to plunge the city into perpetual darkness. Time is of the essence if Carlos and Sarah are to succeed in their mission.

6.5 Babbitt, Lucy Cullyford. **Where the Truth Lies.** Orchard Books, 1993. 199 pp. ISBN 0-531-05473-X.

Kyra has been given a great honor by the Elders. The problem is that she does not view her mission as an honor; she feels confused, abandoned, and apprehensive. Kyra has been instructed to join two outsiders for a dangerous journey. Fundamental religious differences separate the three travelers, differences which may spell disaster for their mission. If the three are successful, peace may return to the three nations who inhabit the land.

6.6 Banks, Lynne Reid. **The Adventures of King Midas.** Illustrated by Jos. A. Smith. Avon/Camelot, 1993. 153 pp. ISBN 0-380-71564-3.

King Midas longs for only one thing: gold and lots of it! When his wish to have more gold is granted, everything he touches turns to gold, even his beloved daughter and the family dog. Now he must search out someone who can "un-spell" him. A crafty witch and a baby monster compound his problems. Midas is determined to find a way to change things from gold back to flesh and blood.

6.7 Banks, Lynne Reid. **The Mystery of the Cupboard.** Illustrated by Tom Newsom. Avon/Camelot, 1994. 246 pp. ISBN 0-380-72013-2.

This book continues the drama begun in *The Indian in the Cupboard*. Omri feels he has outgrown the magic cupboard and the miniature figures which occupy it. However, Omri changes his mind after he discovers an old journal written by a distant relative that reveals the secret of the cupboard and its magical properties. The secret compels him to open the cupboard once more and allow it to work its magic.

6.8 Bedard, Michael. **The Painted Devil.** Atheneum, 1994. 226 pp. ISBN 0-689-31827-8.

When Alice takes a part-time job at the local library, she is not prepared for the sinister events which follow. She and the new librarian plan a puppet show for the kids. The antique puppets they discover in the basement of the library are terrifying to look at. They seem to emanate evil. With the help of Alice's Aunt Lela, Alice tries to solve the mystery surrounding the puppets and the dark magic they possess.

6.9 Bradshaw, Gillian. **Beyond the North Wind.** Greenwillow Books, 1993. 184 pp. ISBN 0-688-11357-5.

The Greek god Apollo fears a shadow has fallen across the land. He sends Aristeas to seek out the source of this ill omen. They learn that the source lies with fearsome Arimaspians, one-eyed giants who intend to enslave humans and use them for food. The dragon-like griffins are also endangered by these beasts. Aristeas pledges to use his magic to foil the evil plans of the Arimaspians and their witch queen Colaxis.

6.10 Breathed, Berkeley. **Goodnight Opus.** Little, Brown and Company, 1993. 32 pp. ISBN 0-316-10853-7.

When Opus's Grandma reads him for the two hundred tenth time his favorite bedtime story, which sounds and looks suspiciously like Margaret Wise Brown's *Goodnight Moon*, she falls asleep and he "departs the text" going on a wild adventure. If you remember bedtime stories or love the comic strip character Opus, you'll enjoy this funny story.

6.11 Brennan, J. H. **Shiva Accused.** HarperTrophy, 1993. 275 pp. ISBN 0-06-440431-5.

Shiva stumbles across the body of an old woman in a river. While she is attempting to protect the body from predators, members of a rival tribe, the Barradiks, approach. They accuse Shiva of murdering the woman, who turns out to be The Hag, spiritual leader of the Barradiks. The penalty for murder is death by stoning—unless someone from Shiva's tribe can rescue her.

6.12 Brennan, J. H. **Shiva's Challenge: An Adventure of the Ice Age.** HarperTrophy, 1993. 224 pp. ISBN 0-06-440-460-9.

In another Shiva adventure, Shiva is rudely awakened and taken to the lodge of the ruler of the Crones, the magicians of the tribe. In front of her are six bowls, all but one filled with poison. She must choose, but how? A sudden calm falls over her when she hears a voice, that of her dead mother, inside her head guiding her toward the correct bowl. Shiva drains the bowl, falls unconscious, and awakens in a cave. She has survived the first test. Now she must prove herself worthy of becoming her tribe's next Crone.

6.13 Brooke, William. **A Brush with Magic.** Illustrated by Michael Koelsch. HarperCollins, 1993. 137 pp. ISBN 0-06-022973-X.

In ancient China, an elderly man discovers an abandoned baby in his rice paddy. With the baby is a magical brush that transforms any picture drawn with the brush into reality. The young child, called Liang, creates beauty with his magic brush, but this talent is not much appreciated in his village. When Liang's wish to display his talent for the Emperor is granted, he learns that magic can be used for evil as well as for beauty.

6.14 Bunyan, John. **Pilgrim's Progress.** Retold by Gary D. Schmidt. Illustrated by Barry Moser. William B. Eerdman's Publishing, 1994 (Originally published in 1678). 76 pp. ISBN 0-8028-5080-4.

Christian leaves his wife and four children to travel to the faraway Celestial City. Along the way, he must fight a knight, deal with wild animals, and face a fearsome, fire-breathing, winged monster. As he travels, he constantly sees the bones and bodies of others who have tried and failed to reach this goal. Is this Christian's destiny, too?

6.15 Carroll, Lewis. **Through the Looking Glass and What Alice Found There.** Illustrated by John Tenniel. William Morrow and Company, 1993 (Originally published in 1872). 228 pp. ISBN 0-688-12049-0.

In this filled-with-nonsense sequel to *Alice in Wonderland*, Alice goes beyond the looking glass to meet Humpty Dumpty, Tweedledee and Tweedledum, the Jabberwock, and the Red Queen who says, "It takes all the running you can do to stay in the same place." Illustrations made from Tenniel's original woodblocks, which were discovered in a bank vault in 1985, make this classic fantasy more fun.

6.16 Cassedy, Sylvia. **Lucie Babbidge's House.** Avon/Camelot, 1993. 243 pp. ISBN 0-380-71812-X.

Lucie is the target of a great deal of taunting at Norwood Hall, an orphanage where she has lived since her parents were killed. When things are too difficult, Lucie takes refuge in a dollhouse she discovers in Norwood Hall's cellar. A wonderful family of dolls lives in the house. The china "Lucie" is treasured by her make-believe family, and the real Lucie uses the dollhouse and its occupants to escape from the cruel torment of her roommates.

6.17 Charnas, Suzy McKee. **The Kingdom of Kevin Malone.** Harcourt Brace Jovanovich, 1993. 211 pp. ISBN 0-15-200756-3.

Skating in Central Park, Amy runs into the school bully, Kevin Malone. As she chases after him, Amy skates through one of the arches of Central Park into a kingdom created in Kevin's mind. Somehow she must escape and save Kevin. As she travels back into reality, she begins to understand why Kevin has built such an elaborate kingdom.

6.18 Chenoweth, Russ. **Shadow Walkers.** Charles Scribner's Sons, 1993. 153 pp. ISBN 0-684-19447-3.

Sara, her brother Peter, and their friend Tom are young water rats who adventure across the beaches of Cape Cod to deliver some much-needed insulin to a neighboring town. During their journey, they discuss the books they are reading (Sara is into *Moby Dick*), save a heart-attack victim, and foil a bank robbery by using their intelligence and their wits.

6.19 Chetwin, Grace. **The Chimes of Alyafaleyn.** Bradbury Press, 1993. 234 pp. ISBN 0-02-718222-3.

Tamborel saves Caidy from death when she is an infant. His remarkable bravery creates a strong bond between the two children. The children's magical powers cause the villagers to be suspicious of them. Eventually, Caidy's life is endangered. Unless Tamborel finds a way to help her control her powers, she will die. For this task, he needs the assistance of a powerful healer. As Caidy flees the village in search of safety, Tamborel follows in hope of finding a healer to help them both.

6.20 Cooper, Susan. **The Boggart.** Macmillan Publishing Company, 1993. 196 pp. ISBN 0-689-50576-0.

Strange things begin happening in the Volnik household after they return from vacation at an ancient Scottish castle. Emily and Jessup discover the reason for all the mayhem: a mischievous boggart. A boggart is a magical creature that's not exactly a ghost but behaves like a poltergeist. This boggart steals food (it's partial to pizza and fudge sauce) and rearranges the furniture. The problem is how do Em and Jess send the boggart back to Castle Keep. Can you mail a boggart?

6.21 Coville, Bruce. **Into the Land of the Unicorns.** Scholastic, 1994. 161 pp. ISBN 0-590-45955-4.

In Book One of the Unicorn Chronicles, when Cara's grandmother instructs her to jump off the top of a tower to elude a threatening stranger, she hesitates, but then does as she is told. Her fall lands her in Luster, the land of the unicorns. There she meets these beautiful creatures and befriends one named Lightfoot. Cara vows to help him protect the unicorns against hunters who would end their existence. To do this, Cara must battle one who holds much power in her life: her father.

6.22 Dickinson, Peter. **Time and the Clockmice Etcetera.** Illustrated by Emma Chichester-Clark. Delacorte Press, 1994. 128 pp. ISBN 0-385-32038-8.

The Branton Town Hall Clock is a wonder—never skipped a tick or a tock for ninety-nine years. But now it needs repair. When the repair man arrives, he discovers the existence of the clockmice. Unlike ordinary mice, clockmice are quite intelligent. The mice might be the key to keeping the Branton Clock in working order for centuries to come *if* the clock maker can save them from the cat and the researcher, each of whom has a different idea about what should happen to these mice.

6.23 Downer, Ann. **The Books of the Keepers.** Atheneum, 1993. 245 pp. ISBN 0-689-31519-8.

The Consort Pending to the Elven Queen has been used by agents who wish the throne returned to its rightful occupant, the Goblin Pretender. When the Consort Pending escapes from the Elven Kingdom known as Below, he locates his real parents. Thus begins a chain of events in which a wolf-girl, a leopard-woman, and other unusual creatures attempt to solve the ancient riddles. This sequel completes the story begun in *The Spellkey* and *The Glass Salamander*.

6.24 Farmer, Penelope. **Thicker than Water.** Candlewick Press, 1993. 205 pp. ISBN 1-56402-178-5.

Will, an orphan, goes to live with his cousin Becky and her parents. There, he struggles to adjust to his mother's death and his new life. His problems are compounded by Becky's jealousy of the attention he receives and the ghostly voice he hears at night. Will is certain of what he hears, however, and is compelled to solve the mystery. But his search for the origin of the nightmare voice may prove hazardous to his health.

6.25 Fine, Anne. **The Chicken Gave It to Me.** Illustrated by Cynthia Fisher. Little, Brown and Company, 1993. 77 pp. ISBN 0-316-28316-9.

Gemma and Andrew are classmates. One day Andrew plunks down a book entitled "The True Story of Harrowing Farm." It is, he insists, written by a chicken. Gemma is skeptical but agrees to read the manuscript. What follows is an amazing story of extraterrestrials who come to Earth on a sort-of grocery trip to find some nice juicy people to eat. Gemma and Andrew become involved in the fight against these aliens as they try to save the planet.

6.26 Fletcher, Susan. **Flight of the Dragon Kyn.** Atheneum, 1993. 213 pp. ISBN 0-689-31880-4.

Ever since a childhood illness, Kara has possessed the special ability to call birds. Now this gift has drawn the interest of the king. Kara's rapport with birds may be his means of ridding the kingdom of dragons, as dragons are known to follow the bidding of anyone who can charm birds. Once Kara witnesses the slaughter of a dragon, however, she knows she cannot be a part of the king's plot. She must find a means of escape.

6.27 Friesner, Esther M. **Wishing Season.** Illustrated by Frank Kelly Freas. Atheneum, 1993. 138 pp. ISBN 0-689-31574-0.

Khalid is one of the best students in his class. He may graduate as the top genie. Unfortunately, he has one major flaw: his pride. Perhaps his first encounter with a mortal will teach him a valuable lesson. His initial encounter, however, is with a curious cat who rubs against his lamp. Khalid may never escape his lamp unless he pays a bit more attention to the rules governing genies, especially the "However Clause" which prohibits anyone from wishing for more wishes.

6.28 Hunter, Mollie. **The Mermaid Summer.** HarperTrophy, 1994. 118 pp. ISBN 0-06-440344-0.

Twelve-year-old Anna and her brother Jon miss Grandpa Eric. He left their home to sign on as a seaman after a skirmish with a mermaid nearly killed the crew of his fishing boat. If Grandpa is ever to return, Jon and Anna must tame the mermaid which has placed a curse upon their grandfather. This feat will prove quite difficult as the mermaid is a cunning and temperamental creature.

6.29 Jacques, Brian. **Martin the Warrior.** Philomel Books, 1993. 376 pp. ISBN 0-399-22670-2.

In the sixth book of the Redwall series, Martin, a young mouse warrior, lies in Marshank Prison along with Brome and Felldoh.

They are slave labor for Badrang the Tyrant. When Rose, Brome's sister, helps the three escape, they undertake a journey toward home. All must return to Marshank to free the others who remain under Badrang's control. It is an extremely dangerous mission; not all who enter the battle will survive.

6.30 Jacques, Brian. **Salamandastron.** Illustrated by Gary Chalk. Philomel Books, 1993. 391 pp. ISBN 0-399-21992-7.

Ferahgo, the weasel assassin, is again on the prowl for victims. He attacks the fortress Salamandastron, looking for buried treasures within its mountain. An unusual band of heroes and heroines comes to the rescue of Salamandastron including the badger maid Mara and her friend Pikkle the hare. They are assisted in their battle by Samkin the young squirrel and his mole friend Arula. This is the sequel to *Mariel of Redwall*.

6.31 Jarrow, Gail. **Beyond the Magic Sphere.** Harcourt Brace & Company, 1994. 208 pp. ISBN 0-15-200193-X.

Eleven-year-old S. B. is angry with her father when he takes off for Europe without her. Even worse, he makes arrangements for her to spend the summer out in the boonies with an aunt she has never met. Over the course of a magical summer, though, S. B. acquires two new friends who join her to help defeat an evil presence in the woods surrounding Aunt Brenda's house.

6.32 Jones, Diana Wynne. **Witch Week.** Greenwillow Books, 1993. 213 pp. ISBN 0-688-12374-0.

Someone leaves a note in Mr. Crossley's room: a member of the class is a witch! Of course, this is entirely possible, since the school caters to witch-orphans. But who is the witch? It could be Charles; he seems to be able to make himself invisible. Perhaps Dulcinea is the culprit. After all, she is named after the greatest arch-witch of all time. There are plenty of suspects in this quirky, humorous mystery.

6.33 Jordan, Sherryl. **Winter of Fire.** Scholastic, 1993. 321 pp. ISBN 0-590-45288-6.

In a dark and cold future, the only source of fuel is firestone, a mineral mined from deep in the earth. The Quelled are made to slave in these mines to extract firestone for The Chosen. Elsha, born of The Quelled, believes it is her destiny to free her people from the tyranny of The Chosen. Selected by the leader of The Chosen as his handmaiden, Elsha uses her magical powers to ensure that The Quelled and The Chosen will someday live as equals.

6.34 Jordan, Sherryl. **Wolf-Woman.** Houghton Mifflin, 1994. 162 pp. ISBN 0-395-70932-6.

Tanith has grown up as the adopted daughter of Ahearn's clan after her rescue from a wolves' den. It is the wolves, however, whom Tanith considers her real family. When she returns to play among them, she is shunned and eventually cast out from her clan. Tanith is torn between her love for the wolves and her need for a human family.

6.35 Kassem, Lou. **The Druid Curse.** Avon/Camelot, 1994. 118 pp. ISBN 0-380-77593-X.

To escape her classmates and their teasing about her dyslexia, Penny enjoys hiking the trails and sketching the woods near her home. That is how she meets Chris, the new boy in town. When he confides his story to her, Penny agrees to help him locate the ancient Druid oak. This tree is rumored to be evil; whenever it appears, young girls disappear and die. Penny and Chris must solve the riddle of the oak to save their own lives and the lives of their friends and neighbors.

6.36 Kaye, M. M. **The Ordinary Princess.** Illustrated by M. M. Kaye. Dell/Yearling, 1993. 112 pp. ISBN 0-440-40880-6.

Amethyst Alexandra Augusta Araminta Adelaide Aurelia Anne is the seventh daughter born to royal parents. She is destined to become as lovely as her sisters until an ill-tempered fairy gives her an unusual christening gift: the gift of being ordinary. As a young princess, her plainness keeps eligible princes from being interested in her. So she runs away, becoming a servant in the castle of a far-off kingdom. Her enchanting adventure is one which transforms her from ordinary to extraordinary.

6.37 Kindl, Patrice. **Owl in Love.** Puffin Books, 1994. 204 pp. ISBN 0-14-037129-X.

Fourteen-year-old Owl is a shape shifter, able to change effortlessly into an owl. She has a crush on her science teacher, Mr. Lindstrom, and flies nightly to his house to observe him. That is when she discovers that a wild boy is camping in the woods near Mr. Lindstrom's house. As she strives to protect her beloved teacher, Owl learns that there are other shape shifters like her.

6.38 Lee, Tanith. **Gold Unicorn.** Atheneum, 1994. 149 pp. ISBN 0-689-31814-6.

Tanaquil and her familiar, a talking peeve, travel across different lands. Everywhere they journey they hear of the Empress Veriam and her goal to conquer all the lands. Tanaquil is frightened when she is apprehended by some of Veriam's soldiers and is shocked to learn that Veriam is in fact her half-sister, Lizra. Lizra enlists Tanaquil's ability as a mender to finish construction of an enormous black unicorn which will figure prominently in Veriam's plans to control all of the lands in the kingdom.

6.39 Levy, Robert. **Clan of the Shape-Changers.** Houghton Mifflin, 1994. 183 pp. ISBN 0-395-66612-0.

An order from the King decrees that all green-eyed people must report to the village of their birth or face execution. Green eyes are considered a mark of the Elders, a race now vanished but thought to have had magical powers. Susan bears the Elders' mark. She is a shape-changer, one who can transform from human to animal. She discovers there are others like her; together they attempt to learn the intent behind the King's decree.

6.40 Levy, Robert. **Escape from Exile.** Houghton Mifflin, 1993. 171 pp. ISBN 0-395-64379-1.

Daniel becomes lost in a violent snowstorm. A sudden flash of lightning renders him unconscious. When he awakens, he is in a strange new country, a place inhabited by warriors and weird animals. Daniel finds that he can communicate with these animals telepathically. Perhaps they can assist him as he tries to find the way back to his own time and place. Before he returns, though, Daniel faces fierce battles and other dangerous adventures involving kings, princesses, and snakes.

6.41 Lisle, Janet Taylor. **Forest.** Orchard Books, 1993. 150 pp. ISBN 0-531-06803-X.

Twelve-year-old Amber loves to steal away to the woods which surround her home, especially when her father seems unbearable. One night, Amber discovers an amazing community of squirrels in the forest. She is startled to realize that these animals are quite intelligent. When the squirrel and human communities conflict, Amber and her brother are determined to end the war peacefully with the assistance of the squirrels.

The Fantastic World of Fantasy

6.42   Mahy, Margaret. **Dangerous Spaces.** Puffin Books, 1993. 154 pp. ISBN 0-14-036362-9.

Flora and Anthea should be immediate friends. After all, Flora has longed for a friend close to her own age. However, Flora sees Anthea more as an intruder even though the two of them share the same nightmarish dream world. Places and people which exist only in old photographs frighteningly come to life within each girl's dreams. They discover that the old house in which they live possesses some dangerous spaces, spaces they must help each other navigate.

6.43   McGowen, Tom. **A Question of Magic.** Dutton/Lodestar, 1993. 138 pp. ISBN 0-525-67380-6.

The day of Earthdoom for ancient Earth is rapidly drawing nearer. Soon, the mages predict, alien creatures will arrive, intent on taking all of Earth's resources. Alone, each of the five races on Earth is powerless to combat this attack force. Mages from each race, however, may be able to concentrate their powers and save the planet. A young boy named Lithim may have the answer, but first he will have to gain the acceptance of the other races.

6.44   Pierce, Tamora. **Wolf-Speaker.** Atheneum, 1994. 182 pp. ISBN 0-689-31833-2.

In this sequel to *Wild Magic,* Daine must use her "magic" to help save the lives of the wolves and the other animals whose forests and hills are threatened by evil forces. Daine's gifts enable her to make contact with the animals and to help them join forces to end the overmining of the hills and the stripping of the forests.

6.45   Salsitz, Rhondi Vilott. **The Twilight Gate.** Illustrated by Alan M. Clark. Walker and Company, 1994. 181 pp. ISBN 0-8027-8213-2.

It has been a tragic year for George, Leigh, and Mindy. First, their father was killed in a car crash. Now their mother is undergoing chemotherapy for cancer. They must spend the summer with Dave Stoner, their mother's first husband. They are miserable at the prospect of being away from their mother when she is so sick, and there seems to be more trouble ahead. The Twilight Gate has allowed evil beings into their world. George, Leigh, and Mindy must help defeat the beings in order to survive.

6.46   Seidler, Tor. **Wainscott Weasel.** Illustrated by Fred Marcellino. HarperCollins, 1993. 194 pp. ISBN 0-06-205032-X.

He cuts quite a dashing figure with his eye patch, but there is an air of mystery about Bagley Brown, better known as the Wainscott Weasel. What happened to his father? Is he really missing an eye? Bagley is a different sort of weasel; thankfully he is a courageous one. When an osprey threatens the life of a nearby pond, Bagley is ready to put himself in danger to help save his friends.

6.47 Sherman, Josepha. **Gleaming Bright.** Walker and Company, 1994. 170 pp. ISBN 0-8027-8296-5.

The kingdom is in trouble. To complicate matters, an unscrupulous king proposes marriage to Finola whose father presses her to accept the offer to save the kingdom. Instead, Finola searches for the magic box bestowed upon her grandfather by one wizard and stolen by another. Aided by a bewitched stag, Finola finds the evil wizard. If she can wrest the magic box from his possession, she may be able to save the kingdom.

6.48 Sherman, Josepha. **Windleaf.** Illustrated by Rick Farley. Walker and Company, 1993. 121 pp. ISBN 0-8027-8259-0.

As young Count Thierry gazes out into a ferocious storm, he sees a figure lying drenched in the darkness. Thierry rushes out to rescue this sodden person and discovers a beautiful young woman named Glinfinial. Glinfinial, he soon learns, is half-human, half-fairy. Despite their differences, they fall in love. Glinfinial's father, the powerful, cold-hearted Lord of the Fairies, disapproves and kidnaps his daughter. He sets three tasks before Thierry. If Thierry fails, Glinfinial will be forever lost to him.

6.49 Shetterly, Will. **Nevernever.** Harcourt Brace & Company, 1993. 226 pp. ISBN 0-15-257022-5.

In Bordertown, things are seldom as they seem. Certainly, that is the case for Wolfboy, a human turned into a werewolf by an angry elf's spell. In this sequel to *Elsewhere,* Wolfboy becomes unwittingly involved in a series of escapades including kidnapping and murder as he attempts to find a way to break the spell and become a human once more.

6.50 Sinykin, Sheri Cooper. **Sirens.** Lothrop, Lee & Shepard, 1993. 183 pp. ISBN 0-688-12309-0.

At first, only Chantal can hear the strange music which emanates from the statue of the sea queen at the local art fair. When the elderly artist makes her a present of the statue, Chantal is unprepared for the events which unfold. Those whom she likes find themselves in accidents; even Chantal's older sister is stricken with a mysterious illness. Chantal is puzzled by the power of her statue and determined to uncover its secrets before someone is seriously hurt.

6.51 Smith, Sherwood. **Wren's Quest.** Harcourt Brace Jovanovich, 1993. 199 pp. ISBN 0-15-200976-0.

Apprentice magician Wren and her companion Prince Connor journey in search of Wren's "history." All Wren remembers of her childhood is the orphanage; she wants to find some trace of her parents. Connor joins in Wren's quest in order to escape from the turmoil in the kingdom. However, it appears that their departure did not go unnoticed; they are being followed. Who is after them? It could be an evil magician or even someone from Connor's own court.

6.52 Snyder, Zilpha Keatley. **Black and Blue Magic.** Illustrated by Gene Holtan. Macmillan, 1994. 184 pp. ISBN 0-689-71848-9.

Summer stretches endlessly in front of twelve-year-old Harry Marco. While his friends are off on vacation, Harry is stuck at home helping his mom run their boarding house. Enter Tarzack Mazzeeck. Harry is certain that Tarzack is not really a traveling salesman, but he is hardly prepared for what is about to happen. This may be the summer when Harry Houdini Marco grows into his name.

6.53 Snyder, Zilpha Keatley. **Song of the Gargoyle.** Dell/Yearling, 1994. 232 pp. ISBN 0-440-40898-9.

Thirteen-year-old Tymmon awakens in the middle of the night to discover his father, the court jester, being kidnapped by errant knights. Why would they want to take away a harmless fool? That is the question Tymmon ponders as he flees the castle in search of his father. Along his journey, he is befriended by a dog-like creature, a gargoyle named Troff. Troff's menacing looks and enchanting powers may be just what Tymmon needs to find his father.

6.54 Somtow, S. P. **The Wizard's Apprentice.** Illustrated by Nicholas Jainschigg. Atheneum, 1993. 132 pp. ISBN 0-689-31576-7.

Aaron Maguire was not looking for magic the day he ran into Anaxgoras, the wizard. He was on his way to meet Penelope at the mall. But that's the way fate works. One minute you're an ordinary high school student, the next you're apprenticed to a two-thousand-year-old magician. Aaron's apprenticeship is a bit bizarre: his first spell involves a clogged drain. Magic, Aaron learns, has its ups and downs.

6.55 Sterman, Betsy, and Samuel Sterman. **Backyard Dragon.** Illustrated by David Wenzel. HarperCollins, 1993. 189 pp. ISBN 0-06-020783-3.

When Owen finds a dragon in his backyard, he does the logical thing and tells his parents. However, they chide him for making up stories to get attention. Next, he tells his classmates, who tease him about his overactive imagination. But everyone is suitably impressed when they finally meet Wyrdryn, the dragon accidentally zapped from the Middle Ages to the twentieth century by a confused wizard. Owen and his friends must figure out a way to help Wyrdryn go home.

6.56 Tarr, Judith. **His Majesty's Elephant.** Harcourt Brace & Company, 1993. 193 pp. ISBN 0-15-200737-7.

Rowan creeps close to see the elephant, which has just been given to her father, the Emperor Charlemagne, along with a talisman containing a holy relic. Although the elephant is majestic, Rowan never thinks she would need its assistance. But when she learns of a deadly spell that has been placed on her father, she needs the help of the elephant, its keeper Kerric, and her own magical powers to save her father.

6.57 Voigt, Cynthia. **The Wings of a Falcon.** Scholastic, 1993. 467 pp. ISBN 0-590-46712-3.

After fourteen winters of beatings, hunger, fear, and horror, fourteen-year-old Oriel and his friend Griff escape from the Damall's island to the mainland. Griff, a boy who had always feared the Damall's anger, and Oriel, the one who always faced it bravely, find themselves alone on the mainland facing new dangers with only one hope: the Damall's greatest treasure, a green gemstone carved into a falcon with its wings unfolding.

6.58 Waugh, Sylvia. **The Mennyms.** Greenwillow Books, 1994. 216 pp. ISBN 0-688-13070-4.

The Mennyms are a close-knit family with a well-guarded secret: they are actually dolls. They live peacefully, managing to come out in disguise or at night to fool the neighbors. Now their serene life is about to be shattered. A letter arrives from Albert Pond indicating that he will be visiting the "family" in the near future. Albert's visit threatens their heretofore peaceful existence unless they can come up with a plan to persuade him to change his plans.

6.59 Winthrop, Elizabeth. **The Battle for the Castle.** Holiday House, 1993. 211 pp. ISBN 0-8264-1010-2.

In this sequel to *The Castle in the Attic*, William and Jason are still best friends. For his twelfth birthday, William's old nanny sends him the magic token from his earlier adventure. This token allows William once again to enter the miniature castle in his attic and travel back in time to the Middle Ages. This time he takes Jason with him. They face danger and adventure as they battle evil forces trying to destroy the castle and its occupants.

6.60 Wrede, Patricia. **Talking to Dragons.** Harcourt Brace & Company, 1993. 272 pp. ISBN 0-15-284247-0.

On his sixteenth birthday, Daystar is sent into the Enchanted Forest by his mother Cimorene. He is instructed not to return until he discovers the reason for his adventure. In this fourth installment of the Enchanted Forest Chronicles, Daystar is reunited with his lost father. Kazul, the dragon, and Shiara, a temperamental fire witch, help him defeat the horde of wizards who long to capture the magic sword that Daystar wears.

6.61 Yep, Laurence. **Dragon Cauldron.** HarperTrophy, 1994. 312 pp. ISBN 0-06-440398-X.

Shimmer, the Dragon Princess, must repair the crack in the magic cauldron. Accompanied by Monkey Boy, Thorn, Civet the witch, and Indigo, she journeys in search of help from The Smith and the Snail Woman. Along the way, the group encounters danger in many forms. They become trapped by the Nameless One, the most powerful and evil wizard known. If they fail to escape, the dragon world may be lost, and the human world is, too, at peril.

6.62 Yep, Laurence. **Dragon War.** HarperTrophy, 1994. 313 pp. ISBN 0-06-440525-7.

The Boneless King has managed to steal the dragon cauldron from Shimmer, the Dragon Princess. With the aid of this powerful magic he can destroy the dragons' home and gain absolute control over all living things. Shimmer, along with Indigo and Monkey, must unite all dragons if they are to foil this most evil plan and defeat the Boneless King.

6.63 Yolen, Jane. **Here There Be Unicorns.** Illustrated by David Wilgus. Harcourt Brace & Company, 1994. 128 pp. ISBN 0-15-209902-6.

Poems, stories, and ballads about unicorns present some of the collected lore about this mythical beast of long ago. How can you capture a unicorn? What do unicorns eat? Are unicorn horns magical? Yolen's work answers these and many other questions with her magical tales and mystical poems.

6.64 Zambreno, Mary Frances. **Journeyman Wizard: A Magical Mystery.** Harcourt Brace & Company, 1994. 240 pp. ISBN 0-15-200022-4.

Jermyn has come to the distant village of Land's End to be trained as a journeyman wizard by Lady Jean. He is frustrated that Lady Jean will not permit him to cast spells; he is anxious to develop his talents. Jermyn will need all his talents and those of his new friend, Brianne, after Lady Jean is found dead in her chambers. It is Jermyn who stands accused of her murder.

6.65 Zindel, Paul. **Loch.** HarperCollins, 1994. 209 pp. ISBN 0-06-024542-5.

Many believe the Loch Ness monster to be only a mythical creature. Fifteen-year-old Loch Perkins knows better; he has seen the creature with his own eyes. While his father is off tracking the elusive creature with sophisticated sonar devices, Loch literally stumbles across one of its young. What Loch is now able to provide is proof that this mythical creature really does exist. That proof, however, may mean death to these ancient animals.

7 Science with a Twist: Science Fiction

7.1 Adkins, Jan. **A Storm without Rain.** Beech Tree Books, 1993. 179 pp. ISBN 0-688-11852-6.

Jack Carter, fifteen, does not have a good relationship with his grandfather, so when Jack is chosen to give a speech at his grandfather's ninety-third birthday, he escapes on his sailboat. A strange storm transports Jack back in time, where he again meets his grandfather. Only this time, they are the same age. Jack wonders whether or not he should reveal his true identity to his grandfather, and how he will get back to his own time.

7.2 Brittain, Bill. **Shape-Changer.** HarperCollins, 1994. 108 pp. ISBN 0-06-024238-8.

Twelve-year-old Frank Dunn and his friend, Lauren Kyle, are awakened by a loud noise and a flash of light. They begin the strangest adventure of their lives with the appearance of Zymel, an alien policeman from the planet Shilad. Zymel and the criminal he is chasing, Fek, are shape changers. Frank and Lauren become Zymel's deputies. They outwit the U.S. government, their parents, and their teachers as they chase the elusive Fek in all his disguises.

7.3 Christopher, John. **A Dusk of Demons.** Macmillan, 1994. 175 pp. ISBN 0-02-718425-0.

It is only after the Master's death that Ben learns about his heritage. Now, as the new Master of Old Isle, Ben faces many dangers. He manages to escape his island home only to be pursued by people who wish to use his power for their own gain. There are other dangers as well, from the demons which haunt Ben's nightmares and the towns to which he flees.

7.4 Farmer, Nancy. **The Ear, the Eye and the Arm.** Orchard Books, 1994. 301 pp. ISBN 0-531-06829-3.

The future world of Zimbabwe, in the year 2194, is populated with talking blue monkeys, robotic Dobermans, street gangs, toxic waste dumps, a woman known as the She-elephant, a detective agency staffed by mutants, and a tribal village as ancient as time.

Thrown rudely into this mix are the Matsika children, Tendai, Rita, and Kuda. When kidnapped by the She-elephant to work in a toxic-waste dump, Tendai struggles to lead his brother and sister safely home again.

7.5 Gilden, Mel. **The Pumpkins of Time.** Harcourt Brace & Company, 1994. 211 pp. ISBN 0-15-200889-6.

Myron plans to be an accountant when he grows up; however, a summer with his uncle Hugo may change those plans. Hugo's experiment with time launches Myron and his friend Princess into a dangerous adventure in which they encounter slimy monsters driving trucks, zombie-like pod people, and a curious cat named H. G. Wells. Myron, Princess, and H. G. must learn the secrets of time travel if they are to have a future of their own.

7.6 Griffin, Peni R. **Switching Well.** Macmillan, 1993. 218 pp. ISBN 0-689-50581-7.

In 1891, Ada stands at a wishing well wishing that she could live when the lot of women is better. At the same time, but one hundred years later, Amber makes a wish at the same well, wishing that she lived when life was simpler and parents never split up. Their wishes are granted, and they are transported to each other's worlds. Unhappy with their granted wishes and living in orphanages, they struggle to return to their original places.

7.7 Hesse, Karen. **Phoenix Rising.** Henry Holt and Company, 1994. 182 pp. ISBN 0-8050-3108-1.

Life on the Vermont sheep farm where Nyle lives with her grandmother will never be the same. A nuclear accident has killed thousands; thousands more are dying. As long as the wind keeps blowing contamination to the east, the farm is safe. Ezra and his mother, evacuees from the center of the leak, come to stay with Nyle and Gram. Nyle is increasingly attracted to Ezra, but is terrified that time may be running out for all of them.

7.8 Howarth, Lesley. **Maphead.** Candlewick Press, 1994. 154 pp. ISBN 1-56402-416-4. Twelve-year-old Booth Powers and his father reside in Subtle World, a world parallel to our own. But Booth's mother is human, and Booth must meet her as he enters the year of his Dawn of Power. Known as Maphead for his ability to project maps on his forehead, Booth struggles with the love he feels for his father, and with the longing he feels to acknowledge his existence to his mother. Feelings he has never known before begin to control him, and he almost destroys both relationships. Struggling with the complexities of human language, Maphead must depend upon the language of his heart.

7.9 Hughes, Monica. **The Crystal Drop.** Simon and Schuster, 1993. 212 pp. ISBN 0-671-79195-8.

Poor environmental practices have left the western half of North America a near desert by the year 2011. Upon their mother's death, Megan and Ian Dougal are left alone to fend for themselves. Short on food and water, Megan decides they must travel across the wasteland to find their Uncle Greg, last heard from nearly six years ago. Their journey leads them to excitement, danger, and an understanding of their relationship to each other and to the world around them.

7.10 Jones, Diana Wynne. **Hexwood.** Greenwillow Books, 1994. 295 pp. ISBN 0-688-12488-7.

Ann, ill in bed for an interminably long time, is bored. When she notices the strange comings and goings at Hexwood, she sets up a system for spying on the old farmhouse. Her curiosity leads her into the woods surrounding Hexwood, where she meets Mordion, a wizard awakened after centuries of sleep. Then she discovers that the entire village area is controlled by a machine sent by extraterrestrial beings.

7.11 Klause, Annette Curtis. **Alien Secrets.** Delacorte Press, 1993. 227 pp. ISBN 0-385-30928-7.

Twelve-year-old "Puck" Goodfellow finds herself involved in an interplanetary adventure with her new friend, the Shoowa called Hush. Smugglers have stolen the symbol of freedom for the Shoowa people, the Soo. Hush is traveling home in shame, and Puck feels sympathy, having recently flunked out of school, shaming herself and her parents. Together they decide to find the Soo. In doing so they must fight smugglers, thieves, and Hush's natural enemies, the Grakk. To make matters worse, they don't know whom amongst the crew of fellow passengers they can trust.

7.12 Leigh, Stephen. **Dinosaur Planet.** Avon/AvoNova, 1993. 280 pp. ISBN 0-380-76278-1.

Time Safari, Inc. offers safaris to any year in the past for hunters to shoot any type of animal they can name. This leads to a disastrous situation in which both history and the future of humankind are changed. Aaron Cofield travels back in time in an effort to rectify the disaster. He confronts two races of talking dinosaurs, a psychotic time traveler, and other curious creatures in his quest to save humanity. This is Book Two in the Ray Bradbury Presents series, following Book One, *Dinosaur World*, also by Stephen Leigh.

7.13 Lindbergh, Anne. **Nick of Time.** Little, Brown and Company, 1994. 204 pp. ISBN 0-316-52629-0.

Thirteen-year-old Jericho Fugleman attends a private school run by his father and is in love with Allison. When he discovers a time warp in the kitchen of the school, he meets Nick, a citizen of the year 2094, who leads Jericho and Allison into the future. Jericho soon discovers that the uniformity of people and things in the future is not for him, but Allison seems to prefer it to her current life. Can Jericho convince her to come back to her own time? Is Nick his friend, or is he trying to steal Allison? Follow the humorous adventure as Jericho and Allison find their places in time.

7.14 Lowry, Lois. **The Giver.** Houghton Mifflin, 1993. 180 pp. ISBN 0-395-64566-2.

Being chosen as the new Receiver for his community is the highest honor twelve-year-old Jonas can imagine. His world of sameness (no colors, no music, no choices) changes rapidly once his training begins. He discovers memories and feelings unknown to anyone else in his world other than his trainer, The Giver. Some of this knowledge is so terrible that Jonas must face decisions beyond his experience and maturity.

7.15 Lyons, George Ella. **Here and Then.** Orchard Books, 1994. 114 pp. ISBN 0-531-06866-8.

To please her parents, Abby agrees to go on a Civil War reenactment weekend with them. But going to Camp Robinson also means going back in time. Seventh grader Abby is playing the past of Eliza Hoskins, a Civil War nurse. Eliza needs help in getting supplies for the wounded. Abby is whom she chooses to use. With the help of her friend, Harper, Abby decides to deliver the needed supplies. Going back in time is easy. Leaving the 1860s is the difficult part. Abby's desire to help may be fatal.

7.16 McKean, Thomas. **The Haunted Circus.** Simon and Schuster, 1993. 168 pp. ISBN 0-671-72998-5.

In Book Two in the Doors in Time trilogy, twelve-year-old Edith Byrom is visiting her cousins at Bluebird Hall for the summer when she encounters a ghost. The ghost, a female ancestor of

Edith's, shows her a door in time. Edith is sent on a quest to find the young boy who will eventually become her grandfather, but only if Edith can change history. Magical forces are on Edith's side, but time is against her.

7.17 Oppel, Kenneth. **Dead Water Zone.** Joy Street Books/Little, Brown and Company, 1993. 152 pp. ISBN 0-316-65102-8.

Paul Berriker's younger brother, Sam, has disappeared. A cryptic phone call sends Paul to Watertown, a futuristic city of criminals and smugglers surrounded by a chemically polluted lake. Paul meets Monica Shanks and enlists her aid in finding his brother. His only hope lies in understanding his brother's addiction to the polluted waters of Watertown.

7.18 Pace, Sue. **The Last Oasis.** Delacorte Press, 1993. 230 pp. ISBN 0-385-30881-7.

Teenagers Phoenix and Madonna live in a world nearly destroyed by a vanishing ozone layer, nuclear contamination, and a lack of water. Life centers around malls, where everyone goes to bathe, eat, and seek relief from the effects of intensified sunlight. Pursued by the police, and with nothing to hold them, Phoenix and Madonna decide to seek a better life in Idaho, where hydroponic gardens are rumored to exist. Their journey is interrupted by smugglers, thieves, a religious fanatic, and by fights with each other. Can they survive the journey to reach their last oasis?

7.19 Peck, Richard. **Blossom Culp and the Sleep of Death.** Dell/Yearling, 1994. 185 pp. ISBN 0-440-40676-5.

Blossom's research on ancient Egypt gets a bit of a hand from an ancient princess who calls upon Blossom's remarkable psychic powers for assistance. Blossom must help Princess Sat-Hathor locate the items stolen from her burial chamber or wind up being cursed! With Alexander, her classmate and fellow psychic, Blossom sets off on a quest which transports them to ancient Egypt and the dangers of the past.

7.20 Peck, Richard. **Ghosts I Have Been.** Dell/Yearling, 1994 (Originally published in 1979). 214 pp. ISBN 0-440-421864-5.

Blossom Culp has a gift (or curse?) which enables her to see into the past and future. When she travels to the past and befriends a young boy aboard the Titanic, Blossom's life changes. She becomes famous for her talents and is even granted a visit with the Queen of England. Blossom would be happier, however, if

Alexander Armsworth would pay more attention to her. This hilarious misadventure is a sequel to *The Ghost Belonged to Me*.

7.21 Peck, Richard. **The Dreadful Future of Blossom Culp.** Dell/Yearling, 1994 (Originally published in 1983). 183 pp. ISBN 0-440-42154-3.

Blossom Culp is at it again. Her power to see into the future takes her on an astonishing trip from 1914 to the 1980s. Her visit to her hometown, Bluff City, amazes and saddens her. She is not sure she likes this strange new world, but she is also not sure if she can return to her own time. Perhaps Jeremy, a young boy in the future, can help.

7.22 Pinkwater, Jill. **Mister Fred.** Dutton Children's Books, 1994. 211 pp. ISBN 0-525-44778-4.

When the best teacher in the school leaves to participate in a teacher-exchange program, students in 6-A vow to drive away anyone who tries to replace her. Five weeks and seven substitutes later, the students think that their spitballs, screaming, and paper airplanes will frighten off anyone—until Mr. Fred arrives. When Mr. Fred ignores the students' behavior and excites them about learning, the students are sure that he is an alien, and they set out to prove it.

7.23 Rodda, Emily. **Finders Keepers.** Beech Tree Books, 1993. 184 pp. ISBN 0-688-11846-1.

Sunglasses that aren't there. Earrings that disappear. A drawer full of socks that don't match. Nobody thinks much about these oddities until Patrick finds himself drawn into a parallel world through a computer game. The game becomes real on the other side and Patrick is the contestant. The barrier between worlds is weak in spots, and objects close to the barrier are often pulled from one side to the other. Patrick must recover three lost items, but he has only poetic clues. Can he beat the time limits and locate these objects?

7.24 Rodda, Emily. **The Timekeeper.** Illustrated by Noella Young. Greenwillow Books, 1993. 156 pp. ISBN 0-688-12448-8.

In this sequel to *Finders Keepers*, Patrick Minter is once again called across the barrier between our world and the world parallel to ours. The barrier is collapsing, and only Patrick can stop the destruction of both worlds. Unfortunately, Patrick's brother Danny and his sister Claire accidentally find themselves transported across the barrier as well. The timestream on one side is moving faster than the timestream on the other, bringing the destruction of both worlds ever closer.

7.25 Ryan, Mary C. **Me Two.** Avon/Camelot, 1993. 179 pp. ISBN 0-380-71826-X.

Seventh grader Wilf Farkus doesn't like school. When his science project comes due, he takes the easy way out and orders one through the mail. When it backfires on him, Wilf suddenly finds himself cloned. He quickly devises a plan to substitute the cloned Wilf for the real Wilf. Everything goes well until Wilf starts feeling lost and invisible. Now he must find a way to tell his parents about the other Wilf. Somehow, he must reclaim his life.

7.26 Scott, Michael. **Gemini Game.** Holiday House, 1993. 159 pp. ISBN 0-8234-1092-7.

Welcome to the twenty-first century, where virtual reality computer games are incredibly realistic and complex. The fabulously wealthy fifteen-year-old twins, Liz and B. J., are on the run from VR police after their Gemini Corporation's most popular VR game creation, Night Castle, mysteriously caused players to lapse into comas. In a race against time, the "Game Makers" enter their own game of Virtual Reality to solve the programming mystery before they, too, are stricken.

7.27 Sleator, William. **Others See Us.** Dutton Children's Books, 1993. 163 pp. ISBN 0-525-45104-8.

When sixteen-year-old Jared makes his annual summer trip to the family home, he accidentally falls into a toxic waste dump. The chemicals in the dump somehow give him powers of extrasensory perception. These new powers, which he struggles to keep secret, give him horrifying knowledge about his family. Complicating matters, he discovers that his grandmother and evil cousin, Annelise, also have these powers. Now he's caught in a battle of mind control that becomes a fight for life.

7.28 Slepian, Jan. **Back to Before.** Philomel Books, 1993. 170 pp. ISBN 0-399-22011-9.

Linny Erda and his cousin Hilary both wish they could have the previous year to live over. Linny has lost his mother to cancer, and Hilary's dad has divorced her mother. The discovery of a strange golden ring sends them on the journey they wish for. Linny realizes this is his chance to change things, to relieve his guilt over the death of his mother, and to prove his love. Hilary sees it as a chance to save her parents' marriage and to find the love missing in her life.

7.29 Sobol, Donald J. **"My Name Is Amelia."** Atheneum, 1994. 105 pp. ISBN 0-689-31970-3.

Falling overboard, Lisa is sure she's a goner until she notices a wooden raft in the water. After drifting for two days, she spots land and swims to safety, where she is greeted by a ten-year-old Amelia Earhart. Lisa soon discovers she is on an uncharted island with Abe Lincoln, Beethoven, and other notables. Lisa is trapped in time with only one way out—and that way is nearly impossible.

7.30 Sweeney, Joyce. **Shadow.** Delacorte Press, 1994. 216 pp. ISBN 0-385-32051-5.

Eighth grader Sarah Shaheen's beloved cat, Shadow, dies unexpectedly. But has the cat really gone? Sarah begins seeing her cat at home and in her dreams. She feels Shadow is trying to warn her about an impending disaster. But no one believes Sarah— not her parents, not her brothers, not even her boyfriend, Julian. Can she discover what Shadow is trying to tell her?

7.31 Ure, Jean. **Plague.** Puffin Books, 1993. 218 pp. ISBN 0-14-036283-5.

Teenager Fran Latimer returns from a month-long primitive camping trip to a London devastated by a deadly disease. She finds her parents dead and her best friend, Harriet, mentally deranged. The army has cordoned off their section of London, so they decide to try to reach a relative's home in the country. Out of food and nearly out of hope, they begin their journey into a world reshaped by something deadlier than any nuclear bomb.

7.32 Woodruff, Elvira. **The Disappearing Bike Shop.** Dell/Yearling, 1994. 169 pp. ISBN 0-440-40938-1.

All Tyler wants is a bicycle chain, but when he first sees Quigley's Bicycle Shop, it is rising in the air in a puff of smoke! When it settles to the ground, Tyler and his friend Freckle can't resist going inside. Mr. Quigley is as mysterious and fascinating as the artwork and inventions in his shop. Trapped in one of those inventions, the boys travel back in time with the frightening possibility that they will never return.

Science with a Twist: Science Fiction **111**

7.33 Wu, William F. **Predator.** Avon/AvoNova, 1993. 223 pp. ISBN 0-380-76510-1.

The Laws of Robotics dictate the actions of a futuristic robot that governs an entire human city. Capable of splitting into six different robots, it does just that when similar robots begin to fail. The six different robots send themselves back in time. Then, a hunter robot and his human helpers launch a massive hunt for the escaped robots. Their first stop is prehistoric time, where human emotion and robot logic clash. First in the Robots in Time series.

7.34 Wu, William F. **Marauder.** Avon/AvoNova, 1993. 243 pp. ISBN 0-380-76511-X.

The robot Hunter launches into the second in the Robots in Time time-travel adventures, seeking one of six robots that have escaped into the past. Hunter and his team of human experts travel back in time to the city of Port Royal, Jamaica, in the year 1668. There they confront pirates, buccaneers, privateers, and a fellow time traveler, all wishing to get their hands on the escaped robot, MC-2.

III Shudder and Shake!

To me, detective stories are a great solace, a sort of mental knitting, where it doesn't matter if you drop a stitch.

Rupert Hart-Davis, English publisher

8 Whodunnit? Mysteries

8.1   Alcock, Vivien. **A Kind of Thief.** Dell/Yearling, 1994. 179 pp. ISBN 0-440-40916-0.

Police officers come to the house early one morning and arrest Elinor's father for stealing money from his company. Elinor is certain of his innocence at first, but gradually she must come to accept the fact that her father has committed a crime. When he slips her a claim ticket for a briefcase, she feels sure that it contains the stolen money, but she is afraid to let anyone else know. With her dad in jail, the family may need this money to survive.

8.2   Arkin, Anthony Dana. **Captain Hawaii.** HarperCollins, 1994. 242 pp. ISBN 0-06-021508-9.

Fifteen-year-old Aaron is not content sitting by the pool while on a family vacation in Hawaii. Wanting excitement, he signs up for an island tour. On the tour, he meets a beautiful girl. Unfortunately, she isn't there to help when the boat is blown up or when three men with dogs chase him through the jungle and shoot at him.

8.3   Avi. **"Who Was That Masked Man, Anyway?"** Avon/Camelot, 1994. 170 pp. ISBN 0-380-72113-9.

During World War II, Frankie is caught up in the adventurous world of the radio drama. The Lone Ranger, the Green Hornet, The Shadow, and Captain America fill his head with notions of becoming a master spy. Frankie's parents, however, think that homework is more important! When Frankie becomes convinced that a spy is in the family's midst, he has a tough time persuading others to believe him. His alter ego, Chet Barker, Master Spy, comes to the rescue.

8.4   Burgess, Barbara Hood. **The Fred Field.** Delacorte Press, 1994. 180 pp. ISBN 0-385-31070-6.

Oren Bell's best friend Fred was murdered last summer. Oren's family and friends have established a playing field in Fred's honor. Oren is still bothered, however, by the fact that Fred's killer has never been found. The "Friends of Fred" decide to commit their summer vacation to solving the mystery of Fred's murder and improving the neighborhood in which they live.

8.5   Byars, Betsy. **The Dark Stars: A Herculeah Jones Mystery.** Viking, 1994. 130 pp. ISBN 0-670-85487-5.

As Herculeah passes "Dead Oaks," her hair begins to frizzle, a sure sign that a mystery is about to happen. She sees her father, a police detective, investigating a reported prowler, though none is found. She returns home to find her mother, a private detective, in conference with a menacing man with deep, piercing eyes. When her mother refuses to tell her what is going on, Herculeah immediately recruits her friend Meat to start her own investigation.

8.6   DeFelice, Cynthia. **The Light on Hogback Hill.** Macmillan, 1993. 139 pp. ISBN 0-02-726453-X.

Eleven-year-old Hadley Patterson has been intrigued by the light from the house on Hogback Hill since she and her mom moved to Possum Hollow. Townspeople say that a frightening old hunchback lives there. Often alone while her mother is working, Hadley wonders about the stories of the old woman. Once Josh Carter arrives, Hadley and Josh join forces and together begin to unlock the mystery of the hunchbacked woman.

8.7   Ferguson, Alane. **Poison.** Bradbury Press, 1994. 246 pp. ISBN 0-02-734528-9.

Chelsea misses her stepmother Diane and resents her father for divorcing Diane. Since the divorce, Chelsea's father seems determined to make her life miserable. He refuses to answer questions Chelsea has about Diane, refuses to let Chelsea talk to her, and becomes furious whenever Chelsea mentions Diane's name. Then, by accident, Chelsea overhears a conversation which leads her to a dead body: Diane's. The problem is that now the murderer knows who Chelsea is.

8.8   Geras, Adèle. **Pictures of the Night.** Harcourt Brace Jovanovich, 1993. 182 pp. ISBN 0-15-261588-1.

Bella sings with a band of seven Bohemian musicians during the summer before college. After narrowly escaping injury several times, she searches for a connection between the appearance of two mysterious old women and her jealous, vindictive stepmother. Bella finds that both romance and death may be waiting at her final performance with the band. Book Three of the Egerton Hall Trilogy.

8.9   Haynes, Betsy. **Deadly Deception.** Delacorte Press, 1994. 212 pp. ISBN 0-385-32067-1.

How can seventeen-year-old Ashley get her boyfriend Drew to get the help he needs to stay off of drugs permanently? Her problem becomes more complicated when the school counselor, Mrs. Rothlis, is found murdered. Drew was the last person seen near her office, and his name was on her appointment calendar. Drew is arrested. While Ashley tries to help him by finding the real killer, she discovers strange secrets about her own past.

8.10 Heisel, Sharon E. **Wrapped in a Riddle.** Houghton Mifflin, 1993. 140 pp. ISBN 0-395-65026-7.

Strange things have been going on in the inn since Miranda arrived to live there with her grandmother. First, the housekeeper is attacked. Next, some valuable letters written by Mark Twain are stolen. Miranda works to solve these mysteries with the help of her new school friends. All of the clues seem to be pointing in the direction of one of the boarders, but she disappears before Miranda can confirm her suspicions.

8.11 Keene, Carolyn. **Dance till You Die.** Archway/Pocket Books, 1994. 149 pp. ISBN 0-671-79492-2.

When Nancy Drew's friend Bess disappears from the club where she works, Nancy is on the case immediately. Even after Bess is found, Nancy keeps working. When the DJ from the same club is found murdered, Nancy knows something is terribly wrong. Soon she finds her own life in danger, but still she keeps looking for the murderer—someone who is also looking for her.

8.12 Kerr, M. E. **Fell Down.** HarperKeypoint, 1993. 191 pp. 0-06-447086-5.

Seventeen-year-old John Fell of the two previous titles, *Fell* and *Fell Back*, becomes involved in a parallel mystery while investigating his best friend's death. The mystery unfolds as Fell relates the events of the present while a ventriloquist's journal, written in the voice of the dummy, provides the ventriloquist's version of the past. The intertwining stories raise an interesting question. Could a demented ventriloquist's dummy drive a man to murder?

8.13 L'Engle, Madeleine. **Troubling a Star.** Farrar, Straus, and Giroux, 1994. 296 pp. ISBN 0-374-37783-9.

Vicky Austin can't believe her eyes: a trip to the Antarctica as a birthday present! After convincing her parents that the trip is well-chaperoned and safe, Vicky starts off only to learn that safety is not what this trip is about. Unknowingly, Vicky has become part of a group more interested in drug smuggling than studying penguins. Finally, when she knows too much, she is placed adrift on an iceberg. Stranded and freezing, Vicky struggles to stay alive.

8.14 Miklowitz, Gloria. **The Killing Boy.** Bantam Books, 1993. 168 pp. ISBN 0-553-56037-9.

When Brian's parents die in a strange fire, he is sent to live with his cousin Tim's family. At first, Tim is overjoyed; he finally has a brother his own age, someone to have fun with. But Tim's elation soon fades as he discovers a darker side to Brian. Tim begins to wonder just what really happened to Brian's family and then begins to fear for his own family's safety.

8.15 Nixon, Joan Lowery. **Shadowmaker.** Delacorte Press, 1994. 197 pp. ISBN 0-385-32030-2.

Katie moves from the big city of Houston to a small town, so that her mom can complete a book she is writing. Katie thinks that small-town life will be sleepy and boring. Nothing could be further from the truth once her mom exposes the illegal dumping of toxic waste by some of the town residents. Now Katie and her mom are in real danger from the shadowy people who lurk outside their trailer at night, threatening them into silence.

8.16 Nixon, Joan Lowery. **The Name of the Game Was Murder.** Delacorte Press, 1993. 182 pp. ISBN 0-385-30864-7.

Samantha, a would-be writer, is thrilled to be spending the weekend with her great uncle, an acclaimed mystery writer. Once at this house, though, she is dismayed to learn that he is not a very nice person. As a matter of fact, he is in the process of blackmailing all his weekend guests. When he ends up murdered, Samantha's sleuthing powers may be the only way she can escape being the next victim of the murderer.

8.17 Patneaude, David. **Someone Was Watching.** Albert Whitman & Company, 1993. 220 pp. ISBN 0-8075-7531-3.

Missing and presumed drowned: that was the police's conclusion about Chris's baby sister, Molly. Chris and his family have a tough time dealing with their loss but decide to confront their grief directly by viewing the video they shot the day Molly disappeared. Watching the video, Chris spots the van. He begins to believe that Molly has been kidnapped and is still alive. Feeling both hopeful and fearful, he starts off on a journey to find Molly.

Whodunnit? Mysteries

8.18 Pfoutz, Sally. **Missing Person.** Viking, 1993. 177 pp. ISBN 0-670-84663-5.

At seventeen, Carrie's life begins to unravel when she comes home and finds that her dog has been killed. While Carrie buries Zinc, her mom disappears and does not return. The only clue is a note in her mom's handwriting: "I've gone to the movies." Carrie feels her mom was trying to tell her something, but no one seems to care. Carrie's father and sister seem almost relieved to be rid of her mom, a former alcoholic with an unstable past.

8.19 Roberts, Willo Davis. **The Absolutely True Story . . . How I Visited Yellowstone Park with the Terrible Rupes.** Atheneum, 1994. 154 pp. ISBN 0-689-31939-8.

Twelve-year-old Lewis and his twin sister Alison are excited to be invited on a trip to Yellowstone Park with their neighbors, the Rupes. Things don't go quite the way they plan, though. Mr. Rupe can't drive the motor home; Mrs. Rupe chain smokes; the two younger Rupes are allowed to do whatever they want! To add to his woes, Lewis notices that two men are following them. Could they be after the money that Billy Rupes found?

8.20 Roberts, Willo Davis. **Caught.** Atheneum, 1994. 151 pp. ISBN 0-689-31903-7.

Victoria's parents have separated. While her mother is away on business, she and her younger sister, Joanie, stay with Gram, a domineering woman whom Victoria hates. The girls run away to their dad, who is not expecting them. The janitor lets them into their dad's apartment, but their dad never comes home. There is evidence that something is wrong—unfamiliar possessions, suspicious bloodstains. It is clear that Dad is in trouble, and it is up to the girls to set things right.

8.21 Ruckman, Ivy. **Pronounce It Dead.** Bantam/Skylark, 1994. 167 pp. ISBN 0-553-48176-2.

Katy and Andrea are helping cousin Susan tend her pigs at the Elgin Fair when the mysterious disappearances begin. First, one of the magician's assistants and then Susan's runt pig seem to vanish into thin air. When Katy and Andrea try to help solve these mysteries, their own lives may be at risk.

8.22 Ruckman, Ivy. **Spell It Murder.** Bantam/Skylark, 1994. 150 pp. ISBN 0-553-48175-4.

Summer camp should be loads of fun, but Katy and Andrea seem to spend most of their time working in the camp kitchen. When they decide to run away one night, they don't count on running into two men dumping bodies into the camp's lake. Now the girls are in serious trouble.

8.23 Taylor, Theodore. **The Weirdo.** Avon/Flare, 1993. 222 pp. ISBN 0-380-72017-5.

When a prize-winning dog she is in charge of heads off into the swamp, Samantha must go after it. While in the swamp, she sees someone dump a body. She also becomes lost, but she is finally rescued by Chip Clewt, whom everyone calls The Weirdo because of his scarred face and reclusive nature. Slowly the two become friends, and then together they search for the person who dumped the body.

8.24 Vigor, John. **Danger, Dolphins, and Ginger Beer.** Atheneum, 1993. 180 pp. ISBN 0-689-31817-0.

Sally is camping on an island with her two younger brothers while her father is away. They rescue an injured dolphin and save a mysterious man and woman who have had a boating accident. Sally goes to the mainland for supplies. Upon returning, she discovers that her brothers have been kidnapped by the boaters that they had saved.

8.25 Wallace, Bill. **Blackwater Swamp.** Holiday House, 1994. 185 pp. ISBN 0-9234-1120-6.

The first thing Ted hears about when his family moves to Louisiana is the witch living in Blackwater Swamp. Next, he hears about the robberies plaguing the townspeople. Ted finds the witch and discovers she isn't a witch, but an eccentric woman living in the swamp caring for sick or hurt animals. The town is convinced, however, that she is responsible for their troubles, and soon Ted finds his own life threatened as he tries to save the "witch."

8.26 Westall, Robert. **A Place to Hide.** Scholastic, 1994. 199 pp. ISBN 0-590-47748-X.

After her mother's death, Lucy's father behaves strangely. First, he sells her mother's Rembrandt, and then, he gives Lucy a suitcase filled with cash and tells her that she needs to run away and change her identity. Lucy's only link with her father will be through a secret code in the obituary section of a small newspaper. Lucy knows she is fleeing from the British government, but she doesn't know why.

9 Occult, Horror, Ghosts, and Unexplained Phenomena

9.1   Adams, Carmen. **The Band.** Avon/Flare, 1994. 133 pp. ISBN 0-380-77328-7.

Megan is not happy about the move from Colorado to California at the beginning of her junior year. She knows how hard it is to make new friends. So, when she gets to California, she is excited about being included in "the band," a mysterious group that wears black, drives classic sports cars, and listens to old rock songs. But why don't they come to school? Do they have jobs? Why are they only seen in the late afternoon and at night? Torn between wanting to be popular and feeling very uncomfortable with the group, Megan begins her own research to find out more about them.

9.2   Bauer, Marion Dane. **A Taste of Smoke.** Clarion Books, 1993. 106 pp. ISBN 0-395-64341-4.

Sisters Caitlin and Pam go camping in order to spend some time together. When Pam's boyfriend comes to visit them at the state park, they go to see a movie about a mill fire that killed an abandoned orphan boy in 1894. Later, when Caitlin meets an oddly dressed boy in the woods, she realizes that he is the ghost of the boy who died in the fire. What does he want from her?

9.3   Bellairs, John (completed by Brad Strickland). **The Vengeance of the Witch-Finder.** Dial Books for Young Readers, 1993. 153 pp. ISBN 0-8037-1450-5.

A European vacation for Lewis Barnavelt and his uncle Jonathan seems like the perfect opportunity to visit their English cousin. At Barnavelt Manor, the ancestral home, Lewis decides to explore the house and grounds for family history. What might have been an enjoyable stay turns into a nightmare when Lewis and his new friend, Bertie, open a grave that holds more than the remains of Lewis's ancestor.

9.4 Bellairs, John (Completed by Brad Strickland). **The Drum, the Doll, and the Zombie.** Dial Books for Young Readers, 1994. 153 pp. ISBN 0-8037-1426-9.

Two thirteen-year-old boys, Johnny Dixon and Fergie Ferguson, are invited to a party that Professor Childermass throws for his friend, Dr. Coote. At the party, everyone is talking about the voodoo drum that was given to Dr. Coote. When Fergie decides to play a drum solo on it, he puts himself and others in danger from Baron Samedi, the Lord of the Dead. Strange illnesses, voodoo dolls, attacks by zombies, and a kidnapping test the creativity of these resourceful young men.

9.5 Bellairs, John. **The Ghost in the Mirror.** Dial Books for Young Readers, 1993. 169 pp. ISBN 0-8037-1370-3.

When Mrs. Zimmermann begins to have visions, she and Rose Rita decide they must get to the bottom of the problem. Their investigation leads them to Pennsylvania where, in the summer of 1951, they calmly begin driving through a tunnel. It is the winter of 1898 when they exit. Mrs. Zimmermann and Rose Rita must help the Hermann Weiss family fight rumors that Grandpa Drexel is a magician who makes deals with the devil.

9.6 Butler, Beverly. **Witch's Fire.** Dutton/Cobblehill Books, 1993. 135 pp. ISBN 0-525-65132-2.

Thirteen-year-old Kirsty Hamilton has been learning to live with a wheelchair since the automobile accident that killed her mom and sister two years ago. Her dad has remarried and wants Kirsty to live with him, his new wife, and her daughter Pam. Kirsty moves in, but the house that is supposed to help her feel like part of this new family is haunted. Neighbors tell stories about girls who moved to this house and then mysteriously disappeared. Kirsty must face the unknown force that is trying to pull Pam and herself to another world—or risk the fate that has taken the lives of others.

9.7 Carmody, Isobelle. **The Gathering.** Dial Books, 1994. 279 pp. ISBN 0-8037-1716-4.

From the moment of his initial introduction to Cheshunt, Nathaniel knew that something was wrong. His father's death and a strange school add to his uneasy feelings. Then he is "chosen" by a group of misfits who are trying to find out about an evil that has occurred. None of the adults in town want to talk about what is happening. In fact, some of the adults seem to be a part of this evil. Ultimately, Nathaniel and his friends must have a showdown with "The Gathering." This isn't a game they can afford to lose.

9.8 Cheetham, Ann. **The Pit.** HarperTrophy, 1993. 186 pp. ISBN 0-06-440448-X.

Nine-year-old Oliver Wright is not excited about summer vacation. The weather is cold and rainy, his father is in the hospital, and his mother doesn't want him exploring the demolition site near his home. Then odd things begin to happen. A worker runs screaming from the site and can't return to work. An old man suddenly appears and wants to rent a specific room in Oliver's house. And Oliver is transported to London of the 1600s, where the plague is killing everyone.

9.9 Clapp, Patricia. **Jane-Emily.** Beech Tree Books, 1993. 160 pp. ISBN 0-688-04592-8.

Eighteen-year-old Louisa is going to spend the summer in an elegant old mansion, but that means she must leave Martin, her boyfriend; her companions will be elderly Mrs. Canfield and nine-year-old Jane. What Louisa fears will be a boring summer becomes a summer of romance and battle with the forces of evil. A handsome young doctor and the ghost of Emily, Jane's long dead aunt, come together to create a memorable yet very dangerous summer.

9.10 Cohen, Daniel. **The Ghost of Elvis and Other Celebrity Spirits.** G.P. Putnam's Sons, 1994. 100 pp. ISBN 0-399-22611-7.

Elvis, Houdini, and Edgar Allan Poe are among the famous ghosts whose stories are in this book. The names of the three lighthouse keepers in Scotland aren't remembered, but their strange disappearances and frequent sightings are. Ghosts seem to be everywhere: in people's homes, on the beach, in castles, on ships, and even in the White House. No place is safe from ghosts. Another Cohen book about ghosts is *Ghosts of the Deep.*

9.11 Cohen, Daniel. **The Mummy's Curse: 101 of the World's Strangest Mysteries.** Avon/Camelot, 1994. 213 pp. ISBN 0-380-77093-8.

One of many strange happenings and mysteries reported in this book is the Mummy's Curse. Legend says that anyone who defiles the final resting place of the Egyptian kings will die. But not all of the mysteries in this book are thousands of years old. In 1971, D. B. Cooper threatened to blow up a plane if his $200,000 demand was not met. After getting his money and four parachutes, he jumped from a plane. Cooper was never caught! Cohen tells about 101 of the world's strangest mysteries.

9.12 Cusick, Richie Tankersley. **Silent Stalker.** Archway/Pocket Books, 1993. 214 pp. ISBN 0-671-79402-7.

Jenny Logan doesn't want to spend her vacation with people she does not know. But when Ed Logan gets a chance to write an article about the annual fair held at Worthington Hall, Jenny finds herself left alone in a household of strange people and stranger happenings. Trapped in this house with an ancient curse that could lead to her death, Jenny doesn't know which twin, Malcolm or Derrick, to trust.

9.13 Cusick, Richie Tankersley. **Someone at the Door.** Archway/Pocket Books, 1994. 243 pp. ISBN 0-671-88742-4.

Hannah and her younger sister, Meg, are in the house alone when they hear that a killer has escaped from a mental hospital and is headed in their direction. Because of a raging blizzard, their phone doesn't work. They are frightened, but they finally fall asleep. Suddenly there is a pounding on their front door. Afraid to let someone in, but not wanting to let anyone freeze to death, they open the door for Lance and Jonathan. The girls become increasingly alarmed when first an ax and then their dog disappears.

9.14 Davidson, Nicole. **Night Terrors.** Avon/Flare, 1994. 181 pp. ISBN 0-380-72243-7.

Maggie Johnson fears the night and sleep. As long as Maggie can remember, she has had a nightmare about a crazed woman who chases her down a long corridor with a knife. Her parents have resisted getting professional help for her to find the reason for the nightmare, until Maggie falls from a moving car and must be hospitalized. During therapy in the hospital's sleep disorder clinic, she uncovers the murderer of several elderly patients and then discovers the source of her recurring nightmares.

9.15 Favors, Jean M. **My Soul to Keep.** Avon/Flare, 1994. 154 pp. ISBN 0-389-77478-X.

April is torn among three guys: Sherman, her cousin, who is always wanting her to help with one of his experiments; Patrick, her friend since childhood; and Doug, the star athlete, the one she most wants to impress. This Halloween, April makes two decisions: to help Sherman with an ESP experiment and to take a ride with Doug without telling anyone where she is going. The ride leads to a cemetery, where April is to become a slave to Xanthu, exalted guardian of the everlasting flames.

9.16 Ferguson, Alane. **Overkill.** Avon/Flare, 1992. 168 pp. ISBN 0-380-72167-8.

A girl dancing in the breeze is suddenly stabbed. This is the nightmare that continues to awaken Lacey Brighton every night. When the principal announces that Lacey's friend Celeste has been murdered, Lacey realizes that she has been dreaming about her friend's death. After she tells the police about her recurring dream, and after they learn of Lacey's and Celeste's recent argument, Lacey becomes the prime murder suspect. Lacey's days become the nightmare as she realizes that everyone thinks she is guilty.

9.17 Garth, G. G. **Nightmare Matinee.** Bantam Books, 1994. 134 pp. ISBN 0-553-56566-4.

Aaron, a horror movie fan, is delighted when the ultimate 3-D horror movie *Still Life: The Best of the Worst* comes to town. But the movie becomes addictive to him and his friends at Westlake High School. Each time they see it there is a subtle change in the movie and a big change in them. Aaron begins to grow fangs and claws, and his girlfriend has fat green worms oozing out of her face.

9.18 Gorman, Carol. **Graveyard Moon.** Avon/Flare, 1993. 153 pp. ISBN 0-380-76991-3.

Kelly McLees wants to become part of a group at her new school. When seniors Tracy, Alice, and Colette suggest a party in the cemetery, Kelly knows she must go along with this initiation. The "dead body" Kelly is supposed to discover when sent on an errand turns out to be real, instead of the joke the other girls had planned. Kelly's terror begins when she becomes the target of the murderer.

9.19 Hardy, Robin. **Call of the Wendigo.** Bantam Books, 1994. 179 pp. ISBN 0-553-29828-3.

The legend of the wendigo becomes too real for four high school students. Kyla and Mark have come from opposite coasts for the Keewatin tennis camp. Marla, a model in New York, just needs a rest, so she accompanies her friend Kyla. Tyrone lives and works at the lodge and is the only one of the four who truly understands the power of this force that resides in the Canadian wilderness. Can the wind really steal your mind?

9.20 Harrell, Janice. **Fatal Magic.** Avon/Flare, 1994. 119 pp. ISBN 0-380-77327-9.

Blythe and Quentin have been a couple for over a year, and Blythe is ready for a change. Harry seems to be just the reason for the break-up. He is attentive, knows just the right things to say, and is an amateur magician. Blythe agrees to tutor him in algebra and is introduced to a house of mystery where tigers roam the grounds freely. Her curiosity and Harry's need for revenge put everyone in danger.

9.21 Hawks, Robert. **Summer's End.** Avon/Flare, 1994. 164 pp. ISBN 0-380-77440-2.

Summer on the island is sure to be a bore. At least that is what Amy thinks at first. Once the children begin to vanish, though, summer is far from boring. It may be deadly unless Amy can successfully defeat a vampire and his minions who now inhabit most of the island and its residents.

9.22 James, J. Alison. **Runa.** Atheneum, 1993. 138 pp. ISBN 0-689-31708-5.

Runa is thrilled at the idea of spending the summer with her Grandfather Morfar at his home in Sweden. Her thirteenth birthday is approaching, and Runa is looking forward to the celebration she will have. However, the celebration is delayed when she and her friend Luci stumble across an ancient mystery concerning the Vikings and Norse gods of ancient times. Runa's delight swiftly changes to terror.

9.23 Kuraoka, Hannah. **The Last Victim.** Avon/Flare, 1994. 136 pp. ISBN 0-380-77375-9.

Kelly and her parents move to Astoria. People there are frightened after a series of murders, especially the murder of Susan Wells. Although they are told that the murderer has been found, Kelly knows differently. She has evidence that proves Joey couldn't have killed his girlfriend Susan. Knowing too much almost costs Kelly her life.

9.24 Lasky, Kathryn. **A Voice in the Wind.** Harcourt Brace & Company, 1993. 255 pp. ISBN 0-15-294102-9.

In this third Starbuck Family Adventure, telepathic twins Liberty and July find themselves trying to solve a six-hundred-year-old murder mystery. While exploring their surroundings in New Mexico, they discover the ghost of an ancient Native American.

The ghost lets them know that she was murdered and that her killers were never caught. Determined to help, the twins use their special powers to solve the crime and escape the danger they now face.

9.25 Leroe, Ellen. **H.O.W.L. High Goes Bats.** Pocket Books/Minstrel, 1993. 131 pp. ISBN 0-671-79838-3.

A fun-filled Halloween is what fourteen-year-old Drac (Dragomir) Johnson and his friends are expecting after winning the "Design the Ultimate Dracula Attraction" for Terror Town Scream Park. But a strange purple mist, a gargoyle from Transylvania, and a Dracula folklore expert lead Drac and the Fang Gang on a night of horror they won't forget!

9.26 Leroux, Gaston. **The Phantom of the Opera.** Puffin Books, 1994 (Originally published in 1911). 322 pp. ISBN 0-14-036813-2.

Mysterious things are happening at the Paris Opera, and several people hint that there might be a ghost in the building, but no one takes these rumors seriously until the night beautiful singer Christine Daae disappears. Then the phantom reveals himself, threatens the opera company, and puts everyone into the hidden sanctuary he's created deep beneath the opera floors. Compare this original story to the current Broadway musical based on it.

9.27 Locke, Joseph. **1-900-Killer.** Bantam Books, 1994. 185 pp. ISBN 0-553-56079-4.

When students from Trenton Memorial High get bored, they call 1-900-PARTY-ON. What seems to be a fun and harmless pastime turns deadly after the "Phantom" begins to join in the conversations. When two regular callers are found murdered and friends begin to disappear, Heather decides to become involved in the investigation. Jumping to conclusions too quickly causes her to give the police the wrong information. Now that she knows who the killer is and is in danger herself, no one will listen to her.

9.28 Locke, Joseph. **Game Over.** Bantam Books, 1993. 178 pp. ISBN 0-553-29652-3.

Joe is the best player in town; there's not a video game that he can't beat. Then Mr. Everett Blacke opens HADES, a video arcade with all new games. This challenge is more than Joe can resist. Even Lorinda, his girlfriend who hates video games, gets hooked. Then the figures on the scene begin to look like people from school. Since these people haven't been too nice to Joe and

Lorinda, he enjoys destroying them. When real murders and suicides begin to happen, Joe realizes that he'll have to play the ultimate game for his own life.

9.29 Maugham, Somerset W. **Appointment.** Adapted by Alan Benjamin. Illustrated by Roger Essley. Simon and Schuster, 1993. Unpaged. ISBN 0-671-75887-X.

Long ago in Baghdad, a servant, Abdullah, goes to the marketplace where he is frightened by Death, who is disguised as an old woman. His master sends Abdullah to Samarra to question the woman to find out the reason for her strange look. This scary story is based on Somerset Maugham's "Appointment in Samarra."

9.30 Morse, Eric. **Road Trip (Friday the 13th).** Berkley Books, 1994. 187 pp. ISBN 0-425-14383-X.

Winning the opening football game should have meant a celebration for the Carville Hornets. Instead, it meant disaster. The van carrying three star players, their girlfriends, the coach, and Teddy gets lost and wrecks. Everyone blames Teddy because he was reading the map; therefore, he is left at the van while the others look for help. Finding a hockey mask that gives him superhuman strength, Teddy seeks revenge on his companions. Will Jason and his legend ever die?

9.31 O'Neal, Michael. **Haunted Houses.** Greenhaven Press, Inc., 1994. 111 pp. ISBN 1-56510-095-6.

In this book from the Great Mysteries: Opposing Viewpoint series, you can read about the ghosts of well-known historical figures such as Abraham Lincoln, Marie Antoinette, and General George Custer. You can also get tips on the best places to go as well as what to look for if you want to see a ghost. If you are a skeptic, you can learn how to investigate hauntings and how to tell hauntings from hallucinations. When things go bump in the night, you'll know what to do!

9.32 Peel, John. **Alien Prey.** Grosset & Dunlap, 1993. 154 pp. ISBN 0-448-40529-6.

Josh, Paul, Beth, and Ben would be juvenile delinquents in any other town, but in Baine's Hollow none of their acts of vandalism are taken seriously. All they want is attention and understanding. No one questions the strangeness of the town until two surveyors arrive and the sheriff tries to discourage them from doing their work or even staying. The surveyors decide to investigate.

Occult, Horror, Ghosts, and Unexplained Phenomena

What they find out leads them to spiders, aliens, and the war between good and evil.

9.33 Peel, John. **Blood Wolf.** Grosset & Dunlap, 1993. 159 pp. ISBN 0-448-40527-X.

After King Kardak is murdered, his well-liked son Numin must flee for his life. Duroc, his older brother, fears Numin wants to challenge him for the throne. As Numin tries to escape from his brother, he is helped by Senza and her magic. Her magic is to keep the wolves at bay, wolves that Senza "sees" gnawing his dead body. Numin must escape the assassins sent after him by his brother, as well as the wolves.

9.34 Peel, John. **Night Wings.** Grosset & Dunlap, 1993. 157 pp. ISBN 0-448-40526-1.

The artificial neck that makes Rob Jensen feel like a freak is exactly what makes him the best vampire hunter. So, when Ferenc Veszali, fourteenth Duke of Pestroseni, and his daughter, Katica, ask Rob to come to Romania to fight vampires, he accepts. Rob does his job exceptionally well and becomes a hero. But there's always a price to pay.

9.35 Peel, John. **Shattered.** Archway/Pocket Books, 1993. 211 pp. ISBN 0-671-79406-X.

Stephanie avoids conflict. She won't respond to Kimberly's cruel remarks or stand up to Blake, her boss, when he makes her do the menial jobs at Burger Heaven. But she does confront Dolman because no one would possibly believe that this old man who sells antiques could be the cause of two murders. But how can Stephanie convince the police that a comb and scarab pin come to life to kill people or that a magic mirror can give or take away life?

9.36 Peel, John. **Talons.** Archway/Pocket Books, 1993. 196 pp. ISBN 0-671-79405-1.

"This has got to be the dullest spot on the face of the earth," states Kari about her home in Radford, Maine. Little does she realize that the summer before her senior year in high school will be unforgettable. The excitement begins when the mother of her friend Ryan decides to renovate a store. The excavation leads to an intriguing discovery that frightens Kari and Ryan. Vikings, twelve silver game pieces, and a corpse wrapped in silver chains teach the two that history is more than stuff in books.

9.37 Phillips, Ann. **A Haunted Year.** Macmillan, 1994. 175 pp. ISBN 0-02-774605-4.

Florence is lonely. She wishes for a playmate but gets George, the ghost of a long-dead twelve-year-old cousin. At first he is a good friend and playmate, but soon he is ruling her life. When she tries to break away from his control, he turns her life into terror. To break the spell George has over her, Florence needs information about his life. But no one is willing to talk about George, dead or alive.

9.38 Piazza, Linda. **Call of the Deep.** Avon/Flare Books, 1994. 153 pp. ISBN 0-380-77330-9.

Three years ago a flash flood broke sixteen-year-old Dilly's leg and killed her mom, leaving her with a strong fear of water. A vacation to Galveston Island with her dad and new stepmother is supposed to help conquer this fear. Zachary and Jason, the Galveston flood of 1900, and a ghost who walks the beach before someone is about to drown, all come together to show Dilly that things aren't always as they seem.

9.39 Pickford, Ted. **Bobby's Watching.** Bantam Books, 1993. 155 pp. ISBN 0-553-56089-1.

When they were twelve years old, Leigh Millen, her twin sister Jamie, and three other friends played a trick on Bobby Wimmer, the guy they always called a "dweeb" and a "wimper." Now that the group has grown up and gone off to college, Bobby is set on revenge. Leigh is his first target, but Bobby feels that just killing her is not enough. Bobby must make her suffer as he suffered that day so long ago when he was left trapped in the haunted house.

9.40 Pierce, Richard. **Frankenstein's Children: Book One—The Creation.** Berkley Books, 1994. 200 pp. ISBN 0-425-14361-9.

Sara Watkins believes the love between Josh Frank and herself is true and will last forever. Then Josh commits suicide. In the midst of her grief, Grandfather Frank shows Sara the link between his family and the original Dr. Frankenstein. He wants Sara to show her love for Josh by being the one to bring him back to life. Can she, along with Josh's younger sister Jessie and Eddie Perez, the school's computer genius, perform such a miracle? Will the person who is created really be Josh?

9.41 Pike, Christopher. **The Last Vampire 2.** Archway Hardcover Pocket Books, 1994. 196 pp. ISBN 0-671-87258-3.

Alisa can't understand why she is running into vampires. She and Ray are supposed to be the last ones. Alisa has lived for centuries, taking her victims only for survival. But Eddie and his followers are evil and are killing for power. The struggle between good and evil is played out in the midst of an FBI investigation. Alisa must make decisions about her own future and the lives of people she has grown to love—something a vampire should avoid.

9.42   Posner, Richard. **Sweet Sixteen and Never Been Killed.** Archway/Pocket Books, 1993. 211 pp. ISBN 0-671-86506-4.

Cara Nelson has everything under control. She's the only junior who has ever been editor of the *Tempest*. Her boyfriend is a baseball star. She negotiates at the Swan Club to get exactly what she wants for her Sweet Sixteen party. But, checking out a news story, Cara visits a psychic who turns her world upside down. The psychic's predictions have Cara's destiny intertwined with that of Cyann, a writer for the *Tempest*. Cara must find a way to regain control of her life in order to keep from being killed.

9.43   Reiss, Kathryn. **Dreadful Sorry.** Harcourt Brace Jovanovich, 1993. 340 pp. ISBN 0-15-224213-9.

Molly is deathly afraid of water. After a near-fatal accident at a swimming party, Molly decides she needs time away from her friends, especially Jared. Spending the summer in Maine with her father seems like a good idea until she becomes obsessed with the life and disappearance of a girl who, eighty years ago, lived in the Victorian house Molly's father is renovating.

9.44   Scott, Michael. **October Moon.** Holiday House, 1994. 158 pp. ISBN 0-8234-1110-9.

At first Rachel is happy to be in Ireland on the horse-breeding farm her father has purchased. Then the accidents begin. A fire is set outside the barn, her waterbed is slashed, and the library is destroyed. The destruction only happens when Rachel is near, and the destroyer leaves no clues. The constable blames Rachel. To prove her innocence, she must discover what kind of person leaves no traces and reaches rooftops without ladders.

9.45   Siegel, Barbara, and Scott Siegel. **Final Frenzy.** Archway/Pocket Books, 1993. 151 pp. ISBN 0-671-75948-5.

Sixteen-year-old Andy Moser would like to be a typical teenager, but he finds himself in a world of ghosts. Elizabeth Teller, also sixteen, is a ghost who needs Andy's help. Before she can go to her final peace, Elizabeth and Andy must find out who stole the "Secret of Death" and stop the thief before the secret is released into the world of the living.

9.46 Smith, L. J. **Dark Visions: The Strange Power.** Archway/Pocket Books, 1994. 230 pp. ISBN 0-671-87454-3.

The students at this Ohio high school think Kaitlyn is a witch. Her prophetic drawings frighten those who don't understand them. Kaitlyn doesn't understand the drawings either, but the drawings just come to her; she has no choice about making them. She finally finds an understanding of her unusual talent when she is asked to attend the Zetes Institute in California. There, with four other psychically talented students, Kaitlyn feels accepted. Then she and her friends discover that their talents are being used for evil.

9.47 Steiner, Barbara. **Deathline.** Avon/Flare, 1993. 164 pp. ISBN 0-380-77066-0.

Unlike most eighteen-year-olds, Erika doesn't like phones, but she agrees to join friends on the local Rapline. Erika's famous intuition is tested when she takes a call from a guy who says that he has just murdered a girl. What everyone hopes is a crank call turns into a nightmare. Three girls are killed, and the killer will talk only to Erika. He calls her at home, on dates, and even while she is jogging. Her friends want to help, but Erika doesn't know whom to trust.

9.48 Steiner, Barbara. **Night Cries.** Avon/Flare, 1993. 132 pp. ISBN 0-380-76990-5.

The head of the Shoreview High School Drama Department wants to take the students recently cast for a new play away for the weekend to help them become a tightly knit group. Suzanne and the other students are not sure how well this will work, but they are willing to give a weekend on deserted Thunder Island a try. The strange cries of the loon make for great scary jokes until cast members begin to disappear one by one.

9.49 Steiner, Barbara. **The Photographer II: The Dark Room.** Avon/Flare, 1993. 165 pp. ISBN 0-380-77064-4.

SueAnne is missing. Then she suddenly appears in her prom dress with flowers in her hair, a smile on her face, and quite dead. The same thing happens to Belle. Who is killing these beautiful girls? Vicki and her boyfriend Scott are determined to stop the killings. Could the new photographer in town be responsible?

9.50 Stine, R. L. **Fear Street Saga: The Betrayal.** Archway/Pocket Books, 1993. 161 pp. ISBN 0-671-86831-4.

In *The Betrayal* and its sequel *The Secret*, R. L. Stine gives you the history behind the Simon Fear mansion on Fear Street. As Nora Goode watches the Fear mansion burn in 1900, the past history of the house and its inhabitants flashes before her. In 1692 Susannah Goode's betrayal by her fiancé begins a series of events that are still affecting the lives of the descendants of the Goodes and the Fiers today.

9.51 Stine, R. L. **Silent Night 2.** Archway/Pocket Books, 1993. 196 pp. ISBN 0-671-78619-9.

Reva Dalby is beautiful, rich, and spoiled. Paul Nichols and Diane Morris, wanting some easy money for Christmas, construct a plot to kidnap Reva. The plot backfires when they take the wrong girl, but they get the right person on the second attempt. This time the kidnappers decide that Reva must be killed.

9.52 Stine, R. L. **The Mind Reader.** Archway/Pocket Books, 1994. 148 pp. ISBN 0-671-78600-8.

Ellie Anderson has visions. She tries to keep them a secret, but sometimes she can't. Last time, these visions caused her to lose her boyfriend. Now they've started again, and Ellie is losing her best friend Sarah. While walking her dog, Ellie finds the body of Sarah's sister who ran away from home two years earlier. When Brian Tanner, a handsome stranger, begins to follow Ellie, she knows she must bring the visions into focus before there is another murder.

9.53 Thesman, Jean. **Cattail Moon.** Houghton Mifflin, 1994. 197 pp. ISBN 0-395-67409-3.

Julie Foster wants to study and perform classical music. Her mother wants her to be a cheerleader or homecoming queen. Their fights force Julie into making a decision: will she stay in Seattle and continue her music and the fights, or will she live with her father in the Cascade Mountains? On her fifteenth birthday she chooses the mountains. This brings Luke Sutherland into her life, but it also brings the ghost of Christine Woodmark.

9.54 Westall, Robert. **The Stones of Muncaster Cathedral.** Farrar, Straus, and Giroux, 1993. 97 pp. ISBN 0-374-37263-2.

The restoration of historic Muncaster Cathedral is the job of his dreams for steeplejack Joe Clarke. But his dream quickly turns into a nightmare. Strange accidents begin to occur in the southwest tower and lead to the death of a young boy. In order to save his and his son's lives, Joe must find out why this tower holds so much evil.

9.55 Westwood, Chris. **Calling All Monsters.** HarperCollins, 1993. 218 pp. ISBN 0-06-022461-4.

Joanne loves to read horror stories by Martin Wisemann. Could they be giving her nightmares, or is she really seeing strange monsters? Not until she has to contend with the death of her ex-boyfriend does Joanne realize that her vivid imagination could be the cause of these creatures coming to life. Her nightmares become reality, and only Mr. Wisemann can tell her how to stop it.

9.56 Wright, Betty Ren. **The Ghosts of Mercy Manor.** Scholastic, 1993. 172 pp. ISBN 0-590-43601-5.

Gwen has been orphaned twice now that Aunt Mary has died. Her dream is to live with her older brother and his wife, but that doesn't work out. What does work out is moving to an old house in the country with the Mercys. Gwen is made to feel like one of the family until she begins seeing the ghost of a young girl. Mr. and Mrs. Mercy refuse to believe Gwen or even to let her tell them what she is seeing. Gwen must solve this mystery or she may be orphaned again.

9.57 Wyss, Thelma Hatch. **A Stranger Here.** HarperCollins, 1993. 132 pp. ISBN 0-06-021438-4.

Jada Sinclair, sixteen, writes poetry, looks at her curly hair, and wonders if she belongs to some family other than her own. Reluctantly, she agrees to spend the summer taking care of her ailing aunt. At her aunt's house, life gets more interesting after she discovers an antique gramophone and Starr Freeman, who died in World War II on the very day that Jada was born. Why is Starr back? Why isn't he still dead? And why can't anyone else see him?

10 Staying Alive! Adventure and Survival

10.1 Bosse, Malcolm. **Deep Dream of the Rain Forest.** Farrar, Straus, and Giroux, 1993. 179 pp. ISBN 0-374-31757-7.

Bayang, an Iban warrior from Borneo, has a powerful dream that he must act upon to fulfill his destiny. He sets off into the jungle with Tambong, a guide known as Duck Foot, in the lead. They encounter Harry, a war orphan, and kidnap him, thinking he is the key to achieving the dream. Nothing can stop them, not even the headhunters who are nearby.

10.2 Campbell, Eric. **Shark Callers.** Harcourt Brace & Company, 1994. 232 pp. ISBN 0-15-200007-0.

Knowing that the volcano is about to erupt, Andy and his family board their boat and head toward deep water and safety. At the same time, Klaleku is preparing to become a sacred Shark Caller; he, too, leads his canoe to deep water. His mission is to capture a shark, the final ritual to complete his apprenticeship. Little do Andy and Klaleku know that a tidal wave will force their paths to cross, leaving only one of them alive.

10.3 Cavanaugh, Helen. **Panther Glade.** Simon & Schuster, 1993. 147 pp. ISBN 0-671-75617-6.

The last thing Bill wants to do is spend the summer in the Florida Everglades with an aunt he hardly knows. But Bill feels different once he becomes involved in Aunt Cait's archeology project: exploring an ancient tribal burial ground. He becomes fascinated with the legend of the cat god, a panther-man who tested the courage of young warriors. Bill believes he'd never be able to pass the cat god's test. Then, one night, he finds himself alone, stranded on a remote island in the midst of a raging storm, facing his own test of courage.

10.4 Cohen, Peter Zachary. **Deadly Game at Stony Creek.** Puffin Books, 1993. 107 pp. ISBN 0-14-036476-5.

As the last day of school ends, Cliff prepares himself for a boring summer working on his parents' farm and practicing baseball by himself. Then his friend, Eddie, convinces him that together they can track and kill a pack of wild dogs that viciously attacked a classmate. With only a shotgun for protection against the five wild dogs, the boys begin the life-threatening hunt. If they survive, this is a day that the two boys will never forget.

10.5 Cowley, Marjorie. **Dar and the Spear-Thrower.** Clarion Books, 1994. 118 pp. ISBN 0-395-68132-4.

Dar, a Cro-Magnon cave boy, knows his manhood initiation is approaching. Dar is not certain that he is ready to assume the role of a hunter for his people. He is too short; many things frighten him. When Dar encounters a member of a neighboring clan, he discovers a way to help combat his fears and to become a better hunter. Perhaps he will be prepared to assume his rightful place among his people.

10.6 Crew, Gary. **No Such Country.** Simon & Schuster, 1994. 248 pp. ISBN 0-671-79760-3.

There are signs that things are about to change in Rachel's quiet community. The death of her mother is only one of them. When a stranger appears to conduct archeological research, he uncovers more than just the traces of the Aborigines who once inhabited Rachel's village. His discovery causes Rachel to question the life she and others have lived. Could her village, her neighbors, be deadly?

10.7 Cross, Gillian. **The Great American Elephant Chase.** Holiday House, 1993. 193 pp. ISBN 0-8234-1016-1.

How do you hide a full-grown Indian elephant? Fifteen-year-old Tad never dreams he'll have to worry about that when he runs away from his aunt's boarding house. Before he knows it, Tad becomes part of a traveling show and is swept up in a desperate attempt to keep Khush, the elephant, with his rightful owner. He's running from two villains who will stop at nothing to claim the elephant for themselves.

10.8 DeFelice, Cynthia. **Devil's Bridge.** Avon/Camelot, 1992. 95 pp. ISBN 0-380-72117-1.

The annual Striped Bass Derby holds special meaning for Ben. Years before Ben was born, his father set the record for the biggest bass ever caught on Martha's Vineyard. Since his dad's death, Ben misses the fishing adventures they shared. When Ben overhears two men plotting to win the prize money illegally, Ben sets out on a dangerous chase to expose them and protect his father's record.

10.9 Dickens, Charles. **Oliver Twist.** Abridged by Robin Waterfield. Puffin Books, 1994 (originally published in 1837–1839). 346 pp. ISBN 0-14-036814-0.

All young Oliver Twist wants to do is escape the horrible orphanage where he has lived for all of his nine years. But when he runs away, he ends up on the streets of London and in the midst of a gang of pickpockets led by Fagin and the Artful Dodger, a boy not much older than Oliver. Has Oliver gone from a bad situation to a worse one?

10.10 Dickinson, Peter. **AK.** Dell/Laurel Leaf, 1994. 229 pp. ISBN 0-440-21897-7.

Paul is growing up in a war-torn Africa. After his parents' death, he joins a commando unit and becomes a child guerrilla. Paul learns to trust only his instincts and his gun, an AK. Later, with the promise of peace, he buries the gun and goes away to school. But peace fails; as soldiers come for him, he leaves with his friend Jilli to search for his gun. His goal is to free his commando unit leader.

10.11 Gabhart, Ann. **Secrets to Tell.** Avon/Flare, 1994. 169 pp. ISBN 0-380-76610-8.

Emily has horrifying nightmares. To overcome them, she reluctantly goes on a group camping trip her therapist arranges, but things begin to go wrong the moment the group enters the forest. A severe thunderstorm, a nighttime brush fire, and an injured camper make survival difficult. Emily goes for help but soon finds herself lost and in the middle of her worst nightmare—only, she is awake.

10.12 Garland, Sherry. **The Silent Storm.** Harcourt Brace Jovanovich, 1993. 240 pp. ISBN 0-15-274170-4.

Ever since she saw her parents drown during a hurricane, Alyssa has not spoken a word. Now, three years later, another hurricane is heading toward her Galveston home, and Alyssa finds herself a prisoner on a boat sailing away from the shore. How can Alyssa persuade the owner to turn around so she can reach her seriously ill grandfather before it is too late?

10.13 George, Jean Craighead. **Julie.** Illustrated by Wendell Minor. HarperCollins, 1994. 240 pp. ISBN 0-06-023528-4.

After spending months in the Arctic wilderness with only wolves for companions, Julie goes to live with her father and his non-

Eskimo wife. Life is very different now. Julie's stepmother is expecting a baby, and her father is the corporate leader of the village musk-ox business. Julie's father has promised to shoot any wolves that attack the oxen. But these are the same wolves that saved Julie's life. How can she remain loyal to her father and also save her beloved wolves?

10.14 Goldman, E. M. **Money to Burn.** Viking, 1994. 213 pp. ISBN 0-670-85339-9.

Matt and Lewis are resigned to spending another hot and boring summer with nothing to do. After they literally stumble upon a briefcase full of money, summer is suddenly filled with possibilities. Before the summer is over, Matt and Lewis have managed to amass quite a few new items—stereos, computers, and the like. There is just one problem: the $400,000.00 is drug money, and the owner wants it back.

10.15 Gregory, Kristiana. **Jimmy Spoon and the Pony Express.** Scholastic, 1994. 128 pp. ISBN 0-590-46577-5.

Jimmy Spoon ran away when he was twelve years old to live with the Shoshoni, and has returned home at age seventeen. He soon becomes bored working in his father's store, so he eagerly signs on with the newly formed Pony Express. Jimmy is mindless of the dangers on the trail, finding the narrow escapes he has with bandits and Indians exciting.

10.16 Gutman, Bill. **Across the Wild River.** HarperCollins, 1993. 169 pp. ISBN 0-06-106159-X.

James and his family leave Independence to join a wagon train heading for Oregon. James knows it is going to be an exciting trip when, as he is getting supplies, he sees a man get shot. The trip begins, and James realizes this trip is more than exciting—it is dangerous. Soon his family is stampeded by buffalo, and Indians appear.

10.17 Gutman, Bill. **Along the Dangerous Trail.** HarperCollins, 1993. 167 pp. ISBN 0-06-106152-2.

James and his family have been on the trail for many months when his father becomes ill with cholera. Slowly, the family falls behind the rest of the wagon train and is left alone in the territory with the very ill father. James and his brother leave the family briefly to hunt for food. Upon returning, they discover that their family is being held captive by desperados. Now, not only is their father's life at stake, but so is everyone else's.

10.18 Hahn, Mary Downing. **The Spanish Kidnapping Disaster.** Avon/Camelot, 1993. 132 pp. ISBN 0-380-71712-3.

Twelve-year-old Felix and her stepsister Amy are traveling with their parents in Spain when they get lost. Grace, a mysterious stranger, helps them find their parents and then offers to take the girls sightseeing. But, once Grace gets them away from everyone, she takes Amy and Felix to a cave high in the mountains where two sinister-looking men join them. The girls are afraid their captors are killers.

10.19 Hite, Sid. **It's Nothing to a Mountain.** Henry Holt and Company, 1994. 214 pp. ISBN 0-8050-2769-6.

After the death of their parents, Lisette and Riley go to live with their grandparents. To escape all the sadness, Riley heads for the mountains. While camping, a strong gust of wind picks him up and leaves him dangling high above a ravine. He is rescued by Thorpe, a runaway, and from that point on, Riley spends as much time as he can with Thorpe, learning how to survive in the forest. But will those skills help him survive the loss of his parents?

10.20 Hobbs, Will. **Beardance.** Atheneum, 1993. 197 pp. ISBN 0-689-31867-7.

In this sequel to *Bearstone,* Cloyd, of the Ute tribe, is on his spirit-finding mission when he finds two orphaned bear cubs. He is determined to do everything possible to keep the cubs alive. He begins by wearing the fur of the dead mother grizzly so the cubs will accept him as their surrogate mother. But soon Cloyd is facing a freezing winter where his survival is as much at issue as the cubs' survival.

10.21 Hobbs, Will. **The Big Wander.** Avon/Camelot, 1994. 192 pp. ISBN 0-380-72140-6.

Fourteen-year-old Clay and his older brother Mike leave for a long-awaited trip—their Big Wander throughout the west. Unexpected events cause Mike to return home, but Clay continues. He finally comes to the Navajo Mountains accompanied only by a lost dog and a burro. To survive, he must face the desert, the raging storms, the mountains, and Indians. Facing these things will change him, but is survival worth the changes he must make?

10.22 Karr, Kathleen. **Gideon and the Mummy Professor.** Farrar, Straus, and Giroux, 1993. 137 pp. ISBN 0-374-32563-4.

In 1855, twelve-year-old Gideon travels around the United States with his father. Together they perform shows about ancient Egypt. The main attraction of their show is a mummy that Gideon calls George. After one disastrous show, they leave hurriedly to escape an angry audience and head toward exotic New Orleans. What Gideon and his father don't realize is that a mysterious man from his father's past is following them. Is his target the unraveling mummy, or the father, or both?

10.23 Kehret, Peg. **Night of Fear.** Cobblehill/Dutton, 1994. 138 pp. ISBN 0-525-65136-5.

Recent arson and a bank robbery have thirteen-year-old T.J. and his family worried. Left home one night to care for his Grandma Ruth, who has Alzheimer's disease, T. J. finds himself face to face with a sinister man. Forced to go with the man, T. J. leaves Grandma Ruth alone. Then, both Grandma and T. J. survive horrors as Grandma gets lost in the woods, and as T. J. accompanies a man who could care less whether T. J. lives or dies.

10.24 Mayne, William. **Low Tide.** Delacorte Press, 1993. 198 pp. ISBN 0-385-30904-X.

Charlie, Wiremu, and Elizabeth expect a nice fishing trip in New Zealand. What they get is a tidal wave that sweeps all three of them to the top of a mountain. There they encounter the dreaded Koroua—the wild mountain man whose teeth are black from eating people. They realize only their wits will save them from this creature whose goal is to kill them.

10.25 McClung, Robert M. **Hugh Glass, Mountain Man: Left for Dead.** Beech Tree Books, 1993. 166 pp. ISBN 0-688-04595-2.

In 1823, trapper Hugh Glass is horribly wounded by a grizzly bear, and his companions are sure he will die. Leaving two men to guard and bury him, the trappers move on. After five days, the two remaining men, fearing Indian attacks, take Glass's rifle and supplies and abandon the dying man. Hugh Glass, however, survives, and he vows to track and kill the traitors. Half dead, Glass crawls 200 miles to seek his revenge. What is most amazing about Hugh Glass's story is that it is true!

10.26 Mikaelsen, Ben. **Rescue Josh McGuire.** Hyperion Books, 1994. 266 pp. ISBN 1-56282-523-2.

Thirteen-year-old Josh finds a bear cub after his father shoots the cub's mother. Learning that the cub is to be used for laboratory testing, Josh takes it and runs away to the forest near his home. An unexpected snowstorm and a serious accident put both Josh and the cub in a dangerous situation.

10.27 Mikaelsen, Ben. **Sparrow Hawk Red.** Hyperion Books, 1993. 185 pp. ISBN 1-56282-387-6.

When thirteen-year-old Ricky Mendoza learns that his mother was murdered by drug smugglers from Mexico, he is determined to get even with the smugglers. He crosses the border into Mexico disguised as a homeless street child. His plan is to sneak into the cartel's compound, steal their plane used for drug smuggling, and make his escape in it. His plan goes awry when all his money is stolen, but he doesn't give up!

10.28 Morpurgo, Michael. **Twist of Gold.** Viking, 1993. 246 pp. ISBN 0-670-84851-4.

Sean and Annie O'Brien leave a plague-ridden Ireland to find their father in America. They carry with them the family heirloom, a golden necklace which is supposed to protect them. Instead of offering protection, this golden charm causes problems. The necklace is stolen, and Sean has to work on the ship. Just before the ship sinks, they recover the charm. With the heirloom, they finally reach America and begin the perilous search for their lost father.

10.29 Myers, Edward. **Climb or Die.** Hyperion Books, 1994. 180 pp. ISBN 0-7868-0026-7.

It is dangerous for Danielle and her younger brother Jake to consider climbing a mountain during a blizzard, but what choice do they have? Their parents have been badly injured in an accident. If help doesn't arrive soon, they will die. Using only the tools found in their car, Danielle and Jake try to reach safety at the weather station on the top of Mount Remington.

10.30 Myers, Walter Dean. **The Righteous Revenge of Artemis Bonner.** HarperTrophy, 1994. 140 pp. ISBN 0-06-020844-9.

In 1882, Artemis goes west to Tombstone, Arizona, to avenge the death of his uncle, the Ugly Ned Bonner. Catfish Grimes has murdered Uncle Ugly and stolen his treasure map. Artemis and his friend Frolic want to find the treasure first, but encounters with Catfish and his lady friend, Lucy Featherdip, don't go as planned. Artemis is left with one of his ears partially shot off and the other bitten off.

10.31 Paulsen, Gary. **Winterdance: The Fine Madness of Running the Iditarod.** Harcourt Brace & Company, 1994. 256 pp. ISBN 0-15-126227-6.

Though published for adults, readers who enjoyed the tales of sled dogs and the Iditarod from *Woodsong* are sure to want to read Paulsen's graphic day-by-day account of the Alaskan race which pits man and dog against the powerful forces of nature. Paulsen entered the harsh 1,108-mile race across Alaska to fulfill a dream. In the seventeen-day journey, he learned a great deal about the Arctic terrain and the dangers waiting for the inexperienced sledder.

10.32 Regan, Dian Curtis. **The Initiation.** Avon/Flare, 1993. 160 pp. ISBN 0-380-76325-7.

During the summer they spend in Cripple Creek, Parie is completely responsible for her younger brother Jeff, who begins disappearing for long periods of time with his new friend Amber. Amber wants to join "The Club" and is ready to be initiated by spending the night in an old mine. Jeff knows no one has ever survived that particular mine and is determined to go with Amber. Will Parie find out what is going on before it is too late to stop them?

10.33 Snyder, Zilpha Keatley. **Fool's Gold.** Delacorte Press, 1993. 214 pp. ISBN 0-385-30908-2.

Rudy will do anything, including baby-sitting the M&M's, his constantly fighting sisters, for the entire summer rather than take a chance that his best friend will find out he is terrified to explore the abandoned mine. He also suggests giving horseback riding lessons to his neighbor, Heather. These distractions work for a while, but soon talk of the mine returns. Maybe he can cure his claustrophobia before the summer is over.

10.34 Stevenson, Robert Louis. **Treasure Island.** Henry Holt and Company, 1993 (Originally published in 1883). 379 pp. ISBN 0-8050-2773.

Young Jim gets the chance of a lifetime when he discovers a treasure map in the sea chest of a dead seaman. Jim narrowly escapes torture at the hands of ruthless pirates, is frightened out of his wits by an animal-like man marooned on Treasure Island for years, and risks his life to save the ship from the unscrupulous crew that has mutinied.

Staying Alive! Adventure and Survival   **143**

10.35   Taylor, Theodore. **Sweet Friday Island.** Harcourt Brace & Company, 1994. 173 pp. ISBN 0-15-200009-7.

As soon as fifteen-year-old Peg and her father step onto the island, Peg senses something is wrong, particularly when she feels eyes staring at her. Her father says the island is uninhabited and suggests they go for a swim. Returning to their camp, they discover their raft, the only means of leaving, is cut to pieces. Peg's glasses are smashed, her clothing is slashed, and the ax is gone. With no defenses and no escape, their survival is questionable.

10.36   Taylor, Theodore. **Timothy of the Cay.** Harcourt Brace & Company, 1993. 161 pp. ISBN 0-15-288358-4.

Two lives are forever linked when Timothy, an elderly black man, and Phillip, an eleven-year-old white boy, are shipwrecked on a Caribbean island during World War II. This successor to *The Cay* opens with Phillip's rescue. From there, we go back in time to get a glimpse of Timothy's early brutal life as a slave and follow Phillip's quest to regain his lost sight. Phillip's parents want their son to put the harrowing island experience behind him, but Phillip is determined to visit the island that he shared with the man who gave up his life for Phillip's.

10.37   Wangerin, Walter. **The Crying for a Vision.** Simon & Schuster Books for Young Readers, 1994. 273 pp. ISBN 0-671-79911-8.

Waskn Mani—Moves Walking—cares nothing for hunting or making war. His mysterious powers, which come from being half human and half celestial being, scare the people of his tribe. A Lakota orphan, Moves Walking seeks to learn the truth about the strange disappearance of his mother, a search that propels him into a fierce confrontation with Fire Thunder, leader of the Lakotas.

10.38   Westall, Robert. **The Kingdom by the Sea.** Farrar, Straus, and Giroux, 1993. 176 pp. ISBN 0-374-44060-3.

Since England is at war with Hitler, Harry is used to air raids. So when the siren sounds, he grabs his suitcase and heads for the shelter. He wonders where his parents and sister are, but before he can worry long, a bomb hits. When Harry is rescued, he sees his destroyed house. Not waiting for explanations, he runs away. Alone, except for a new-found dog, he faces a country torn by war.

10.39   Yolen, Jane. **Children of the Wolf.** Puffin Books, 1993. 136 pp. ISBN 0-14-036477-3.

It takes every bit of his courage to make fourteen-year-old Mohandas go into the jungle to help capture the "ghosts of Godamuri." No one, however, is prepared for what the searchers find—a two-headed ball of fur with four glowing eyes. This "creature" turns out to be two young girls who have been raised by wolves! Can they be civilized, or are they destined to remain savage forever? This incredible story is based on fact.

IV People, Problems, and Places: Yesterday and Today

"The things I want to know are in books. My best friend is the man who will get me a book I ain't read." Since early youth he was possessed by a passion for books and borrowed any he could lay his hands on "in a radius of fifty miles." He kept with him even when working in the field some books to read during periods of rest. . . . When he travelled over the circuit, he often carried with him a volume of Shakespeare to read during spare moments.

M. L. Houser, American writer, describing Abraham Lincoln, Sixteenth President of the United States

11 Looking Back: Historical Fiction

11.1 Alcott, Louisa May. **Jo's Boys.** Little, Brown and Company, 1994 (originally published in 1886). 316 pp. ISBN 0-316-03103-8.

Jo's Boys is the third book of Louisa May Alcott's trilogy. The twelve boys we met earlier in *Little Men* have scattered all over the world, but in this book they reunite with our favorite characters from *Little Women* to reminisce about the fun they had growing up and to describe their experiences in the adult world.

11.2 Alcott, Louisa May. **Little Men.** Little, Brown and Company, 1994 (originally published in 1871). 332 pp. ISBN 0-316-03104-6.

In *Little Men*, the second volume of Louisa May Alcott's trilogy, Jo, the tomboy of *Little Women*, has grown up and married. She and her husband, Professor Bhaer, run Plumfield, a school for boys. We see how all those at Plumfield, including the orphan Nat, the strong-willed Nan, and the selfish Stuffy, learn about life together under the loving guidance of Jo and her husband.

11.3 Alcott, Louisa May. **Little Women.** Little, Brown and Company, 1994 (originally published in 1868). 502 pp. ISBN 0-316-03107-0.

In conjunction with the release of a new movie of an old classic, the original publisher of Alcott's trilogy, *Little Women, Little Men*, and *Jo's Boys*, has released a new hardback and paperback edition of the trilogy. Drawn from events in her own growing-up in the nineteenth century as part of a family of four sisters, Alcott tells how the March family loved, played, and shared in each other's romances in *Little Women*.

11.4 Antle, Nancy. **Tough Choices: A Story of the Vietnam War.** Illustrated by Michele Laporte. Viking, 1993. 55 pp. ISBN 0-670-84879-4.

Samantha is so excited that her oldest brother Mitch is finally coming home from the war in Vietnam. His homecoming, however, is spoiled when Mitch is greeted by angry war protesters and when he learns that his own older brother Emmett agrees with the protesters. Mitch becomes moody, jumpy, and distant. Samantha wonders what this war has done to her brothers and if her family life will ever be the same again.

11.5 Avi. **The Barn.** Orchard Books, 1994. 106 pp. ISBN 0-531-06861-7.

In 1855, Oregon homesteading is difficult at best. When nine-year-old Ben's father has a completely incapacitating stroke, Ben is the only one of the three motherless children who believes his father can recover. Though he is the youngest of the children, Ben takes over caring for their father and the building of the barn, convinced that the barn will give his father a reason to live.

11.6 Avi. **Captain Grey.** Illustrated by Charles Mikolaycak. Beech Tree Books, 1993. 141 pp. ISBN 0-688-12234-5.

Kevin and Cathleen follow their father into the New Jersey wilderness of 1783. Their father has been fighting the hated English for seven years, and they are searching now for peace. They walk instead into a band of pirates, who kill Kevin's father and sister and take Kevin captive. Kevin's determination to escape is bolstered when the message he sends by carrier pigeon is answered. But is this a trick or a sincere offer of help?

11.7 Avi. **Punch with Judy.** Illustrated by Emily Lisker. Bradbury Press, 1993. 167 pp. ISBN 0-02-707755-1.

In 1870, the orphan Punch joins Joe McSneed's traveling medicine show, assured of food, shelter, and Mr. McSneed's care. Then business tapers off and Mr. McSneed dies, leaving his daughter Judy in charge of a disgruntled and impoverished troupe now wanted by the sheriff. The entertainers devise a plan that will either revive the show and clear their names or land them all in jail. It's up to Punch to save the show.

11.8 Baylis-White, Mary. **Sheltering Rebecca.** Puffin Books, 1993. 99 pp. ISBN 0-14-036448-X.

It is 1938 in England, and Sally Simpkins is not excited when the teacher assigns her the job of helping the new student, Rebecca Muller, settle in. Rebecca, a Jewish refugee from Nazi Germany, speaks little English and is quiet and sad. Gradually, the girls become good friends. Sally learns that Rebecca had to leave all her family behind in Germany. As the war touches England and news from Germany filters in, Sally wonders how she will help Rebecca cope with the possible permanent loss of her family.

11.9 Beatty, Patricia. **Bonanza Girl.** Beech Tree Books, 1993. 210 pp. ISBN 0-688-12280-9.

The 1880s brought thousands of people into the Idaho Territory, from miners and gamblers to shopkeepers and school teachers.

After her husband's death, Katherine Scott catches gold rush fever and moves with her children to a mining camp. Not at all prepared for what is in store, Mrs. Scott teams up with a new friend, Helga Storkersen. Neither woman had anticipated the hardships of this new life, and they both wonder if any amount of gold is worth the dangers they face.

11.10 Beatty, Patricia. **Eight Mules from Monterey.** Beech Tree Books, 1993. 192 pp. ISBN 0-688-12281-7.

Five "desperate ladies" write to the librarian in Monterey, begging for books. It's 1916, and the only way to get to their remote area is by mule train. When thirteen-year-old Fayette Ashmore's mother gets the job of not only taking books to the ladies in Big Tree Junction, but also establishing library outposts throughout the California mountains, Fayette, her brother, and her mother have a most memorable summer.

11.11 Berry, James. **Ajeemah and His Son.** HarperTrophy, 1994. 83 pp. ISBN 0-06-440523-0.

In 1807, the slave traders are capturing Africans and sending them to America and the Caribbean. Ajeemah and his son Atu are taking a dowry of gold to his fiancée's parents when they are captured, bound, and sent with hundreds of other Africans, against their will, to Jamaica. Ajeemah longs for his home and his family and never knows that he and Atu are actually only a few miles apart.

11.12 Bosse, Malcolm. **The Examination.** Farrar, Straus, and Giroux, 1994. 296 pp. ISBN 0-374-32234-1.

Lao Chen, a brilliant scholar, journeys from his hometown to take the provincial exam, then to Beijing for the nationals, necessary for advancement in public office. With the help of his younger yet braver brother, Hong, the two travel across medieval China, confronting floods, poverty, pirates, as well as their own personal limitations and values.

11.13 Calvert, Patricia. **Bigger.** Charles Scribner's Sons, 1994. 137 pp. ISBN 0-684-19685-9.

Tyler Bohannon is sure his father does not realize how much he is missed at home, so the twelve-year-old sets out alone on foot for Mexico, where Black Jack Bohannon is still with General Jo Shelby, refusing to surrender to the Yankees. Tyler is joined on the difficult trip by Bigger, a strange dog who becomes Tyler's companion, confidant, and protector.

11.14 Carter, Peter. **The Hunted.** Farrar, Straus, and Giroux, 1993. 326 pp. ISBN 0-374-33520-6.

With the surrender of Mussolini to the Allies, Italian soldiers begin their journey home, leaving Jewish refugees in southern France at the mercy of the Gestapo and the French secret police. Italian corporal, Vito Salvani, and his commander, Major Balbo, try to save a wealthy French perfume manufacturer and his young son Judah from the Gestapo.

11.15 Choi, Sook Nyul. **Echoes of the White Giraffe.** Houghton Mifflin, 1993. 137 pp. ISBN 0-395-64721-5.

An old man shouting, "Good morning, refugees," across the mountains gives Sookan delight and hope. Running from Seoul for their very lives, being parted from family members, and living high up the rocky mountain in a shabby refugee village, fifteen-year-old Sookan, her mother, and her brother work against tremendous odds to find missing relatives and return to their former home. But can Sookan leave her first love and her reunited family to travel alone to America?

11.16 Choi, Sook Nyul. **Gathering of Pearls.** Houghton Mifflin, 1994. 163 pp. ISBN 0-395-67437-9.

Since coming from Seoul, Korea, to college in New York City, Sookan Bak has had to learn a new language, adapt to a very different society, and keep up a demanding college schedule, while constantly striving to meet her family's expectations. New friends help Sookan adjust to a very different lifestyle. This is the sequel to *Year of Impossible Goodbyes* and *Echoes of the White Giraffe.*

11.17 Clark, Clara Gillow. **Annie's Choice.** Boyds Mills Press, 1993. 196 pp. ISBN 1-56397-053-8.

Annie's sister Mae has the right idea. Just as soon as you can manage it, leave this dreary farm with all its chores and children. Annie's dreams don't seem to matter. Since Mae left home, her mother really needs her, especially with another baby on the way. But Annie dreams of high school and maybe even being a teacher someday. Those dreams seem impossible in the early 1920s on a farm in rural New York.

11.18 Collier, James Lincoln, and Christopher Collier. **With Every Drop of Blood.** Delacorte Press, 1994. 229 pp. ISBN 0-385-32028-0.

Fourteen-year-old Johnny will have a long time to regret breaking the promise to his dying father not to get involved in the war.

Looking Back: Historical Fiction 151

But teamsters for the Confederate Army convince him that the trip to get food to President Jeff Davis and other Confederates in Richmond is a safe and easy one. "This is not fighting; it is teamstering," they tell him. When Johnny is captured by a black Union soldier, he discovers that nothing is safe and easy about the Civil War.

11.19 Cushman, Karen. **Catherine, Called Birdy.** Clarion Books, 1994. 164 pp. ISBN 0-395-68186-3.

Spinning is so boring for Catherine, called Little Bird or Birdy, that she bargains with her mother to write in a daily journal instead. It is 1290 in Stonebridge, England, and being the daughter of a country knight, fourteen-year-old Birdy is expected to marry well and be a quiet, agreeable, obedient wife. But marriage to old Shaggy Beard? Not while she is still breathing!

11.20 Cutler, Jane. **My Wartime Summers.** Farrar, Straus, and Giroux, 1994. 153 pp. ISBN 0-374-35111-2.

Ellen's summers from 1942 to 1945 are filled most notably with corresponding with her Uncle Bob, who goes from boot camp all the way to the Battle of the Bulge during the war years. Ellen, eleven when the story begins, gets to know Lisa-Lotte, a Jewish refugee; auditions for a part in a radio program; and does her share for the war effort. Uncle Bob comes back a changed person, and Ellen realizes that everyone has changed during her wartime summers.

11.21 Davis, Russell G., and Brent K. Ashabranner. **The Choctaw Code.** Linnet Books, 1994. 152 pp. ISBN 0-208-02377-1.

Tom Baxter's father works for the railroad and is transferred to Choctaw Territory. The Baxters do not know what to expect in their new home. It is 1892 and fifteen-year-old Tom is not prepared for the exciting outdoor life or for his friendship with Jim Moshulatubbee, a Choctaw who has broken Choctaw law and has been sentenced to die within the year.

11.22 DeFelice, Cynthia. **Lostman's River.** Macmillan, 1994. 157 pp. ISBN 0-02-726466-1.

The MacCauleys fled New York five years ago when Tyler's father was accused of murder. Now, in 1906, still dodging the law, the MacCauleys are suspicious when a stranger appears at their remote settlement on Florida's Lostman's River, asking a for a guide for a scientific expedition. They are finally convinced to let young Ty take Mr. Strawbridge up the river, but the trip turns out totally different than Ty anticipated, and his experiences change his family dramatically.

11.23 de Trevino, Elizabeth Borton. **Leona: A Love Story.** Farrar, Straus, and Giroux, 1994. 144 pp. ISBN 0-374-34382-9.

Leona is a *criolla,* the daughter of a Spanish mother and a Mexican father. She is wealthy and well-educated and, at sixteen, betrothed to a Spanish widower. But when Leona falls in love with Andres, a young poet, they join the Mexican revolutions of 1810 to 1821 and take part in forming a new Mexican government. Years later, Leona is honored as "Heroine of the Independence" and Andres becomes president of the Chamber of Deputies.

11.24 Dorris, Michael. **Guests.** Hyperion Books, 1994. 128 pp. ISBN 0-7868-0047-X.

Upset with his tribe's decision to invite the strangers to the yearly harvest feast, Moss, a young Native American, leaves the tribal grounds and wanders into the forest on his own vision quest. While looking for answers, Moss discovers that in becoming a man, he has much to learn and that many of life's questions do not have clear-cut answers.

11.25 Drucker, Malka, and Michael Halperin. **Jacob's Rescue: A Holocaust Story.** Dell/Yearling, 1993. 117 pp. ISBN 0-440-40965-9.

Eight-year-old Jacob Gutgeld had once lived in Warsaw, Poland, in a lovely home with his family. Now he and his family are forced into the Warsaw Ghetto, starving and waiting to be sent to a Nazi death camp. But Alex Roslan, a Polish Christian, agrees to become Jacob's new "uncle," hiding Jacob and his brother, risking everything.

11.26 Duffy, James. **Radical Red.** Charles Scribner's Sons, 1993. 152 pp. ISBN 0-684-19533-X.

When twelve-year-old Connor O'Shea stops to talk to a woman handing out pamphlets, she doesn't realize she will become caught up in the Votes for Women Movement of 1894, headed by Susan B. Anthony herself. The encounter angers Connor's father who threatens to "strap her" if she talks to the "crazy woman" again. But Connor sees the movement as a way to help her mother out of their abusive home. Will Connor cross her father and risk yet another beating?

Looking Back: Historical Fiction

11.27 Fleischman, Paul. **The Borning Room.** HarperKeypoint, 1993. 101 pp. ISBN 0-06-447099-7.

Georgina Lott's entire life can be chronicled around the borning room in her family's Ohio farmhouse. She was born in that sparsely furnished room, pine walls painted white, as were other members of her family. And from that room, family members left this life. Now on her own deathbed, Georgina looks back on her life, remembering the Civil War, the end of slavery, and life on the Ohio frontier.

11.28 Gaeddert, Louann. **Breaking Free.** Atheneum, 1994. 136 pp. ISBN 0-689-31883-9.

Richard is a city boy. He has lived with his aunt and uncle since his parents died, going to school and helping in the store. When Aunt Ruth dies, her brother, Lyman, always looking for another farm hand, insists on taking Richard. It is 1800 and farming is hard. Nothing about the farm or Uncle Lyman's family or his treatment of his slaves is pleasant for Richard. Only by outsmarting his uncle can Richard or any of the slaves ever escape.

11.29 Greene, Bette. **Summer of My German Soldier.** Dell/Laurel Leaf, 1993. (Originally published in 1973). 199 pp. ISBN 0-440-21892-6.

What was Patty Bergen thinking when she, a Jewish girl with a very strict father, found herself helping a German prisoner escape from a prisoner-of-war camp? Why is this foreigner the only person on earth besides Ruth, the housekeeper, who seems to truly understand her? Is breaking the law as well as defying her family worth risking her own freedom, perhaps even her life?

11.30 Greene, Jacqueline Dembar. **One Foot Ashore.** Walker and Company, 1994. 196 pp. ISBN 0-8027-8281-7.

In 1654, sixteen-year-old Maria Ben Lazar escapes from the Portuguese friars who had kidnapped her and her sister and enslaved them in Brazil. She stows away on an Amsterdam-bound ship and arrives in Amsterdam with no money or friends. There she begins the search for her sister and her parents. She is befriended by the artist Rembrandt, and with his support she continues her intense search to reunite her family. Sequel to *Out of Many Waters*.

11.31 Hildick, E. W. **Hester Bidgood: Investigatrix of Evill Deedes.** Macmillan, 1994. 141 pp. ISBN 0-02-743966-6.

The Massachusetts town of Willow Bend is full of rumors of the witch hunt in nearby Salem in 1692. When Goody Willson's unconscious cat, its fur branded with the symbol of the cross, is left outside the Meeting House, people panic and assume Goody Willson to be a witch. But thirteen-year-old Hester Bidgood and her friend Rob team up to find the real culprit.

11.32 Holland, Isabelle. **Behind the Lines.** Scholastic, 1994. 194 pp. ISBN 0-590-45113-8.

Fleeing poverty in Ireland after the potato blight, the O'Farrells emigrate to New York City. This only transfers their poverty to another location. The Civil War is in progress, and some young Irish men are being paid to take the places of wealthy young men in the Union Army. But fourteen-year-old Katie O'Farrell is against any war, most certainly one that is not their war. With race riots tearing apart the city, Katie does not know where to turn.

11.33 Houston, Gloria. **Mountain Valor.** Illustrated by Thomas B. Allen. Philomel Books, 1994. 236 pp. ISBN 0-399-22519-6.

Valor was named after her father's Medal of Valor. He and the other men in the family are gone, some fighting against each other in the Civil War. As an eleven-year-old girl, Valor feels helpless, but she wants to fight to protect her family at home. Posing as a boy, she enters the war, heeding Aunt Becky's words that "Courage is not lack of fear. Courage is being afraid, but doing a thing anyway."

11.34 Irwin, Hadley. **Jim-Dandy.** Macmillan/Margaret K. McElderry Books, 1994. 135 pp. ISBN 0-689-50594-9.

Caleb cannot understand his stepfather, Webb Cotter. Caleb's father died in the Civil War battle at Shiloh; his mother died soon after marrying Webb Cotter; and now twelve-year-old Caleb finds that pleasing this stepfather is almost impossible. He is overjoyed when Dandy, the new colt, is born. But when Webb must sell Dandy, Caleb follows Dandy and Colonel Custer to fight the Cheyennes.

11.35 Jones, Adrienne. **Long Time Passing.** HarperKeypoint, 1993. 244 pp. ISBN 0-06-447070-9.

With his father in Vietnam, seventeen-year-old Jonas wrestles with the many faces of courage, patriotism, honor, and betrayal. When his father is listed as missing in action, Jonas believes honor dictates that he follow his father to Vietnam. But Jonas is involved in a love affair with an anti-war flower child named Auleen; Auleen offers Jonas herself and Canada instead. At seventeen, Jonas does not know that decisions can carry regrets that last a lifetime.

11.36   Karr, Kathleen. **The Cave.** Farrar, Straus, and Giroux, 1994. 165 pp. ISBN 0-374-31230-3.

Her great-grandfather had homesteaded the farm in the Black Hills of South Dakota, but now, because of the drought, it is part of the Dust Bowl. The Great Depression grips the country. One day, as twelve-year-old Christine is walking in the hills, she discovers a large, unexplored cave. The cave may have resources to help her family, but can its beauty be preserved if she shares its secrets?

11.37   Krisher, Trudy. **Spite Fences.** Delacorte Press, 1994. 283 pp. ISBN 0-385-32088-4.

Maggie Pugh's hometown of Kinship, Georgia, hardly lives up to its name. In the 1960s the town's long history of segregation is under attack, and violence is in the air. In fact, Maggie herself is the target of violence from her white neighbors and from her own distressingly temperamental mother. At thirteen, Maggie is more mature than most of her elders, and her only sources of support are her beloved camera and a handful of allies in the black community.

11.38   Lasky, Kathryn. **Beyond the Burning Time.** Blue Sky/Scholastic, 1994. 176 pp. ISBN 0-590-47331-X.

It is 1691, a dangerous time in Salem Village. Several of Mary's friends have begun to act strangely. The girls blame their behavior on witchcraft. Mary does not believe the girls are truly possessed, but their accusations are being taken seriously by some in the community. When Mary's mother becomes one of those accused of witchcraft, Mary must gather all the courage she can to confront the accusers and free her mother.

11.39   Lehne, Judith Logan. **When the Ragman Sings.** Illustrated by Michael Dooling. HarperCollins, 1993. 116 pp. ISBN 0-06-023316-8.

In the 1920s, the sound of the ragman's voice sends terror through the children of Baltimore. They hear stories about how Stubs, the ragman, will get them if they are naughty. So ten-year-old Dorothea is confused as she watches her mother give the old black man rags and talk with him. When Dorothea's mother dies and Dorothea sees Stubs with her mother's precious leather book, she knows she must find the ragman regardless of the fright she feels.

11.40 Levitin, Sonia. **Escape from Egypt.** Little, Brown and Company, 1994. 267 pp. ISBN 0-316-52273-2.

A Hebrew slave, sixteen-year-old Jesse suffers from the cruel treatment of the Egyptians. Jennat, half-Egyptian, half-Syrian, is also a slave, but enjoys kind treatment from her wealthy mistress, Memnet. Their exodus from Egypt to the Promised Land is filled with conflicting personal feelings and with responsibilities for the welfare of the Israelite people.

11.41 Lingard, Joan. **Between Two Worlds.** Puffin Books, 1993. 186 pp. ISBN 0-14-036505-2.

In this sequel to *Tug of War,* the Peterson family puts World War II and their escape from Latvia behind them for a new life in Canada. Upon arriving, however, Mr. Peterson suffers a massive heart attack and cannot take the teaching position waiting for him. As a result, Astra and Hugo Peterson must give up their dreams and memories of the old world to meet the demands thrust upon them in this strange new environment.

11.42 MacBride, Roger Lea. **Little House on Rocky Ridge.** Illustrated by David Gilleece. HarperCollins, 1993. 353 pp. ISBN 0-06-020842-2.

Living in the "little house on the prairie" has become increasingly difficult, so Almanzo and Laura Wilder take seven-year-old Rose and leave Laura's family in South Dakota for the land of the Big Red Apple, Missouri. Traveling with the Cooleys and their boys makes the trip bearable. They find just the right parcel of land, Rocky Ridge Farm. A barn-raising pulls the community together and welcomes the Wilders into their bright new future.

11.43 MacLachlan, Patricia. **Skylark.** HarperCollins, 1994. 86 pp. ISBN 0-06-023328-1.

In this sequel to *Sarah, Plain and Tall,* Sarah loves Jacob and his children, Anna and Caleb, so much that she is willing to give up her beloved home on the Maine coast, with the roses, green fields, water, and her relatives. But living through a drought is different. When Sarah must take the children to Maine and leave Jacob behind to try to save their prairie farm, they both fear for the future.

Looking Back: Historical Fiction 157

11.44 Matas, Carol. **The Burning Time.** Delacorte Press, 1994. 113 pp. ISBN 0-385-32097-3.

In sixteenth-century France, a woman is burned at the stake if she confesses to being a witch. Fifteen-year-old Rose Rives's mother has been a midwife and healer to many families in their town, but she is accused of being a witch and is tortured for a confession. Rose must eventually decide whether her own death will be worse than the pain of life on her own.

11.45 Matas, Carol. **Daniel's Story.** Scholastic, 1993. 131 pp. ISBN 0-590-46920-7.

Daniel's photographs help him remember life in Germany before the Germans sent the Jews away. His Jewish family flees Frankfurt with none of their possessions except the precious pictures Daniel carries with him. These pictures, and the memories they invoke, sustain him during his journey to the Lodz ghetto in Poland and then to Auschwitz, the Nazi death camp.

11.46 Matas, Carol. **Sworn Enemies.** Bantam Books, 1993. 132 pp. ISBN 0-553-08326-0.

Sixteen-year-old Aaron Chruchinsky, a Russian Jew, never thinks about having an enemy, never thinks about being kidnapped, and never thinks about being betrayed by a fellow Jew. But all three things happen when his former classmate, Zev Lobonsky, betrays him by kidnapping him for Czar Nicholas's army. Vowing to escape and return to his betrothed, Aaron finds himself trapped with Zev, his sworn enemy. Now they must put aside their hatred and join forces in order to survive.

11.47 McKissack, Patricia C., and Fredrick L. McKissack. **Christmas in the Big House, Christmas in the Quarters.** Illustrated by John Thompson. Scholastic, 1994. 58 pp. ISBN 0-590-43027-0.

Christmas on a Virginia plantation in 1859 is a picture of contrasts: the Big House elegant, beautiful, and comfortable, with presents lavished on everyone; the slave Quarters cramped, cold, and uncomfortable, with the best present being a week off from hard work. In the Big House, the youngest occupants dream of gifts soon to be opened; in the Quarters, a young slave dreams of bringing his mother a "store-bought gift" next year because he's "gon' run away to freedom."

11.48 Merino, Jose Maria. **Beyond the Ancient Cities.** Translated by Helen Lane. Farrar, Straus, and Giroux, 1994. 209 pp. ISBN 0-374-34307-1.

Miguel never dreamed that the trip with his godfather from Mexico to Panama would be such a perilous journey. The cruel conquistadors, shipwrecks, and pirates, along with Indian princesses and misguided priests, make for dangerous travel in sixteenth-century New Spain.

11.49 Meyer, Carolyn. **White Lilacs.** Harcourt Brace & Company, 1993. 242 pp. ISBN 0-15-200641-9.

It's 1921, and Rose Lee has lived in Freedomtown, Texas, all her life. She can't imagine living anywhere else, but the white residents who live around this black community want to relocate the black residents, forcibly if necessary, to tear down Freedomtown to build a park there. Can Rose Lee's family and neighbors fight these plans, or will they have to give up their homes, businesses, churches, and friends? This story is based on actual events that happened in Denton, Texas, in 1922.

11.50 Myers, Anna. **Rosie's Tiger.** Walker and Company, 1994. 121 pp. ISBN 0-8027-8305-8.

Rosie misses her older brother, Ronny, and wants him back home in their small Oklahoma town. She still misses her mother who died four years earlier and worries about Ronny fighting in Korea. When he does return, Ronny brings a Korean wife and her young son. Rosie resents them all until she learns to accept the new family structure.

11.51 Myers, Walter Dean. **The Glory Field.** Scholastic, 1994. 375 pp. ISBN 0-590-45897-3.

The 250-year history of the Lewis family is told through the descendants of Muhammad Bilal, an African captured in 1753 and sold to a plantation owner on Curry Island, South Carolina. This rich family ancestry is firmly rooted in a small piece of land in South Carolina they call the Glory Field.

11.52 Nixon, Joan Lowery. **A Dangerous Promise: The Orphan Train Adventures.** Delacorte Press, 1994. 148 pp. ISBN 0-385-32073-6.

The Civil War is tearing the nation apart and twelve-year-old Mike Kelly wants to be in the action. Mike and his best friend Todd manage to join the Union Army as drummers and make the long and difficult march into Missouri, where Todd is brutally killed. Mike has promised Todd that he will return his heirloom pocket watch to his sister. When it is stolen from Todd's body, Mike makes it his mission to retrieve Todd's watch, a mission that further endangers Mike's life.

11.53 Nixon, Joan Lowery. **Land of Dreams.** Delacorte Press, 1994. 152 pp. ISBN 0-385-31170-2.

In this book from the Ellis Island Trilogy, Kristen, a teenage immigrant, yearns for independence from her old-fashioned Swedish family newly settled in Minnesota. She finds that her new community, comprised of Swedish immigrants, has kept all the old customs, but she is ready for a change.

11.54 Nixon, Joan Lowery. **Land of Promise.** Bantam/Skylark, 1993. 167 pp. ISBN 0-553-008111-X.

In this first book of the Ellis Island Trilogy, everything is strange for fifteen-year-old Rose Carney in America. Her father drinks too much and can't hold a job. Her brothers meet with a radical group of transplanted Irishmen whose tactics frighten Rose. She works to save money in order to bring her mother and sisters over from Ireland, but something always happens to the money. When all her dreams seem shattered, Rose realizes that she must be the one to keep the family together.

11.55 O'Dell, Scott, and Elizabeth Hall. **Thunder Rolling in the Mountains.** Dell/Yearling, 1992. 128 pp. ISBN 0-440-40879-2.

Sound of Running Feet sees the white settlers moving her people off their homelands and hears her father's prediction that this is only the beginning of their losses. She watches as Swan Necklace becomes a member of the warriors and worries that their wedding blanket will never be used. She moves with her father, Chief Joseph of the Nez Perce, and faces starvation, destruction, and personal dangers, as he tries to lead their people far away from the Blue Coats.

11.56 Orlev, Uri. **Lydia, Queen of Palestine.** Translated from Hebrew by Hillel Halkin. Houghton Mifflin, 1993. 168 pp. ISBN 0-395-65660-5.

Lydia, a young Jewish Romanian girl, lives in a world of chaos: her parents are headed toward divorce, her country is headed toward war, and her very life is headed toward turmoil as her mother sends her alone to a kibbutz in Palestine. After months of waiting for her mother to join her, Lydia decides to leave the kibbutz and search for her father. Even with her wild imagination,

Lydia never suspects the truth about her parents and "That Woman."

11.57 Paulsen, Gary. **Mr. Tucket.** Delacorte Press, 1994. 166 pp. ISBN 0-385-31169-9.

For his fourteenth birthday, Francis Alphonse Tucket expects no celebration. He is heading west with his family on the Oregon Trail, and there is no time for birthday parties. What excitement he feels, then, when his father gives him his very own rifle. But the excitement makes him careless, and Pawnees capture him. The one-armed Mr. Grimes rescues him, but Francis Alphonse Tucket is not sure that life with Mr. Grimes is that much better.

11.58 Paulsen, Gary. **Nightjohn.** Delacorte Press, 1993. 92 pp. ISBN 0-385-30838-8.

Old Delie has raised Sarny since she was four years old and her birth mother was sold. It is the 1850s on Clel Waller's plantation, and he buys and sells slaves as he does crops. But the slave Nightjohn is different. He can read and wants to teach letters to other slaves, even knowing he could be dismembered or killed for doing so. Twelve-year-old Sarny risks everything to meet secretly with Nightjohn and learn those precious letters.

11.59 Peck, Robert Newton. **A Part of the Sky.** Alfred A. Knopf, 1994. 163 pp. ISBN 0-679-43277-9.

In this sequel to *A Day No Pigs Would Die*, Rob assumes the role of the man of the house. With his father dead, Rob and his mother are faced with the prospect of running the farm on their own. Keeping the farm going was difficult when his dad was alive, but now with him gone and with the country moving into the Great Depression, Rob isn't sure he can raise the money needed for mortgage payments.

11.60 Polacco, Patricia. **Pink and Say.** Philomel Books, 1994. 32 pp. ISBN 0-399-22671-0.

Say Curtis, a soldier in the Union Army, but still just a boy, lies wounded in a field in Georgia when he is found by Pinkus, whose skin is the color of mahogany. Pinkus, also a Union soldier, helps Say get to the safety of his mother's house, where his wounds can heal, but where they are all in danger of being killed by Confederate troops. This story of the goodness and evil in people is one that has been handed down from generation to generation in the author's family.

11.61 Ray, Karen. **To Cross a Line.** Orchard Books, 1994. 154 pp. ISBN 0-531-06831-5.

In 1938, seventeen-year-old Egon Katz is a baker's apprentice in a small German town until he becomes the target of a police search after a traffic accident. As a Jew, he must avoid arrest at all costs, so he decides to flee Germany. With the help of his brother, he walks across the border into Denmark. Just as he begins to think he is safe, he is caught by a Danish police officer, who holds Egon's fate in his hands.

11.62 Reeder, Carolyn. **Grandpa's Mountain.** Avon/Camelot, 1993. 171 pp. ISBN 0-380-71914-2.

Carrie loves the security of her grandparents' farm in Virginia's Blue Ridge Mountains. She enjoys her summers there, helping in the general store and lunchroom and playing with her friends. With her parents struggling in the city because of the Great Depression, Carrie savors the safety of the mountains. But when the government decides to create a national park in the midst of their land, Grandpa's refusal to leave changes their lives forever.

11.63 Reeder, Carolyn. **Moonshiner's Son.** Macmillan, 1993. 206 pp. ISBN 0-02-775805-2.

Even Prohibition did not stop the Blue Ridge Mountain moonshiners from continuing a family tradition of making corn whiskey. June Higgins and his son, Tom, outsmart the federal agents and ignore the new preacher's call to obey the law. However, when Tom sees the destruction of property and the family abuse caused by people drinking too much, he stands up to his father, which proves harder than he ever expected.

11.64 Reuter, Bjarne. **The Boys from St. Petri.** Translated by Anthea Bell. Dutton Children's Books, 1994. 215 pp. ISBN 0-525-45121-8.

With little fanfare, yet cold calculation, the Germans have moved into Denmark. Most people are going on with their lives as usual, hoping the war will end soon and that they will not be too involved. But for the boys from St. Petri, freedom is everything, even if it means losing their lives.

11.65 Rinaldi, Ann. **A Stitch in Time.** Scholastic, 1994. 305 pp. ISBN 0-590-46055-2.

Nathaniel Chelmsford is a bitter man. Life on the frontier is difficult. His wife's death while giving birth to their younger son has left him with five children. He cares little for his sons and wants to control the lives and marriages of his daughters. A quilt divided into three pieces, one for each daughter, helps hold the fragile family together.

11.66 Rinaldi, Ann. **In My Father's House.** Scholastic, 1993. 303 pp. ISBN 0-590-44730-0.

Oscie thinks the worst thing that could have happened is her father's death. Then her mother marries Will McLean, a Southerner with Northern attitudes, and Oscie decides *that* is the worst. When the Civil War begins on McLean land in Manassas, Virginia, Oscie is sure that *that* is the worst. But the worst is only beginning. After four years of savage war, peace treaties are finally signed in the McLean parlor in Appomattox. As Oscie witnesses this history, she wonders if the worsts are over.

11.67 Rinaldi, Ann. **The Fifth of March: A Story of the Boston Massacre.** Gulliver Books/Harcourt Brace & Company, 1993. 321 pp. ISBN 0-15-227517-7.

Being the nursemaid for the children of John and Abigail Adams in Boston in 1770 puts limits on how fourteen-year-old Rachel Marsh is expected to behave. To befriend a British soldier charged with murdering Boston citizens and to stay friends with people the Adams consider "rabble" could cost Rachel her reputation, as well as her job. But how can she show she is a true friend if she runs from trouble and ignores people's pain?

11.68 Robinet, Harriette Gillem. **Mississippi Chariot.** Atheneum, 1994. 116 pp. ISBN 0-689-31960-6.

Shortning Bread Jackson is a share cropper's son in Mississippi in 1936. His daddy has been on the Mississippi chain gang for two years, falsely convicted of car theft. Shortning Bread knows something must be done to free his father, but the rumor he decides to spread may end in disaster, unless a certain white boy proves to be a true friend.

11.69 Rosen, Sidney, and Dorothy Rosen. **The Magician's Apprentice.** Carolrhoda Books, 1994. 153 pp. ISBN 0-87614-809-7.

Roger Bacon's scientific experiments have the thirteenth-century Church convinced that he is practicing black magic. When fifteen-year-old Jean, a friar and French student, is accused of heresy, he is ordered by the Inquisition to Oxford University on the pretense of being a student, but actually to spy on Master Bacon. What he discovers changes the course of his life.

11.70 Ross, Ramon Royal. **Harper & Moon.** Atheneum, 1993. 181 pp. ISBN 0-689-31803-0.

Harper's family befriends Paddie the traveling sign painter and his family—his wife Tessie, who never comes out of the little delivery wagon, and Moon, their mysterious son. When Harper's friend Olinger is found dead at a mountain cabin, all evidence points to Moon. It's up to Harper to find the truth.

11.71 Rupert, Janet E. **The African Mask.** Clarion Books, 1994. 125 pp. ISBN 0-395-67295-3.

Layo loves working with the clay and shows talent as a potter in her Yoruba village in Africa in the 1200s. She wants to follow the traditions of her grandmother and fashion handsome pottery. But at twelve years old, she is nearing marriageable age and will have to learn whatever craft her husband chooses. Layo is delighted when her parents let her accompany her grandmother to the city of Ife, until she learns she has been set up for matrimony.

11.72 Salisbury, Graham. **Under the Blood-Red Sun.** Delacorte Press, 1994. 244 pp. ISBN 0-385-32099-X.

Tomi's buddies on the eighth-grade baseball team, the Rats, show their true friendship when Pearl Harbor is attacked by the Japanese on December 7, 1941. Though Tomi and his family now live in Hawaii, his grandfather and parents were born in Japan. When the United States declares war on Japan, Tomi's father and grandfather are arrested. His mother is scared and his little sister terrified. Tomi must hold the family together, and the Rats help out.

11.73 Savage, Deborah. **To Race a Dream.** Houghton Mifflin, 1994. 245 pp. ISBN 0-395-69252-0.

Even from a distance, the very sight of the brilliant white buildings of the International Stock Feed Farm makes fifteen-year-old Theodora's heart pound with excitement. Her dream is to drive Dan Patch, the famous harness-racing champion from the nearby farm. But it is 1906; girls are not allowed in the stables, and most certainly not as drivers. Could disguising herself as a boy help her dream come true?

11.74 Schur, Maxine Rose. **The Circlemaker.** Dial Books for Young Readers, 1994. 179 pp. ISBN 0-8037-1354-1.

In the mid-1800s, when the news reaches his Russian village that all Jewish boys thirteen or older are to be taken into the czar's army for a twenty-five year term, twelve-year-old Mendel plans to escape to America. He keeps remembering his father's words that "only the closed circle can keep us whole" and agrees to rescue an old enemy in order to complete his dangerous escape.

11.75 Sierra, Patricia. **Echoes in the Grove.** Avon/Flare, 1994. 115 pp. ISBN 0-380-76940-9.

Rebecca's life changes suddenly when her mother dies from an epidemic in 1854. A move to her Aunt Sarah's affords luxuries that Rebecca has never had. Though this life seems easier than the one she'd known as daughter of a backwoods trapper, she is faced with new challenges. Uncle Ash forces Sarah to make choices that will forever change her life.

11.76 Snyder, Zilpha Keatley. **Cat Running.** Delacorte Press, 1994. 168 pp. ISBN 0-385-31056-0.

The Perkins are migrant workers living in a tent in "Okietown" after they fled the 1930 dust bowls of Oklahoma and Texas to find a better life in California. Eleven-year-old Cat Kinsey has been told to stay away from the migrant workers and is frightened when the Perkins find the hideout she uses to escape from her unhappy home. Slowly, Cat becomes involved with the Perkins in spite of her parents' warnings to keep away from the dust-bowl refugees.

11.77 Stolz, Mary. **Cezanne Pinto.** Alfred A. Knopf, 1994. 279 pp. ISBN 0-679-84917-3.

Cezanne Pinto is at least ninety years old. After escaping slavery to Canada, returning to fight in the Union army, working as a cowboy in Texas, then moving to Chicago and becoming a teacher, Cezanne now writes his memoirs. It is his story of adventure, courage, and victory.

11.78 Taylor, Theodore. **Walking up a Rainbow.** Harcourt Brace & Company, 1994. 307 pp. ISBN 0-15-294512-1.

Left alone in 1852 when her parents drown, fourteen-year-old Susan Carlisle must fight to save her home from an unscrupulous debt collector. Moving her sheep from Iowa to California with the help of a drover and his crew seems the only solution. But she soon discovers she is ill-prepared for the adventure.

11.79 Temple, Frances. **The Ramsay Scallop.** Orchard Books, 1994. 310 pp. ISBN 0-531-06836-6.

Elenor and Thomas have been betrothed for years. It is the year 1299, and Thomas is returning from the Crusades while Elenor,

Looking Back: Historical Fiction 165

only fourteen, worries about their approaching marriage. Their village priest, Father Gregory, intervenes by sending the couple on a holy pilgrimage to Spain to pray for the sins of the people of Ramsay. Their encounters on this most difficult journey bond their spirits and prepare them for their life together.

11.80 Turner, Glennette Tilley. **Running for Our Lives.** Drawings by Samuel Byrd. Holiday House, 1994. 198 pp. ISBN 0-8234-1121-4.

Three days after Thanksgiving, 1855, Luther, a slave, escapes from a plantation in Missouri with his parents, sister, and the baby of a friend. They make it to Quincy, Illinois, but there they are separated on the Underground Railroad. Luther and his sister must not only find their way to Canada, but then try to reunite with the rest of the family.

11.81 Vos, Ida. **Anna Is Still Here.** Translated by Terese Edelstein and Inez Smidt. Houghton Mifflin, 1993. 139 pp. ISBN 0-395-65368-1.

Following *Hide and Seek,* Ida Vos's story of a Jewish child in hiding in World War II, Vos now uses her own memories to tell the story of thirteen-year-old Anna's struggles to adjust to a very different world after the War. Becoming friends with an older survivor helps both move forward with their lives.

11.82 Wisler, G. Clifton. **Jericho's Journey.** Lodestar Books, 1993. 135 pp. ISBN 0-525-67428-4.

The Wetherbys "have been creeping westward by degrees" since coming to America, and now Jericho's father decides to leave Tennessee and take his family to join Ma's people in Texas. Traveling in 1852 proves exciting but also difficult for the family of six. Twelve-year-old Jericho may be short in stature, but this journey helps him grow in other ways.

11.83 Woodruff, Elvira. **Dear Levi: Letters from the Overland Trail.** Alfred A. Knopf, 1994. 119 pp. ISBN 0-679-84641-7.

Austin Ives has been left with only his younger brother, Levi, and his father's promise of land in Oregon Territory. Since the cross-country trip is extremely difficult, twelve-year-old Austin leaves Levi in Pennsylvania, promising to send for him as soon as he stakes claim. Austin writes letters to Levi, giving a detailed account of the three-thousand-mile journey in 1851.

11.84 Wosmek, Frances. **A Brown Bird Singing.** Illustrated by Ted Lewin. Beech Tree Press, 1993. 120 pp. ISBN 0-688-04596-0.

Anego knows she is Chippewa and that Hamigeesek, her real father, might return someday and take her from Mama and Pa and Sheila. But that is "someday," and for years Anego has felt loved and safe with the white family. News of the arrival of Hamigeesek sends Anego running and scared into the woods, right into his path.

11.85 Yep, Laurence. **Dragon's Gate.** HarperCollins, 1993. 272 pp. ISBN 0-06-022971-3.

Otter was dreaming of ways to get to the "Land of the Golden Mountain" to join his father and Uncle Foxfire, but never had he included killing a Manchu as his ticket out of China. Forced to run for his life, the hardships of getting to California are nothing compared to what he faces helping the Chinese workers build the great transcontinental railroad. Furthermore, once he is in the labor camps, Otter learns that his uncle is not the hero Otter thought he was.

12 Understanding the Past: History

12.1 Altman, Linda Jacobs. **The Pullman Strike of 1894.** Millbrook Press, 1994. 64 pp. ISBN 1-56294-346-4.

In May 1894, Pullman Palace Car Company workers walked off their jobs because of a wage cut. This started a chain of events that continues to affect American labor relations. Eugene Debs of the American Railway Union became the center of the huge controversy and was eventually jailed. President Cleveland called out federal troops to control Chicago rioters. This six-month period was the beginning of American laborers' continuing struggle for fair treatment and decent wages.

12.2 Andryszewski, Tricia. **The Dust Bowl: Disaster on the Plains.** Millbrook Press, 1993. 64 pp. ISBN 1-56294-272-7.

In the mid-1930s, terrible dust storms swept across Kansas, Oklahoma, Texas, New Mexico, and Colorado. These states were soon called the Dust Bowl. Long periods of drought kept the soil dry so any wind swept it away. This erosion made the already difficult farming even more difficult. As the soil dried up, so did crops and income. Soon people fled the Dust Bowl, carrying all their possessions in their cars, looking for work.

12.3 Avi-Yonah, Michael. **Dig This! How Archaeologists Uncover Our Past.** Runestone Press, 1993. 96 pp. ISBN 0-8225-3200-X.

Who knows what treasures lie hidden beneath the lands and seas of the world? Archaeologists do! How do they locate buried cities? What equipment do they use to explore ancient shipwrecks? What do they do with the coins, art, and bones that they find? These questions and many more are answered in *Dig This!* You may even be inspired to dig for buried treasure yourself.

12.4 Ayoub, Abderrahman, Jamila Binous, Abderrazak Gragueb, Ali Mtimet, and Hedi Slim. **Umm El Madayan: An Islamic City through the Ages.** Translated by Kathleen Leverich. Illustrated by Francesco Corni. Houghton Mifflin, 1994. 62 pp. ISBN 0-395-65967-1.

You can follow the growth and development of the North African Mediterranean Coast with this series of detailed black and white drawings of fourteen crucial periods in its history. See the prehistoric prelude to the age of the Phoenicians, an iron-age village, a Roman fortress, and the Islamic beginnings in the seventh and eighth centuries as you proceed to present times. Each two-page drawing is followed by two pages of fascinating details, cross sections, and illustrations.

12.5 Bachrach, Susan D. **Tell Them We Remember: The Story of the Holocaust.** Little, Brown and Company, 1994. 110 pp. ISBN 0-316-69264-6.

Photographs from the collection of the U.S. Holocaust Memorial Museum highlight stories of individuals whose lives were touched by the Nazis' attempt to exterminate Jews, Gypsies, and others. Follow the story of children like Sandor Braun, a three-year-old whose parents bought him a violin. The book's clear and brief overview of events in Europe is supported by the individual stories of young people like Sandor whose pictures appear in the margins. An extensive bibliography suggests further reading about the Holocaust.

12.6 Barrett, Tracy. **Harper's Ferry: The Story of John Brown's Raid.** Millbrook Press, 1993. 64 pp. ISBN 1-56294-380-4.

In this book from the Spotlight on American History series, meet John Brown and the others who were against slavery. Read about how they seized a federal armory and attempted to make it the center of their struggle to free the slaves.

12.7 Bial, Raymond. **Frontier Home.** Houghton Mifflin, 1993. 40 pp. ISBN 0-395-64046-6.

They came in Conestoga wagons, on horseback, and by foot, and they settled the American West with grit and courage. These early pioneers built their own homes; grew their own food; and made their own clothes, furniture, and toys. Some left, some died, but many survived. Here's their story told through what remains of their early homesteads, their furnishings, and their crafts.

12.8 Bial, Raymond. **Shaker Home.** Photography by Raymond Bial. Houghton Mifflin, 1994. 37 pp. ISBN 0-395-64047-4.

Using exquisite photographs author/photographer Bial provides a respectful look at the life of the Shakers. This religious group is known for its beliefs in pacifism and equality of the races and the sexes, as well as many inventions such as the circular saw, the clothespin, and the slotted spoon. The Shakers are the oldest communal society in the United States.

12.9 Brimner, Larry Dane. **Voices from the Camps.** Franklin Watts, 1994. 110 pp. ISBN 0-531-11179-2.

In addition to the loss of lives suffered by Americans, the attack on Pearl Harbor by the Japanese brought another casualty. Ten weeks after the bombing, President Roosevelt signed an order that began a time described as the most racist period in our history. Over one hundred thousand Japanese Americans were herded into internment camps to satisfy this country's fears of Japanese sabotage. Their story is retold here through the voices of those who survived this breach of individual rights.

12.10 Carrick, Carol. **Whaling Days.** Illustrated by David Frampton. Clarion Books, 1993. 40 pp. ISBN 0-395-50948-3.

Between 1825 and 1860 the American whaling fleet grew to 735 ships, and whaling was a major business in New England. Life was dangerous and difficult for the crews of the crowded ships that sailed the seas for many months at a time. On a successful trip, the whalers filled 2,400 barrels of whale oil from as many as seventy whales. Frampton's beautiful woodcuts will enhance your understanding of how the whalers slaughtered these giants of the seas and why we now have laws protecting whales.

12.11 Carter, Alden R. **Battle of the Ironclads: The Monitor and the Merrimack.** Drawings, maps, and photographs from various archives and museums. Franklin Watts, 1993. 64 pp. ISBN 0-531-20091-4.

To keep their ships away from the Confederacy, Union naval officers at the Norfolk, Virginia, shipyards destroyed many vessels, including the five-year-old *Merrimack*. From the sunken wreckage of the *Merrimack*, the Confederacy built a new ironclad ship named the *Virginia*, but it was still called the *Merrimack* by many. At the same time, the North built the *Monitor*. This book tells of the construction of these ironclads and the eventual clash between the two forerunners of our modern naval vessels.

12.12 Carter, Alden. **China Past—China Future.** Franklin Watts, 1994. 143 pp. ISBN 0-531-11161-X.

Three thousand years of customs, cultures, and political strife are recounted in this moving narrative researched by a Chinese scholar. Find out why Chinese children never strike their parents and why girls bind their feet. This book suggests that being Chinese often means suffering, but with dignity, hope, and a firm belief in the "eternal greatness" of China. From the emperors, dynasties, and mandarins, through years of turmoil, to the events of Tiananmen Square, China has a rich past and has the possibility of a future embracing some form of democratic ideal.

12.13 Clare, John D., editor. **Fourteenth-Century Towns.** Harcourt Brace & Company, 1993. 64 pp. ISBN 0-15-200515-3.

Did you know that children in the Middle Ages often played a game like jacks, with the dried knucklebones of sheep? Or that apartment buildings were common in ancient Rome? Two volumes in the Living History series explore these historical periods. *Fourteenth-Century Towns* is filled with photographs that recreate the world of medieval merchants and peasants and the devastating famines and plagues that haunted their lives. *Classical Rome*, also edited by Clare, recreates important aspects of Roman life from the first century B.C. until the fourth century A.D.—the life of the privileged, their government, their military, and their homes.

12.14 Collins, James. **Settling the American West.** Franklin Watts, 1993. 64 pp. ISBN 0-531-20070-1.

Miners, railroaders, cattlemen, and farmers all played a vital role in settling the American West in the post–Civil War years of the nineteenth century. This slim, easy-to-read volume explores the contributions of each group to our country's expansion and wealth. Photographs, drawings, maps, and a bibliography for further reading are included.

12.15 Colman, Penny. **Toilets, Bathtubs, Sinks, and Sewers: A History of the Bathroom.** Atheneum, 1994. 65 pp. ISBN 0-689-31894-4.

Did you know that ancient Egyptians sometimes buried sink basins in tombs of people who died? Ancient Romans built elaborate baths, but early American settlers rarely bathed. One colonial woman said she had not been wet all over for twenty-eight years. As recently as the 1830s in Leeds, England, "Whole streets were floating in sewage." Today, Americans flush 4.8 billion gallons of water a day. Explore the history of bathrooms, and speculate on the future of this important room.

12.16 Cooper, Kay. **Who Put the Cannon in the Courthouse Square?** Avon, 1993. 81 pp. ISBN 0-380-71298-9.

Don't let professional historians have all the excitement of discovering what used to be around you. Follow these steps to discover your past: ask questions, search for clues, find facts, take field trips, and interview people. This how-to guide will help you uncover local stories, as well as report them, showing you how to take history out of the textbooks and put it into your own backyard.

12.17 Cox, Clinton. **The Forgotten Heroes: The Story of the Buffalo Soldiers.** Scholastic, 1993. 180 pp. ISBN 0-590-45121-9.

After the Civil War, many African Americans joined the Army, forming the ninth and tenth Cavalry divisions, which were designed to help settle the West. Known as the Buffalo Soldiers, they spent more time fighting than any other regiment and continued to be a force until World War II. But, because of bigotry and prejudice, they were denied the very freedoms they fought to preserve. Their deeds were seldom noticed, and their heroism was ignored. Now, by learning about these brave men, we can belatedly honor them.

12.18 Dawson, Imogen. **Food & Feasts in the Middle Ages.** New Discovery Books, 1994. 32 pp. ISBN 0-02-726324-X.

Want to prepare a feast fit for a medieval king or one fit for a Roman king? If so, you need the books in this series, Food and Feasts. They tell all about the food eaten by peoples in ancient cultures and time periods, its cultivation and preparation, and the social customs surrounding eating. *Food and Feasts in the Middle Ages* and *Food and Feasts in Ancient Rome* by Philip Steele use photographs of ancient artifacts and art works that show food and its preparation in rural areas, in the cities, and for travelers in-between. Each book contains recipes, actual menus from writings of the time period, a glossary of terms, and a bibliography for future reading.

12.19 Duncan, Lois. **The Circus Comes Home.** Photographs by Joseph Janney Steinmetz. Delacorte, 1993. 64 pp. ISBN 0-385-30689-X.

Award-winning author Lois Duncan grew up in Sarasota, Florida, the winter home of the Ringling Brothers' Circus. Joining her childhood memories with her father's photographs, she chronicles the history of the Ringling Brothers and Barnum and Bailey Circus, which toured the United States until 1956. Peek behind the scenes of the "Greatest Show on Earth," and meet the circus crews and stars such as the famed Flying Wallendas, the Doll family of midgets, Gargantua the Gorilla, and the Fat Lady.

12.20 Ehrlich, Amy. **Wounded Knee: An Indian History of the American West.** Adapted from Dee Brown's **Bury My Heart at Wounded Knee.** Henry Holt and Company, 1993. 180 pp. ISBN 0-8050-2700-9.

When settlers began moving west of the Mississippi River, Native Americans of the Southwest and the Great Plains knew that their independence would soon be taken from them if they did not resist. Cochese, Geronimo, Red Cloud, and Sitting Bull were all proud leaders who fought to defend their lands, their people, and their way of life from the settlers who threatened them. They saw their people suffer the worst kind of injustices: hunger, sickness, forced migrations, and near annihilation at Wounded Knee in 1890.

12.21 Eschle, Lou. **The Curse of Tutankhamen.** Lucent Books, 1994. 48 pp. ISBN 1-56006-152-9.

Was there a curse on Tutankhamen's tomb? In 1922, Lord Carnarvon funded the expedition to find the tomb, with Howard Carter as the leader. Carter was filled with excitement as they broke through the door and entered the tomb. Shortly after, Carter became gravely ill, and Lord Carnarvon died. By 1929, twenty-two people who had worked on the opening of the tomb were dead. Cursed or not? You decide in this new addition to the series Exploring the Unknown.

12.22 Fleischman, Paul. **Bull Run.** Woodcuts by David Frampton. HarperCollins, 1993. 102 pp. ISBN 0-06-021446-5.

Fleischman finds the human element in war by showing how sixteen individuals, including a black soldier, a young musician, a photographer, and a doctor, all felt about the first battle of the Civil War. Each tells a personal story, but, taken as a whole, these narratives form a full-blown view of armed conflict in general and the Battle of Bull Run in particular.

12.23 Fraser, Mary Ann. **Ten Mile Day and the Building of the Transcontinental Railroad.** Illustrated by Mary Ann Fraser. Henry Holt and Company, 1993. 34 pp. ISBN 0-8050-1902-2.

Two companies laying track for the first transcontinental railroad—the Union Pacific, starting in Omaha, and the Central Pacific, starting in Sacramento—became fierce competitors. Challenged by their rivals, the Central Pacific crew built ten miles of track in one day, laying 3,520 rails with eight track layers, lifting 125 tons of iron each. This book describes the manpower, the materials, the problems, and the determination required to accomplish this incredible feat.

12.24   Freedman, Russell. **Kids at Work: Lewis Hine and the Crusade against Child Labor.** Clarion Books, 1994. 104 pp. ISBN 0-395-58703-4.

In 1911, five-year-olds worked shelling shrimp, eight-year-olds worked in cotton mills, and ten-year-olds worked in the mines. They toiled eleven or twelve hours a day and often lost fingers, toes, or their lives. A former teacher, Lewis Hine, was so disturbed about the misuse of children in the work force that he traveled around taking photographs to document the horrors of child labor. His photographs mobilized public opinion for laws protecting children from abusive and dangerous working conditions.

12.25   Fremon, David K. **The Trail of Tears.** New Discovery Books, 1994. 96 pp. ISBN 0-02-735745-7.

With no warning, the Cherokee, nearly 17,000 strong, were herded by United States soldiers from their homeland to a reservation in Oklahoma. *The Trail of Tears* relates events leading to the cruel, forced migration of these Native Americans from their home east of the Mississippi to strange new lands. This book, part of the American Events series, provides insight into a significant event in North American history.

12.26   Fritz, Jean. **Around the World in a Hundred Years.** G. P. Putnam's Sons, 1994. 128 pp. ISBN 0-399-22527-7.

Jean Fritz weaves together history, biography, travelogues, and humor as she tells of ten explorers who helped map the unknown. Prior to the discoveries of these explorers, people believed that along the west coast of Africa, water boiled, people turned black, and ships caught fire in the poisonous air. Prince Henry the Navigator initiated a century of discovery that began around 1421. Cabral, Ponce de Leon, Magellan, and others were ambitious explorers seeking gold, fame, adventure, or eternal youth.

12.27   Fry, Annette R. **The Orphan Trains.** New Discovery Books, 1994. 96 pp. ISBN 0-02-735721-X.

This new series called American Events provides well-documented information about significant happenings in American history. One such event, which began in the 1850s and lasted for seventy-five years, involved the movement of 100,000 orphaned or abandoned children. These children from eastern cities such as New York and Boston were placed on trains, called Orphan Trains, and sent west. As trains made stops, children were lined up at the stations for families to adopt. This movement, begun by the Children's Aid Society, was meant to provide homes to homeless children; but in some cases, it was a means of providing cheap labor for farmers.

12.28 Fry, Plantagenet Somerset. **The Dorling Kindersley Illustrated History of the World.** Dorling Kindersley, 1994. 384 pp. ISBN 1-56458-244-2.

Scientists believe that life began on Earth some 4,600 million years ago. So that's where this book begins—with a quick look at the Paloezoic, Mesozoic, and Cenozoic eras. Then it moves into the time when modern humans begin to populate the world, around 4,000 to 5,000 B.C. From there, this history provides a summary of the major events and people throughout time, with thoughts about what the future holds. Timelines, maps, photographs, and illustrations make this volume fun to read, as well as informative.

12.29 Gonen, Rivka. **Charge! Weapons and Warfare in Ancient Times.** Runestone Press, 1993. 72 pp. ISBN 0-8225-3201-8.

With the findings of archeologists, ancient artwork, and ancient writings, historians have been able to discover much about weapons used throughout history. Read about weapons used for defense and survival from the beginning of time, like clubs or sabers; weapons used at distances, such as the javelin, the sling, or the bow and arrow; and heavy artillery like the catapult and the battering ram.

12.30 Gonzalez, Christina. **Inca Civilization.** Children's Press, 1993. 36 pp. ISBN 0-516-08380-5.

Inca Civilization is one volume in the World Heritage series, which focuses on cultural and historical sites UNESCO has targeted for preservation around the world. Each volume features maps, drawings, and outstanding photographs of ancient sites, as well as timelines to give the historical perspective. In *Inca Civilization*, read how the records of the Incas come from oral tradition because the culture had no writing system. The people of this civilization, which covered the Andes Mountain regions of South America from the 1200s to the late 1500s, were responsible for many remarkable achievements.

12.31 Granfield, Linda. **Cowboy: An Album.** Ticknor & Fields, 1993. 96 pp. ISBN 0-395-68430-7.

The world of the cowboy was far from the romantic, glamorous view that the media often portrays. Over 100 photographs and historical drawings in this book realistically depict this world and show that the cowboy myth has been perpetuated by artists, authors, movies, and television. You might even find a cowboy song to sing, a trail recipe you would like to try, or some "cowboyspeak" you can test out as you browse through this fact-filled volume.

12.32 Greenfeld, Howard. **The Hidden Children.** Ticknor & Fields, 1993. 118 pp. ISBN 0-395-66074-2.

During World War II, Jewish parents often hid their children so that the children might survive Nazi terrorism. Thirteen adult survivors share their remembrances of being "hidden" children, forced into silence during a time when laughter, tears, or childhood chatter would endanger their lives. They hid in convents, orphanages, attics, and even haystacks, often suffering starvation, fear, cruelty, and emotional neglect. These thirteen tell their stories so that others might not forget.

12.33 Greenlaw, M. Jean. **Ranch Dressing: The Story of Western Wear.** Lodestar Books, 1993. 79 pp. ISBN 0-525-67432-2.

Jeans. Boots. Ten-gallon hats. Behind every item of clothing lies a tale—not of how clothes make the person, but of the men and women who make the clothes. Read about fashion pioneers like Levi Strauss, who peddled his trademark pants to miners in California, Enid Justin, who started the Nacona Boot Company, or John B. Stetson, who set out for Pike's Peak and created a large, ugly hat for his own protection. Contemporary and historical photographs complement the stories.

12.34 Hakim, Joy. **A History of US: The First Americans.** Oxford University Press, 1993. 164 pp. ISBN 0-19-501145-8.

This series, called A History of US, offers nine volumes of U.S. history. This volume, *The First Americans,* introduces you to the Stone-Age tribes of the Bering Strait and guides you to the early settlers of America. Other volumes carry you through American history with vignettes, trivia, fascinating facts, interesting writing, and plenty of illustrations.

12.35 Hamilton, Virginia. **Many Thousand Gone: African Americans from Slavery to Freedom.** Illustrated by Leo and Diane Dillon. Alfred A. Knopf, 1993. 151 pp. ISBN 0-394-82873-9.

In thirty-four concise chapters, Virginia Hamilton relates true accounts of the well-known and the unnamed, as she takes you on a fascinating journey from freedom to slavery to escape to abolition to war to a new freedom. Personal accounts and historical facts are interwoven into a rich fabric of history, adventure, courage, and triumph.

12.36 Haskins, James. **The March on Washington.** HarperCollins, 1993. 144 pp. ISBN 0-06-021289-6.

On August 28, 1963 hundreds of thousands of individuals marched on Washington to show support for racial equality. On that day, Dr. Martin Luther King, Jr. delivered his famous "I have a dream" speech. This event was a long time coming, and Haskins traces its development. You'll find leaders here, but the emphasis is on the grassroots power of individuals, community groups, and congregations who traveled to Washington—where they came from, what they hoped for, and how they realized their own dreams.

12.37 Haskins, James. **The Scottsboro Boys.** Henry Holt and Company, 1994. 118 pp. ISBN 0-9050-2206-6.

Over sixty years ago, when nine Alabama black youths were unjustly accused of raping two white women, issues of racial inequality came to the attention of the whole country. Just two weeks after being accused, and without benefit of lawyers until the day of the trial, the youths were quickly found guilty. In this fast-paced historical narrative, the deeply ingrained racism in our country surfaces through the tragic abuses suffered by these young men in courts and prisons.

12.38 Haskins, James. **Get on Board: The Story of the Underground Railroad.** Scholastic, 1993. 152 pp. ISBN 0-590-45418-8.

Stations, stationmasters, conductors, train robbers! These all sound like terms associated with trains and railroads, but in this case they refer to the places and people that helped slaves in their escape to freedom, during the troubled times prior to the Civil War. The principal players in this organization, such as stationmasters Thomas Garrett and Levi Coffin, and conductors Bill Fairfield and Harriet Tubman, are highlighted in this well-documented history of the secret, underground network that moved people to freedom.

12.39 Heyes, Eileen. **Children of the Swastika: The Hitler Youth.** Millbrook Press, 1993. 96 pp. ISBN 1-56294-237-9.

When Hitler became Chancellor of Germany in 1933, he knew he needed to shape the minds of young people so they would be his followers in the future. The Hitler Youth turned two million young people, beginning at age six, into servants of Hitler and the terrorist regime of the Nazis. Motivated by extra food rations, fun activities, and respect, these young people were taught to exercise unquestioning loyalty to the state; often they would turn in their own family members who made anti-Nazi remarks.

12.40 Howarth, Sara. **The Middle Ages.** With see-through illustrations by Bill Le Fever. Viking, 1993. 48 pp. ISBN 0-670-85098-5.

This book is from a series called See Through History, which focuses on ancient civilizations. This volume looks at the Middle Ages, the period from the fifth century A.D. to the fifteenth century. See-through illustrations of a monastery, a castle, a guild shop, and a water mill, make this ancient time more real. Another title in the series, *The Renaissance,* by Tim Wood, covers the blossoming of the arts and sciences in the fifteenth and sixteenth centuries. See-through illustrations of the printing and paper-making process, a Florentine palace, St. Peter's Cathedral, and one of Columbus's ships complete this volume.

12.41 Hull, Robert, selector and editor. **A Prose Anthology of the First World War.** Millbrook Press, 1993. 64 pp. ISBN 1-56294-223-9.

Using actual documents such as letters, journals, and memoirs, this book gives us a close-up, personal view of the people in World War I. You will read the words of prisoners of war on both sides, front-line soldiers, doctors, nurses, and even the German ace pilot Manfred von Richthofen. Another book by Hull, *A Prose Anthology of the Second World War,* offers a similar intimate look at the people who fought in that war.

12.42 Kalman, Bobbie. **18th Century Clothing.** Crabtree Publishing, 1993. 32 pp. ISBN 0-86505-492-4.

In *18th Century Clothing,* readers learn how children of the 1700s dressed, how they brushed their teeth, why men wore wigs, how the wigs were made, and what kind of makeup the ladies wore. The text and illustrations bring these topics and others up-close, so today's readers can see what one part of life in the eighteenth century was like. In *19th Century Clothing,* by the same author, readers see how fashions have changed to include derby hats and mobcaps, gaiters and scarves. Other titles in this Historic

Communities series include *A Colonial Town,* which offers a look at Williamsburg, and *Colonial Life,* a book about colonists.

12.43 Karl, Jean. **America Alive: A History.** Illustrated by Ian Schoenherr. Philomel Books, 1994. 120 pp. ISBN 0-399-22013-5.

America is a nation built upon the diversity and strengths of the people who have lived here: Native American tribes skilled in architecture and agriculture; explorers looking for riches; settlers; and immigrants who wanted a new life. This brief history of our nation will whet your appetite for more reading about some of the interesting topics and people you will meet here.

12.44 Kent, Zachary. **World War I: "The War to End Wars."** Enslow Publishers, 1994. 128 pp. ISBN 0-89490-523-6.

When the lookout for the Lusitania shouted, "Torpedo coming on the starboard side!" little did he know that his ship would sink and that with its sinking, America would enter World War I. America's involvement in the war escalated so swiftly that American soldiers had to drill using broomsticks until enough firearms were available. In this latest addition to the American War series, you will learn about World War I and why it was called "The War to End Wars."

12.45 Kort, Michael. **China under Communism.** Millbrook Press, 1994. 175 pp. ISBN 1-56294-450-9.

Now a nuclear power, with a fifth of the world's population, China is a dominant political force in the twentieth century. This book describes with vivid details the years between 1949 and 1989, beginning with China's Communist revolution and civil war, and ending with the Tiananmen Square massacre. If you're interested in exploring the roots of the new China, you'll find this book helpful.

12.46 Levine, Ellen, editor. **Freedom's Children.** Avon/Flare, 1994. 204 pp. ISBN 0-380-72114-7.

Many people think the civil rights activists of the 1950s and 1960s were all adults. However, some of the most daring activists were children and teenagers. Claudette Colvin was fifteen years old in 1955 when, on a Montgomery city bus, she refused to give up her seat to a white person. Ben Chaney was a seasoned demonstrator against segregation by the time he was twelve. The author of this book has tracked down thirty individuals who, as children,

Understanding the Past: History 179

were a part of those violent times, and she has recorded their stories.

12.47 Levinson, Nancy Smiler. **Turn of the Century.** Lodestar Books, 1994. 134 pp. ISBN 0-525-67433-0.

Robber barons, westward expansion, immigration, civil rights, the workers' rights struggle, Theodore Roosevelt, Thomas Edison—these are among the issues, events, and personalities that propelled this country into the twentieth century. We can read about them in Nancy Levinson's chronicle of the late 1800s in America.

12.48 Macauley, David. **Ship.** Houghton Mifflin, 1993. 96 pp. ISBN 0-395-52439-3.

An underwater diver discovers an encrusted anchor on the ocean floor. This find leads to others: guns, ballast stones, and squared timber. Working with a team of archeologists and historians, the diver reconstructs a shipwreck, guessing the ruin to be a sixteenth-century caravel. Macauley extends the find through a fictitious diary, purportedly written in 1504 by the widow of a shipyard owner. This book allows you to speculate about the construction, destruction, and recreation of a voyage undertaken over 400 years ago.

12.49 Marrin, Albert. **Cowboys, Indians, and Gunfighters: The Story of the Cattle Kingdom.** Atheneum, 1993. 196 pp. ISBN 0-689-31774-3.

Columbus's second voyage to the new world brought more than people and supplies. It also brought the "noble beasts of Spain"—cattle and horses—which were unknown in the Americas until then. The cattle provided food for conquering Spaniards, and the horses made the Spaniards nearly invincible. From this beginning, author Marrin brings you the magic of that period in American history when ranchers and cowboys ruled the Great Plains of the United States.

12.50 Martin, Ana. **Prehistoric Stone Monuments.** Children's Press, 1993. 36 pp. ISBN 0-516-08386-4.

This book from the World Heritage series highlights the stone megaliths erected during the Neolithic Age thousands of years ago. These ancient structures, found mostly in Western Europe and the British Isles, date from 2000 to 1500 B.C. Each stone slab weighs around 100 tons. The slabs are usually arranged in rows or in a circle. Some people believe they might have had a religious meaning.

12.51 McKissack, Patricia, and Fredrick McKissack. **The Royal Kingdoms of Ghana, Mali, and Songhay: Life in Medieval Africa.** Henry Holt and Company, 1994. 140 pp. ISBN 0-8050-1670-8.

Much of the history of medieval western Africa comes to us from the griots, the oral historians whose stories are still recited today. The people of the ancient kingdoms of Ghana, Mali, and Songhay, called the Land of Blacks by the ancient Arabs, have endured, and their significant history is only beginning to be reconstructed. This book uses current and sometimes conflicting sources to recreate the history of the Western Sudan for young readers.

12.52 Mettger, Zack. **Till Victory is Won: Black Soldiers in the Civil War.** Lodestar Books, 1994. 118 pp. ISBN 0-525-67412-8.

Because black men felt the Civil War was about ending slavery, they demanded their right to fight. When finally given the opportunity, over 200,000 black men fought, and 39,000 lost their lives. Often saddled with the most labor-intensive duties, many of these men worked harder in the army than as slaves, and they endured cruel disciplinary actions. While white soldiers rested, black soldiers often dug ditches and buried the dead, but they only earned half the salary of a white soldier.

12.53 Mettger, Zack. **Reconstruction: America after the Civil War.** Lodestar Books, 1994. 122 pp. ISBN 0-525-67490-X.

Serious problems, including homelessness, starvation, and fear of retaliation faced our country in the years following the Civil War. Using first-person accounts, actual photographs, and vintage drawings, this volume explores the challenges of rebuilding cities and farms, rejoining families torn apart, easing strife between southerners and the newly freed slaves. The freed slaves were struggling for the rights of citizenship and coping with the emergence of white supremacy groups.

12.54 Monroe, Jean Guard, and Ray A. Williamson. **First Houses: Native American Homes and Sacred Structures.** Houghton Mifflin, 1993. 150 pp. ISBN 0-395-51081-3.

Whether they built longhouses, hogans, kivas, or tipis, Native Americans designed their dwellings to be in harmony with the earth, to conform to particular legends and myths, and to take advantage of the natural resources available. Beginning with the buildings of the Iroquois, and including the patterns of the Navaho, Pueblo, Mohave, Pawnee, Delaware, and Plains Indians, the authors construct a solid foundation for understanding our country's earliest houses and those who lived in them.

12.55 Morris, Jeffrey. **The Jefferson Way.** Lerner Publications, 1994. 128 pp. ISBN 0-8225-2926-2.

United States Presidents often make decisions that affect Americans for years to come. This volume, from a series on Presidential decisions, explores four decisions made by Thomas Jefferson, our third president. The Louisiana Purchase in 1803, Jefferson's most significant decision, doubled the size of our country and encouraged westward exploration and expansion. However, his decision to try Aaron Burr for treason endangered the civil liberties of a citizen and symbolized a growing political issue in our country. Others books in the Great Presidential Decisions series include *The Washington Way, The Truman Way, The Lincoln Way, The FDR Way,* and *The Reagan Way*.

12.56 Morris, Juddi. **The Harvey Girls: The Women Who Civilized the West.** Walker & Company, 1994. 101 pp. ISBN 0-8027-8302-3.

By 1880, over 100 Harvey House Restaurants prepared quality meals for Santa Fe Railroad passengers. Those meals were served by "Harvey girls": farmers' daughters, adventurers, immigrants, college students. Owner Fred Harvey provided excellent training and benefits. He required his employees to live in company dormitories and follow strict codes of behavior both in and out of the dining rooms. Period photographs, personal anecdotes, and lively text tell the story of Fred Harvey's restaurants and the girls and women who loyally worked for him.

12.57 Moser, Barry. **Fly! A Brief History of Flight Illustrated.** Willa Perlman Books, 1993. 56 pp. ISBN 0-06-022893-8.

Splendid watercolor paintings, accompanied by a brief text, bring aviation history to life. The book highlights sixteen key historical events, beginning with the invention of the hot-air balloons, moving to the Wright Brothers' flight, and ending with the space shuttle. A timeline accompanying each of the events indicates concurrent milestones in world history. More illustrations and detailed background information concerning the sixteen events can be found in the historical notes.

12.58 Murdoch, David H. **Cowboy.** Illustrated by Geoff Brightling. Dorling Kindersley, 1993. 64 pp. ISBN 0-679-84014-1.

The life of the cowboy, often glorified, sometimes romanticized, was always hard, exciting, and an important part of the development of this country. In *Cowboy* you get an up-close look at guns and gunslingers, charros and vaqueros, the South American gauchos, cowboys from down under, North American cowboys, and cowboys who are girls. *Cowboy* talks about boots, spurs, chaps, saddles, trail drives, branding irons, and gunslingers—all a part of the cowboy's rugged life.

12.59 Murphy, Jim. **Across America on an Emigrant Train.** Clarion Books, 1993. 150 pp. ISBN 0-395-63390-7.

In the late 1800s, over sixteen million European immigrants arrived in America, and many used our fledgling railroad system to move westward. One such traveler was a young Scottish writer, Robert Louis Stevenson. Using archival photographs and Stevenson's diary, author Jim Murphy weaves a fascinating story of Stevenson's trip to California, of railroad travel in the United States, and of the endurance of the immigrants who came to this country for a new way of life.

12.60 Nardo, Don. **Democracy.** Lucent Books, 1994. 128 pp. ISBN 1-56006-147-2.

America isn't the first democracy, but rather represents a form of government developed over several centuries. Nardo traces the history and reality of this concept, while other books in the Overview Series touch on institutions that influence the system: *The U.S. Congress* by Don Nardo and *The United Nations* by Adam Wong.

12.61 Nirgiotis, Nicholas. **Erie Canal: Gateway to the West.** Franklin Watts, 1993. 64 pp. ISBN 0-531-20146-5.

Using photographs, drawings, and maps, this book tells about the construction of the Erie Canal, a waterway to the new, rich farmlands of the midwest and a gateway to thriving commerce and trade. Begun in 1817 and completed in 1825, the 363-mile-long Erie Canal, with its intricate series of locks, provided a connection between the Hudson River and Lake Erie and served as a major means of transportation prior to the coming of the railroad.

12.62 Platt, Richard. **The Smithsonian Visual Timeline of Inventions.** Illustrated with photographs. Dorling Kindersley, 1994. 64 pp. ISBN 1-56458-675-8.

Understanding the Past: History 183

When was the bottle cork invented? Who invented the first set of false teeth? What was a bicycle originally called? When were the first toilets invented? To find out the answers to these questions, and learn about hundreds of other inventions, you need this book! Photographs, illustrations, timelines, and brief historical notes carry you from 600,000 B.C., when the early hominids made the first crude tools, to visions of the future, when zero-emission vehicles, virtual reality, and human genome mapping will be everyday occurrences.

12.63 Platt, Richard. **Man-of-War.** Illustrated by Stephen Biesty. Dorling Kindersley, 1993. 32 pp. ISBN 1-56458-321-X.

In this intriguing book, from Stephen Biesty's Cross-Sections series, historically accurate illustrations slice a British warship into ten cross-sections. Fact-filled text accompanies each cut-away and informs you about life aboard this Napoleonic-era vessel—from navigation to cooking and eating, from sleeping to fighting, from the horrible living conditions of the crew to the luxurious quarters of the admiral. Through these detailed cut-away illustrations, step back in time, board an ancient warship, and see how sailors of another time and place lived.

12.64 Platt, Richard. **Castle.** Illustrated by Stephen Biesty. Dorling Kindersley, 1994. 32 pp. ISBN 1-5648-467-4.

Castle, another book from Stephen Biesty's Cross-Sections series, offers ten incredibly detailed cross-sections of a medieval castle. These cross-sections will transport you into the exciting world of dungeons and feasts, enemy attacks, and jousting knights. You can see every nook and cranny of a castle and meet the people who live and work within its walls, from the lord of the manor to the court jester, from the stonemasons who shape the complex structures to the castle cooks who prepare the lavish feasts.

12.65 Reid, Struan. **Exploration by Sea.** New Discovery Books, 1994. 48 pp. ISBN 0-02-775801-X.

In this book from the Silk and Spice Route series, you will sail the more than 9,300 miles of the spice routes. You will see the hardships of sea trade and the adventures of early sea-going traders. You will visit many ports and various cultures along the routes, and you'll be amazed at all the riches of the spice trade.

12.66 Rochelle, Belinda. **Witnesses to Freedom: Young People Who Fought for Civil Rights.** Lodestar Books, 1993. 97 pp. ISBN 0-525-67377-6.

This book chronicles the role of young people in the civil rights movement in our country. From bus boycotts to sit-ins to children's marches to freedom rides, African American children took an important role in this twentieth-century struggle for freedom. Each chapter introduces a young person such as Barbara, who organized a high school boycott; Elizabeth, one of the "Little Rock Nine"; or nine-year-old Sheyann, a marcher in Selma. All of them were indeed witnesses to freedom.

12.67 Sandler, Martin W. **Cowboys.** HarperCollins, 1994. 91 pp. ISBN 0-06-023318-4.

Using the vast resources of the Library of Congress, author Martin Sandler has created a fascinating historical series called A Library of Congress Book. In *Cowboys*, readers discover the hard and often lonely life of the cowboy on the open range, as well as the cowboys of movies and rodeos. Over 100 photos and illustrations explore life on the trail, the open range, "cutting" new calves, the relationship of cowboys and outlaws, and famous movie and rodeo cowboy legends. Another book by Martin Sandler, *Pioneers*, shows readers why and how men and women went west.

12.68 Sattler, Helen Roney. **The Earliest Americans.** Illustrated by Jean Day Zallinger. Clarion Books, 1993. 125 pp. ISBN 0-395-54996-5.

What is the history of the people whom Columbus encountered on his first visit to the Americas? Most archeologists believe the ancestors of these Native Americans arrived more than 15,000 years before 1492 and had achieved levels of culture that rivaled any others of the ancient world. Using information from archeological discoveries at sites of ancient peoples and theories of origin of the earliest Americans, this book explores the characteristics and accomplishments of the peoples who populated the American continents before Columbus arrived.

12.69 Senna, Carl. **The Black Press and the Struggle for Civil Rights.** Franklin Watts, 1993. 160 pp. ISBN 0-531-11036-2.

An institution that figures prominently throughout African American history is the black press. It has exposed injustices; led the fight for civil rights; and produced outstanding, talented, and dedicated individuals. Meet some of those individuals: Thomas Fortune, whose fiery editorials condemned racism at the end of the nineteenth century; John Harold Johnson, who founded *Ebony* magazine; and Frederick Douglass, who escaped from slavery and then started *The North Star*, a strong abolitionist newspaper.

12.70 Siegel, Beatrice. **Murder on the Highway: The Viola Liuzzo Story.** Four Winds Press, 1993. 125 pp. ISBN 0-02-782632-5.

Viola Liuzzo, a suburban Detroit middle-class white mother of five, joined the March 25, 1965, civil-rights trek from Selma to Montgomery, Alabama. After the demonstration, Mrs. Liuzzo was murdered by members of the Ku Klux Klan. Why did Viola Liuzzo feel compelled to travel south to be part of this historic event? Beatrice Siegel tells the story of an ordinary person who contributed to an extraordinary event.

12.71 Silverman, Jerry. **Songs and Stories from the American Revolution.** Millbrook Press, 1994. 134 pp. ISBN 1-56294-429-072.

You probably know the song "Yankee Doodle," but what about other songs of the American Revolution, like "Bunker Hill," "The Swamp Fox," or "In the Days of Seventy-Six"? Each of the ten songs in this book is presented as sheet music and preceded by an explanation of its historical significance, interesting notes about meanings of archaic words, and, when possible, a sketch about the writer.

12.72 Smith-Baranzini, Marlene, and Howard Egger-Bovet. **Book of the American Indians.** Illustrated by T. Taylor Bruce. Little, Brown and Company, 1994. 96 pp. ISBN 0-316-22208-9.

Do you want to be actively involved in learning about your country's history? Here is your opportunity. Each of the books in the series called USKids History uses first-hand accounts, letters, speeches, songs, and cartoons to make history come alive. You will also find fun activities to do. In this book, read about the Native American tribes of North America, including the Hopi, the Crow, and the Pauite. Then weave a basket, make a medicine bag, or even a pair of moccasins. The instructions are all there.

12.73 Smith, Carter, editor. **Prelude to War.** Millbrook Press, 1993. 96 pp. ISBN 1-56294-261-1.

This book, from a series that uses visual documents from the Library of Congress's rich pictorial record of the Civil War, describes the causes of that war. It visually sets the historical background and takes you to the war's beginning. *Behind the Lines,* also edited by Smith, explores the life of civilians and of Union and Confederate soldiers during the Civil War. These volumes are easy to read and provide thorough timelines to support the array of maps, photographs, cartoons, and sheet music. If you want a more complete understanding of the Civil War, then you'll want to spend time with this series.

12.74 Stanley, Jerry. **I Am an American: A True Story of Japanese Internment.** Crown, 1994. 102 pp. ISBN 0-517-59786-1.

On February 19, 1942, the United States placed all Japanese living on the west coast into relocation centers for the duration of World War II. With thousands of others, California citizen Shiro Nomura had to leave his home and school to enter the camp at Manzanar. This forced move meant leaving behind more than friends and possessions; it also meant a loss of self-worth and dignity. This true story of the Japanese internment recounts the plight of those whose lives were drastically altered simply because of their Japanese ancestry.

12.75 Stein, R. Conrad. **The Mexican Revolution 1910–1920.** New Discovery Books, 1994. 160 pp. ISBN 0-02-786950-4.

The Mexican Revolution began in 1910 with the overthrow of Porfirio Diaz who had ruled ruthlessly for thirty years. During this conflict called the "hacienda war," over two million Mexicans lost their lives. You can read about the conflicts; the leaders who emerged, such as Pancho Villa and Emiliano Zapata; and the eventual outcomes of this decade-long struggle against the wealthy descendants of Spaniards, in an effort to return control of the country to the common people.

12.76 Stein, Richard C. **The Montgomery Bus Boycott.** Children's Press, 1993. 32 pp. ISBN 0-516-06671-4.

Books in this series, called Cornerstones of Freedom, highlight African Americans who made significant contributions in the struggle for equal rights. Jim Crow laws imposed on southern blacks were humiliating, particularly one that forced them to sit in the back of a public bus and to give up even those seats if there were no available seats for whites. In *The Montgomery Bus Boycott*, readers meet Rosa Parks, who challenged those laws when she refused to give up her seat for a white person, an event that led to the famous bus boycott and the beginning of the end of segregation.

12.77 Stein, R. Conrad. **World War II: America Goes to War.** Enslow Publishers, 1994. 128 pp. ISBN 0-89490-525-2.

From the air war over Britain to the invasion of France, from the battles on the Russian front to the United States' entry into the war, from North Africa to Italy, you will follow World War II from its beginnings in 1939 to the ultimate surrender of the Germans in *World War II: America Goes to War,* part of the American War Series. In a second volume from this series, *The Korean War: The Forgotten War,* read about a war the American public largely ignored, even though 54,000 Americans died during the period from 1950 to the signing of the peace treaty at Panmunjom in 1953.

12.78 Stewart, Gail B. **The New Deal.** New Discovery Books, 1993. 111 pp. ISBN 0-02-788369-8.

What were the conditions in our country that brought about the Great Depression of the 1930s? This book explores the problems that led to the closing of banks and businesses and to mass unemployment. Franklin D. Roosevelt was the leader who soothed angry Americans with his promise of a "new deal for the American people." FDR led the country out of troubled times, sometimes making bitter enemies, often seeing his reforms fail, but never giving up his quest to reform the American government.

12.79 Strathern, Paul. **Exploration by Land.** New Discovery Books, 1994. 48 pp. ISBN 0-02-788375-2.

Silk, supposedly discovered when an emperor's wife accidentally dropped a cocoon in a cup of tea, was only one of the goods exchanged along the silk routes, the overland routes of trade between China and Europe that have existed for over 1600 years. In this book from the Silk and Spice Routes series, you can follow these routes and read of diverse peoples, difficult terrain, and the many adventures of the early traders as they traveled the silk routes.

12.80 Sullivan, George. **The Day the Women Got the Vote: A Photo History of the Women's Rights Movement.** Scholastic, 1994. 96 pp. ISBN 0-590-47560-6.

On November 2, 1920, American women voted for the first time. That historic moment, the culmination of efforts beginning in the early 1800s, was only a first step in achieving social, economic, legal, and political rights equal to those enjoyed by men in this country. Leaders such as Lucretia Mott, Susan B. Anthony, Mary McLeod Bethune, Barbara Jordan, and Betty Friedan are among those highlighted in this pictorial chronicle of the Women's Rights Movement in the United States.

12.81 Tanaka, Shelley. **The Disaster of the Hindenburg.** Scholastic Madison Press, 1993. 64 pp. ISBN 0-590-45750-0.

Many say the Hindenburg was the greatest airship ever built, a luxurious flying hotel over three times larger than today's largest passenger jet and as tall as a fifteen-story building. In the 1930s these airships, called zeppelins, carried passengers and cargo across the Atlantic and helped scientists gain information about the earth's atmosphere. This narrative details the disastrous final voyage of the Hindenburg, which crashed in flames in 1937. Photographs, diagrams, and survivors' memoirs present the horror of this tragedy.

12.82 Terkel, Susan Neiburg. **Colonial American Medicine.** Franklin Watts, 1993. 112 pp. ISBN 0-525-67412-8.

Because many religions did not permit human dissection, no one in colonial times really knew how the human body worked. Such ignorance led to long-time acceptance of the practices of bloodletting, purging, and blistering, practices which prevailed into the early 1800s. This detailed, well-documented account of the astoundingly primitive colonial medical practices provides fascinating reading for anyone curious about colonial medicine, the training or lack of training of doctors, and the eventual establishment of hospitals and schools of medicine. Another book in this series, *Colonial American Craftspeople,* offers as close a look at the people who provided the early colonists with everything from wigs to hats to buildings. For more information on Colonial America, look at *Colonial American Holidays and Entertainment* and *Colonial American Home Life.*

12.83 van der Linde, Laurel. **The Pony Express.** New Discovery Books, 1993. 72 pp. ISBN 0-02-759056-9.

Bob Haslam was just nineteen in 1860 when he rode horseback for 360 miles in 36 hours across some of the most dangerous parts of our country. He earned twenty-five dollars per week for his heroic efforts. He was one of eighty teenagers who became a part of the legendary Pony Express. This book traces the eighteen-month life of the Pony Express, the role it played in our expanding nation, and the reasons why it was such a colorful part of American history.

12.84 Ventura, Piero (with the collaboration of Max Casalini, Laura Battaglia, Marisa Murgo Ventura, and Antonella Toffolo). **Clothing: Garments, Styles, and Uses.** Houghton Mifflin, 1993. 64 pp. ISBN 0-395-66791-7.

What will I wear today? That's a question we ask each morning, and one that's been asked for thousands of years. And the answer remains the same. We want to wear something that's in style and comfortable, and that makes us look good. Over the years the particulars have changed, as people don all sorts of outfits to show off different colors, fabrics, and parts of their bodies. From skins to hoops to flappers, this history of clothing covers what has covered us.

12.85 Ventura, Piero (with the collaboration of Max Casalini, Pierluigi Longo, and Marisa Murgo Ventura). **Houses: Structures, Methods, and Ways of Living.** Houghton Mifflin, 1993. 64 pp. ISBN 0-395-66792-5.

While building a house may not create a home, it certainly says something about the people who live in it. Castle dwellers followed a different lifestyle from those who lived in slums. By looking at houses throughout history, along with their building materials, heating and plumbing conveniences, and furnishings, we can begin to understand our attempts to define ourselves by where we live.

12.86 **Visual Dictionary of Ancient Civilizations.** Dorling Kindersley, 1994. 64 pp. ISBN 1-56458-701-0.

This illustrated dictionary relating to ancient civilizations uses pictures of objects found in archeological sites to help you establish a minimal vocabulary for further explorations. The page on Greek architecture, for example, identifies each of the parts of the Temple of Hera, from pediment to frieze, from Doric column to cornice.

12.87 Wakin, Edward (with Daniel Wakin). **Photos That Made U.S. History: Volume 1, From the Civil War Era to the Atomic Age.** Walker & Company, 1993. 50 pp. ISBN 0-8027-8230-2.

In this series, Photos That Made U.S. History, you will see first hand the actual photographs from historic events. In *Volume 1, From the Civil War Era to the Atomic Age,* you see Dorothea Lange's photo of a migrant mother during the Great Depression and the image of the mushroom cloud over Hiroshima. *Volume 2, From the Cold War to the Space Age* brings us more close-ups, as we see photos of the earth from the moon, and Huynh Ut's famous picture of a nine-year-old Vietnamese girl, caught in the horrors of the Vietnam War. The images captured in photographs here have influenced the opinions and actions of Americans for decades.

12.88 Walker, Lou Ann. **Hand, Heart, & Mind: The Story of the Education of America's Deaf People.** Dial Books, 1994. 136 pp. ISBN 0-8037-1225-1.

The struggle for any minority to gain recognition is often a difficult one, and the education of deaf people in America is no exception. First, America's deaf people needed a method of communication, and then they had to work to obtain their civil rights. This story begins many years ago in Europe with the first steps toward a universal sign language, and concludes dramatically at Gallaudet University as deaf students fought for and won approval for their first president of the deaf.

12.89 Wills, Charles A. **A Historical Album of California.** Millbrook Press, 1994. 64 pp. ISBN 1-56294-479-7.

Whether you are doing research on a state for a class assignment, learning about states for fun, or looking to see how your home state became a part of the United States, the books in this series will help. For instance, in *A Historical Album of California,* you will read about how California got its name, what the gold rush meant to its growth, and how it influences the United States today. Other books in the series by Charles A. Will include *A Historical Album of Florida* and *A Historical Album of Illinois.*

12.90 Wormser, Richard. **The Iron Horse.** Walker & Company, 1993. 182 pp. ISBN 0-8027-8221-3.

Would you travel on a train if you had to jump off occasionally and chop down a few trees to keep it running? Passengers often endured that inconvenience and many more when they rode on the early trains. Richard Wormser takes you on a historical journey through the nineteenth and twentieth centuries. He shows how the railroad changed America forever and unified a sprawling nation.

12.91 Wormser, Richard. **Three Faces of Vietnam.** Franklin Watts, 1993. 158 pp. ISBN 0-531-11142-3.

The Vietnam War, a war that divided our own country, caused great tragedy in both Vietnam and the United States. Using the actual voices of participants and survivors, this book explores the controversial war from three different viewpoints: the American students who protested, the American soldiers who fought, and the Vietnamese people who suffered.

Understanding the Past: History

12.92 Yancey, Diane. **The Reunification of Germany.** Lucent Books, 1994. 128 pp. ISBN 1-56006-143-X.

For over forty years, the German people dreamed of being one country, and on October 3, 1990, the dream came true. The two former countries, East and West Germany, were different and not just because of the Berlin Wall that divided them. West Germany experienced democracy and financial growth while East Germany was repressed by communism. Joining the two countries meant merging social, economic, and environmental issues. In this book from the World in Conflict series, watch the Germans who worked together to make reunification a reality.

12.93 Zall, P. M. **Becoming American: Young People in the American Revolution.** Linnet Books, 1993. 196 pp. ISBN 0-208-02355-0.

What was it like to be a teenager during the American Revolution? These first-person accounts of twenty-three young people under the age of twenty-one provide us with a different view of this period in our history. From Solomon Drawn, age fourteen, in 1767 Newport, Rhode Island, to Sam Webb, a young lieutenant at the Battle of Bunker Hill in 1775, the diaries, journals, and letters of young people take us through the turbulent revolutionary years in our country.

12.94 Zevin, Jack, editor. **The Kingfisher Illustrated History of the World: 40,000 B.C. to Present Day.** Foreword by Magnus Magnusson. Contribution by Hazel Martell. Kingfisher Books, 1993. 795 pp. ISBN 1-85697-862-1.

Did you know that while the Great Wall of China was being built (214–204 B.C.), any builder who left a crack large enough to hold a nail was hanged on the spot? Did you know that the first piano was made in 1709? Did you know that in 1212 A.D. several thousand children crusaded to save the Holy Lands? All of these facts and thousands more are in this concise history of the world. Beginning with the Ice Age at about 40,000 B.C. and continuing to the 1990s, this book not only offers fun reading, but also supplies important information.

13 People to Know: Autobiography and Biography

13.1 Anderson, Kelly C. **Thomas Edison.** Lucent Books, 1994. 112 pp. ISBN 1-56006-041-7.

If you like science and enjoy reading about scientists, then check out this series called The Importance of . . . . It has books about scientists such as Thomas Edison, the famous inventor; Albert Einstein, the Nobel Prize–winning physicist famous for his theory of relativity; and Sir Isaac Newton.

13.2 Anderson, Madelyn Klein. **Edgar Allan Poe: A Mystery.** Franklin Watts, 1993. 158 pp. ISBN 0-531-13012-6.

This book, part of the Impact Biography series, chronicles the life of Edgar Allan Poe, poet and mystery author, known as the father of detective stories. Poe's life was as sad and mysterious as some of his tales. Orphaned at the age of three and dead at the early age of forty, Poe spent much of his life depressed. Mysteries continue to surround him, even long after his death; each year, on the anniversary of his birthday, an unknown person leaves a bottle of brandy and three roses at his grave. Other books in the series include *Lyndon Baines Johnson* by Dennis Eskow; *Ella Fitzgerald, Jazz Singer Supreme* by Carolyn Wyman; and *Louis Armstrong, Swinging, Singing Satchmo* by Sandford Brown.

13.3 Anderson, Margaret J. **Charles Darwin: Naturalist.** Enslow, 1994. 128 pp. ISBN 0-89490-476-0.

If you like to read about the lives of scientists, then you will enjoy the series called Great Minds of Science. For example, in one book, *Charles Darwin: Naturalist,* you learn about Charles, a quiet boy who liked to take long walks and to collect shells, rocks, insects, birds' eggs, and coins. Nobody expected him to grow up to be a famous naturalist whose book, *The Origin of Species,* would cause much controversy. Other books in this series include *Marie Curie: Discoverer of Radium* by Margaret Poynter and *William Harvey: Discoverer of How Blood Circulates* by Lisa Yount.

13.4 Andronik, Catherine M. **Prince of Humbugs: A Life of P. T. Barnum.** Atheneum, 1994. 136 pp. ISBN 0-689-31796-4.

Taylor Barnum's reputation for being the laziest boy in town did not keep him from making and losing fortunes. He discovered that the public is entertained by and will pay money to see human and animal oddities. He eventually became the owner of the "Greatest Show on Earth."

13.5 Andronik, Catherine M. **Kindred Spirit: A Biography of L. M. Montgomery, Creator of Anne of Green Gables.** Atheneum, 1993. 160 pp. ISBN 0-689-31671-2.

Maud's mother died when she was very young, and she was raised by her grandparents on Prince Edward Island, the place which became the setting for her most famous book, *Anne of Green Gables*. She wanted to get an education and to write, but her family thought she should marry a local farmer. She worked as a teacher and a journalist and kept on writing in spite of disappointments along the way.

13.6 Archbold, Rick. **Deep-Sea Explorer: The Story of Robert Ballard, Discoverer of the Titanic.** Scholastic, 1994. 144 pp. ISBN 0-590-47232-1.

Dr. Robert Ballard had explored many parts of the ocean depths in his tiny submarine, and he knew that finding the Titanic, the most famous ship to sink to the bottom of the ocean, would take a lot of skill and a lot of luck. He had both. His crew's time underwater was almost gone when they spotted the huge hulk two miles down!

13.7 Archer, Jules. **They Had a Dream: The Civil Rights Struggle from Frederick Douglass to Marcus Garvey to Martin Luther King to Malcolm X.** Viking, 1993. 258 pp. ISBN 0-670-84494-2.

Frederick Douglass freed himself and others from slavery; Marcus Garvey organized the Universal Negro Improvement Association and encouraged blacks to have pride and to seek power and control of their own lives; Martin Luther King organized peaceful civil disobedience and urged integration to achieve equality; and Malcolm X felt that violence and separation were the only paths to liberation. Archer tells their stories and explains their impact on American society.

13.8 Averill, Esther. **King Philip: The Indian Chief.** Illustrated by Vera Belsky. Linnet Books, 1993. 147 pp. ISBN 0-208-2357-7.

King Philip's father believed that the new colonists could live in peace with the Wampanoags and the other tribes who lived in what is now New England. But as more settlers came, the natives decided to fight for their lands. Bravery, treachery, greed, and misunderstanding were all parts of King Philip's War, 1675-1676, when an entire Native American community was wiped out.

13.9 Baldwin, Joyce. **DNA Pioneer: James Watson and the Double Helix.** Walker & Company, 1994. 152 pp. ISBN 0-8027-8297-3.

This book tells the story of James Watson, the genius who discovered the double helix, the twisting spiral which defines the genetic makeup of all organisms. As a young man, he was a shy contestant on the "Quiz Kid" radio show, and at age fifteen, he entered the University of Chicago. As an adult, he won the Nobel Prize.

13.10 Bentley, Bill. **Ulysses S. Grant.** Franklin Watts, 1993. 64 pp. ISBN 0-531-20162-7.

Did you know that Ulysses S. Grant was named Hiram Ulysses Grant at birth? Did you know that those who served with him in the Civil War considered him a "soldier's soldier" and would have followed him anywhere? This informative biography of our eighteenth President goes beyond his fame as a Civil War leader and President of the United States, to reveal information about his childhood, his formal and informal education, and his devotion to his family.

13.11 Bruce, Harry. **Maud: The Life of L. M. Montgomery.** Seal Bantam Books, 1994. 166 pp. ISBN 0-553-56584-2.

From the time she was a girl living on Prince Edward Island in Canada, Lucy Maud Montgomery dreamed of becoming a writer. Although her family disapproved, Maud wrote constantly, drawing on her own experiences and creating the beloved character Anne of Green Gables. If you've loved her books or enjoyed the television series based on them, you'll enjoy learning more about this spirited woman who was determined to make her dream come true.

13.12 Burchard, Peter. **"We'll Stand by the Union": Robert Gould Shaw and the Black 54th Massachusetts Regiment.** Facts on File, 1993. 132 pp. ISBN 0-8160-2609-2.

Robert Gould Shaw, the son of abolitionists, grew up to be the white commander of the first regiment of black soldiers to be formed after the Emancipation Proclamation. This book tells of his youth, but mostly about his bravery and that of the African American soldiers under his command, who knew that if they were captured, they would probably be killed rather than taken as prisoners of war.

13.13 Burford, Betty. **Al Gore: United States Vice President.** Enslow, 1994. 128 pp. ISBN 0-89490-496-5.

Al Gore, born into a political family, grew up with two separate lives, one in Washington D.C., when Congress was in session, and one on his family's 250-acre farm in Tennessee. Although both he and his father opposed the Vietnam War, he enlisted shortly after college graduation and his marriage to his childhood sweetheart. His experiences in Vietnam troubled him. Eventually he decided upon a political career—one that has taken him to high office as Vice President of the United States.

13.14 Ryan, Cary, compiler and editor. **Louisa May Alcott: Her Girlhood Diary.** Illustrated by Mark Graham. BridgeWater Books, 1993. 56 pp. ISBN 0-8167-3139-X.

Louisa May Alcott, who wrote *Little Women* and other stories, destroyed most of her girlhood diary. Here, remaining excerpts, letters, and poems are combined with the editor's notes to show you the real "Jo March," with her "dreadful" temper. Experiencing extreme poverty as a child, Louisa May vowed that she would earn enough to give her family necessities and more.

13.15 Colman, Penny. **A Woman Unafraid: The Achievements of Frances Perkins.** Illustrated with family photographs. Atheneum, 1993. 129 pp. ISBN 0-689-31853-7.

Frances Perkins, Secretary of Labor under President Franklin Roosevelt, was the first woman cabinet member. A career woman when few women were, she commuted to Washington for her new job because her husband wanted to stay in New York. Feeling a real mission to better the lives of workers, she was instrumental in setting up Social Security, unemployment insurance, fairer wages, and safer working conditions.

13.16 Cooper, Floyd. **Coming Home: From the Life of Langston Hughes.** Philomel Books, 1994. 32 pp. ISBN 0-399-22682-6.

As a little boy, Langston Hughes would sit on the porch listening to his grandmother tell stories of black heroes. While growing up, he dreamed of living with his actress mother and his lawyer father, who had left him and moved to Mexico. As an adult, he moved to Harlem, where he wrote stories and poems and came to realize that home was within himself.

13.17 Cytron, Barry, and Phyllis Cytron. **Myriam Mendilow: Mother of Jerusalem.** Lerner Publications, 1994. 128 pp. ISBN 0-8225-4919-0.

Myriam was born in 1909 in Safed, a town overlooking the sea of Galilee and the Jordan Valley. Her mother wanted for her daughters more than her father and local custom encouraged. So Myriam learned to read. She grew up and became a social worker, committed to making life better for the elderly in Jerusalem.

13.18 Denenberg, Barry. **The True Story of J. Edgar Hoover and the FBI.** Scholastic, 1993. 202 pp. ISBN 0-590-43168-4.

As the United States' top law-enforcement officer for nearly half a century, J. Edgar Hoover changed the image of the Federal Bureau of Investigation (FBI) from a bungling, corrupt organization to a highly regarded government division. Under Hoover's leadership, the FBI fought organized crime and communism with new scientific law enforcement. But, Hoover's domain began to topple in the early 1970s when the FBI's Domestic Security files were stolen. Then, some people realized that the agency had often been operating outside the law.

13.19 Dolan, Ellen M. **Susan Butcher and the Iditarod Trail.** Walker & Company, 1993. 103 pp. ISBN 0-8027-8211-6.

When Susan Butcher was eight years old, she wrote a paper, "I Hate the City." Her love for the out-of-doors led to participation in field hockey, basketball, softball, swimming, and sailing. Eventually, she became a champion musher in the Iditarod dog-sled race in Alaska. This yearly race from Anchorage to Nome, Alaska, is a grueling challenge for drivers and dogs. To win it once is outstanding; to win it three times in a row, as Susan did, is close to incredible.

13.20 Douglas, William O. **Muir of the Mountains.** Illustrated by Daniel San Souci. Sierra Club Books for Children, 1994. 105 pp. ISBN 0-87156-505-6.

John Muir's earliest memories were of his love for wild places and creatures in both his native Scotland and in Wisconsin, where he moved in 1849 at the age of eleven. He grew up to be a naturalist and an inventor. Among his inventions was a clock that caused his bed to tip, dumping him on the floor when it was time to get up! He walked over much of the country and, believing that wilderness must be preserved, he worked to create national parks and helped to found the Sierra Club.

13.21 Duran, Gloria. **Malinche: Slave Princess of Cortez.** Linnet Books, 1993. 221 pp. ISBN 0-208-02343-7.

Astrologers told Teteotcingo, an Aztec prince, that his child would rule over all the Aztec empire. When Malianali was born, her father held a huge celebration, even though she was a girl. But after his death, Malianali's mother sold her into slavery, drastically changing the life of the little princess. She became La Malinche, translator, interpreter, and mistress to Cortez, the Spanish conquistador.

13.22 Durrett, Dean. **Jim Henson.** Lucent Books, 1994. 112 pp. ISBN 1-56006-048-4.

Whether you like dance, classical art, classical music, or the fun world of puppets, the books in this series called The Importance of . . . can give you information about the people involved in those arts. *Jim Henson* takes a close look at the creator of the Muppets. *Louis Armstrong* by Adam Wong tells jazz lovers the story of that famous trumpeter. *Martha Graham* by Paula Bryant Pratt describes the life of the famous dancer. *Wolfgang Amadeus Mozart* by Roger K. Blakely and *Michelangelo* by William W. Lace take you back in time to those two famous artists, one a concert pianist and the latter a painter and sculptor.

13.23 Evans, J. Edward. **Charles Darwin: Revolutionary Biologist.** Lerner Publications, 1993. 112 pp. ISBN 0-8225-4914-X.

Charles, a shy and lonely boy, could not decide what he wanted to be when he grew up. His father wanted him to be a doctor or a clergyman, certainly not a biologist. But he allowed Charles to go on a voyage from 1831 to 1836, during which he collected plants and animals to study. This trip around the world changed his life.

13.24 Filipovic, Zlata. **Zlata's Diary.** Viking Penguin, 1994. 220 pp. ISBN 0-670-85724-6.

Eleven-year-old Zlata lived in Sarajevo when the war began. She wrote about the war in her diary. In September of 1992, she wrote, "Another innocent victim of this disgusting war, another child among the thousands of other children killed in Sarajevo. Oh, God, what is happening here? Hasn't there been enough?" Later, in October 1993 she wrote, "Life in a closed circle continues . . . a life of waiting, of fear, a life where you want the circle to open and the sun of peace to shine down on you again." Like Anne Frank, Zlata has offered us a child's view of a tragic situation, with clarity and wisdom.

13.25 Fireside, Bryna J. **Is There a Woman in the House . . . or Senate?** Albert Whitman & Company, 1994. 144 pp. ISBN 0-8075-3662-8.

The first Congress of the United States met in 1789, but it was not until 1916 that a woman served in Congress. The percentage of women in the House and Senate is still small, considering that women make up more than half the nation's population. This book tells the stories of ten women from different ethnic backgrounds, different parts of the U.S., and different political parties, who have been elected to Congress.

13.26 Fleming, Alice. **P. T. Barnum: The World's Greatest Showman.** Walker & Company, 1993. 160 pp. ISBN 0-8027-8324-5.

Phineas Taylor Barnum was born in 1810 in a society which loved nothing better than practical jokes. Young Taylor learned early to laugh at adversity. Disastrous fires and getting caught with "fakes" in his museum could not stop him from becoming a great promoter, bringing to America tiny General Tom Thumb, opera singer Jenny Lind, and Jumbo the elephant. His name became almost synonymous with the circus, the "Greatest Show on Earth."

13.27 Fleming, Thomas. **Harry S Truman, President.** Walker & Company, 1993. 136 pp. ISBN 0-8027-8267-1.

Harry Truman was an ordinary boy who grew up to be an extraordinary soldier and then became distinguished as a President who could make hard decisions and was willing to take responsibility for them. He really believed the sign on his desk which said, "The buck stops here." In this book, you can read about a man who knew what he believed in and stood by his convictions.

13.28 Fox, Mary Virginia. **Bette Bao Lord: Novelist and Chinese Voice for Change.** Children's Press, 1993. 107 pp. ISBN 0-516-03291-7.

Bette Bao, author of *Spring Moon* and *The Year of the Boar and Jackie Robinson,* is a product of two cultures. Born in China, but living in the United States when the communists took over in China, she and her family could not go home because her father had worked for the Nationalists. She grew up, married, raised a family, wrote, and eventually returned to China as the wife of the American ambassador.

13.29 Freedman, Russell. **Eleanor Roosevelt: A Life of Discovery.** Photographs from various sources. Clarion Books, 1993. 198 pp. ISBN 0-89919-862-7.

Eleanor Roosevelt, niece of President Teddy Roosevelt and wife of President Franklin Roosevelt, regarded herself as an "ugly duckling." Her mother called her "Granny," and she described herself as a "child without beauty and painfully shy." Orphaned at a young age, she was raised by her grandmother. Eventually, she was regarded by many as "First Lady of the World." She was not only the President's wife, but also a public figure in her own right.

13.30 Fritz, Jean. **Harriet Beecher Stowe and the Beecher Preachers.** G. P. Putnam's Sons, 1994. 144 pp. ISBN 0-399-22666-4.

When Harriet Beecher was born in 1811, her father said, "Wish it had been a boy." He wanted her eight brothers to be preachers, but he paid little attention to his four daughters. Harriet "longed to do something" and "to make some declaration on my own account." As an adult, she did make that declaration as she wrote articles and books, including *Uncle Tom's Cabin,* which influenced the way people felt about slavery.

13.31 Gallo, Don. **Presenting Richard Peck.** Dell/Laurel Leaf, 1993. 194 pp. ISBN 0-440-21888-8.

Unlike many writers, Richard Peck did not begin writing until he was thirty-seven years old. But when he did begin, he created books that lots of people now call their favorites. His books include *Are You in the House Alone?, Father Figure, Princess Ashley, Unfinished Portrait of Jessica,* and *Bel-Air Bambi and the Mall Rats.* In Gallo's book about Peck, you can read about Peck as a teacher, a writer, and a person.

13.32 Gherman, Beverly. **E. B. White: Some Writer!** Beech Tree, 1994. 136 pp. ISBN 0-688-12826-2.

Elwyn White, as a child, trembled when he was called on to recite in class. As an adult, he refused to speak in public even when he was presented awards. At Cornell, friends predicted he would go far, nicknaming him "Andy" for Andrew White, the first president of the college. This book tells of the personal life and career of E. B. White, who wrote extensively for both adults and children, but who is most remembered for *Charlotte's Web.*

13.33 Graff, Nancy Price. **Where the River Runs: A Portrait of a Refugee Family.** Photographs by Richard Howard. Little, Brown and Company, 1993. 71 pp. ISBN 0-316-32287-3.

Buttra, Oudom, and their mother Sohka Prek immigrate to America to escape the civil war in their native Cambodia. In Boston, their apartment is in a neighborhood of newcomers. Sohka works and attends school to learn English. The book enters the life of these modern pilgrims, as they attend school, watch TV, and shop in America. All the while, they remember their former home, retaining many Cambodian customs as they learn new ways.

13.34 Greenfield, Eloise and Lessie Jones Little. **Childtimes: A Three-Generation Memoir.** Drawings by Jerry Pinkney; photographs from the authors' family albums. HarperTrophy, 1993. 178 pp. ISBN 0-06-446134-3.

Three African American women—grandmother, mother, and daughter—relate charming recollections of their "childtimes" in Parmele, North Carolina. Over a seventy-year time span, Parmele evolves from a bustling mill town to a train town and finally to a going-back-to-visit-in-the-summer hometown. Three voices communicate the simple, everyday pleasures and challenges of childhood: "dumb" suppers, friends, frog houses, new shoes, siblings, chores. Their lives are separate from mainstream America and are not untouched by racism, but their days are rich and full in spite of it.

13.35 Handler, Andrew, and Susan V. Meschel, compilers and editors. **Young People Speak: Surviving the Holocaust in Hungary.** Franklin Watts, 1993. 160 pp. ISBN 0-531-11044-3.

Eva remembers sleeping in a dog house in winter. Peter remembers being forced into a Swiss safe house and living with sixteen other relatives in one room. Susan remembers always hunting for food or something to chew. These are three of the eleven contributors to this volume, people who were children in Hungary during World War II. While none were sent to concentration camps, they recount their personal memories of the other horrors thrust on European Jews.

13.36 Heyes, Eileen. **Adolf Hitler.** Millbrook Press, 1994. 168 pp. ISBN 1-56294-343-X.

Adolf Hitler, as a child, adored his mother but disagreed with his father about almost everything. His ambition to be an artist was thwarted when he was turned down by the Fine Arts Academy in Vienna. He buried his disappointment by getting involved with anti-Semitic groups flourishing at the time, and then he went on to become the leader of the infamous SS and Germany's Third Reich.

13.37 Hurwitz, Johanna. **Leonard Bernstein: A Passion for Music.** Illustrated by Sonia O. Lisker. Jewish Publication Society, 1993. 72 pp. ISBN 0-8276-0501-3.

Leonard Bernstein loved music from the time he was a little boy, but his father told him to quit playing the piano. He did not want Lennie to be a musician because he was afraid that he would not be able to support himself. But nothing stopped this young man from pursuing his passion. He became a pianist, a composer, and a conductor of classical and popular music, one of the most beloved musicians of his time.

13.38 Kerr, M. E. **Me Me Me Me Me: Not a Novel.** HarperTrophy, 1994 (originally published in 1983). 212 pp. ISBN 0-06-446163-7.

Maryjane Meaker relates many funny episodes from her growing-up years, including how she became M. E. Kerr, the author of *Fell, Linger,* and *Dinky Hocker Shoots Smack,* among others. In this book, she shares excerpts from her diary and tells about the real people behind some of the fictional characters in her novels.

13.39 Klausner, Janet. **Sequoyah's Gift: A Portrait of the Cherokee Leader.** HarperCollins, 1993. 111 pp. ISBN 0-06-021235-7.

Sequoyah, a Cherokee Indian, was born around 1770 in what is now Tennessee. An artistic young man, Sequoyah grew up fascinated by the white man's "talking leaves" or letters of the alphabet. At the time, the Cherokee language had no written form. But Sequoyah changed that by giving his people a way to write down their language. A leader of his people in many ways, he represented the Cherokees in Washington, attempting to keep the Cherokee on their homelands.

13.40 Knudson, R. R. **The Wonderful Pen of May Swenson.** Macmillan, 1993. 112 pp. ISBN 0-02-750915-X.

Swenson was considered one of America's finest poets. In this biography, you'll read the story of her gritty determination to become a first-rate poet and to support herself through her writing. The early years were marked by May's move from a large and loving family in Utah to New York City, where she would pursue her dream. She eventually overcame poverty and rejection, when national magazines began to publish her work. Here's a biography for aspiring writers who share Swenson's dream.

13.41 Krull, Kathleen. **Lives of Musicians: Good Times, Bad Times (And What the Neighbors Thought).** Illustrated by Kathryn Hewitt. Harcourt Brace Jovanovich, 1993. 96 pp. ISBN 0-15-248010-2.

Which German composer was so small when he began taking piano lessons that he had to stand on the piano bench to reach the keys? Which Austrian composer was afraid of ghosts and had a pet grasshopper? Which American composer once pounded the piano keys so hard during a concert that he had to stop and bandage his hands? Find out the answers to these questions along with many more lesser-known facts in this fascinating book that looks at twenty famous musicians.

13.42 Linnea, Sharon. **Raoul Wallenberg: The Man Who Stopped Death.** Jewish Publication Society, 1993. 168 pp. ISBN 0-8276-0448-3.

Raoul Wallenberg, a Swedish diplomat, saved the lives of thousands of Jews in Hungary in the closing days of World War II by issuing them Swedish identification papers. He also established safe houses, places where Jews could hide to avoid arrest by Nazi soldiers. While we know what has happened to the people he helped, no one knows what happened to him after his arrest by the Russians at the end of the war.

13.43 Lewis-Ferguson, Julinda. **Alvin Ailey, Jr.: A Life in Dance.** Walker & Company, 1994. 84 pp. ISBN 0-8027-8239-6.

Alvin Ailey, African American dancer and choreographer, combined the gospel, blues, and dance-hall songs of his childhood with his knowledge of ballet, to create dances of his own making, such as "Revelations" and "Blues Suite." He has helped to make modern dance an art form appreciated by many instead of a few.

13.44 Marrin, Albert. **Unconditional Surrender: U. S. Grant and the Civil War.** Atheneum, 1994. 200 pp. ISBN 0-689-318370-5.

Lyss Grant, as his family called him, was an unknown shop clerk at the start of the Civil War. However, within three years, he led the United States armies to victory and became the eighteenth President of our country. From Shiloh to Vicksburg to Appomatox, this well-documented account uses diaries, letters, and vivid prose to tell the story of U. S. Grant and his role in ending our country's most destructive war.

13.45 McCurdy, Michael, editor. **Escape from Slavery: The Boyhood of Frederick Douglass in His Own Words.** Illustrated by Michael McCurdy. Alfred A. Knopf, 1994. 65 pp. ISBN 0-679-84652-2.

Frederick Augustus Washington Bailey was born a slave. Always longing for freedom, Frederick educated himself so that when he was a young man, he was able to escape to freedom. He ran away to Massachusetts, and to protect himself, he changed his name to Frederick Douglass. In Massachusetts he worked to end slavery. Now, Michael McCurdy has brought together Douglass's comments and thoughts about his life and put them into this version of his boyhood.

13.46 McPherson, Stephanie Sammartino. **Peace and Bread: The Story of Jane Addams.** Carolrhoda Books, 1993. 96 pp. ISBN 0-87614-792-9.

Jane Addams, born in 1861, grew up in a wealthy close-knit family, busy with school, dating, and parties. As a young woman, she became interested in doing something for those less fortunate than she. Eventually, she founded Hull-House, one of the first settlement homes for immigrants. She worked hard to implement child labor laws. Later she became a women's rights activist and a proponent for international peace. Her life's work culminated in winning the Nobel Peace Prize.

13.47 Medearis, Angela Shelf. **Little Louis and the Jazz Band: The Story of Louis "Satchmo" Armstrong.** Illustrated by Anna Rich. Lodestar Books, 1994. 42 pp. ISBN 0-525-67424-1.

Little Louis and the Jazz Band, part of the Rainbow Biography series, explains how seven-year-old Louis Armstrong discovered that when he took the end off the horn that announced his presence to his coal customers, he could play tunes. From an early age, he loved the music he heard around his New Orleans neighborhood, and he grew up to be one of the great jazz musicians of all time.

13.48 Meltzer, Milton, editor. **Lincoln: In His Own Words.** Illustrated by Stephen Alcorn. Harcourt Brace & Company, 1993. 226 pp. ISBN 0-15-2454387-3.

Lincoln tells us that for as long as he could remember, he liked to read—*The Bible, Pilgrim's Progress, Robinson Crusoe,* or anything! We learn this and many other things about this nation's sixteenth

President in *Lincoln: In His Own Words.* Meltzer pulls excerpts from Lincoln's speeches, letters, and papers to give us a good look at the man who led the nation from division to unity.

13.49 Myers, Walter Dean. **Malcolm X: By Any Means Necessary.** Scholastic, 1993. 210 pp. ISBN 0-590-46484-1.

Malcolm Little's earliest memories were of his father speaking out for the rights of blacks. When Malcolm was six, his father was run over by a streetcar, leaving his mother a widow with ten children to raise. He grew up to become a street-wise teenager and later a controversial leader of the Nation of Islam, respected by thousands, but a target of the FBI. His influence is still felt, thirty years after his assassination.

13.50 Pflaum, Rosalynd. **Marie Curie and Her Daughter Irene.** Illustrated with family photographs. Lerner, 1993. 144 pp. ISBN 0-8225-4915-8.

Manya Sklodowska was born into a poor family in Poland in 1867. After graduating with honors from high school, she moved to Paris and excelled at her scientific studies at the Sorbonne. She met Pierre, a promising young physicist, whom she married. Together, they discovered radium and helped in the fight against cancer. Their daughters, Eve and Irene, grew up in their parents' lab, and Irene became a scientist, too. Between them, Irene and Marie won three Nobel Prizes.

13.51 Plowden, Martha Ward. **Famous Firsts of Black Women.** Illustrated by Ronald Jones. Pelican Publishing Company, 1993. 155 pp. ISBN 0-99289-973-2.

If you are interested in finding out about African American women who have made notable contributions to America, read this collection of biographical sketches. You'll read about bank presidents and sports figures, poets, abolitionists, and ambassadors. Included are such women as Barbara Jordan and Shirley Chisholm, U.S. Representatives; Marion Anderson and Leontyne Price, opera singers; Wilma Rudolph, an Olympic Gold Medalist; and Althea Gibson, tennis star.

13.52 Quiri, Patricia Ryan. **Dolley Madison.** Franklin Watts, 1993. 64 pp. ISBN 0-531-20097-3.

Dolley Payne Todd, left widowed with a young son, was courted by James Madison, already an important man in the young United States. As his wife, during the War of 1812, she saw Washington burned and the White House destroyed. However, she helped to keep up spirits and to get women interested in politics. Other biographies in the First Books series include: *Robert E. Lee* by Marian G. Cannan, the story of the general who commanded the Confederate forces during the Civil War; *Helen Keller* by Lois Markam, the story of Keller's triumph over blindness and deafness; and *Martha Washington* by Joan Marsh, the story of the first First Lady.

13.53 Rainey, Richard. **The Monster Factory.** New Discovery Books, 1993. 128 pp. ISBN 0-02-775663-7.

Mary Shelley, wife of poet Percy Bysshe Shelley, wrote *Frankenstein.* How did she come to create such a monster? It happened one night in June, 1816, when the Shelleys and friends were telling ghost stories. Lord Byron, the poet, suggested that each tell a story, and Mary's story was about Frankenstein. Learn how other writers created their monsters, such as Robert Louis Stevenson's Dr. Jekyll and Mr. Hyde, Washington Irving's headless horseman, and Bram Stoker's Dracula.

13.54 Reiss, Johanna. **The Journey Back.** HarperCollins, 1993. 212 pp. ISBN 0-690-01252-7.

In her autobiography, *The Upstairs Room,* Annie tells of spending three years hiding during World War II with the Oosterveld family, whom she comes to love. In this sequel, she tells about the difficulties when her own family reunites after the war. She feels guilty for missing the Oostervelds and frustrated that she never seems to please her new stepmother. Annie survives the hardships of postwar Holland and discovers that she can love both her own family and her wartime family.

13.55 Schraff, Anne. **Women of Peace: Nobel Peace Prize Winners.** Enslow Publishers, 1994. 112 pp. ISBN 0-89490-493-0.

Mairead Corrigan is horrified when her niece and nephews, ages eight, two, and six months, are killed, and their mother is badly injured. Betty Williams, a terrified witness to the accident, starts a petition against the violence between Catholics and Protestants in Northern Ireland. These two ordinary women begin a peace movement which ultimately earns them the Nobel Prize. Their story, along with the stories of other women including Mother Teresa, Jane Addams, and Alva Myrdal, is told in this book about Nobel Peace Prize winners.

13.56 Sherrow, Victoria. **Mohandas Gandhi: The Power of the Spirit.** Millbrook Press, 1994. 128 pp. ISBN 1-56294-335-9.

Mohandas Gandhi, born into India's middle class, developed a profound sense of right and wrong. Instead of living the comfortable life he could have had, he chose to work for equality in South Africa, freedom from British rule for India, and peace between India and Pakistan.

13.57 Sinnott, Susan. **Extraordinary Asian Pacific Americans.** Children's Press, 1993. 269 pp. ISBN 0-516-03052-X.

This book is a collection of biographies of Americans who have their roots in the Far East—politicians, athletes, artists, musicians, writers, actors, and scientists. The author provides an introductory chapter about each ethnic group, then follows with biographies of people from that culture, who have made a difference in American history. Skater Kristi Yamaguchi and diver Greg Louganis share the spotlight with Senator Hiram Fong, writer Bette Bao Lord, and many others.

13.58 Slater, Jack. **Malcolm X.** Children's Press, 1993. 32 pp. ISBN 0-516-06669-2.

Malcolm X by Jack Slater, in the Cornerstones of Freedom series, tells of one of the most influential black leaders in the civil rights movement. Follow Malcolm X, born Malcolm Little, from his childhood in Nebraska to his troubled youth in Boston and finally to his emergence as an articulate spokesman for the Nation of Islam. In 1965, he was murdered by three assassins.

13.59 Sleator, William. **Oddballs.** Dutton Children's Books, 1993. 134 pp. ISBN 0-525-45057-2.

With apologies to his family, popular science-fiction writer Sleator presents in this volume nine stories about one family—his—which reflect the growing-up years. In this loosely autobiographical collection, readers meet Bill, the older brother, Vicky, the only sister, and Danny and Tycho, the competitive younger siblings. Readers of all ages will identify with and delight in the stories in this collection.

13.60 St. George, Judith. **Crazy Horse.** G. P. Putnam's Sons, 1994. 192 pp. ISBN 0-399-22667-2.

A young Sioux, Curly, so called because of his wavy hair, watches as the soldiers and his tribe battle over who will control his family's hunting grounds. As he grows up, bravery earns him his adult name, Crazy Horse, and ultimately a part in the Battle of Little Big Horn.

13.61 St. George, Judith. **Dear Mr. Bell . . . Your Friend, Helen Keller.** Beech Tree Press, 1993. 96 pp. ISBN 0-688-12814-9.

It was Alexander Graham Bell, inventor of the telephone, who first advised Helen Keller's father to get a private tutor for her, one trained in working with deaf children. Later that year, when Helen was seven, she wrote to thank him for freeing her from her "prison" of deafness and blindness. This story tells of their lives and of their friendship, which lasted until his death thirty-five years later.

13.62 Stacey, T. J. **Hillary Rodham Clinton: Activist First Lady.** Enslow Publishers, 1994. 128 pp. ISBN 0-89490-583-X.

In this People to Know series, you can learn about the life of the woman who serves as First Lady during the Clinton administration, Hillary Rodham Clinton. Young Hillary, hoping to become an astronaut, discovered that females were ineligible for the space program. Her parents had taught her that all people who worked for their goals could achieve them, yet as a female she was stymied. Later, Martin Luther King and John F. Kennedy taught her that others were oppressed, sparking her interest in the law. She became a lawyer and eventually assumed the role of First Lady. Another book in this series, *Alex Haley, Author of Roots,* by Doreen Gonzales, introduces you to Haley and his writings. After twelve years researching his family's history, Haley published the story of his past.

13.63 Stanley, Diane, and Peter Vennema. **Cleopatra.** Morrow Junior Books, 1994. 32 pp. ISBN 0-688-10413-4.

In 30 B.C., Cleopatra became queen of Egypt; she was only fifteen years old! She dreamed of a world under Egyptian rule. Legend has it that she was powerful because of her beauty, but the authors tell us that she was strong because of her intelligence, her courage, and her charm. This beautiful picture book not only teaches us about an amazing woman, but also shows us what her world might have looked like.

13.64 Stanley, Diane, and Peter Vennema. **Charles Dickens: The Man Who Had Great Expectations.** Illustrated by Diane Stanley. Morrow Junior Books, 1993. 48 pp. ISBN 0-688-09110-5.

When he was a boy, Dickens's father showed him a huge house, advised him to work hard, and told him that one day he would live there. However, soon after his twelfth birthday, his father ended up in debtors' prison, and Charles went to work in a factory. Though his family fortunes finally changed for the better, he never forgot the misery of poverty. Many of his stories, *A Christmas Carol, Oliver Twist,* and *David Copperfield,* for example, reflect these memories, colored by his imagination.

13.65 Stefoff, Rebecca. **Herman Melville.** Silver Burdett Press, 1994. 156 pp. ISBN 0-671-86771-7.

Herman Melville, one of America's literary giants, had nearly been forgotten when at age sixty-six, he retired to "put his papers in order." Little did anyone at the time know that what he was doing was writing another masterpiece, *Billy Budd.* Certainly not forgotten today, Melville, author of *Moby Dick,* had a rough childhood and adventurous young adulthood. In Stefoff's biography of this man, you can read about his challenges, his motivations, and the books he wrote.

13.66 Sullivan, George. **Mathew Brady: His Life and Photographs.** Cobblehill/Dutton, 1994. 136 pp. ISBN 0-525-65186-1.

As a young man, Brady became skilled at the new art of photography, and as time went by, he photographed most of the prominent people of his day, recognizing that photographs were one way to provide a record of events and people. His pictures of the dead and wounded in the Civil War showed people the horrors of war, and it is for these photos that he is most remembered.

13.67 Taylor, Richard L. **The First Solo Flight around the World: The Story of Wiley Post and His Airplane.** Franklin Watts, 1993. 64 pp. ISBN 0-531-20160-0.

Wiley Post refused to give up his dreams of being a pilot, even after losing an eye in an oil-field accident. This biography traces the famous aviator's life from his early years as a farm boy, to his days of glory as a record breaker, and finally to his fatal crash in Alaska with Will Rogers, the famed humorist. A major focus of the story is Wiley's record-setting solo flight around the world in 1933 aboard the *Winnie Mae.*

13.68 Toll, Nelly S. **Behind the Secret Window: A Memoir of a Hidden Childhood during World War II.** Dial, 1993. 160 pp. ISBN 0-8037-1362-2.

Nelly Toll, a Jewish girl, survived World War II by hiding in the bedroom of neighbors. To keep herself quiet and occupied, she spent her days painting with watercolors. She painted the things that were important to her: pictures of school, her friends, her family celebrations, flowers, and trees in the park. Some of her pictures are reproduced in this book.

13.69 van der Rol, Ruud, and Rian Verhoeven. **Anne Frank, beyond the Diary: A Photographic Remembrance.** Translated by Tony Langham and Plym Peters. Viking, 1993. 112 pp. ISBN 0-670-84932-4.

Diary excerpts, interviews, numerous photographs, illustrations, maps, and historical essays reveal the lives behind Anne Frank's remarkable diary. This handsome and informative photobiography, prepared by the Anne Frank House in Amsterdam, uses numerous photos from the personal collections of Otto Frank and Miep Gies to take the reader to Anne's life before the Frank family went into hiding in the Annex and to answer questions about the influences on her early life.

13.70 Watkins, Yoko Kawashima. **My Brother, My Sister, and I.** Bradbury, 1994. 275 pp. ISBN 0-02-79526-9.

The fortunes of thirteen-year-old Yoko and her family, who have lived in Korea, change as she and her brother and sister try to make their way in a Japan where they discover that they are no longer welcome. Their father is in prison. When their mother dies, they face homelessness, poverty, illness, and false accusations in this hostile land. Sequel to *Far from the Bamboo Grove*.

13.71 Zassenhaus, Hiltgunt. **Walls: Resisting the Third Reich—One Woman's Story.** Beacon, 1993. 248 pp. ISBN 0-8070-6345-2.

Hiltgunt Zassenhaus, a person with strong convictions, was seventeen years old in 1933 when Hitler took over Germany. Taking several trips to Denmark and to England gave her a taste of the freedom that was scarce in Germany. Fluent in Scandinavian languages, she was able to get a job as translator for political prisoners. As the war continued, she smuggled food and medicine to these prisoners at great risk to her own life, acts which later won her a Nobel Peace Prize.

13.72 Zindel, Paul. **The Pigman & Me.** Bantam Books, 1993. 168 pp. ISBN 0-553-56456-0.

Paul Zindel, author of many books for young adults, tells his own story of growing up in New York with his sister, his mother, and his best friend Jennifer. Mostly, he shares his feelings about his English teacher, his fist fights, and his own Pigman.

14 Customs, Cultures, and Lands

14.1 Bandon, Alexandra. **Chinese Americans.** New Discovery Books/Macmillan, 1994. 112 pp. ISBN 0-02-768149-1.

Through the years, people have come to America to make money, flee from wars, and escape political oppression. In the 1840s, many Chinese came to this country for the Gold Rush or to work on the transcontinental railroad. The personal narratives in this book tell why some Chinese people come to the United States today. Another book by Bandon in the Footsteps to America series is *West Indian Americans.*

14.2 Bial, Raymond. **Amish Home.** Houghton Mifflin, 1993. 40 pp. ISBN 0-395-59504-5.

Here's your chance to take a photographic tour of Amish settlements in Pennsylvania. You won't find people in these pictures because the Amish believe "it is prideful" to draw attention to themselves. Instead, you'll see what they've created: their homes, their clothes, their farms, and their horse-drawn buggies. These scenes paint a portrait of a complex community of individuals determined to take charge of their own lives. The text accompanying the photographs outlines the common beliefs and habits of the Amish.

14.3 Bonvillain, Nancy. **The Haidas: People of the Northwest Coast.** Millbrook Press, 1994. 64 pp. ISBN 1-56294-491-6.

Wouldn't it be fun to get a present every time you went to a friend's house for dinner? The Haidas, a tribe of Native Americans who live on the northwest coast of Canada, give gifts to guests. Another custom of the Haidas is for men and women to work together, gathering clams, crabs, and scallops. If you're interested in other Native American tribes, you may also want to read *The Apaches: People of the Southwest,* by Jennifer Fleischner, another book in the Native American series.

14.4 Cavan, Seamus. **Coming to America: The Irish-American Experience.** Millbrook Press, 1993. 64 pp. ISBN 1-56294-218-2.

Customs, Cultures, and Lands 211

During the 1840s and 1850s, the people of Ireland were devastated by the Potato Famine. Facing starvation and disease, as well as eviction by English landlords, hundreds of thousands of Irish Catholics fled to America on "coffin ships," searching for better lives. This book examines the movement of Irish people to the United States: their roots, their reasons for immigration, their arduous journey, their difficulties with hardships and prejudices encountered upon arrival in a heavily Protestant nation, and their many victories.

14.5   Kreikemeier, Gregory Scott. **Come with Me to Africa: A Photographic Journey.** Golden Books/Golden Press, 1993. 62 pp. ISBN 0-307-15660-5.

Spending six months traveling across Africa was just the adventure photojournalist Kreikemeier wanted. Along with eleven other people, he explored thirteen countries spread over sixteen thousand miles. From the explanation of necessary gear (each person was allowed only 47 pounds, but his camera equipment alone weighed 32 pounds!), to the descriptions of scenery and people, this picture book of Africa is one to savor.

14.6   Krull, Kathleen. **City within a City: How Kids Live in New York's Chinatown.** Photographs by David Hautzig. Lodestar Books, 1994. 48 pp. ISBN 0-525-67457-3.

This easy-to-read text with colored photos, from the A World of My Own series, provides a glimpse of what it's like to live in New York's Chinatown. Two young Chinese Americans who live in Chinatown, Sze Ki Chau and Chao Liu, share information about family life, school, traditions, and special interests. Other books in this series by Kathleen Krull describe life in Milwaukee's Indian community and California's Latino neighborhoods.

14.7   Langone, John. **In the Shogun's Shadow: Understanding a Changing Japan.** Illustrated by Steven Parton. Little, Brown and Company, 1994. 202 pp. ISBN 0-316-51409-8.

Start by answering 100 true-false questions to determine "what you know about the Japanese." Then examine this society to learn the answers to many of the questions. Japan's history and geography, beliefs and customs, home life, and crime rates are just a few of the topics covered in this comprehensive look at Japan and its people. In comparing Americans and Japanese, the frank discussion of cultural differences and similarities should clear up common myths and misconceptions.

14.8 Lankford, Mary D. **Quinceañera: A Latina's Journey to Womanhood.** Photographs by Jesse Herrera. Millbrook Press, 1994. 47 pp. ISBN 1-56294-363-4.

All birthdays are special, but the fifteenth one marks an important ceremony, or *quinceañera,* for Latinas. The *quinceañera* signals both a religious and social transformation from girl to woman and may be observed in many ways, ranging from an informal celebration to an elaborate commemoration. Martha Jiminez, an eighth grader in Austin, Texas, spent a year planning her *quinceañera* and a special day enjoying it. This is her story.

14.9 Lasky, Kathryn. **Days of the Dead.** Hyperion Books, 1994. 48 pp. ISBN 0-7868-0022-4.

A holiday called Days of the Dead might sound sad, but in Mexico this day is for celebration. Children dress up and ask for candy, as children in the United States do on Halloween. Adults remember their ancestors. The deceased ancestor's favorite foods are made, a candle for the dead is lit, and the family gathers to share memories of the dead. The next morning the entire family goes to the cemetery to clean and decorate the graves.

14.10 Liptak, Karen. **Coming-of-Age: Traditions and Rituals around the World.** Millbrook Press, 1994. 126 pp. ISBN 1-56294-243-3.

In some cultures, coming-of-age is symbolic of death and new birth; therefore, the initiates go into isolation for a period of time and then emerge. Other cultures make physical changes to the bodies of those who are coming of age, such as tattoos or piercings. Cleansing is a common tradition and can include ritual baths, haircuts, or new clothes. Often there are tests of bravery, endurance, or competence. In several African and South American tribes, a young man must kill a large animal and share the meat with his future in-laws.

14.11 Ricciuti, Edward R. **War in Yugoslavia: The Breakup of a Nation.** Millbrook Press, 1993. 64 pp. ISBN 1-56294-375-8.

After World War I, various people and small countries were forced together by the European powers under a new umbrella identity, Yugoslavs. Ethnic hatreds and religious differences brewed for many years, and in 1991, they exploded in a bloody conflict that has resulted in the deaths of many thousands of people, created millions of refugees, and contributed to terrible atrocities, such as torture, murder, and rape. As Serbians and Croatians fight for control of Bosnia, innocent civilians become war victims.

Customs, Cultures, and Lands

14.12 Rodgers, Mary, Tom Streissguth, and Colleen Sexton, editors. **Kazakhstan.** Lerner, 1993. 56 pp. ISBN 0-8225-2815-0.

With the breakup of the Soviet Union in 1991, Kazakhstan became a fully independent state. This book provides detailed information about the land, people, economy, and future challenges of this area, which consists of one million square miles in central Asia. As part of the Then and Now series, which focuses on the republics that have emerged from the former Soviet Union, this resource provides up-to-date information about this little-known area of the world.

14.13 Seymour, Tryntje Van Ness. **The Gift of the Changing Woman.** Henry Holt and Company, 1993. 38 pp. ISBN 0-8050-2577-4.

This book describes the initiation ceremony performed when young Apache females become women. The ritual is based on Apache mythology. An Apache medicine man, an Apache artist, and a participant in many of these ceremonies, called Na'ii'ees, talk about the history and significance of the ritual. Illustrations are by Apache artists and come from museum collections.

14.14 Sita, Lisa. **The Rattle and the Drum.** The Millbrook Press, 1994. 71 pp. ISBN 1-56294-420-7.

Every culture has its traditions, rituals, and ceremonies. Native American customs have been popularized by television and movies, sometimes inaccurately. This book explains the original meanings of many of the ceremonies. For example, the Snake Ceremony of the Hopi is performed so that rain will come, while the Green Corn Dance of the Creek is done to ensure a good harvest. Suggested games, crafts, and recipes will allow you to experience some of these traditions.

14.15 Siy, Alexandra. **The Eeyou: People of Eastern James Bay.** Dillon Press, 1993. 80 pp. ISBN 0-87518-549-5.

Harnessing the hydroelectric power to maintain civilization in Montreal, Canada, and in some United States cities threatens the lifestyle and very existence of the Eeyou, a Native American tribe which has great respect for the land and its other inhabitants. A proposed project violates the current treaty. Do the Eeyou have a future? Alexandra Siy offers a straightforward account of the Eeyou (Cree) of Canada, that is sensitive to the social customs and cultural beliefs that have sustained this people for thousands of years.

14.16 Siy, Alexandra. **The Waorani: People of the Ecuadoran Rain Forest.** Dillon Press, 1993. 80 pp. ISBN 0-87518-550-9.

Imagine living in a world where the largest percentage of deaths is due to snake bites and to accidents like falling from trees. For centuries, the Waorani have lived in such a world in the jungles of Ecuador, isolated from the western world. Now, industrialization threatens their ancient lifestyle. This book describes their customs, their celebrations, and their daily living.

14.17 Strom, Yale. **Uncertain Roads.** Four Winds Press, 1993. 111 pp. ISBN 0-02-788531-3.

Roma, or Gypsies as they are commonly called, are often depicted as a mysterious, romantic people. *Uncertain Roads* traces the roots of this ethnic group from ancient India to modern Europe and presents the everyday life of this colorful, often persecuted people. Their contributions in all fields, especially in art, literature, and music, are documented here.

14.18 Zeleza, Tiyambe. **Maasai.** Rosen Publishing, 1994. 64 pp. ISBN 0-8239-1757-6.

Maasai and *Pokot*, both from the Heritage Library of African Peoples, describe two African tribes with similarities as well as differences. Both groups practice polygamy, which means that men may have more than one wife. The Pokot live an agricultural lifestyle, while the Maasai have been forced to take jobs as wage earners. Each group is trying to maintain a lifestyle that goes back many generations, but this is often difficult in a world where progress means changing old ways.

15 Analyzing Issues of Today

15.1 Aaseng, Nathan. **Jobs vs. the Environment: Can We Save Both?** Enslow Publishers, 1994. 112 pp. ISBN 0-89490-574-0.

This book from the Issues in Focus series addresses the conflicts that sometimes arise between environmentalists and workers. Should forests be saved to protect endangered owls? What about the loggers who work in that forest? Conflicts arise when jobs are threatened, the environment is endangered, or natural resources become scarce or unsafe. Aaseng says, "The challenge of future generations will to be choose the course that best protects the environment with the least disruption to lives of working people."

15.2 Abodaher, David J. **Puerto Rico: America's 51st State?** Franklin Watts, 1993. 95 pp. ISBN 0-531-13024-X.

This Impact series book shows us that the history of Puerto Rico is the story of one upheaval after another. After fifty years of American possession, the island became a semi-independent commonwealth of the United States, governing itself and electing its own leaders. Now Puerto Ricans are divided on the issue of their future. Will it be independence, continued commonwealth status, or statehood?

15.3 Anderson, Kelly C. **Immigration.** Lucent Books, 1993. 112 pp. ISBN 1-56006-140-5.

Immigrants provide the substance of our culture and often become the subject of national debate. Should immigration be limited? Should undocumented workers have medical care? Should our borders be open or closed? Look for discussion of these challenging and complex issues, as you read about how our country has become a nation of immigrants.

15.4 Archer, Jules. **Rage in the Streets: Mob Violence in America.** Illustrated by Lydia J. Hees. Browndeer Press/Harcourt Brace, 1994. 175 pp. ISBN 0-15-277691-5.

Violent protest has been an American tradition since the American Revolution. Archer examines riots which have occurred because of unjust laws, abuses of power, unfair court rulings, unpopular government decisions, and inequality. The only hope for preventing future riots is to understand the reasons why groups erupt into angry mobs and to look for solutions, not scapegoats.

15.5 Ashabranner, Brent. **A New Frontier: The Peace Corps in Eastern Europe.** Cobblehill/Dutton, 1994. 104 pp. ISBN 0-525-65155-1.

In his inaugural address, John F. Kennedy issued his famous challenge: "Ask not what your country can do for you. Ask what you can do for your country." Brent Ashabranner met that challenge when he started the first Peace Corps in Nigeria in 1961. Now, over thirty years later, Ashabranner writes about the Peace Corps in Eastern Europe—who the participants are, how they live, what they do. Meet volunteers up close and personal, and see how they are helping both themselves and others.

15.6 Ashabranner, Brent. **Still a Nation of Immigrants.** Cobblehill/Dutton, 1993. 131 pp. ISBN 0-525-65130-6.

"Immigration is as American as Apple Pie," states a headline from the *Washington Post*, underscoring the quarter of a million immigrants who become American citizens each year. Who are these individuals? Why do they choose America as home? The immigrants interviewed here offer answers to these questions. While responses vary, each person voices a strong commitment to this adopted country and a new life, while trying to hold on to the best of the land left behind.

15.7 Atkin, S. Beth. **Voices from the Fields: Children of Migrant Farm Workers Tell Their Stories.** Little, Brown and Company, 1993. 96 pp. ISBN 0-316-05633-2.

Voices filled with pride, fear, love, frustration, and hope—"let us be the key that opens new doors to our people,"—rise from the pages of this compelling book. The photographs, poems (in both English and Spanish), and interviews dispel many myths and prejudices about the children of migrant farm workers. Through this book, you may see that the cycles of poverty, displacement, and teen pregnancy can be broken with the help of migrant programs and education, and through the perseverance of migrant youths looking for a brighter future.

15.8 Biskup, Michael. **Criminal Justice: Opposing Viewpoints.** Greenhaven Press, 1993. 213 pp. ISBN 0-89908-623-3.

Persons accused of crimes have rights: the right to a trial, the right to fair representation, the right to know why they've been arrested. But what about victims and their families? Do they have rights as well? If so, what are they? A series of paired essays, each taking a different stance on relevant questions concerning the rights of the accused and the accuser, explores these and other volatile questions, which form the backbone of America's criminal justice system.

15.9   Black, Christine M. **The Pursuit of the Presidency '92 and Beyond.** Oryx Press, 1994. 201 pp. ISBN 0-89774-845-X.

Politics can be an interesting, exciting, and important aspect of life. Christine Black, a political reporter for the *Boston Globe*, took extensive notes about the 1992 presidential campaign as she traveled with the candidates. Now, in this book, those notes are turned into anecdotes, explanations, and information about the 1992 election, when Bill Clinton became president.

15.10 Blue, Rose, and Corrine J. Naden. **Working Together against Hate Groups.** Rosen, 1994. 64 pp. ISBN 0-8239-1776-2.

"No one is born with hatred and intolerance. They are taught at an early age by others." Many of those who have been taught this hatred and intolerance are joining hate groups. The animosity of the people who join these groups is directed toward people who do not fit the hate group's vision of an ideal society. This book offers suggestions for stopping these groups and the violence they inflict.

15.11 Carter, Jimmy. **Talking Peace: A Vision for the Next Generation.** Dutton Children's Books, 1993. 177 pp. ISBN 0-525-44959-0.

Americans have been fortunate; we have not fought a war on American soil since the last century. However, we face other kinds of war daily: wars against hunger, homelessness, and crime. Former President Jimmy Carter, the author of this book, has a vision and a plan to help eliminate hunger and crime. In this book, he describes the Carter Center programs throughout the world and presents specific actions young adults can take to further the cause of peace at home and abroad.

15.12 Cheney, Glen Alan. **Chernobyl: The Ongoing Story of the World's Deadliest Nuclear Disaster.** New Discovery Books, 1993. 126 pp. ISBN 0-02-718305-X.

We think of a nuclear disaster as the subject of science fiction. But this story came true in 1986 in Chernobyl. Now, distortions, cover-ups, political upheaval, and poor data gathering make it almost impossible to determine accurately all the effects of that nuclear-power-plant explosion in the Ukraine. However, there is evidence that Chernobyl is a nuclear nightmare that will affect thousands of people and the world's ecosystem for many years.

15.13 Cohen, Daniel. **Animal Rights: A Handbook for Young Adults.** Millbrook Press, 1993. 128 pp. ISBN 1-56294-219-0.

The ideas and actions of animal rights activists may influence what you eat or what you wear. Practices recommended by animal rights activists include eating only a vegetarian diet, opposing animal testing, campaigning against hunting and trapping, and protesting against the ill treatment of animals in zoos, circuses, and other entertainment venues. This book not only explains the issues that surround animal rights, but also lets you know how to become involved in the animal-rights movement.

15.14 Cohen, Daniel. **Cults.** Millbrook Press, 1994. 128 pp. ISBN 1-56294-324-3.

What is a cult? Are all cults evil? Who joins a cult? Is a cult a group of fanatics, a group of people who will die a violent death, or a group of dedicated individuals? Do all cult leaders brainwash their members? Cohen demystifies cults by tracing their origins and studying their methods.

15.15 Davies, Nancy Millichap. **Foster Care.** Franklin Watts, 1994. 112 pp. ISBN 0-531-11081-8.

Foster care is full-time, substitute care of children outside their own homes, by caretakers other than biological parents. About 340,000 young people were in foster care in the United States in 1991. Although foster care is designed to protect children, being placed in a foster home is often a traumatic experience for them. This book, part of the Changing Family series, looks at controversies surrounding foster care and explores alternatives to the current system.

15.16 Day, Nancy. **Animal Experimentation: Cruelty or Science?** Enslow Publishers, 1994. 128 pp. ISBN 0-89490-578-3.

Does saving the lives of humans justify using animals in medical and scientific research, or is animal experimentation morally wrong and unnecessary? This book from the Issue in Focus series documents the arguments on both sides. The best hope for resolving this controversy lies in current and future technology, such as cell cultures and computer models.

15.17 Echo-Hawk, Roger, and Walter Echo-Hawk. **Battlefields and Burial Grounds: The Indian Struggle to Protect Ancestral Graves in the United States.** Lerner Publications, 1994. 80 pp. ISBN 0-8225-2663-8.

If the federal government informed you that they were digging up the graves of all your family members who had died and been buried, how would you react? In the name of science, Native American graves have been dug up freely, despite the strong religious concerns many tribes have about protecting their dead from disturbance. This book chronicles the struggle of tribal governments to reclaim the remains of their ancestors for reburial.

15.18 Eisaguirre, Lynn. **Sexual Harassment: A Reference Handbook.** ABC-CLIO, 1993. 217 pp. ISBN 0-87436-723-9.

In a 1992 Minnesota survey of 250 students, approximately 50 percent of the teenage girls who responded to the survey reported having been sexually harassed at school, either verbally or physically; another 30 percent stated that they had been harassed at work. The whole issue of sexual harassment and the laws concerning it are still relatively new and evolving, but the bottom line is this: sexual harassment is illegal. This book looks at people who have been harassed and at the laws being designed to protect them.

15.19 Gay, Kathlyn. **The New Power of Women in Politics.** Enslow Publishers, 1994. 128 pp. ISBN 0-89490-584-B.

Have you ever wondered how the feminist movement got started and why it was necessary? Did you know that prior to the movement, women in the United States were not allowed to own property, to vote, or to hold office? Trace the triumphs of fascinating women and their struggle for independence, rights, and change. The author packs this interesting book with facts and insights from the suffrage movement to current and recent political leaders, including Supreme Court Justice Ruth Bader Ginsburg, Attorney General Janet Reno, and former Texas Governor Ann Richards.

15.20 Goldish, Meish. **Crisis in Haiti.** Millbrook Press, 1994. 64 pp. ISBN 1-56294-553-X.

Deye mon ge mon ("Beyond the mountains there are more mountains") is a Haitian Creole proverb which reflects Haiti's struggles for democracy and better economic conditions. The flood of Haitian refugees into the United States and the terrorism against

Haitians by the ruling military prompted President Clinton to help Jean-Bertrand Aristide, the last democratically elected Haitian president, return to power in the fall of 1994. The future of Haiti is still very uncertain.

15.21 Gottfried, Ted. **Privacy: Individual Right v. Social Needs.** Millbrook Press, 1994. 112 pp. ISBN 1-56294-403-7.

Your locker is searched. Does that violate your rights? The right to privacy is not guaranteed by the Constitution. Issues of privacy are decided through court decisions. Many of these issues affect young people: random drug testing, searches of individuals and lockers or belongings, access to personnel or school records. Should you be able to tell authorities that they can't search you or your things? Should they ever be allowed to do so? These questions are explored in this book from the Issue and Debate series.

15.22 Grady, Sean M. **Illiteracy.** Lucent Overview Books, 1994. 96 pp. ISBN 1-56006-139-1.

As you read this, keep in mind that millions of Americans would not be able to. They are illiterate; they cannot read or write. In 1992 thirty-five million to eighty million people in America suffered from some degree of illiteracy. These people can't read the newspaper or magazines, signs or directions, menus, forms, or labels. They often try to hide their disability. What causes illiteracy, and what can society do to help solve the problem?

15.23 Guernsey, JoAnn Bren. **Abortion: Understanding the Controversy.** Lerner Publications, 1993. 112 pp. ISBN 0-8225-2605-0.

This book, from Lerner's Pro/Con series, reveals that many Americans are uninformed about the abortion issue. Abortion debaters lack a common language, are often unwilling to consider the other side's arguments, and hold established beliefs that contribute to emotionally charged disputes. When does life begin? This central question is explored from both sides.

15.24 Guernsey, JoAnn Bren. **Should We Have Capital Punishment?** Lerner Publications, 1993. 96 pp. ISBN 0-8225-2602-6.

Should convicted murderers be executed? If the convicted murderer is under eighteen years old, mentally retarded, or is the product of an abusive childhood, should he or she be exempt from the death penalty? Death penalty opponents say that there is no justification for taking human life. Death penalty advocates say that capital punishment prevents more murders. Testimony, sta-

Analyzing Issues of Today

tistics, and straightforward information will help you take a stand on this difficult issue. Another book in Lerner's Pro/Con series.

15.25 Haas, Carol. **Engel vs. Vitale: Separation of Church and State.** Enslow Publishers, 1994. 104 pp. ISBN 0-89490-461-2.

The people, the historical context, and the arguments behind landmark Supreme Court decisions shed light not only on history, but on many of today's current controversies. Will it become more difficult to maintain the separation of church and state as legislators fight to return prayer to schools? Have we achieved equal schooling for all? Why must an accused person be informed of his or her rights, and how might this affect the rights of victims? Should there be a death penalty? Can freedom of the press endanger national security? These small books in the *Landmark Supreme Court Cases Series* include *Furman v. Georgia*, *Miranda v. Arizona*, *Brown v. Board of Education*, and *New York Times v. United States National Security and Censorship*.

15.26 Hackman, Peggy, and Oldenbury, Don, editors. **Dear Mr. President.** Avon Books, 1993. 130 pp. ISBN 0-380-77473-9.

What would you like to tell the president of the United States? The *Washington Post* sponsored a contest for children who wanted to write to President Clinton. This book is a collection of many of the letters young people wrote. While many issues, questions, and concerns were raised, most children expressed a thought that Philip Croom shared with the president: "I am young and not able to vote, but I am also a child of the future so my feelings count."

15.27 Hoose, Phillip. **It's Our World, Too! Stories of Young People Who Are Making a Difference.** Joy Street Books/Little, Brown and Company, 1993. 176 pp. ISBN 0-316-37241-2.

Some people believe their individual ideas don't make much difference. But some people think differently; they know that a few strong voices can change things. More important, they know that those voices don't have to come from the rich and the powerful to be powerful. Sometimes they come from kids. In this book you will meet young people who decided to do something about a problem they saw. For example, Dwaina, a fifth grader, started a soup kitchen in her own home for the homeless of her community.

15.28 Kent, Zachary. **The Persian Gulf War: "The Mother of All Battles."** Enslow Publishers, 1994. 128 pp. ISBN 0-89490-528-7.

Saddam Hussein, president and dictator of Iraq, ordered an invasion of his country's middle-eastern neighbor Kuwait in August 1990. American president George Bush, with the aid of many nations, immediately acted to free Kuwait. The swiftness of the American troops, the high technology used in battles, and the hardships of the desert location are described in this book, through the personal stories of men and women who fought in the war, as well as through excerpts from speeches and news stories.

15.29 Kronenwetter, Michael. **The Peace Commandos: Nonviolent Heroes in the Struggle against War and Injustice.** Macmillan, 1994. 160 pp. ISBN 0-02-751051-4.

Peaceful warriors fight with ideas, words, and nonviolent protest, in contrast with the United States military forces, which have been involved in more than 300 conflicts, one for each year of the nation's existence. Throughout this history, there have been individuals—some famous, some ordinary citizens—who refused to participate in war. This *Impact* book provides a readable account of the pacifist movement. It offers insights into the difficult decisions peace commandos make and explores the dangers nonviolent heroes face.

15.30 Kuklin, Susan. **Speaking Out: Teenagers Take On Race, Sex, and Identity.** G. P. Putnam's Sons, 1993. 165 pp. ISBN 0-399-22532-3.

Reporter Susan Kuklin had unlimited access to students, teachers, administrators, and activities at Bayard Rustin High School for the Humanities, in New York City. Culturally and socioeconomically diverse students at the school tell in their own words how they feel about themselves, other students of different cultural backgrounds, and the world around them. Carrie says, "There is something decent and good about caring for people who are different from you." America's best hope for fighting prejudice is getting to know one another in settings like Rustin High, where students talk about their differences and find out they have much in common.

15.31 Landau, Elaine. **The Right to Die.** Franklin Watts, 1993. 96 pp. ISBN 0-531-13015-0.

The stories are heartbreaking, and there are no definite answers. Do family members have the right to remove life support if there is no proof of the injured or ill person's wishes? Can doctors know absolutely that certain patients will never recover? When a teenager faces cancer and wishes not to take treatment, can the parents force their child to undergo therapy? In this Impact book, Landau uses real cases to explore difficult issues related to sustaining life through medical technology.

15.32 Landau, Elaine. **Sexual Harassment.** Walker and Company, 1993. 93 pp. ISBN 0-8027-8265-5.

Sexual harassment is sexual pressure—physical or verbal—at school or work, which places a person in a position that makes refusal difficult. Often the person who is doing the harassing is someone in authority who has some power over the other person, but there are incidents of harassment by peers. Landau explores the issues of harassment through widely publicized cases and through the stories of ordinary workers, students, and others.

15.33 Lang, Susan S., and Paul Lang. **Censorship.** Franklin Watts, 1993. 126 pp. ISBN 0-531-10999-2.

Can parents demand that objectionable television programs be taken off the air? Does the government have the right to control what the media can publish or broadcast about government activities if national security is not at risk? Should there be special restrictions on music, television, or movies that glamorize violence? These are tough censorship questions. The answers come from the Constitution and from understanding the First Amendment. This book explores what happens when censorship becomes the issue.

15.34 Lindop, Edmund. **Presidents versus Congress: Conflict and Compromise.** Franklin Watts, 1994. 176 pp. ISBN 0-531-11165-2.

Government gridlock, the inability to accomplish legislation because of disagreements between political parties, is not a recent phenomenon. Lindop tells the story of fifteen major conflicts between presidents and Congress, beginning with the problems George Washington had with his Congress, and concluding with President Bush's congressional struggles.

15.35 Liptak, Karen. **Adoption Controversies.** Franklin Watts, 1993. 158 pp. ISBN 0-531-13032-0.

Unplanned pregnancies among teenagers have reached "epidemic proportions." Those dealing with a teenage pregnancy must ask, "Are we ready to take on the financial, emotional, and time commitments of being full-time parents?" If the answer is no, offering the child for adoption is one of the possible choices.

Liptak gives non-judgmental advice and information about the adoption process and discusses the debates about adoption issues. Additional sources of information are provided. This is one of the Changing Family books.

15.36 Liptak, Karen. **Endangered Peoples.** Franklin Watts, 1993. 160 pp. ISBN 0-531-10987-9.

Most indigenous tribes, those native to an area, have survived because they have adapted to harsh realities of climate, scarcity of food, and the danger of predators and enemies. Liptak studies five native tribes that, despite centuries of survival, face extinction in the near future as they are displaced by modern life. Even when the tribe is protected, modern curiosity and the desire to study tribal culture bring lifestyle changes among the natives and endanger their future existence.

15.37 Meisel, Jacqueline Drobis. **South Africa at the Crossroads.** Millbrook Press, 1994. 64 pp. ISBN 1-56294-511-4.

For many years, groups in South Africa have clashed violently in an attempt to end racism and human-rights violations in their country. The government's policy of apartheid, separate laws for black and white people, assured whites a superior status, but people all over the world opposed apartheid and put pressure on South African leaders to change the system. Nelson Mandela's release from prison and his election in 1994 as South Africa's first black leader now provides hope for real change.

15.38 Meltzer, Milton. **Cheap Raw Material: How Our Youngest Workers Are Exploited and Abused.** Viking/Penguin, 1994. 167 pp. ISBN 0-670-83128-X.

You want a job so you can buy a stereo, a horse, or clothes. You apply and discover that there are laws that govern the types of jobs you can have and the number of hours you can work. Why? Basically because throughout history, children have been abused and forced to do difficult and dangerous work on farms, in factories, and in sweatshops. Even today, with laws regulating child labor, there are frequent violations and abuses of children in workplaces.

15.39 Miller, Maryann. **Working Together against Gun Violence.** Rosen Publishing, 1994. 64 pp. ISBN 0-8239-1779-7.

The leading cause of death among teenagers is gunshot wounds. Would getting rid of all the guns solve the problem? Probably not, say those who oppose gun control. "The problem of gun violence is not just the guns. It's the people who use them and how they are used." Thought-provoking questions, arguments on both sides of the issue, reference information, and sample speeches make this small book from the Library of Social Activism series a useful tool.

15.40 Nichelason, Margery G. **Homeless or Hopeless?** Lerner Publications, 1994. 112 pp. ISBN 0-8225-2606-9.

There is no single description for homeless people nor a single reason people become homeless. However, all homeless people face hunger, danger, loss of self-respect, illness, and the countless other problems of having little or no income and no permanent residence. What should society do about these people? Support them? Educate them? Leave them alone? In this book from Lerner's Pro/Con series, you can gather statistics and information about the homeless that will help you make decisions about this complex issue.

15.41 Owen, Marna. **Animal Rights: Yes or No?** Lerner, 1993. 112 pp. ISBN 0-8225-2603-4.

The books in the Pro/Con series are designed to help you understand both sides of an issue. In this book, that issue is the rights of animals. Facts help you place yourself on the continuum of several positions: (1) Humans are superior to animals, so we can use them as we please. (2) Animals should be used only in ways that greatly benefit humankind. (3) Animals have basic rights just as humans do and should be allowed to live their lives naturally and without cruelty.

15.42 Parker, Rev. Julie F. **Careers for Women as Clergy.** Rosen Publishing, 1993. 176 pp. ISBN 0-8239-1424-0.

"If you are a young woman considering a career in clergy, you were born at the right time!" Today, one third of the students in seminaries are female, although forty years ago few women were permitted this choice. How does a girl know if this career is right for her? Take Parker's advice: examine specific strengths and weaknesses, learn about the various forms the career can take, understand what's involved in serving a congregation, and talk with others.

15.43 Patent, Dorothy Hinshaw. **The Vanishing Feast: How Dwindling Genetic Diversity Threatens the World's Food Supply.** Gulliver Green Books/Harcourt Brace & Company, 1994. 180 pp. ISBN 0-15-292867-7.

Large industries and governmental policies move farmers and breeders towards increasing specialization in the crops they grow and the animals they breed. While specialization appears to be a good thing, some believe it ruins diversity. Without diversity, unreliable soil conditions arise, and animals become more susceptible to common diseases. To keep specialization but protect diversity, scientists are experimenting with new techniques such as gene storage, embryo transplantation, and splitting and cloning of embryos.

15.44 Rosen, Roger, and Patra McSharry Sevastiades. **On Heroes and the Heroic: In Search of Good Deeds.** Rosen Publishing, 1993. 177 pp. ISBN 0-8239-1384-8.

"The truth about John Wayne is that he was indeed the great American cowboy hero, throwing his stalking shadow across the continent and beyond. And he did, in fact, make everything up, reinventing himself during an incredible career." John Wayne is one of many heroes you will read about in this book. These essays and stories include a variety of ancient retellings of legends, the true stories behind historic figures who have become legendary, explanations of how popular figures became mythical, and accounts of modern events that involve brave men and women.

15.45 Sherrow, Victoria. **The U.S. Health Care Crisis: The Fight over Access, Quality, and Cost.** Millbrook Press, 1994. 144 pp. ISBN 1-56294-364-2.

Most Americans agree that health care needs reform but disagree about how to fix it. Annual national health costs are approaching a trillion dollars. In addition to being costly and inefficient, the current system denies services to many poor people and minorities. This book explores the history of medical care and current proposals for reform, in this moment of national health care crisis.

15.46 Snodgrass, Mary Ellen. **Japan and the United States: Economic Competitors.** Millbrook Press, 1993. 64 pp. ISBN 1-56294-374-X.

Social and economic factors are at the core of the sometimes rocky relationship between Japan and America, as shown in this Headliner series book. The bottom line is that the two countries need each other. Intense competition and cultural differences create conflicting emotions, but cooperation between the economic superpowers is a sure key to survival for both countries.

15.47 Thompson, Sharon Elaine. **Hate Groups.** Lucent Books, 1994. 112 pp. ISBN 1-56006-144-8.

Members of hate groups believe that their race, their faith, and their country are threatened by large-scale immigration, poor economics, and massive social changes. Acting on these fears, many members of hate groups are commiting acts of violence against those they hate. Sadly, many hate crimes are random acts of violence committed by young people who do not even know their victim. The only reason for inflicting harm is that the victim is a member of the group they hate.

15.48 Whitehead, Fred, editor. **Culture Wars: Opposing Viewpoints.** Greenhaven Press, 1994. 216 pp. ISBN 1-5610-100-6.

Movie ratings of *G, PG, PG-13,* and *R* are designed to help parents decide if a movie is appropriate for their child. Often, television shows carry a warning about violence or language that some may find offensive. Now, some people are suggesting that record covers should carry labels warning listeners about explicit lyrics. One of those advocates, Tipper Gore, wife of the Vice-President of the United States, presents her argument for labeling, in this detailed book that explores many of the issues surrounding pop culture.

15.49 Woods, Geraldine. **Drug Abuse in Society: A Reference Handbook.** ABC-CLIO Contemporary World Issues, 1993. 269 pp. ISBN 0-87436-720-4.

Americans spend more money on drugs than on food. How many Americans abuse drugs? Who are the drug abusers? Why do they use drugs? How can society prevent drug abuse? Since illegal drug use is a secret activity, these are difficult questions to answer fully. Real-life stories, statistics, a historical overview, and many charts and graphs offer insight, however, and make this book a valuable reference tool.

V Science All around You

Reading furnishes the mind only with materials for knowledge; it is thinking [that] makes what we read ours.

John Locke, English philosopher

16 Physical Science

16.1 Barnes-Svarey, Patricia. **Traveler's Guide to the Solar System.** Sterling, 1994. 80 pp. ISBN 0-8069-8675-1.

Have you ever wanted to get into a spaceship and take a tour of the solar system? This book is the next best thing. Dramatic photographs will take you to each of the planets, as you learn interesting facts about them. On which planet will you find volcanoes three times higher than Mt. Everest? Which planet's moon has ice, perhaps even a frozen ocean? How did the rings of Saturn form? Hop into your spaceship and take a celestial ride.

16.2 Branley, Franklyn M. **It's Raining Cats and Dogs: All Kinds of Weather and Why We Have It.** Avon Books, 1993. 112 pp. ISBN 0-380-71849-9.

What will the weather be tomorrow? After reading this informative book, you will be able to answer this question, as well as amaze your friends with knowledge of weather facts. Directions are given for constructing your own weather instruments.

16.3 Branley, Franklyn M. **Keeping Time: From the Beginning and into the 21st Century.** Houghton Mifflin, 1993. 105 pp. ISBN 0-395-47777-8.

Why are there twenty-four hours in a day? Seven days in a week? Sixty minutes in an hour? These are just a few of the questions answered in Franklyn Branley's book, *Keeping Time*. In clear language, Branley describes the history of time and of time-keeping devices (including directions for building your own clocks). He explains why we have time zones and daylight-saving time. If you have the time, this book has everything that you have ever wanted to know about time.

16.4 Branley, Franklyn M. **Venus.** HarperCollins, 1994. 56 pp. ISBN 0-06-020298-X.

Hop aboard the Magellan Space Craft, and take a close-up look at the surface of Venus. Beneath that thick cloud layer, you will find mountains and valleys, plateaus and plains, just like on Earth. You will also see craters, some as large as twenty miles across, and volcanoes, some perhaps still active. The book is filled with dramatic photographs of the surface of Venus.

16.5 Breckenridge, Judy. **Simple Physics Experiments with Everyday Materials.** Sterling Publishing, 1993. 128 pp. ISBN 0-8069-8606-9.

Have you ever wondered how to make a coin talk? Or how to stick a needle into a balloon without making it burst? These are just a few of the mysteries of physics that you can explore with this book. Each experiment lists all materials (simple and easily obtained), provides clear directions, describes what happens, and gives a clear explanation of the scientific principles involved.

16.6 Butterfield, Moira. **Space: Look Inside Cross-Sections.** Dorling Kindersley, 1994. 32 pp. ISBN 1-56458-682-0.

Want to see what it's like on board the space shuttle? Intricate cross-section diagrams allow readers to actually look inside twelve different spacecraft. Two-page colored illustrations highlight the design and construction of such famous spacecraft as Mercury, Skylab, Voyager, and the space shuttle. A space timeline, beginning with Sputnik in 1957 and ending with the repair of the Hubble telescope in 1994, illustrates the milestones of space exploration.

16.7 Canault, Nina. **Incredibly Small.** Macmillan/New Discovery Books, 1993. 47 pp. ISBN 0-02-718650-4.

Open your eyes to the magic of the world around you. You will see amazing pictures of some of the tiniest living creatures. In other books in the Frontiers of the Invisible series, *Incredibly Hidden, Incredibly Fast,* and *Incredibly Far,* you will learn about photographing a speeding bullet and about worlds millions of miles away. These books celebrate the photographer's art and show how photography and science are closely related.

16.8 Cash, Terry. **101 Physics Tricks: Fun Experiments with Everyday Materials.** Sterling Publishing, 1994. 104 pp. ISBN 0-8069-8785-5.

How do you make a parachute? How does a hovercraft work? How can you make your own magnetic hockey game? These are just a few of the questions answered in this book. Experiments that you can do using simple materials will teach you the basic principles of physics. Chapters include topics such as "puff, squeeze, bang, blow" and "click, flash, buzz, whirr."

16.9 Cobb, Vicki, and Josh Cobb. **Light Action.** Illustrated by Theo Cobb. HarperCollins, 1993. 198 pp. ISBN 0-06-021436-8.

What is light? This book will take you on a journey of discovery through physics, as you conduct experiments to learn more about light. How can you bend light? How can you bounce light? What makes something a particular color? You will even learn how to catch a beam of light.

16.10 Cobb, Vicki. **Science Experiments You Can Eat.** Revised edition. HarperTrophy, 1994. 214 pp. ISBN 0-06-023534-9.

Who doesn't like to eat? And when you can eat and learn science at the same time, you have the best of everything. This book gives you recipes for cooking up some delicious science. Learn about freezing, as you make ice pops. Learn about emulsions as you make mayonnaise. Conduct a simple chemistry experiment as you make a lemon fizz. Do a series of investigations to learn about your microwave. What a yummy way to do science!

16.11 Cobb, Vicki, and Kathy Darling. **Wanna Bet? Science Challenges to Fool You.** Illustrated by Meredith Johnson. Avon/Camelot, 1994. 132 pp. ISBN 0-380-71722-0.

Want a sure-fire way to fool and amaze your friends? You'll find it in *Wanna Bet?*, Vicki Cobb's follow-up book to *Bet You Can* and *Bet You Can't*. Make a bionic arm. Tie a bone into a knot. Make fire with blood (the hamburger variety, of course). These are just a few of the amazing "tricks" of science in this book. Scientific explanations are given for all of the tricks.

16.12 Deem, James M. **How to Catch a Flying Saucer.** Avon, 1993. 192 pp. ISBN 0-380-71898-7.

UFOs exist. They've been spotted since the thirteenth century. But just because they exist doesn't mean that they come from far-away galaxies or that they house alien creatures. There are as many explanations for UFOs as there are recorded encounters. But how does someone evaluate a sighting? These are the tools of a UFOlogist: learning as much as possible about previous UFOs, keeping an open mind, and classifying and assessing often conflicting information.

16.13 Docekal, Eileen M. **Sky Detective: Investigating the Mysteries of Space.** Sterling Publishing, 1993. 128 pp. ISBN 0-8069-8404-X.

Next time you are going to look at the night sky, this is a book that you need to take along. You will learn about the constellations and planets, read about the lives of stars from birth to maturity to death, and find instructions for constructing stargazing equipment.

16.14 Englehart, Steve. **Countdown to the Moon.** Avon/Camelot, 1994. 88 pp. ISBN 0-380-77538-7.

On July 20, 1969, the dream came true as astronauts Neil Armstrong and Buzz Aldrin landed the lunar module, *Eagle*, and a human being first set foot on the moon. The intense preparation, the blastoff on the *Columbia*, the exploration of the moon, the journey back to Earth, and the splashdown are all documented in this chronology. Aspiring astronauts will find the appendix with qualifications and application procedures for astronaut candidates particularly helpful.

16.15 Gardner, Robert. **Experimenting with Science in Sports.** Franklin Watts, 1993. 128 pp. ISBN 0-531-12543-2.

Want to be a smarter athlete? Learn about what causes a curve ball to "break," why runners start a race from a crouched position, or how to determine the speed of a hockey puck. As a former coach and science teacher, author Robert Gardner combines science and sports through easily understood experiments that deal with footwear, friction, wind resistance, and bouncing balls. He relates all of these phenomena to laws of physics. Photographs and numerous drawings aid in understanding how science affects sports.

16.16 Gardner, Robert. **Science Projects about Electricity and Magnets.** Enslow Publishers, Inc., 1994. 128 pp. ISBN 0-98490-530-9.

This book and others in this series are a great starting point for your next science-fair project. How can you make your own weather station? Build an electrical motor? Melt ice faster? Can you bend the path of light? You will find enough ideas here for years of science projects, but you can find even more ideas in these other books by Gardner: *Science Projects about Temperature and Heat, Science Projects about Light, Science Projects about Chemistry,* or *Science Projects about Weather*.

16.17 Gribbin, John, and Mary Gribbin. **Time and Space.** Dorling Kindersley Publishing, 1994. 64 pp. ISBN 1-56458-478-X.

Learn about the universe, black holes, and the birth of the earth in this beautiful book. You can even amaze your friends with your understanding of Einstein's Theory of Relativity. In Astronomy, by Kristen Lippencott, another book in this series, you will learn about the development of the telescope from the first telescope of Luppershey to the modern radio telescope. You will also take a trip through the solar system to each of the planets. Both of these books are dramatically illustrated, and each takes you through an historical journey of its topic.

16.18 Gustafson, John. **The Young Stargazer's Guide to the Galaxy: Stars, Clusters, and Galaxies.** Julian Messner, 1993. 64 pp. ISBN 0-671-72536-X.

Have you ever looked up at a clear night sky and marveled at what seem to be millions of stars? This book will help you to understand the life story of each of those stars. How are stars born? What are some of the different kinds of star clusters? How do stars die? You will find step-by-step directions for doing stargazing, including how to read a star chart and how to measure the distances in the night sky.

16.19 Herbst, Judith. **Star Crossing: How to Get around in the Universe.** Atheneum, 1993. 187 pp. ISBN 0-689-31523-6.

If you like the tales of Flash Gordon and Star Trek, you will love this book. The story of space exploration, from the first rockets of Robert Goddard to the fanciful musings of scientists dreaming of ships that can navigate black holes, is described in scientific detail. What are the chances that there are intelligent beings in our universe and that we will ever meet them? After reading this book, you will know the answer to that and many other questions about space.

16.20 Kettlekamp, Larry. **Living in Space.** William Morrow and Company, 1993. 104 pp. ISBN 0-688-10018-X.

What's on the drawing board for the space program? Following a brief historical view of the United States' success at placing humans on the moon, this book examines America's plans and aspirations for exploring and "living in space." Future plans for space stations, the space shuttle, and colonization of Mars are just a few of the topics to intrigue space buffs.

16.21 Lancaster-Brown, Peter. **Skywatch: Eyes-On Activities for Getting to Know the Stars, Planets, and Galaxies.** Sterling Publishing, 1994. 136 pp. ISBN 0-8069-8628-X.

Look up into the night sky, and what do you see? Billions and billions of stars. This book will help you to understand what you are seeing. Excellent sky charts will help you to locate stars, constellations, and planets. The book is packed with celestial facts including information about buying a telescope that is best for your needs.

16.22 Markle, Sandra. **Science to the Rescue.** Atheneum, 1994. 48 pp. ISBN 0-689-31783-2.

How is science helping to make our world a better place? This book explores some of the problems facing science and examines how science and technology are being applied to solve these problems. How do we find new land to allow coastal cities to expand? How can we use robots to do jobs that are too dangerous for humans? How do we protect our atmosphere from pollution? For each question, you are challenged to do something in your own home or community to help to solve the problem. There are also suggestions for experiments and ways that you can test your solutions.

16.23 Murphy, Pat. **Bending Light.** Illustrated by Denise Brunkus. Little, Brown and Company, 1993. 48 pp. ISBN 0-316-25851-2.

How do cameras and slide projectors work? These are a few of the mysteries of light that you can explore in this book. You will also learn to build a lens from jello! But you won't really need to because this book comes with a magnifying glass. There is also advice about purchasing lenses.

16.24 Newton, David E. **Making and Using Scientific Equipment.** Franklin Watts, 1993. 157 pp. ISBN 0-531-11176-8.

Want to start your own science laboratory, but you're short on cash? This is the book for you. From an anemometer to a water-temperature gauge, directions are given for building a variety of lab instruments. Want a simple microscope? Want to build some electrical equipment? Build that lab and get started on your own science career.

16.25 Richards, Roy. **101 Science Surprises.** Sterling Publishing, 1993. 104 pp. ISBN 0-8069-8822-3.

Learn about geometric patterns. Work your way through a maze. Make pictures from leaves. These are just a few of the 101 science surprises awaiting you in this book. Simple household materials and clear directions will provide activities to give you hours of science fun.

16.26 Rybolt, Thomas R., and Robert C. Mebane. **Environmental Experiments about Renewable Energy.** Enslow Publishers, Inc., 1994. 96 pp. ISBN 0-89490-579-1.

Interested in energy? This book is full of interesting and easy experiments that you can do to learn more about energy resources.

Physical Science

Topics included are energy, temperature, and heat; sources and savings of energy; cooling and heating; solar energy; and energy from biomass. Can a salt be used for heating and cooling? Can solar energy be concentrated? Can a fuel be made from plant material? You can find out for yourself.

16.27 Skurzynski, Gloria. **Get the Message.** Bradbury, 1993. 64 pp. ISBN 0-02-778071-6.

The phone rings. It may ring in your bedroom, at an outside booth, in your car, or in space. Americans place over 400 billion phone calls a year, and when you include fax and e-mail messages, the number soars. What happens to make these systems work is the focus here; it's up to you to bargain with your parents to stay on the line longer.

16.28 Simon, Seymour. **Science Dictionary.** HarperCollins, 1994. 256 pp. ISBN 0-06-025629-X.

From abacus to zygote, this dictionary contains over 2000 entries of science terms and famous scientists. Many of the definitions are illustrated. An appendix contains several tables and charts, including the classification of living things; information about planets, stars and constellations; common weights and measures; weather terms; and the periodic table. A section of scientific prefixes and suffixes will help you to decipher difficult scientific terms.

16.29 Souza, D. M. **Northern Lights.** Carolrhoda Books, Inc., 1994. 46 pp. ISBN 0-876414-799-6.

Learn what three elements create the beautiful and mysterious northern lights called the aurora borealis. Discover how similar this creation of magnificent color is to the transmission of color to our television sets. Find out how static electricity on a sock and a t-shirt taken from the clothes dryer help to explain the exquisite flash of color in the northern lights. A truly fascinating book with breath-taking photographs of a phenomenon so fantastic that people used to believe they were witnessing a dance of spirits.

16.30 Stein, Wendy. **Dinosaurs: Great Mysteries.** Greenhaven Press, Inc., 1994. 128 pp. ISBN 1-5651-096-4.

Do you feel like all of the great mysteries of science have been solved? If so, dive into the Great Mysteries series and discover some of the unanswered questions that have been troubling scientists for years. The best part about these books is that they present several points of view, and you get to be the judge. Did the dinosaurs die slowly over time, or quickly because of one catastrophic event? Read the evidence, and then *you* decide. Here's another great mystery: Is there life in the universe? What do you think? If this question interests you, read *Mysteries of Space: Great Mysteries,* by Richard M. Rassmussen, another book in the Opposing Viewpoints series.

16.31 Van Rose, Susanna. **Earth.** Dorling Kindersley, 1994. 64 pp. ISBN 1-56458-476-3.

This book is full of pictures and diagrams to help you to better understand your home, the earth. From "What Makes Up the Earth" to geological time, this book will help you understand how the earth is constantly changing. Biographies of famous scientists are woven throughout the book.

16.32 Vogt, Gregory L. **The Search for the Killer Asteroid.** The Millbrook Press, 1994. 72 pp. ISBN 1-56294-448-7.

One theory suggests that the dinosaurs became extinct because a large asteroid collided with Earth, changing Earth's climate. What is the evidence for that collision? This book presents data that supports the theory of an asteroid impact near the Yucatan that sent waves well into what is now central Texas. The book also investigates the possibility that another catastrophic collision could occur. What are scientists doing to look for near-Earth objects (NEO), and what could be done if one were to appear?

16.33 Young, Jay. **The Most Amazing Science Pop-up Book.** HarperCollins/Festival, 1994. 12 pp. ISBN 0-694-00588-6.

This is much more than a book. It is a science lab in twelve pages. Using pop-ups, you can explore sound by making your own phonograph. Magnetism is no mystery with your own compass. The world of miniature is within anyone's grasp when you have your own microscope. Use a pinhole camera or a kaleidoscope to learn about light. Spy on others with your periscope. This book will keep you involved for a long time.

17 Nature, Ecology, and the Environment

17.1 Anderson, Joan. **Earth Keepers.** Gulliver Green Books/Harcourt Brace & Company, 1993. 92 pp. ISBN 0-15-242199-8.

There's hope for the survival of wildlife on Planet Earth! This book chronicles three sites (New York City, the Hudson River Valley, and a Minnesota wilderness) that are supported by environmental groups which save land, air, and water from destructive pollution. Through the combined efforts of groups of people and under the leadership of environmental groups, these sites are now viable homes for wild creatures ranging in size from small bugs to large black bears.

17.2 Bailey, Jill, and Catherine Thomas. **Planet Earth.** Oxford University Press, 1993. 160 pp. ISBN 0-19-910144-2.

Encyclopedic in scope, *Planet Earth* provides useful information about earth formations (volcanoes, mountains, icebergs), as well as about environmental processes (climate, seasons, weather). In addition, there are maps of various parts of the globe. Like the two other books in this series, *The Living World* and *Science and Technology,* this book is amply illustrated with charts, diagrams, and pictures. Each book in the series provides a treasury of useful information. An index to text and pictures makes finding information simple. *The Living World* is a compendium of information about plants and animals, organized by their biological classifications. *Science and Technology* will expose you to the science of the human-made world and tell you how photocopiers, motor bikes, and holograms work.

17.3 Bash, Barbara. **Ancient Ones: The World of the Old-Growth Douglas Fir.** Sierra Club Books for Children, 1994. 28 pp. ISBN 0-87156-561-7.

In the United States today, only 10 percent of the forests are old growth, meaning that they have never been cut before. Old forests support an enormous diversity of plants and animals in a constant recycling of life. In this book, lyrical prose and vivid watercolors depict the life cycle of the Douglas fir, a tree that can live to be 1,000 years old.

17.4 Brandenburg, Jim. **Sand and Fog: Adventures in Southern Africa.** Walker and Company, 1994. 44 pp. ISBN 0-8027-8232-9.

Wildlife photographer Jim Brandenburg tells the story of survival in the harsh, barren, but beautiful world of the Namib Desert. Survival for the animals comes in many different ways. The oryx migrates with the seasons; the lizard licks moisture left by the fog from its own body; the jackal preys on the flamingo. Some of the people make their living by working in the diamond mines, while others follow the more primitive ways of their forefathers. Brandenburg's photographs prove that a desert doesn't have to be just sand.

17.5 Burnie, David. **Dictionary of Nature.** Dorling Kindersley, 1994. 192 pp. ISBN 1-56458-473-9.

Here's science from A to Z. Beautifully illustrated and clearly written, this dictionary uses a thematic approach, grouping similar topics together. Would you like to know about the chemistry of life, fungi, or animal biology? The answers to many fascinating questions are here. There is also a list of more than 150 of the world's great biologists.

17.6 Children's Task Force on Agenda 21. **Rescue Mission—Planet Earth: A Global Handbook for the 21st Century.** Kingfisher Books in association with the United Nations, 1994. 96 pp. ISBN 1-85697-174-0.

Join "Rescue Mission." Read about Agenda 21, which was established at the Earth Summit held in Rio de Janeiro, and see if you'd like to become involved in a project to save our planet. With poetry, art, activities, and information about protecting our Earth's environment, this book clearly establishes the philosophical trade-off between feeding the expanding populations on Earth and saving natural habitats. This is not a book of doom and gloom, but rather a collection of action plans for young people to pursue.

17.7 Cossi, Olga. **Water Wars.** New Discovery Books, 1993. 127 pp. ISBN 0-02-724595-0.

Without water, life on our planet cannot survive. This Earthcare Book presents clearly the case for water and its preservation. It offers suggestions for the future role of water on our planet. The appendix of this book contains a chronology of major federal acts concerning water, as well as other sources to consult on water issues.

17.8 Cozic, Charles P. **Pollution.** Greenhaven Press, 1994. 224 pp. ISBN 1-56510-075-1.

Debaters or report writers will find this book to be a valuable resource for information about pollution and its effects upon our environment. Topics include a discussion of the seriousness of pollution, who is polluting, the effectiveness of the Environmental Protection Agency (EPA), and the effects of recycling. Another title in the series deals with energy alternatives. Other books in the Current Controversies series focus upon political, social, and economic issues.

17.9 Dowden, Anne Ophelia. **From Flower to Fruit.** Ticknor & Fields Books for Young Readers, 1994. 56 pp. ISBN 0-395-68376-9.

How do plants reproduce? This beautifully illustrated book will clearly answer that question. Starting with the flower, you will learn about fertilization, fruits, and how seeds start the whole process over again. Learn the difference between dry fruits (grains and nuts) and fleshy fruits (berries, tomatoes, cucumbers, apples, etc.).

17.10 Dowden, Anne Ophelia. **Poisons in Our Path.** HarperCollins, 1994. 64 pp. ISBN 0-06-020861-9.

Did you know that many of our beautiful house plants are poisonous? Learn which ones are lovely to look at but should never be eaten. Did you know that poison ivy is not really poisonous, but if it is eaten the swelling eruptions could bring on suffocation? This intriguing book is full of colored pictures, and it discusses interesting "plants that harm and heal."

17.11 Dowden, Anne Ophelia. **The Blossom on the Bough.** Ticknor & Fields Books for Young Readers, 1994. 71 pp. ISBN 0-395-68375-0.

This beautifully illustrated guide to trees is as much an art book as a science book. With this book, you can learn about how trees grow, why leaves change colors, and the role that flowers play in tree reproduction. The illustrations can help you identify the trees that you see in your world.

17.12 Duffy, Trent. **The Vanishing Wetlands.** Franklin Watts, 1994. 159 pp. ISBN 0-531-13034-7.

Severe floods! Erosion! Dirty water! No breeding place for fish or fowl! No migratory resting place for birds! These are a few of the disasters that will befall us if we continue to lose wetlands to development and agriculture. Duffy describes the different kinds of wetlands, their importance, the politics and economics influencing decisions about land use, and the kinds of animals and plants the wetlands support. He also offers creative suggestions for the use of wetlands.

17.13 Durrell, Ann, Jean Craighead George, and Katherine Paterson, editors. **The Big Book for Our Planet.** Dutton Children's Books, 1993. 136 pp. ISBN 0-525-45119-6.

Marvel at our planet Earth! Why are weeds important? How can we appreciate the ugly bat? This book holds a collection of poems, stories, and essays centered around the theme "Earth." It challenges the reader to think about how people can learn to live in harmony with their environment on this planet. Over forty respected authors and illustrators represent twenty-eight literary pieces for children and adults to savor.

17.14 Halpern, Robert R. **Green Planet Rescue: Saving the Earth's Endangered Plants.** Franklin Watts, 1993. 64 pp. ISBN 0-531-11095-8.

Plants are the basis for all animal survival, providing medicine, food, shelter, and oxygen. Yet, forests are being destroyed at alarming rates, and with this destruction comes the elimination of many species of plants and animals. This is serious because the bonds between plants and animals are vital to continuing life on Earth! A glossary includes further related readings and the names of organizations involved in saving plant and animal life throughout the world.

17.15 Hirshi, Ron. **Save Our Oceans and Coasts.** Photographs by Erwin and Peggy Bauer and others. Delacorte Press, 1993. 72 pp. ISBN 0-385-31077-3.

This book takes you on a walk along the rocky Pacific Northwest shoreline, where you will begin to understand the interconnections between land and sea, and among the plants and animals which live in the water and along its edge. You will explore beaches, oceans, and swamps to learn about roseate terns, brown pelicans, monk seals, manatees, sea turtles, and crocodiles. This book includes information about political issues and economics, as well as the ecology of shorelines.

17.16 Johnson, Rebecca L. **Investigating the Ozone Hole.** Lerner Publications, 1993. 112 pp. ISBN 0-8225-1574-1.

Nature, Ecology, and the Environment 243

Have you ever wondered why it is dangerous to spend too much time in the sun? This book about ozone depletion explains what has happened to the earth's protective layer. Years of chemicals called chlorofluorocarbons (CFCs) have escaped into the air from refrigerators, styrofoam production, and aerosols, causing ozone depletion. Without a protective layer of ozone, harmful ultraviolet rays damage the earth's plants and animals, including human beings.

17.17 Jordan, Martin, and Tanis Jordan. **Jungle Days, Jungle Nights.** Kingfisher Books, 1993. 40 pp. ISBN 1-85697-885.

Travel into the steamy Amazon Jungle of South America as you flip through this dazzling picture book. The full-page colored paintings and easy-to-read informative text bring to life the plants and animals of this exotic rain forest. You will meet caimans, basilisk lizards, and Orinoco crocodiles. You'll even encounter the world's largest rodent, known as a capybara, as well as the world's tiniest monkey, the pygmy marmoset.

17.18 Keene, Ann T. **Earthkeepers: Observers and Protectors of Nature.** Oxford University Press, 1994. 222 pp. ISBN 0-19-507867-5.

Throughout history, there have been men and women who cared about preserving the natural beauty of our Earth. This book is about those "keepers" and the roles they played. William Bartram, for example, was an eighteenth-century naturalist who lived in Florida. Today, saving the environment is a political issue, as ecologists balance nature and development. Also included is a list of conservation and nature organizations.

17.19 Lavies, Bianca. **Compost Critters.** Dutton Children's Books, 1993. 32 pp. ISBN 0-525-44763-6.

Imagine calling garbage a "veritable banquet!" Bianca Lavies does just that, as she builds a compost pile and then closely observes and photographs the process of decomposition. With enlarged, detailed photos, readers see hyphae on mold, as it turns a piece of old bread to liquid. Earthworms tunnel through the compost, changing the chemical composition of organic material. After reading this book, you'll want a compost pile of your own.

17.20 Lerner, Carol. **Plants That Make You Sniffle and Sneeze.** Morrow Junior Books, 1993. 32 pp. ISBN 0-688-11489-X.

If you find yourself sniffling and sneezing at the same time each year, you might suffer from hay fever. But hay fever is not caused by hay. This book describes a variety of plants, including trees, bushes, grasses, and weeds, which cause allergies. If you suffer from hay fever, you can also learn how to reduce your symptoms.

17.21 Lourie, Peter. **Everglades: Buffalo Tiger and the River of Grass.** Boyds Mills Press, 1994. 47 pp. ISBN 1-878093-91-6.

Chief Buffalo Tiger narrates the story of the Everglades and points out the diversity of species that exists there. He explains the special relationship that the Miccosukee Indians have with this wilderness area, as well as the fragile balance of species of plants and animals, now affected by pollution and development. This is one of five books in a series about rivers. The others discuss the ecology of rivers, as the author journeys down them: Hudson River, Amazon River, Yukon River, and Delaware River.

17.22 Love, Ann, and Jane Drake. **Take Action: An Environmental Book for Kids.** Illustrated by Pat Cupples. Tambourine Books, 1993 (U.S. edition). 96 pp. ISBN 0-688-12465-8.

If pesticides are killing the animals at the top of the food chain, can they also be killing humans? Absolutely! Learning why and where environmental problems have arisen (and how you can help solve some of these problems) is the focus of this book. Published with funds from the World Wildlife Fund, the book offers activities to help readers understand the chain reactions in nature.

17.23 Love, Douglas. **Be Kind to Your Mother (Earth) and Blame It on the Wolf.** HarperCollins/Festival, 1993. 71 pp. ISBN 0-06-021106-7.

The two hilarious plays in this book use satire and perspective shifts to make their points! "Be Kind to Your Mother (Earth)" takes actors through a time warp, revisiting the Boston Tea Party, George Washington and the cherry tree, and the Dodo bird, to discuss lost possibilities: "If only I had..." In the end, the characters find that the future is theirs, for shaping the environment.

17.24 Maynard, Thane. **Endangered Animal Babies.** Franklin Watts, 1993. 57 pp. ISBN 0-531-11077-X.

Imagine a baby who drinks 150 gallons of its mother's milk a day. This baby, the biggest baby in the world, is the blue whale, which weighs about 2,500 pounds at birth. Twenty-eight endangered baby animals, both insects and vertebrates, are discussed in this book, with information bullets, location maps, colorful photographs, and precise text. Always, the threats to these babies are the same: human beings, elimination of breeding grounds, pollution, and overkill. In this Cincinnati Zoo series, another book by the same author is *Saving Endangered Birds*.

Nature, Ecology, and the Environment 245

17.25 McClung, Robert. **Lost Wild America: The Story of Our Extinct and Vanishing Wildlife.** Illustrated by Bob Hines. Linnet Books, 1993. 277 pp. ISBN 0-208-02359-3.

What is the balance between extinction and evolution? What were the U.S. policies that resulted in destruction of nature? This "state of the species" report documents the fate of extinct and endangered species in the United States. Historical accounts of American conservation, as well as current global eco-political issues, are included in this updated version of McClung's 1969 edition.

17.26 McVey, Vicki. **The Sierra Club Kid's Guide to Planet Care and Repair.** Illustrated by Martha Weston. Sierra Club Books for Children, 1993. 84 pp. ISBN 0-87156-567-6.

Too often, we believe that we cannot do anything to protect our earth from further environmental destruction. This book suggests many ways for people of all ages to become involved in improving the environment, including projects, imaginative games, and hands-on activities. McVey's narratives tell of people who have made a difference in saving the earth's environment.

17.27 Oppenheim, Joanne. **Floratorium.** Byron Preiss Visual Publications/Bantam Books, 1994. 47 pp. ISBN 0-553-09365-7.

Floratorium will introduce you to the world of plants, as you join a group of students taking a trip through a science museum. From the briefing room, you will walk to the Hall of Flowering Plants, through the Tropical Rain Forest, and on to investigate freshwater and saltwater plants. In *Oceanarium,* another book by this author, you can visit tidal waters, coastal waters, and a coral reef.

17.28 Pringle, Laurence. **Oil Spills: Damage, Recovery, and Prevention.** Morrow Junior Books, 1993. 56 pp. ISBN 0-688-09860-6.

Millions of plants and animals are killed each year by oil spills! Since the entire world relies upon fossil fuels for energy, fossil fuels are transported all over the globe, and spills can happen anywhere. Pringle explains how oil spills occur, the damage they cause, and how they are cleaned up.

17.29 Russo, Monica. **Tree Almanac: A Year-round Activity Guide.** Photographs by Kevin Byron. Sterling Publishing, 1993. 128 pp. ISBN 0-8069-1252-9.

If you are fascinated by trees, then you will love this book. *Tree Almanac* contains just about everything you might want to know about these magnificent plants. What are the parts of a tree? What are some of the major kinds of trees? What are the changes that trees go through during the seasons?

17.30 Taylor, Dave. **Endangered Ocean Animals.** Crabtree Publishing, 1993. 32 pp. ISBN 0-86505-533-5.

"Shoot on sight!" That was the command of the California Fisheries Commission in 1899 when it was believed that the Steller sea lion was interfering with the fishing industry. Now we know that the sea lions had little impact on the industry. Nevertheless, thousands of these animals were killed. In this book in the Endangered Animals series, the reader also learns about other ocean animals which are endangered. The book concludes with information about research and action for saving endangered ocean species. Other books in this series by Dave Taylor are *Endangered Island Animals, Endangered Wetland Animals, Endangered Forest Animals, Endangered Savannah Animals, Endangered Desert Animals, Endangered Mountain Animals,* and *Endangered Grassland Animals*.

17.31 Vogel, Carole G., and Goldner, Kathryn A. **The Great Yellowstone Fire.** Sierra Club/Little, Brown and Company, 1993. 31 pp. ISBN 0-316-90249-7.

In 1988, a "Great Fire" destroyed a large section of Yellowstone National Park, but firefighters fought desperately and successfully to save the historic Old Faithful Inn. Photographs tell the dramatic story of the progression of the fire, the changes it made to the landscape, and the threat it posed to wildlife that struggled to survive. The authors treat the phenomenon of fire as a natural process in the shaping of the earth.

17.32 Wekesser, Carol, editor. **Water.** Greenhaven Press, 1994. 191 pp. ISBN 1-56510-064-6.

This book discusses the seriousness of water pollution, strategies for management of the water supply, and the real dangers of acid rain. As in other books in the Opposing Viewpoints series, the editor includes multiple perspectives for each topic.

17.33 Whitman, Sylvia. **This Land Is Your Land.** Lerner Publications, 1994. 87 pp. ISBN 0-8225-1729-9.

The conservation movement has changed with evolving national needs. In the 1870s, it was important to preserve beautiful scenery from land development. Conservation also means, however, preservation of all species. Enemies of the conservation movement have included atomic weapons, pesticides, global warming, acid rain, and water pollution. This book tells the story of the conservation movement in the United States.

17.34 Wolfson, Evelyn. **From the Earth to beyond the Sky.** Houghton Mifflin, 1993. 96 pp. ISBN 0-395-55009-2.

Often, when people think of medical discoveries, they picture sterile labs with dedicated scientists studying computer printouts, chemical experiments, or treated animals. But many medical discoveries have taken place far from that mythical lab, in the forests, plains, and coastlines of our country. The discoverers of substances used in aspirin and quinine are the same individuals who realized the importance of hygiene and the concept of contagion. These medical pioneers are Native Americans.

18 The Animal Kingdom

18.1 Booth, Jerry. **Big Bugs.** Harcourt Brace & Company, 1994. 48 pp. ISBN 0-15-200693-1.

Does the idea of "big bugs" give you the creeps? This book promises to "take the 'ug' out of bug." Insects are the most numerous group of animals on the planet. This book will teach you how to observe and study insects, and it will answer many questions: How can you plant a garden that is guaranteed to attract insects to study? How can you collect crickets at night? It will also introduce you to some Greenpatch Kids, students who are making a difference in protecting their environment.

18.2 Bowen, Betsy. **Tracks in the Wild.** Little, Brown and Company, 1993. 32 pp. ISBN 0-316-10377-2.

Betsy Bowen takes you on a tour of the animals who live near her Minnesota North Woods home. How does she find these animals? From their tracks. The book is beautifully illustrated with block-print pictures of each animal, along with life-size footprints. Quotes about nature, many from Native Americans, complete this delightful book.

18.3 Brandenburg, Jim. **To the Top of the World.** Walker and Company, 1993. 44 pp. ISBN 0-8027-8219-1.

Wildlife photographer Jim Brandenburg is assigned to photograph a wolf pack on a remote Alaskan island during the summer, when the sun never sets. Once his presence is accepted by the pack, Jim settles in to record their lives. Despite being almost trampled by a stampeding herd of musk oxen, Jim captures impressive and beautiful moments of the wolves at work and at play.

18.4 Brooks, Bruce. **Making Sense: Animal Perception and Communication.** Farrar, Straus, and Giroux, 1993. 74 pp. ISBN 0-374-34742-5.

Some intelligent animals like dolphins and whales use their brains to receive and interpret sonic feedback. Other, lower forms of animals, like the starfish, depend upon their sense of touch to locate food. No matter how complex or simple the sensory system is, all animals have mechanisms in the brain for translating the meaning of sensations so that they can survive in their own environments.

The Animal Kingdom

18.5 Cerullo, Mary M. **Lobsters: Gangsters of the Sea.** Cobblehill Books, 1994. 52 pp. ISBN 0-525-65153-5.

How big can a lobster get? The largest one caught was over three feet long and weighed over forty-four pounds! Find out why this author calls lobsters "gangsters," and why the lobster man and the lobster are "linked like a trap and a buoy." This picture book is filled with information about the combative lobsters and those who make their living catching them.

18.6 Clark, Margaret Goff. **The Endangered Florida Panther.** Cobblehill Books, 1993. 54 pp. ISBN 0-525-65114-4.

The Florida panther is Florida's state animal and one of the world's most endangered animals. This book provides a lively recounting of efforts to save the Florida panther. To help the panthers share territory with humans, the Highway Department has developed special passageways under the highway to permit their natural migration. Wildlife biologists fit panthers with radio transmitters to learn about them. This book gives an up-close view of this rare and beautiful animal.

18.7 Collard, Sneed B., III. **Sea Snakes.** Boyds Mills Press, 1993. 32 pp. ISBN 1-56397-004-X.

You've probably heard stories about giant sea serpents. The truth is that most snakes living in the sea are quite small but very poisonous. This easy-to-read, illustrated book will tell you all about the two major groups of sea snakes—the sea kraits and the true snakes. You will learn where they live, how they eat, and how they move around in the water.

18.8 Davis, Lloyd Spenser. **Penguin: A Season in the Life of the Adélie Penguin.** Harcourt Brace Children's Books, 1994. 76 pp. ISBN 0-15-200070-4.

Would you like to know what it is like to be a penguin? What is a penguin's daily routine? How does a penguin search for food? This book is written and illustrated from the penguin's viewpoint. The Antarctic landscape is painted as both beautiful and harsh. As these penguins "speak" of their life, you will have a new appreciation for the beauty of nature and the wonder of survival.

18.9 Dewey, Jennifer Owings. **Wildlife Rescue: The Work of Dr. Kathleen Ramsay.** Photographs by Don MacCarter. Boyds Mills Press, 1994. 63 pp. ISBN 1-56397-045-7.

A day in the life of veterinarian Kathleen Ramsay is filled with unexpected events: saving orphaned, newborn beaver kits; treating an owl with a bullet hole in its head; caring for a bobcat with a torn ear; and sewing up a turtle hit by a car. Many color photographs help tell the story of this amazing doctor whose New Mexico clinic is filled with animals recuperating from injuries and waiting to be returned to the wild.

18.10 Dixon, Dougal. **Dinosaurs.** Boyds Mills Press, 1993. 160 pp. ISBN 1-56397-261-1.

Which dinosaur was the most intelligent? Which was the heaviest dinosaur? These are some of the fascinating questions answered in this book, which profiles more than twenty-five different dinosaurs. You will learn about the early days of the dinosaurs, as well as the work of fossil hunters who are trying now to reconstruct the past through fossil records. Each dinosaur is described in a two-page spread with pictures and detailed information.

18.11 Emory, Jerry. **Night Prowlers: Everyday Creatures under Every Night Sky.** Harcourt Brace & Company, 1994. 48 pp. ISBN 0-15-200694-X.

Ever wonder about the hoots and creaks and squeaks that you hear in the night? This book is a how-to manual for investigating the animals of the dark. How can you build a house for an owl? What should you do when observing animals at night? These are just a few of the questions answered in this book.

18.12 Facklam, Margery. **What Does the Crow Know? The Mysteries of Animal Intelligence.** Sierra Club Books for Children, 1994. 45 pp. ISBN 0-87156-544-7.

Can animals think? Can animals paint pictures? One elephant is quite famous for her paintings. Read about animals who can count and discern the difference between colors and shapes. Find out why a trained animal learns to disobey its owner in order to save the master's life. Discover how a dog or monkey can become a valuable helpmate to a disabled human. Fascinating reading, this book opens a new perspective to the animal kingdom and new insights into how learning occurs.

18.13 Gerstenfeld, Sheldon L., D.V.M. **The Aquarium Take-along Book.** Viking, 1994. 104 pp. ISBN 0-670-84386-5.

Would you like to take a trip to an aquarium? With this book, you will go behind the scenes and learn interesting facts from the aquarium veterinarians. Why are jellyfish kept in circular tanks? How do oysters make pearls? How do you give a turtle an X-ray? This book may start you on a new career.

18.14 Gowell, Elizabeth Tayntor. **Sea Jellies: Rainbows in the Sea.** Franklin Watts, 1993. 59 pp. ISBN 0-531-15259-6.

The sea jellies float like rainbow-colored balloons through the sea. They are an amazing class of simple, yet beautiful creatures. Learn about moon jellies, corals, the Portuguese man-of-war, and many other animals. Sea jellies have lived in the oceans for millions of years. Isn't it time you discovered them?

18.15 Grace, Eric S. **Snakes.** Sierra Club Books for Children, 1994. 64 pp. ISBN 0-87156-490-4.

What would you do if you saw a snake in the grass? Run? Scream? Add it to your reptile collection? Snakes are possibly the most feared of all animals, and yet 75 percent of the world's snakes are not poisonous and not threatening to people. This book is full of information about this common reptile that's found in every climate and in every part of the world except Antarctica. Other books about animals in the Sierra Club Wildlife Library include *Wolves,* by R. D. Lawrence, and *Seals,* by Eric S. Grace.

18.16 Hecht, Jeff. **Vanishing Life: The Mystery of Mass Extinctions.** Charles Scribner's Sons, 1993. 149 pp. ISBN 0-684-19331-0.

What happened to the dinosaurs? There are lots of different theories, and this book explores several of them. But that's just the beginning. Did you know that there have been several other examples of mass extinction throughout our planet's history? This book presents clear and detailed scientific evidence reflecting these startling changes in our world.

18.17 Herriot, James. **James Herriot's Cat Stories.** St. Martin's Press, 1994. 161 pp. ISBN 0-312-11342-0.

Are you a cat lover? James Herriot, the famous British veterinarian, tells stories about Moses, the orphan kitten, adopted by a mother pig and nursed along with the piglets; Emily, the gentle tabby who brightens up the life of a lonely old man; Oscar, the socialite, who spends his nights visiting all the action spots in town; and seven other interesting felines.

18.18 Knight, Lindsay. **The Sierra Club Book of Small Mammals.** Sierra Club Books for Children, 1993. 68 pp. ISBN 0-87156-525-0.

If you are interested in learning more about mammals, this book is for you. The technical text is accompanied by outstanding photographs and drawings. The author takes you on a tour of the class *mammalia*, from spiny anteaters, to whales and dolphins, to horses and rhinoceroses, to dogs and cats.

18.19 Landau, Elaine. **Rabies.** Lodestar Books, 1993. 52 pp. ISBN 0-525-67403-9.

Why is it so important to have your pet cat or dog vaccinated? Why should you avoid contact with wild animals, especially if they appear sick? These are just two of the questions answered in Elaine Landau's well-researched book, *Rabies.* You might have thought that rabies is a disease that only wild animals carry. Through case studies and graphic photographs, this book describes how even healthy appearing pets can carry the rabies virus. This book presents ideas to protect not only yourself, but also your pets from this disease.

18.20 Lang, Susan S. **Invisible Bugs and Other Creepy Creatures That Live with You.** Sterling Publishing, 1993. 96 pp. ISBN 0-8069-8209-8.

Imagine being able to shrink to the size of the microscopic creatures that are in your living room carpet. What would you see? This book will take you on a tour of the world of dust mites and other "bugs" that live on and around you all of the time.

18.21 Lasky, Kathryn. **Monarchs.** Gulliver Green Book/Harcourt Brace & Company, 1993. 64 pp. ISBN 0-15-255296-0.

Starting in Maine and ending in Mexico, the monarch butterfly makes a remarkable journey during its lifetime. This book dramatically documents the life of the monarch, along with the lives of the people who have been affected by these butterflies touch. In Penobscot Bay, Maine, Clara Waterman watches as the monarchs emerge from their chrysalises. Several months later in the Mexican state of Michoacan, the monarchs spend their winter. But their safety is being threatened by logging, just as they are being threatened in another of their homes, Pacific Grove, California, where, through a grassroots effort of the community, the winter grove of trees was saved from destruction.

18.22 Lavies, Bianca. **A Gathering of Garter Snakes.** Dutton Children's Books, 1993. 25 pp. ISBN 0-525-45099-8.

Read about a woman who moved into a house vacated by its previous owners because it was full of snakes! The new owner likes to sit in her living room and watch the snakes play. Find out how a snake breathes as it swallows its food. Read about a photographer who had a snake crawl inside his camera and found another one curled up in his back seat! This book is written in a readable essay style, punctuated with dramatic pictures.

18.23 Lavies, Bianca. **Killer Bees.** Dutton Children's Books, 1994. 29 pp. ISBN 0-525-45243-5.

The name "killer bee" conjures up all sorts of images of science-fiction movie monsters. But killer (or more accurately, "Africanized") bees are real. This book describes how the bees were first bred in the late 1950s to produce more honey, how they were accidentally released into the wild, how they have multiplied and migrated to cover nearly all of South and Central America, and how they are beginning to move into North America. The book also describes how Brazilian communities have learned to live in harmony with the bees.

18.24 Lavies, Bianca. **Tundra Swans.** Dutton Children's Books, 1994. 27 pp. ISBN 0-525-45273-7.

Through text and photographs, this book tells a remarkable story of the tundra swan, a bird that migrates from Canada to the Chesapeake Bay. Because their population is shrinking, like that of the trumpeter swans before them, researchers follow their breeding, feeding, and migratory habits through complicated electronic devices.

18.25 Lindblad, Lisa. **The Serengeti Migration: Africa's Animals on the Move.** Photography by Sven-Olof Lindblad. Hyperion Books, 1994. 40 pp. ISBN 1-56282-668-9.

Join the wildebeests and zebras in their annual 700-mile migration, which takes them through Serengeti National Park in Tanzania and Kenya, in search of greener pastures. Impalas, elephants, cape buffalo, and black rhinoceros are just a few of the animals they meet during the nine-month arduous journey. Colored photographs document the landscape and the life cycle of animals which are dependent on rain.

18.26 Morris, Desmond. **The World of Animals.** Viking, 1993. 128 pp. ISBN 0-670-85184-1.

From the armadillo to the zebra, this book will show you the world of animals with interesting facts and stories. Did you know that the koala, often thought of as cute and cuddly, is really one of the most sluggish mammals? It sleeps eighteen hours a day.

Did you know that the American bison was systematically eliminated as a way to control the Native American population? These are just a few of the facts that you will learn in this book.

18.27 Myers, Jack. **Do Cats Really Have Nine Lives?** Boyds Mills Press, 1993. 60 pp. ISBN 1-56397-215-8.

Curious about the world of science? This entertaining resource provides answers to questions kids often ask *Highlights* science editor, Jack Myers. You'll discover how dogs wag their tails, how baby birds breathe inside their eggs, and why giraffes have long necks. You'll even learn about the world's tiniest mammal, the 2 1/2- inch white-toothed pigmy shrew. Other books in this series which answer questions are *Can Birds Get Lost?*, *How Do We Dream?*, and *What Makes Popcorn Pop?*

18.28 Nardo, Don. **The Extinction of the Dinosaurs.** Lucent Books, 1994. 48 pp. ISBN 1-56006-154-5.

What happened to the dinosaur? This book presents several viewpoints with clear and simple explanations. Did extinction occur because of disease? A collision with an asteroid? Changes in climate? Read the evidence and make up your own mind.

18.29 Parker, Steve. **Frogs and Toads.** Sierra Club Books for Children, 1994. 57 pp. ISBN 0-87156-466-1.

Enjoy a wealth of knowledge about the frogs and toads, in this beautifully illustrated book with fold-out pages that provide additional information. You can learn about the variety of frogs and toads, how frogs and toads grow, and what they eat. Another book by Steve Parker, *Whales and Dolphins,* will tell you about a typical day for a dolphin and explain how whales breathe.

18.30 Patent, Dorothy Hinshaw. **Horses: Understanding Animals.** Carolrhoda Books, 1994. 48 pp. ISBN 0-87614-766-X.

Horses, wild or tame, are fascinating animals. They can be strong, fast, and powerful, yet sensitive, gentle, and affectionate. Horses like company and will get bored and lonely if kept by themselves. Often they are paired with a buddy horse or even a goat to keep them happy. Did you know you can adopt a wild horse for $125 from the Bureau of Land Management? This information book, filled with many color photographs, tells you how.

18.31 Patent, Dorothy Hinshaw. **What Good Is a Tail?** Cobblehill Books/Dutton, 1994. 32 pp. ISBN 0-525-65148-9.

The Animal Kingdom

Besides walking upright, humans differ in another way from most animals: we have no tails! Ever wonder why animals and mammals have tails and what purpose they serve? Find out how some animals use their tails as an extra leg, a steering mechanism, or even a communication tool. This short picture book explores the vital uses of tails. Although the book is aimed at a young audience, more mature readers will find this a quick read full of interesting trivia about tails. Illustrated with beautiful color photographs.

18.32 Silverstein, Alvin, Virginia Silverstein, and Robert Silverstein. **The Red Wolf.** Millbrook Press, 1994. 48 pp. ISBN 1-56294-416-9.

Explore the life of a misunderstood and endangered animal, the red wolf. We have grown up with the idea of "the big, bad wolf," but actually wolves are a remarkable and basically shy relative of the domestic dog. Another book by the Silversteins about an endangered species is *The Spotted Owl*. The spotted owl is at the center of the logging debate in the Pacific Northwest. Should the old-growth forests that house these animals be protected or harvested for lumber? These two books will help you make up your own mind about these animals.

18.33 Snedden, Robert. **What Is a Bird?** Sierra Club Books for Children, 1993. 32 pp. ISBN 0-81756-539-0.

What is a bird? What is an insect? How do birds and insects eat? Why don't fish drown? This series of books combines lively photographs from Oxford Scientific Films, accurate illustrations, and good writing to describe the nature of animals. Other books in the What Is a . . . series include *What Is an Insect?* and *What Is a Fish?*.

18.34 Swanson, Diane. **Safari beneath the Sea: The Wonder World of the North Pacific Coast.** Sierra Club Books for Children, 1994. 58 pp. ISBN 0-87156-415-7.

Imagine a place where millions of microscopic creatures create a dazzling light show. Listen to the songs of the humpback whales as they join in a chorus of sighs, chirps, and squeaks. Watch a group of sea lions scampering through the water. This book is beautifully illustrated and presents interesting facts, as well as little-known oddities about one of the world's most nutrient-rich areas, the waters off British Columbia, Washington, Oregon, and Southeast Alaska.

18.35 Taylor, Barbara. **The Bird Atlas.** Dorling Kindersley, 1993. 64 pp. ISBN 1-56458-327-9.

If you have ever wanted to travel around the world exploring the bird life of our planet, this is the book for you! It is organized geographically, with maps of each region, and provides an illustrated glossary to the birds of each area. How do birds in the Arctic differ from those at the Equator? What birds are common to the North American forests and woodlands? What are the colors of birds in the rain forests of South America? You can find out in this book.

18.36 Taylor, David. **Nature's Creatures of the Dark.** Dial Books for Young Readers, 1993. 13 pp. ISBN 0-8037-1631-1.

In this book, you will read about fascinating nocturnal creatures that create their own light. Discover the difference between a firefly and a glowworm, and find out how few bioluminescent beetles it takes to produce enough light to read a book. Read about how an owl's feathers act like a satellite, creating a sound detector as strong as a doctor's stethoscope. And, experience the thrill of three-dimensional, pop-up pictures, with glow-in-the-dark features on every page.

18.37 Van Der Linde, Laurel. **The White Stallions: The Story of the Dancing Horses of Lipizza.** New Discovery Books, 1994. 72 pp. ISBN 0-02-759055-0.

They are the most famous performing horses in the world, and their history goes back four centuries. Many times, their Austrian home has been in danger, but never more than during World War II when Hitler's forces threatened to destroy it. Amazingly, help came from United States' General George Patton himself, who launched Operation Cowboy to rescue the horses by smuggling all 1000 horses to safety!

18.38 **Visual Dictionary of the Horse.** Dorling Kindersley, 1994. 64 pp. ISBN 1-56458-504-2.

Do you like horses but don't know a fetlock from a forelock or a whinny from a hinny? Over 200 photographs and 5000 terms help you learn all about horses, both inside and out, and make this a dictionary resource you'll turn to again and again.

19 Mental and Physical Health

19.1 Anonymous. **It Happened to Nancy.** Beatrice Sparks, editor. Avon/Flare, 1994. 241 pp. ISBN 0-380-77315-5.

Fourteen-year-old Nancy shares, through her diary, a personal and painful story about the reality of HIV and AIDS. Telling the story of how one sexual experience led to a sentence of death, Nancy encourages readers to think about individual responsibility and the need for increased education and understanding. The book concludes with a question-and-answer section about HIV/AIDS and a short list of resources and hotline numbers.

19.2 Bode, Janet. **Death Is Hard to Live With: Teenagers Talk about How They Cope with Loss.** Delacorte Press, 1993. 178 pp. ISBN 0-385-314042-2.

Coping with the loss of a loved one is always difficult. Janet Bode focuses on the special needs of teens who face the grieving process. Interviews with them and with religious and social leaders provide a window to grief and pain, and to the healing process. Source notes, suggested readings, and a list of recommended videos are included.

19.3 Bode, Janet, and Stan Mack. **Heartbreak and Roses.** Illustrated by Stan Mack. Delacorte Press, 1994. 162 pp. ISBN 0-385-32068-X.

All too often, love stories in books are just too perfect: perfect guy, perfect girl, perfect relationship. But not this time. These are real stories, shared by real young adults. Some of them are bittersweet, others just bitter. There are couples respecting each other and couples abusing each other; couples postponing sex and couples having sex; couples falling in love and couples breaking up. In these stories you may see your friends, your parents, and even yourself.

19.4 Boyd, George. **Drugs and Sex.** Rosen Publishing, 1994. 64 pp. ISBN 0-8239-1538-7.

Social pressures often encourage drug use and early sexuality. In this book, a drug counselor explores myths about the effects of drugs on sexuality. A concise fact sheet, a resource list, a brief glossary, a bibliography, and an index make the book particularly useful. Another title in the Drug Abuse Prevention Library, an extensive series about specific substances and issues surrounding their use, is *Designer Drugs*.

19.5 Bryan, Jenny. **Breathing: The Respiratory System.** Dillon Press, 1993. 48 pp. ISBN 0-87518-563-0.

What causes colds and the flu? How do our lungs work? What are the dangers of tobacco? These are just a few of the questions that this book will answer about the respiratory system. With well-written text and excellent diagrams and pictures, this book will help you understand how to build healthy bodies, as well as tell you about some health problems, including asthma, tuberculosis, and cystic fibrosis. Additional books by Jenny Bryan in the Body Talk series explain other systems in the body: *Digestion: The Digestive System; Movement: The Muscular and Skeletal System;* and *The Pulse of Life: The Circulatory System*.

19.6 Crocker, Mary. **The Body Atlas.** Oxford University Press, 1994. 64 pp. ISBN 0-19-520963-X.

Imagine that your body is a well-organized country, and you will have some idea about the organization of *The Body Atlas*. The atlas looks at six major body systems—digestive, transport, skeletal, muscular, nervous, and reproductive—and describes how each works. The book is generously illustrated, and the descriptions are clear.

19.7 Dentemaro, Christine, and Rachel Kranz. **Straight Talk about Student Life.** Facts on File, 1993. 140 pp. ISBN 0-8160-2735-8.

Are you starting to think about high school or just having trouble keeping your grades up and staying focused? Do you have trouble identifying what the real problems are and how you feel about possible solutions? Are you sometimes stretched too tight because you want to be in too many extracurricular activities? This book explores all these situations, offering answers to these questions and many others regarding school and related social situations.

19.8 Dolan, Edward. **Teenagers and Compulsive Gambling.** Franklin Watts, 1994. 140 pp. ISBN 0-531-11100-8.

Dolan investigates the spread of compulsive gambling and the patterns of behavior that characterize the gambler. The special considerations of teens addicted to gambling are addressed throughout the book. If you have a gambling casino or racetrack near your home, are you more likely to become addicted to gambling? Facts and history highlight the unique problems of compulsive gambling.

19.9 Durrett, Deanne. **Organ Transplants.** Lucent Books, 1993. 96 pp. ISBN 1-56006-137-5.

Have you ever thought about whether you would want to donate your kidneys or eyes to someone if you were killed in an accident? Many lives have been saved by organ transplants, but donors or their families have to agree. This book explains the history and process of transplanting organs and explores complex medical, legal, and ethical questions, along with predictions for future transplant techniques. Diagrams, photographs, and other illustrations provide additional information.

19.10 Ford, Michael Thomas. **100 Questions and Answers about AIDS: What You Need to Know Now.** Beech Tree Books, 1993. 202 pp. ISBN 0-688-12697-9.

How long can you live if you are HIV positive? Ford combines up-to-date factual information with personal accounts of what it is like to live and die with the AIDS virus. The interviews with young persons who have AIDS make the cold facts much more real and the danger much more clear. A resource guide, glossary, and index make this a valuable source for anyone who wants to learn more about HIV/AIDS awareness and education.

19.11 Galas, Judith C. **Teen Suicide.** Lucent Books, 1994. 128 pp. ISBN 1-56006-148-0.

Do you have a friend who is depressed or thinking about suicide? As teen deaths from suicide increase, experts continue to search for information and understanding about this tragic societal problem. This book discusses pressures from family, school, and society, from substance abuse, and from peer influences. Graphs, photographs, cartoons, and anecdotes help make this book interesting. An appendix offers a list of common myths about suicidal behavior, a checklist of warning signs, and a self-evaluation for depression.

19.12 Gay, Kathlyn. **Breast Implants: Making Safe Choices.** New Discovery Books, 1993. 128 pp. ISBN 0-02-737955-8.

Newspapers have been filled with court cases about the medical and legal controversies which surround breast-implant surgery, especially the use of silicone gel implants. Why do women choose to have implants? What decisions do they have to make? This book discusses safety, testing, regulation, and societal concerns and presents women's personal stories, which reflect the conflicting reasons for their decisions. Source notes provide additional information, and a bibliography, organizations list, and index are provided.

19.13 Gay, Kathlyn. **The Right to Die: Public Controversy, Private Matter.** Millbrook Press, 1993. 128 pp. ISBN 1-56294-325-1.

As medical technology allows us to live longer lives, complicated legal, ethical, and moral issues surrounding the right to die become more urgent. When should we pull the plug? Kathlyn Gay's book examines the complex emotional, psychological, and medical ramifications of assisted suicide and euthanasia. Current controversies and a look at how other countries approach this problem provide the reader with much to discuss. An extensive bibliography and source notes assist further study of this complicated topic.

19.14 Gravelle, Karen, and Susan Fischer. **Where Are My Birth Parents?** Walker and Company, 1993. 132 pp. ISBN 0-8027-8257-4.

If you are a teenage adoptee, then you've probably wondered about your birth parents and entertained the idea of finding them. What is the process? Is it difficult? Expensive? Legal? Before asking these questions, address a more important one: Should I? Gravelle and Fischer explore the emotional risks and rewards, as well as the mechanics of searching for and identifying birth parents.

19.15 Grollman, Earl A. **Straight Talk about Death for Teenagers: How to Cope with Losing Someone You Love.** Beacon Press, 1993. 146 pp. ISBN 0-8070-2500-3.

People die. Grandparents, parents, friends, siblings. When it happens, how do you deal with it? Grollman offers advice for working through, not getting over, your grief. He talks about how you may feel immediately after a loved one or close friend has died; how different circumstances surrounding the deaths of special people—in accidents, by suicide, or by illness—may affect you differently; and how you can begin to rebuild your life. An appended journal offers a format for recording your feelings.

19.16 Hall, David E., M.D. **Living with Learning Disabilities: A Guide for Students.** Lerner Publications, 1993. 64 pp. ISBN 0-8225-0036-1.

Dr. Hall describes the confusion and uncertainty of living with a learning disorder and lists ways to counteract the negative effects of disabilities. Getting organized and recognizing your own learning strengths is a first step in overcoming learning problems. Practical tips to improve the chances for learning success are combined with suggestions for overcoming frustration and stress. Additional resources, a glossary, and an index are included.

19.17 Harris, Robie H. **It's Perfectly Normal: A Book about Changing Bodies, Growing Up, Sex, and Sexual Health.** Illustrated by Michael Emberly. Candlewick Press, 1994. 88 pp. ISBN 1-56402-199-8.

Biological and psychological changes, masturbation, reproduction, pregnancy, birth, sexual abuse, sexually transmitted diseases, and sexual responsibility are topics teens often ask about. This book answers many questions with humor and understanding. The cartoon-like illustrations add fun and information to this book, which encourages exchanges of information and feelings about sex.

19.18 Krizmanic, Judy. **A Teen's Guide to Going Vegetarian.** Illustrated by Matther Wawiorka. Viking, 1994. 218 pp. ISBN 0-670-85114-0.

To foster and encourage alternative nutrition, Judy Krizmanic has written an informative and persuasive book about being a vegetarian. Read about teens who have chosen to be vegetarians. Learn how they have adapted their diets and lifestyles. To help you become a vegetarian, the author includes varied recipes and practical guidelines for planning meals and snacks.

19.19 Kuklin, Susan. **Surviving Suicide: Young People Speak Up.** G. P. Putnam's Sons, 1994. 128 pp. ISBN 0-399-22605-2.

Susan Kuklin explains that she wrote this book to "help other survivors . . . and to help people understand that suicide is never a way to solve problems." She presents the stories of several suicide survivors—people who cope with the tragic loss of someone they cared for. Whether reading about the teenage boy whose mother ended her life after a long struggle with MS or about the sister who will never understand why her seemingly happy younger brother took his life, you will see a common thread: suicide is not the answer.

19.20 Landau, Elaine. **The Beauty Trap.** New Discovery Books, 1994. 128 pp. ISBN 0-02-751389-0.

The beauty trap is "a way of thinking that asserts that a woman's true value and desirability are essentially tied up in the way she looks." It is a value emphasized throughout society in folk tales, in Barbie dolls, and in beauty pageants. Women frequently resort to surgery and starvation as they try to live up to society's expectations. While the trap may be losing its allure, it still tempts young women. What are those temptations? How can girls avoid them?

19.21 Landau, Elaine. **Teenage Drinking.** Enslow Publishers, 1994. 104 pp. ISBN 0-89490-575-9.

Statistics about teen alcohol abuse only tell part of the story of physical and emotional pain that is caused when drinking gets out of control. The teens interviewed in this book reveal the long-term effects of alcoholism on families and on success in school. This book reviews those costs in health, safety, and personal relationships and discusses resources for families and communities. Issues in Focus series.

19.22 Lukas, Scott E. Ph.D. **Steroids.** Enslow Publishers, 1994. 112 pp. ISBN 0-89490-471-X.

Why do some athletes use anabolic steroids? Should you take steroids so you can be a track star? Scott Lucas' book presents factual and anecdotal information about a misunderstood and dangerous chemical. Particularly informative is an interview with a former steroid user who provides graphic detail about the implications of steroid use. Other books in this health-oriented series, The Drug Library, include *Alcohol, Nicotine, Designer Drugs, Heroin,* and *Cocaine and Crack.*

19.23 Maloney, Michael M.D., and Rachel Kranz. **Straight Talk about Eating Disorders.** Dell Publishing, 1991. 138 pp. ISBN 1-56294-259-X.

Eating disorders, including anorexia nervosa, bulimia, and compulsive eating, plague a significant number of people, young and old. A variety of factors contribute to eating disorders, including pressures of school and family. The authors include checklists, case studies, state and national resources, and practical examples to illustrate the physical and emotional problems of eating disorders. *Straight Talk about Anxiety and Depression* is another title in the High School Help Line series by the same authors.

19.24 Nottridge, Rhoda. **Care for Your Body.** Crestwood House, 1992. 32 pp. ISBN 0-89686-787-0.

This informative and readable work addresses questions about changing bodies and changing relationships. Health and hygiene concerns are examined along with addictions, sexuality, teen pregnancy, and stress. This book emphasizes a healthy respect for self and for others. It includes a glossary, book and resource list, and index.

19.25 Salter, Charles A. **Food Risks and Controversies: Minimizing the Dangers in Your Diet.** Millbrook Press, 1993. 111 pp. ISBN 1-56294-259X.

In a confusing world of food additives, pesticides, and chemicals, choosing foods wisely and managing your diet are increasingly important. This book explores a wide range of food issues and discusses regulation of the food industry. It can help you learn to shop intelligently and to interpret food labels.

19.26 Silverstein, Alvin, Virginia Silverstein, and Robert Silverstein. **Diabetes.** Enslow Publishers, 1994. 128 pp. ISBN 0-89490-464-7.

Learning to live with a disease requires knowledge, support, and patience. In this book from the Diseases and People series, the authors trace the symptoms, causes, and treatment for a disease which affects the daily lives of millions of people. It offers case studies and examples, along with a timeline, a question-and-answer section, a glossary, source notes, and a bibliography. The book also includes a discussion of research into the future prevention and treatment of diabetes.

19.27 Silverstein, Alvin, Virginia Silverstein, and Robert Silverstein. **Mononucleosis.** Enslow Publishers, 1993. 112 pp. ISBN 0-89490-466-3.

You have a sore throat, and you feel tired all the time. Do you have a cold, or is it mononucleosis? Using vignettes and personal stories to illustrate the complexities of mono, the authors discuss problems in diagnosis of the syndrome and also its treatment and prevention. Related diseases, such as Epstein-Barr virus and chronic fatigue syndrome, are also covered. Other books in the Diseases and People series include *Common Cold and Flu, Hepatitis, Rabies,* and *Tuberculosis.*

19.28 Siroff, Harriet. **The Road Back: Living with a Physical Disability.** New Discovery Books, 1993. 144 pp. ISBN 0-02-782885-9.

Like most teens, Trisha, Steven, and Christopher never dreamed they would be faced with serious illness or injury, but they now struggle with the physical and emotional tasks which face anyone who is suddenly disabled. Recovering from an accident, coping with unexpected illness, or facing the physical and mental challenge of rehabilitation requires teamwork from teens, their parents, their doctors, and their therapists. This Open Door Book examines the processes of rehabilitation and recovery from serious physical trauma.

19.29 Smith, Douglas. **Schizophrenia.** Franklin Watts, 1993. 95 pp. ISBN 0-531-12514-9.

Case studies and real-life examples help the reader to understand the complicated and confusing world of the schizophrenic. This book explores the causes and characteristics of schizophrenia and the social and medical issues involved in treating people with this complex mental illness. Readers wanting more information can consult the source notes and bibliography.

19.30 Walker, Richard. **The Children's Atlas of the Human Body.** Millbrook Press, 1994. 64 pp. ISBN 1-56294-503-3.

This book will take you on a journey through the human body using actual-size drawings and diagrams. How do muscles work? What keeps your heart beating? These are just a few of the interesting questions answered by this book. The life-sized drawings will give you a good idea of the size of your stomach, heart, intestines, and other internal organs. An enclosed poster shows a life-sized skeleton.

19.31 Wekesser, Carol, editor. **Health Care in America: Opposing Viewpoints.** David Bender and Bruno Leone, series editors. Greenhaven Press, 1994. 264 pp. ISBN 1-56510-134-0.

Health Care in America uses excerpts from national publications to present diverse opinions about the current state of medical care. By offering a variety of outlooks, from the physician's role in the current system, to the place of alternative medicines, to prospects for reform and the effects of regulation on the quality of care, this book reveals the complexity of the issues and the difficulty of arriving at a just solution to health-care problems in this country. For mature readers who want to explore diverse issues, other titles in the Opposing Viewpoints series include *Abortion, AIDS, Biomedical Ethics, Chemical Dependency, Death and Dying, The Elderly, Genetic Engineering,* and *Suicide.*

19.32 Westheimer, Ruth Dr. **Dr. Ruth Talks to Kids: Where You Came From, How Your Body Changes, and What Sex Is All About.** Macmillan, 1993. 96 pp. ISBN 0-02-792532-3.

When will my body develop? How old should I be when I have my first sexual experience? In her usual open and honest approach, Dr. Ruth answers basic questions about physical growth and sexual maturity. With humor and personal stories, she lets us know that curiosity about sex and growing up is healthy. A major theme of this book is the need to accept personal responsibility for sexual behavior. It presents information about contraception, sexual abuse, AIDS, and other sexually transmitted diseases. Clear definitions of terms and a booklist complete this guide.

VI Words to Remember

There is no Frigate like a Book
To take us Lands away
Nor any Coursers like a Page
Of prancing Poetry—

                                        Emily Dickinson, American poet

20 Poetry

20.1   Angelou, Maya. **On the Pulse of Morning.** Random House, 1993. Unpaged. ISBN 0-679-42894-1.

"On the Pulse of Morning" is the powerful poem written by Maya Angelou and read at President Clinton's inauguration ceremony on January 20, 1993. In this optimistic poem, Angelou celebrates the different races of people who make up America and asks us all to come together in peace. She challenges each American to have the courage and grace "on the pulse of this new day," to look each other in the eye and start anew with hope.

20.2   Duffy, Carol Ann, editor. **I Wouldn't Thank You for a Valentine.** Illustrated by Trisha Rafferty. Henry Holt and Company, 1994. 104 pp. ISBN 0-8050-2756-4.

The poet editor of this collection believes that "poetry is the sharpest and most memorable way of using language." She has collected poems written by women around the world. These strong poetic voices offer varying perspectives on what it means to be female, from Maya Angelou's celebratory "Phenomenal Woman" to Gwen Harwood's "A Simple Story" about sexual harassment.

20.3   Feelings, Tom, compiler. **Soul Looks Back in Wonder.** Illustrated by Tom Feelings. Dial, 1993. Unpaged. ISBN 0-8037-1001-1.

Tom Feelings did the artwork for this beautiful book and then asked thirteen African American writers to create poems to accompany the pictures. Authors from Walter Dean Myers to Margaret Walker celebrate what it means to be "children of African descent, children of the sun." This book offers poetry and art about destiny, creativity, the importance of ancestors and history, the power of reading, and the magic of dreams.

20.4   Fletcher, Ralph. **Poems about Love.** Photographs by Joe Baker. Bradbury Press, 1994. 48 pp. ISBN 0-02-735395-8.

Enjoy thirty-three poems about the various faces of love. The first half of the book contains poems about falling in love—"First Look," "First Touch," and "First Kiss." It includes a poem about an unsigned love note that says simply, "Springtime/and I wish I knew you." The second half is about falling *out* of love—"The First Fight"; results of the springtime love note; and love that is too possessive. Fletcher takes us from first blush to the crush of losing in love.

20.5   Gordon, Ruth, selector. **Peeling the Onion.** HarperCollins, 1993. 94 pp. ISBN 0-06-021727-8.

"Poetry," Gordon writes, "is the onion of readers. It can cause tears, be peeled layer by layer, or be replanted to grow into new ideas. Poetry adds taste, zest, and a sharp but sweet quality that enriches our lives." Peel these onion poems with sharp eyes and keen thoughts, and you'll unwrap appealing poems about cars, body surfing, and sports. The deeper layers of these poems tell about the security of a loving family, the encouragement of a parent, and equality among races.

20.6   Hopkins, Lee Bennett, collector. **Hand in Hand: An American History through Poetry.** Illustrated by Peter M. Fiore. Simon & Schuster, 1994. 144 pp. ISBN 0-671-73315-X.

Hopkins has selected poems and songs that celebrate the history of America. From Myra Cohn Livingston's "First Thanksgiving" to poems about the Civil War, Vietnam, and the future of the United States, *Hand in Hand* offers readers a poetic look at our past through the eyes of some of our finest poets.

20.7   Hopkins, Lee Bennett, compiler. **Extra Innings: Baseball Poems.** Illustrated by Scott Medlock. Harcourt Brace Jovanovich, 1993. 40 pp. ISBN 0-15-226833-2.

America's favorite pastime—baseball—is the subject of the nineteen poems that make up this collection. You'll find poems on umpires, coaches, stealing bases, pitching, winning, and losing. *Extra Innings* is also about hopes and dreams and great players like Joe DiMaggio. From little league to the major league, from Casey at the Bat to Jackie Robinson and Pee Wee Reese, from the infield to the outfield, this book captures the poetry of baseball.

20.8   Hughes, Langston. **The Dream Keeper and Other Poems.** Illustrated by Brian Pinkney. Alfred A. Knopf, 1994. 84 pp. ISBN 0-679-84421-X.

Are you a dreamer? Your dreams are important in this collection. Here are poems featuring tattooed sailors with dreams of foreign ports, and powerful poems about the African American experience, such as "My People." One of the finest poems written about friendship is Hughes' "Poem" which begins—"I loved my friend./He went away from me." Dreamer, keep those dreams alive. Hughes writes, "Hold fast to dreams/For if dreams die/ Life is a broken-winged bird/That cannot fly."

20.9 Janeczko, Paul B. **Stardust otel.** Illustrated by Dorothy Leech. Orchard Books, 1993. 64 pp. ISBN 0-531-05498-5.

Leary is fourteen and lives with his flower-children parents in the Stardust otel. When Leary was born, his father swung on the old hotel sign in joy. The H came off and was never replaced. In these poems, Leary describes his parents; his girlfriend and her abusive father; Charlie Hooper, who can't forget Vietnam; seventeen-year-old, ninth-grade bully Philip Slade, whose joy ride in his mother's car lands him in a wheelchair; and a host of other interesting characters.

20.10 Janeczko, Paul B., compiler. **Looking for Your Name.** Orchard Books, 1993. 144 pp. ISBN 0-531-05475-6.

Janeczko has assembled a collection of 112 contemporary poems about conflict. Poems concerned with war, violence, suicide, and AIDS—the pains and horrors of life—are countered with those about peace, happiness, and loving relationships—the joys of life. Whether it's Robert Morage's gritty and sad poem about killing his faithful but ailing dog or Jonathan Holden's look at the pleasures and pains of playing ice hockey, you'll find poetry that captures the highs and lows of living.

20.11 Janeczko, Paul B., compiler. **Poetry from A to Z: A Guide for Young Writers.** Illustrated by Cathy Bobak. Bradbury Press, 1994. 131 pp. ISBN 0-02-747672-3.

Poems can be about anything from autumn leaves to zebras. Janeczko offers young writers enjoyable poetry-writing exercises. Try your hand writing a blessing poem or a curse poem or a list poem. You'll find examples of each type of poetry along with the basic rules for writing in these forms. If you are really interested in poetry writing, you'll appreciate the how-to-become-a-better-poet advice offered by the twenty-three poets whose work is in this book.

20.12 Johnson, James Weldon. **Lift Every Voice and Sing.** Illustrated by Elizabeth Catlett. Walker and Company, 1993. Unpaged. ISBN 0-8027-8250-7.

Originally, James Weldon Johnson and his brother wrote this song so that children could sing it at a celebration marking Abraham Lincoln's birthday. The brothers wanted a song that would allow

African Americans to express pride in themselves and their achievements. Their song of faith, hope, and a new day is tempered with memories of African American struggles—"silent tears," "weary years," and "the blood of the slaughtered." Johnson's song is known by many today as the African American national anthem.

20.13 Johnson, James Weldon. **The Creation.** Illustrated by Carla Golembe. Little, Brown and Company, 1993. Unpaged. ISBN 0-316-46744-8.

"The Creation" is James Weldon Johnson's retelling of the creation story found in the Bible. In this poem, God creates the universe from out of the darkness. Johnson wanted his poem to sound like a preacher telling the Genesis story, and he does that with the rhythm and sounds of the words he chooses. The illustrator's pictures are filled with bright colors and help to make Johnson's poem beautiful to look at, as well as to listen to or read. For a look at how a different artist has illustrated this poem, see the version done by artist James E. Ransome, published in 1994 by Holiday House.

20.14 Jones, Hettie, selector. **The Trees Stand Shining.** Illustrated by Robert Andrew Parker. Dial Books, 1993. Unpaged. ISBN 0-8037-9084-8.

The poems in this book are really songs: prayers, lullabies, stories, and war chants that Native Americans have sung for hundreds of years. Rainbows, thunder, lightning, mountains, wind, and animals are the subjects of these Native American poems. Parker's beautiful paintings add to the mood and the power of these songs that celebrate the earth and all life.

20.15 Kennedy, Dorothy M., selector. **I Thought I'd Take My Rat to School.** Illustrated by Abby Carter. Little, Brown and Company, 1993. 64 pp. ISBN 0-316-48893-3.

School is the subject of this collection with funny poems about arithmetic, equations, proper English, history, science, recess, and lunch. Here's Jack Prelutsky's popular poem about homework that begins "Homework! Oh, Homework!/I hate you! You stink!" Russell Hoban sees things slightly differently when he writes, "Homework sits on top of Sunday, squashing Sunday flat./Homework has the smell of Monday, homework's very fat." These poems look at school with humor, rhythm, and rhyme.

20.16 Kennedy, X. J. **Drat These Brats.** Illustrated by James Watts. McElderry Books, 1993. 44 pp. ISBN 0-689-50589-2.

Kennedy's third collection of poems about bratty youngsters introduces Gertrude, who ruined the golf course when she stole the riding lawn mower; Lorraine, who yanked the cord that stopped the train; Heloise, who emptied sacks of fleas on Aunt Pru's Pekingnese; and Cora Kotch, who from the rooftop tossed her father's costly watch—" 'Dad, you're mad? What's wrong?' she cries. 'You're always saying, How time flies!' "

20.17 Livingston, Myra Cohn, selector. **Roll Along: Poems on Wheels.** McElderry Books, 1993. 72 pp. ISBN 0-689-50585-X.

Livingston has collected fifty poems about things that roll on wheels. If you like skateboards, cars, jeeps, trucks, taxis, buses, trains, and bikes, you'll find poetry here worth reading. Meet the crusty mechanic who was so fierce that "dead engines turned over in panic!" Read "Riddle," and guess what vehicle has broad antlers, a gleaming eye, and a hungry roar. Don't forget "Traffic Rule 1": "The Mack truck has the right of way."

20.18 McCullough, Frances, editor. **Love Is Like the Lion's Tooth.** HarperCollins, 1993. 80 pp. ISBN 0-06-024139-X.

The editor introduces this collection of love poems with these words: "It seems to me that passion is the special gift of adolescence. . . ." Poets from around the world look at various aspects of love, from ecstasy to pain. In Amichai's "A Painful Love Song," two lovers are together like scissors, "good and useful." But when the couple separate they become "two sharp knives stuck deeply in the world's flesh."

20.19 McNaughton, Colin. **Making Friends with Frankenstein.** Illustrated by Colin McNaughton. Candlewick Press, 1994. 96 pp. ISBN 1-56402-308-7.

McNaughton's poems aren't about death and love. These verses describe cockroach sandwiches, getting sick eating gummy babies, a cross-eyed Cyclops, and a giant pig that attacks the butcher. If you like rhyming, ghoulish poetry with titles like "Another Poem to Send to Your Worst Enemy," "The Forth Worst Pome Wot I Ever Ritted," and "The Ooze-Zombie from the Slime-Pits of Grunge," then prepare for some monstrous laughs as you begin *Making Friends with Frankenstein*.

20.20 Moon, Pat. **Earth Lines: Poems for the Green Age.** Greenwillow Books, 1993. 64 pp. ISBN 0-688-11853-4.

The destruction of the rain forest, our polluted water supply, global warming, and garbage are all subjects here. The killing of dolphins by tuna fishermen is the subject of "Dolphin Mother." "To Make A Fur Hat" begins this way: "Take one gun,/Take one leopard/And shoot it in the head." Moon's verse about the majesty of the elephant ends this way: "Whoever wouldn't rather see/An elephant/Than ivory?" These poems reflect both a love of and a fear for our planet.

20.21 Myers, Walter Dean. **Brown Angels: An Album of Pictures and Verse.** Illustrated with antique photos collected by the author. HarperCollins, 1993. Unpaged. ISBN 0-06-022917-9.

Beautiful old photos of African American children are coupled with Myers's poetry. The result is a celebration of childhood, friendship, and pride in one's heritage. Whether the poet is describing a summer day ("I like hot days, hot days/Sweat is what you got days") or the beauty of African American children ("I never dreamt/that tender blossoms/would be born . . ."), his poems bring you back to the photos and to ideas of your own.

20.22 Panzer, Nora, editor. **Celebrate America in Poetry and Art.** Illustrations provided by the National Museum of American Art—Smithsonian Institution. Hyperion Books, 1994. 96 pp. ISBN 1-56282-665-4.

The multicultural quilt that is America is stitched together in this book with full-color reproductions from the National Museum of American Art and with poems by celebrated writers including Maya Angelou, Emily Dickinson, and Walt Whitman. This attractive anthology offers readers art and poetry that praise our landscape, examine our patriotism, look at our mistakes, and let poets of varied cultures share their views of America.

20.23 Prelutsky, Jack. **The Dragons Are Singing Tonight.** Illustrated by Peter Sis. Greenwillow Press, 1993. 40 pp. ISBN 0-688-09654-X.

Dragons is one of the most beautifully illustrated poetry books published recently. Peter Sis's colorful dragon paintings are the perfect complement to Prelutsky's rhyming verse. "The Dragons Are Singing Tonight," recounts the yearly ritual when dragons "Awake in their lairs underground,/To sing in a cacophonous chorus." You'll find stories of the nastiest little dragon and of a handmade mechanical dragon. If you don't believe in dragons,

Poetry

remember "that the dragons you disparage/Choose to not believe in you."

20.24 Rogasky, Barbara, selector. **Winter Poems.** Illustrated by Trina Schart Hyman. Scholastic, 1994. 40 pp. ISBN 0-590-42872-1.

Winter is the season celebrated in this handsomely illustrated collection of poems. Here you'll find poetry about the geese flying south, signaling the beginning of the season; the quiet, transforming beauty of snow; the howls and hisses of a blustery storm; the animals and birds of the season; the sunny joys of catching snowflakes, and the mysterious early darkness of a winter's night.

20.25 Rylant, Cynthia. **Soda Jerk.** Beech Tree Books, 1993. 64 pp. ISBN 0-688-12654-5.

The teenager in this book works at Maywell's Drugstore. From behind the soda counter, he observes his world through the twenty-eight poems in this collection. His poems look at the rich kids and jocks, the pros and cons of living in a small town, and his dreams of dating that special girl and leaving his hometown to become an actor. About his part-time job in a drugstore, this teen says, "Tips are okay./But the secrets are better."

20.26 Rylant, Cynthia. **Something Permanent.** Photography by Walker Evans. Harcourt Brace & Company, 1994. ISBN 0-15-277090-9.

Walker Evans was one of America's finest photographers. During the 1930s, he traveled across America recording images of the Great Depression. Cynthia Rylant has written a poem to go with each of the Evans photos included in this book. The result is an exquisitely designed book that offers mature adolescents poetic and photographic impressions of the Great Depression. Poems about resilient people struggling to survive are Rylant's poetic addition to Evans's fine photographs.

20.27 Swenson, May. **The Complete Poems to Solve.** Illustrated by Christy Hale. Macmillan, 1993. 116 pp. ISBN 0-02-788725-1.

Swenson writes, "Each of the poems in this selection, in one way or another, is a Poem to Solve. A characteristic of all poetry, in fact, is that more is hidden in it than in prose." If you like looking closely at words, you'll enjoy Swenson's creations and have fun figuring out what riddling poems describe.

20.28 Thomas, Joyce Carol. **Brown Honey in Broomwheat Tea.** Illustrated by Floyd Cooper. HarperCollins, 1993. Unpaged. ISBN 0-06-021087-7.

The thirteen poems contained here are told from one African American girl's point of view. She celebrates her family in poems like "Mama," "Family Tree," and "Sisters." In "Cherish Me" she celebrates herself—"I sprang up from mother earth/She clothed me in her own colors. . . ." You'll find poems about fears and poems about the wisdom of a grandparent. Floyd Cooper's warm, glowing, full-page illustrations of a loving African American family are the perfect complement to Thomas's thoughtful poetry.

20.29 Turner, Ann. **Grass Songs.** Illustrated by Barry Moser. Harcourt Brace Jovanovich, 1993. 64 pp. ISBN 0-15-136788-4.

Turner's poems describe the grit and determination of pioneer women who settled the American West during the 1800s. For some, the journey was a welcome change from "the confinement of women, sitting,/standing, bustled and trussed" to the love of "the needles on my face,/the wind under my dress,/my hair strung out behind." For others it meant the pain of childbirth in a rocking wagon, the horror of having a child kidnapped, or the grief of having to leave behind loved ones dead from cholera.

20.30 UNICEF, editors. **I Dream of Peace: Images of War by Children of Former Yugoslavia.** Illustrated by the children of former Yugoslavia. HarperCollins, 1994. 80 pp. ISBN 0-06-251128-9.

The poems, drawings, and letters are done by youngsters in wartorn former Yugoslavia. The horror of war is clear in a thirteen-year-old's poem about watching his uncle machine-gunned to death. In another poem, a twelve-year-old wishes for Levis and Reeboks. These poems and drawings show youngsters wanting peace, happiness, and a future, but not knowing if they will live another night. One twelve-year-old writes, "War is the saddest word that flows from my quivering lips."

20.31 Volavkova, Hana, editor. **I Never Saw Another Butterfly.** Expanded 2nd edition, with children's drawings and poems from the Terezin Concentration Camp. Schocken Books, 1993. 106 pp. ISBN 0-8052-4115-9.

This collection of poems and drawings created by children held in a concentration camp outside of Prague during World War II is both beautiful and heartbreaking. The Nazis placed 15,000 children in Terezin, and fewer than 100 survived. Their poems speak of tears, fears, and the yearning to be "where no one kills another." But these youngsters also write about the importance of home, family, and the beauty of the natural world beyond the barbed-wire confines of the camp.

20.32 Watson, Jerry, and Laura Apol Obbink, selectors. **Learning to Live in the World: Earth Poems by William Stafford.** Harcourt Brace & Company, 1994. 70 pp. ISBN 0-15-200208-1.

William Stafford was one of America's finest poets and a great listener. He listened to all the people around him and to the natural world that surrounds us all. He writes about the joy of running in the rain. He finds pleasure in spider webs, the smell of roses, and the feel of the sun's warmth. But he also writes about the dark side of nature, such as the death of a doe or having to kill the old dog that was his loyal companion.

20.33 Westcott, Nadine Bernard, selector. **Never Take a Pig to Lunch.** Illustrated by Nadine Bernard Westcott. Orchard Books, 1994. 64 pp. ISBN 0-531-06834-X.

This rollicking collection of verse about food begins with these lines: "Could anything be drearier/Than the food in the school cafeteria?" This book is divided into four funny sections: Look Out Stomach Here It Comes—Poems About Eating Silly Things; We All Scream for Ice Cream—Poems About Eating Foods We Like; Never Eat More Than You Can Lift—Poems About Eating Too Much; and My Mother Says I'm Sickening—Poems About Manners.

21 Short Stories

21.1 Bauer, Marion Dane, editor. **Am I Blue? Coming Out from the Silence.** HarperCollins, 1994. 273 pp. ISBN 0-06-024253-1.

A grandmother who understands better than parents. A twelve-year-old whose summer friendship leads to self-discovery. High school seniors who choose a class video project to "come out." The sixteen stories in this collection focus on the loneliness, the confusion, the pain, and the joy that are a part of growing up gay or lesbian. They also include characters who struggle to understand, when they discover that friends are gay or lesbians. These stories by Jane Yolen, Bruce Coville, William Sleater, M. E. Kerr, and other well-known young-adult authors will help increase understanding and acceptance of differences.

21.2 Berry, James. **Future-Telling Lady and Other Stories.** HarperCollins, 1993. 139 pp. ISBN 0-06-021434-1.

This collection of Jamaican stories will inform and entertain you with characters and situations that reveal the nature of growing up in this West Indies culture. In the title story, two different youngsters are taken by their parents to see Mother Esha, a healer. Through her Grown-up Diary Reading and her Name Stories, she helps Neil, Wendy, and their families. Other stories explore homesickness, ghosts, and magic.

21.3 Bolden, Tonya, editor. **Rites of Passage.** Hyperion Books, 1993. 64 pp. ISBN 1-56282-688-3.

The settings in these stories span the globe from Jamaica to Ghana, from the United States to Costa Rica, from Australia to South Africa, but the characters face similar challenges of growing up. This collection offers a variety of stories that show young people learning about their world and their place in that world as they find a first love, discover boundaries, forge new friendships or mend broken ones, and rise to the occasion of unexpected challenges.

21.4 Brooks, Martha. **Traveling on into the Light and Other Stories.** Orchard Books, 1994. 146 pp. ISBN 0-531-06863-3.

The eleven well-crafted stories in this collection find teenagers on the brink of self-discovery and change, in the midst of confusion,

Short Stories

alienation, and loss. For example, Jamie must deal with the suicide of his father and with his own alcoholism. Laker faces homelessness and rejection from his mother. Samantha must come to terms with the changing lifestyles of her parents, and at age seventeen, Nikki must deal with a difficult marriage and a child.

21.5   Cohen, Daniel. **Phantom Animals.** Pocket Books, 1993. 111 pp. ISBN 0-671-75930-2.

These seventeen short, entertaining, easy-to-read tales will especially appeal to anyone interested in the supernatural. Taken from folklore, legends, and true accounts, some of the creatures in the stories—kangaroos, birds, rabbits, tigers, rats, and more—are ghosts of once-living animals; others are phantoms that simply appear in animal form.

21.6   Cohen, Daniel. **The Beheaded Freshman and Other Nasty Rumors.** Avon/Flare, 1993. 116 pp. ISBN 0-380-77020-2.

Bizarre, frightening, outrageous! Daniel Cohen has collected twenty-one often repeated true stories—perhaps enhanced with each retelling—that are sure to be retold again by many who read this book. Each selection is short, easy to read, great for retelling around the campfire or during a slumber party, and certain to entertain those who love a good scare or an unusual twist.

21.7   Conford, Ellen. **I Love You, I Hate You, Get Lost.** Scholastic, 1994. 134 pp. ISBN 0-590-45558-3.

What, if anything, will help Sally bond with her soon-to-be stepsister, Gruesome Grosman? Can self-centered Renee really do a "good deed" makeover on Suzanne before the big dance? Will Benny La Matta have to stay in Ferret-Face Fraser's American-history class all year? Can Dana survive having to take her little brother Zak on a romantic date with Mitchell? You can read about these and other situations in Ellen Conford's collection of funny short stories.

21.8   Coville, Bruce. **Oddly Enough.** Illustrations by Michael Hussar. Jane Yolen Books/Harcourt Brace & Company, 1994. 122 pp. ISBN 0-15-200093-3.

For a lifetime, Michael carries around, protects, and treasures a box given to him for safekeeping by an angel. Although he never learns its contents, Michael is assured that when he is ninety, this box will change the world. What could be in the box? Bruce Coville says this story "may well be the best thing I will ever write." Stories about unicorns, finding your own identity, ghosts, and freedom of speech are among the other powerful and thought-provoking topics in this collection.

21.9 Cramer, Alexander. **A Night in Moonbeam County.** Charles Scribner's Sons, 1994. 198 pp. ISBN 0-684-19704-9.

Tired of their Chicago life, Chas and Raul ride the rails to escape. To avoid being caught by railroad guards, they jump off the train in the middle of the night, landing in Moonbeam County at the campfire of friendly hoboes, each of whom has a story to tell. Only when daylight comes and the last story has been told, do the boys realize the true identities of their congenial friends. You will enjoy each of the ten eerie campfire tales and the riveting ending.

21.10 Gale, David, editor. **Funny You Should Ask.** Dell/Yearling, 1994. 209 pp. ISBN 0-440-40922-5.

A big sister's wedding! A story-telling cab driver! A Halloween prank that backfires! A seventh grade dance! These are just some of the situations that lead to laughter in this collection of sixteen never-before-published stories from some of the top writers for young people today, including Zelpha Keatley Snyder, Jan Greenburg, Gary Soto, M. E. Kerr and Walter Dean Myers. The stories are followed by autobiographical sketches of the authors.

21.11 Gallo, Donald R., editor. **Join In: Multiethnic Short Stories.** Delacorte Press, 1993. 258 pp. ISBN 0-385-31080-3.

In the seventeen short stories in this volume, you will meet teens from many different cultural backgrounds. There is Lien, struggling for acceptance; Monique, facing the challenges of being a teenage parent; Phuong, building self-confidence and friendships through baseball; Bobby, whose blues guitar is the center of his life; and Sundara, who is struggling with cultural differences. Most important, though, they are all American teenagers with common questions and concerns about relationships, romance, parents, friendships, and their futures.

21.12 Gallo, Donald R., editor. **Within Reach.** HarperCollins, 1993. 179 pp. ISBN 0-06-021440-6.

In this highly appealing volume of mostly first-person narratives, young writers will see that simple, personal incidents can become the heart of a story. Patriotic historical fiction by Pam Conrad and a science fiction tale from Robert Lipsyte enrich this readable collection of ten stories. Also included is a brief note about the origin or background of each story and a biographical sketch about each author.

21.13 Gorog, Judith. **Please Do Not Touch: A Collection of Stories.** Scholastic, 1993. 132 pp. ISBN 0-590-46682-8.

Be careful when you visit the Gallery Pitu, for touching an exhibit makes you a part of it. The twelve stories in this interactive gallery put you in the midst of the weird, or the terrifying. Find out what happens to Jem when he dresses as a mummy for Halloween. And what about Rhoda Green's talking coffee pot? And certainly proceed with caution when you take a tour of the Hillside House with each new set of owners.

21.14 Greenberg, Martin H., and Charles G. Waugh, selectors. **A Newbery Halloween: A Dozen Scary Stories by Newbery Award–Winning Authors.** Delacorte Press, 1993. 188 pp. ISBN 0-385-31028-5.

A witch woman, a camel, a leopard, a sapphire-and-diamond ring, an old plantation house, a beautiful young girl—were these real or figments of a teenage boy's imagination? Madeline L'Engle keeps us reading to find out in "Poor Little Saturday," one of the twelve Halloween tales in this collection of stories meant to be shared in the classroom or at home. Among the Newbery winners included are Virginia Hamilton, Beverly Cleary, Paul Fleischman, Phyllis Reynolds Naylor, and Lloyd Alexander. For more short stories by Newbery authors, look at *A Newbery Christmas*.

21.15 Haskins, James, collector and reteller. **The Headless Haunt and Other African-American Ghost Stories.** Illustrated by Ben Otero. HarperCollins, 1994. 116 pp. ISBN 0-06-022994-2.

Ghosts! Haunts! Plat-eyes! Jack-o'-lanterns! These spirits can be found in ghost stories that combine African and European folklore. According to these traditions, you can see a ghost if your eyebrows meet, if you were born on Christmas Day, if you are the seventh child born in a family, or if you were born with a hole in the lobe of your ear. Don't wait until Halloween to enjoy these stories, firsthand accounts of ghostly experiences, and bits of folk wisdom.

21.16 Jacques, Brian. **Seven Strange & Ghostly Tales.** Avon, 1993. 137 pp. ISBN 0-380-71906-1.

These stories feature ghosts, vampires, and supernatural events. The author introduces each tale with a tantalizing riddle, rhyme, or poem that hints of the characters and events to come. There's Jonathan who receives ghostly help to overcome the taunts of older students, and there's Allie who misuses her role as a community-center volunteer helping the elderly. Find out what happens to Jamie and the vampire he meets. And what happens to Thomas P. Kanne, the compulsive graffiti artist?

21.17 Jennings, Paul. **Unmentionable! More Amazing Stories.** Viking, 1993. 120 pp. ISBN 0-670-84734-8.

A magic cat hat? A homemade lie detector? A magic harmonica that has a mind of its own? Life-like ice statues? An earring that turns people into human magnets? Do these sound a bit unusual? If you don't believe these things exist, then you need to read the nine unusual stories in this volume. They are sometimes funny and sometimes frightening but always entertaining!

21.18 McKinley, Robin. **A Knot in the Grain and Other Stories.** Greenwillow Books, 1994. 195 pp. ISBN 0-688-09201-2.

You will find magic, hidden powers, romance, mystery, and adventure in the five stories of this collection. And if you like Robin McKinley's Newbery Medal winner, *The Hero and the Crown,* you may be pleased to find the familiar setting of the mythical kingdom of Damar in four of the stories. Meet the mage-master Luthe, the Princess Ruen, who would be queen, Maugie the witch, and her troll son Touk, who has built a marvelous house for his beloved Erana.

21.19 Meyer, Carolyn. **Rio Grande Stories.** Harcourt Brace & Company, 1994. 257 pp. ISBN 0-15-200548-X.

Have you ever contributed writing to a class book? The sixteen students in the Heritage Project at Rio Grande Middle School have written about their cultures in this book. For example, Jeremy writes about hidden Jews who pretended to be Catholic, and Ricky writes about Navajo Indians who served in World War II. This book presents a cross-section of cultures in a New Mexico community and gives information about the students who wrote the book.

21.20 Murphy, Jim. **Night Terrors.** Scholastic, 1993. 178 pp. ISBN 0-590-45341-6.

When Brian's university-professor father recreates an Egyptian tomb in his basement at home, mummy and all, Brian makes a secret attempt to bring the mummy back to life. Brian is just one of the ordinary high school students in this collection of spine-tingling tales of vampires, werewolves, witches, and mummies, each introduced by Digger, a wisecracking cemetery caretaker and grave digger.

21.21 Rau, Margaret. **World's Scariest "True" Ghost Stories.** Illustrated by Jim Sharpe. Sterling Publishing Co., 1994. 96 pp. ISBN 0-8069-0796-7.

Twenty-nine scary stories are made all the more frightening because they are true! Learn about the phantom playmate, the ghostly hitchhiker, and other specters who have appeared to ordinary people around the world. Perhaps you will be convinced that ghosts really do exist.

21.22 Razzi, Jim. **The Restless Dead: More Strange Real-Life Mysteries.** Illustrated by John Jude Palencar. HarperTrophy, 1994. 81 pp. ISBN 0-06-44427-7.

A man who survives being swallowed by a whale. Ghost survivors of an airplane crash. A five-year-old boy who lives to tell about being buried alive. An intelligent dachshund who can bark the alphabet. No, these are not the plots of make-believe stories, but rather of real-life accounts of strange occurrences. In this book, a sequel to *Nightmare Island* by the same author, you will find fourteen creepy but true stories that will keep you reading.

21.23 Rochman, Hazel, and Darlene Z. Campbell, selectors. **Who Do You Think You Are?** Little, Brown and Company, 1993. 165 pp. ISBN 0-316-75355-6.

The selections in this collection are about friends and the love and hurt that can come with making friends and keeping them. The talented authors represented in this volume write of the laughs, the dangers, the secrets shared with friends, and also of the way friendships change our lives. Included are the works of such well-known authors as Carson McCullers, Maya Angelou, Sandra Cisneros, Ray Bradbury, and John Updike.

21.24 San Souci, Robert D., reteller. **More Short & Shivery.** Illustrated by Katherine Coville and Jacqueline Rogers. Delacorte Press, 1994. 176 pp. ISBN 0-385-32102-3.

In this collection of scary tales from around the world, you can read about Tom Walker, who mistakenly made a pact with the Devil, Bishop Hatto, who had lots of problems with mice, and the man who stole his dead wife's golden arm. You'll meet creatures such as the yara and the draug, and you'll discover that people from all over the world enjoy a scary tale!

21.25 Sauerwein, Leigh. **The Way Home.** Illustrated by Miles Hyman. Farrar, Straus, and Giroux, 1994. 118 pp. ISBN 0-374-38247-6.

Whether in 1853 or 1992, what binds people together is our feelings: feelings of happiness and of isolation, of bravery and of desolation. These six short stories illustrate those feelings as we watch a widow trying desperately to survive on an isolated farm in the 1860s; witness a daring riverboat escape from slavery; and relive a woman's memories with her, through photographs long kept in a simple white box.

21.26 Soto, Gary. **Local News.** Harcourt Brace Jovanovich, 1993. 144 pp. ISBN 0-15-248117-6.

These fourteen stories provide insights into the Mexican American culture and also reveal similarities of growing up that cross neighborhood or cultural boundaries. Readers will enjoy Soto's easy-to-like characters such as Nacho, who wants to be a vegetarian in order to save the planet; Estela, the racquetball player who wants to be known as Stinger; and dreamy Lorena who revels in wearing her boyfriend's jacket for a day, only to lose it and face the consequences.

21.27 Tashlik, Phyllis, editor. **Hispanic, Female and Young: An Anthology.** Arte Público Press, 1994. 122 pp. ISBN 1-55885-072-4.

In "Las Mujeres Hispanas," a special elective class for eighth-grade girls at a school in Spanish Harlem, the twelve girls in the class not only discovered Hispanic female writers and developed their own writing skills, but also created this book. This collection includes excerpts from novels, short stories, memoirs, and interviews with significant Hispanic females in their community—all selected or written by the students themselves.

21.28 Welch, Sheila Kelly. **A Horse for All Seasons.** Boyds Mills Press, 1994. 159 pp. ISBN 1-56397-415-0.

If you love horses, then you'll want to read this collection of short stories, which includes a story about an escaped mare and her newborn foal lost in the cold; a story about boys who go riding and discover that their father's cattle have been stolen; and a story about how a horse and its rider work to save the family house from burning to the ground. This book offers horse lovers a chance to read about their favorite animal in lots of situations.

21.29 Westall, Robert, selector. **Ghost Stories.** Kingfisher Books, 1993. 253 pp. ISBN 1-85697-884-2.

Diversity is the key to this collection of twenty-one ghost stories which run the gamut from funny to haunting to frightening. From Charles Dickens's "The Lawyer and the Ghost" to Ray Bradbury's "The Emissary" to Franz Kafka's "The Knock at the Manor Gate," these stories reflect collector Westall's view that people want ghosts to exist. Among other authors included in the collection are Kenneth Graham, Guy de Maupassant, and Saki.

VII Facts, Figures, and Fun

He was not a regular, laborious reader, but loved to sup here and sample there, to roam and browse and chew the cud. He frankly admitted a preference even for desultory and idle reading which so many were apt to condemn, but which had its place with him.

Holbrook Jackson, English writer, describing
Montaigne, French essayist

22 The Arts! Music, Dance, Drama, Painting, and Crafts

22.1 Anderson, Joan. **Twins on Toes: A Ballet Debut.** Photographs by George Ancona. Dutton/Lodestar, 1993. 32 pp. ISBN 0-525-67415-2.

Twin dancers Amy and Laurel Foster trained at the School of American Ballet, where they worked hard to develop their skills. Joan Anderson interviewed the girls and followed their careers until they had firm contracts with the Miami Ballet Company. Clear photographs of their daily practice sessions, performances, and even their eating habits offer proof of the arduous task of becoming a professional ballerina.

22.2 Arginteanu, Judy. **The Movies of Alfred Hitchcock.** Lerner Publications, 1994. 80 pp. ISBN 0-8225-1642-X.

Meet the "master of suspense" as film critic Arginteanu looks at themes and techniques used by the prolific and strange Alfred Hitchcock. Whether creating movies that scared us with scenes of birds attacking people or frightened us with a psychotic killer, or producing his weekly television show that introduced us to the bizarre side of human nature, Hitchcock assembled themes, conflicts, and situations that kept audiences on the edges of their seats—and wanting more.

22.3 Balanchine, George. **The Nutcracker.** Photographed by Joel Meyerowitz. Little, Brown and Company, 1993. 88 pp. ISBN 0-316-56921-6.

George Balanchine's version of *The Nutcracker* is retold through words and photographs taken during the film production. The photographs of the ballet as performed by the New York City Ballet, coupled with the text, captures the beauty, magic, and elegance of this well-loved classic. A medley of the most memorable scenes is included at the end of the book. This handsome volume is sure to become a favorite of ballet and film lovers.

22.4 Brust, Beth Wagner. **The Amazing Paper Cuttings of Hans Christian Andersen.** Ticknor & Fields/Houghton Mifflin, 1994. 80 pp. ISBN 0-395-66787-9.

In this fascinating book, you will meet the Danish storyteller Hans Christian Andersen anew. Many already know him for tales such as *The Ugly Duckling*, but few knew of his talent as a paper cutter. This book supplies photographs of Andersen and his intricate paper cuttings. Often Andersen created paper cuttings to accompany his fairy tales, as he struggled to overcome personal poverty.

22.5 Bussell, Darcey, with Patricia Linton. **The Young Dancer.** Dorling Kindersley, 1994. 64 pp. ISBN 1-56458-468-2.

Ballets! Musicals! Dancers! Learn about makeup, mime, jazz, and costume design in this information book written by two ballerinas. Stories about their experiences, snips of the history of dance, information about choreography, and detailed descriptions of their preparations to be a ballerina are also included. Color photographs enhance the descriptions. A glossary of terminology and a reference list of ballet schools across the United States provide helpful information to would-be dancers.

22.6 Davidson, Rosemary. **Take a Look: An Introduction to the Experience of Art.** Viking, 1993. 128 pp. ISBN 0-670-84478-0.

Why is art important to us? Using examples of art through the ages, this collection discusses why art is important for visual pleasure, for telling stories, for decoration in buildings, and most of all for helping us to learn more about ourselves and our cultures. A discussion of faces explains how painting and sculpture have, historically, helped us to understand the beauty and psychology of humanity.

22.7 Fleisher, Paul. **The Master Violinmaker.** Photographs by David Saunders. Houghton Mifflin, 1993. 32 pp. ISBN 0-395-65365-7.

It is still an art to make musical instruments, and fine instrument making is done even today by people, not machines. Violinmakers must know how to choose the types of wood that will make an instrument create the right sounds. They must carve each piece of wood to exactly the right thickness and shape, and then apply special stains and varnishes. This book was inspired by middle-school students who worked with John Larrimore, the violinmaker.

22.8 Fleischman, Paul. **Copier Creations.** HarperCollins, 1993. 122 pp. ISBN 0-06-021052.

The copy machine can be an artist's best friend and can provide artistic fun for those not so artistically inclined. A copy machine allows us to use clip art, as well as original designs, to create invitations, books, decals, and t-shirt transfers. This handy guide is chock full of ideas, patterns, and suggestions for turning a copy machine into an artist's palette.

22.9 Garfunkel, Trudy. **On Wings of Joy: The Story of Ballet from the 16th Century to Today.** Little, Brown and Company, 1994. 194 pp. ISBN 0-316-30412-3.

Enhanced by reproduced drawings, paintings, and photographs, this comprehensive account of ballet contains interesting facts about dance tradition and history. Arranged into four historical periods, the book introduces famous people associated with ballet, from both the past and the present. In this book, you get an inside look at the professional dancer's day and at the dedication and discipline necessary for success.

22.10 Giblin, James Cross. **Be Seated: A Book about Chairs.** HarperCollins, 1993. 136 pp. ISBN 0-06-021537-2.

All chairs have the same function, but they serve that function in hundreds of different ways. Some look like Mickey Mouse, some like automobiles, and some like thrones. Some are comfortable, while others torture the body. Chairs have been around since prehistoric times, and they're coming off the assembly line today. This unusual history of chairs invites you to sit down and study your seat, contemplating its historical, artistic, and economic attributes.

22.11 Greenberg, Jan, and Sandra Jordan. **The Sculptor's Eye.** Delacorte Press, 1993. 128 pp. ISBN 0-385-30902-3.

Can a ballplayer's arch or a horse and rider's hurdle be a sculpture? For the one moment that something hangs motionless in space, it is a sculpture. A sculpture is a three dimensional representation of something, and in this book, the authors have collected an elaborate array of modern sculpture to study and discuss. There are interviews with the artists, who discuss their own creations.

22.12 Guerrier, Charlie. **A Collage of Crafts.** Ticknor & Fields, 1994. 56 pp. ISBN 0-395-68377-7.

Making crafts from newspaper, sand, shells, cardboard, plaster, and stencils can be easy with the step-by-step directions and clear photographs provided in this resource book from the Young Artisan series. A few of the craft projects highlighted include the making of three-dimensional postcards using sand and shells, a comic-strip lamp using newspaper, and a decorative window shade using stencils. Notes interspersed throughout the book provide young artists with historical information on art techniques and materials such as paper, stencils, and batik.

22.13 Haskins, James. **Black Music in America: A History through Its People.** HarperCollins, 1993. 198 pp. ISBN 0-06-446136-X.

Haskins traces the origins of black music in America from early slave music to the music and musicians of the 1970s and 1980s. He explains the influence of black music on jazz, the blues, and rock-and-roll. Along with this historical description, Haskins provides biographical sketches of famous African American performers from Elizabeth Taylor Greenfield, one of the first black opera singers, to James Bland, whose "Carry Me Back to Old Virginny" became the state song of Virginia.

22.14 Hautzig, David. **DJs, Ratings, and Hook Tapes: Pop Music Broadcasting. Photography by David Hautzig. Macmillan, 1993. 48 pp.** ISBN 0-02-743471-0.

So you think that being a disc jockey is the only job available in radio broadcasting? Think again! This book goes behind the scenes to detail everything that contributes to a radio broadcast. From the research department, which determines which new songs will get air play, to the sales department, which sells advertising space, to the engineering department, which keeps the station on the air, you will see how complex broadcasting really is. Black-and-white photos accompany this simple informational book.

22.15 Heslewood, Juliet. **Introducing Picasso.** Little, Brown and Company, 1993. 32 pp. ISBN 0-316-35917-3.

Avant-garde in art means a person who leads the way. Pablo Picasso was such a person. His art shocked the world. Picasso's paintings and sculpture often depicted distorted characters, and sometimes he sculpted with junk. Often his work portrayed the horrors of war against humanity. Clear photographs of his paintings and sculptures accompany this biography. Another book in the Introducing Artists series is *Introducing Rembrandt* by Alexander Sturgis.

22.16   Isaacson, Philip M. **A Short Walk around the Pyramids and through the World of Art.** Alfred A. Knopf, 1993. 120 pp. ISBN 0-679-81523-6.

In this book, adventurous colors, shapes, and images, lead the reader through an entire realm of discoveries, from pyramids and tribal art to modern paintings, sculptures, and architectural wonders. Take a walk in a place called Saqqara where a pyramid, one of the oldest works of art, still stands, or trace modern art forms back to the pyramid structure. Enhanced by photographs, the text explains prominent design features which have impacted civilization.

22.17   Jones, K. Maurice. **Say It Loud! The Story of Rap Music.** Millbrook Press, 1994. 128 pp. ISBN 1-56294-386-3.

Some people like the blues, others appreciate jazz, some prefer heavy metal, and now many enjoy the newest type of music, rap. But what is rap? Who developed it? Why are some people upset with rap lyrics? To answer these questions and many others, take a look at this book. In it, Jones presents a historical perspective of rap music, traces its origins, discusses how it developed within American culture, and looks at the controversial "messages" some claim it carries. Photographs and discussions of "rappers," as well as copies of lyrics, make this a wrap!

22.18   Kalman, Maira. **Roarr: Calder's Circus.** Photographs by Donatella Brun. Delacorte Press/Whitney Museum of American Art, 1993. 32 pp. ISBN 0-385-30916-3.

Imagine an assembly of circus sculptures and an amazing assortment of salubrious words to describe a circus! Photographs of Alexander Calder's movable circus figures are accompanied by a poetic description of a circus coming to town. Calder's Circus, completed in 1926, is currently housed in the Whitney Museum of American Art in New York.

22.19   Kosser, Mike. **Hot Country.** Photography by Alan L. Mayor. Avon Books, 1993. 262 pp. ISBN 0-380-77061-X.

Why is country music so popular? This look at country stars such as Clint Black and Travis Tritt may explain the phenomenon. The book is full of stories about the stars' lives: Garth Brooks, hired as a songwriter, auditions in a producer's office and leaves with a record deal. Vince Gill, even now, dreams of being a professional golfer. Billy Ray Cyrus, famous for "Achy Breaky Heart," really wanted to be a pitcher. The author provides a brief history of country music's meteoric rise in popularity and offers his explanation for the current "hunk" craze.

22.20 Lawrence, Jacob, with a poem by Walter Dean Myers. **The Great Migration: An American Story.** HarperCollins/Museum of Modern Art, 1993. 46 pp. ISBN 0-06-023037-1.

In 1940 and 1941, Jacob Lawrence painted a collection of sixty panels depicting the story of African American migration to the north. These paintings, "bold moving images," and the lyrical expression of Walter Dean Myers tell the story of the great exodus which brought so many African Americans to the industrialized north.

22.21 Lazo, Caroline. **The Terra Cotta Army of Emperor Qin.** New Discovery Books/Macmillan, 1993. 80 pp. ISBN 0-02-754631-4.

In 1974, two Chinese farmers unearthed a life-size figure of a Chinese warrior in a field. This discovery led to a tremendous archeological excavation which has uncovered 7,500 terra cotta warriors who supposedly are guards to the royal tomb of Emperor Qin. The story of his dynasty (259—210 B.C.) and possible explanations of the archeological findings are the subject of this book. Photographs of the site help explain this 2200-year-old "mirror of the ancient world."

22.22 Lyons, Mary. **Master of Mahogany: Tom Day, Free Black Cabinetmaker.** Charles Scribner's Sons, 1994. 42 pp. ISBN 0-684-19675-1.

Tom Day was a famous cabinet and furniture maker of the pre–Civil War era. He was especially noted for his elegant, classical styles of hardwood craftsmanship in furniture and furnishings. In another book about an African American artist, *Deep Blues: Bill Traylor, Self-taught Artist,* Lyons describes Bill Traylor's primitive art style. Traylor's creations depict the life and times of the African American from slavery to freedom and survival. Other books in this series feature African American artists: Horace Pippin and Harriet Powers.

22.23 Marshall, Mary Ann. **Music: Careers in Music.** Crestwood House, 1994. 48 pp. ISBN 0-89686-793-5.

Are you thinking about a career in music but don't know where to begin? Whether you want to work in music, travel, television, or sports, the advice for beginning a career is the same: Do your homework, get yourself "out there," find a mentor, and work your way up. The books in this Now Hiring series outline the career possibilities in these four fields and discuss the qualifications and the everyday routine for a variety of suggested jobs. In addition, each book includes a sample résumé and a glossary of important terms for each specialty area.

22.24 McGuire, Kevin. **Woodworking for Kids: 40 Fabulous, Fun, & Useful Things for Kids to Make.** Sterling/Lark, 1994. 160 pp. ISBN 0-8069-0430-5.

Are you bored, with nothing to do? Why not build something out of wood? The many photographs and clear step-by-step directions make it easy for anyone to build terrific woodworking projects. Make a bookshelf, a rack for your bike, a bird feeder, a toy for your dog, stilts, or a hockey set. The instructions are all here in this great how-to book.

22.25 Mühlberger, Richard. **What Makes a Degas a Degas?** Viking/The Metropolitan Museum of Art, 1993. 48 pp. ISBN 0-670-85205-8(V); 0-87099-674-6(MMA).

The question "What makes a Degas a Degas?" is one that many ask. What is it that distinguishes one artist from another? In this biography and discussion of Degas's life and paintings, the reader learns the distinctive features of this man's paintings: candid effects, so that people in the painting may sometimes appear to be walking off the canvas; views from above; patches of brilliant color; feeling; movement; and large open spaces. The book also discusses events in Degas's life that affected his paintings. Other artists in the What Makes a . . . series focus on Monet, Bruegel, Raphael, Rembrandt, and Van Gogh.

22.26 Roalf, Peggy. **Looking at Paintings: Musicians.** Hyperion Books for Children, 1993. 48 pp. ISBN 1-56282-532-1.

If you like music and you like art, then this book is for you. In *Musicians*, you see nineteen famous paintings of musicians that represent 2000 years of art history. Whether viewing the art of an unknown Roman artist or the work of contemporary artists, you get a chance to learn more about art, more about musicians, and more about how artists interpret the world they see. This series, Looking at Paintings, also includes *Landscapes* and *Families*.

22.27 Roop, Peter, and Connie Roop. **Capturing Nature: The Writings and Art of John James Audubon.** Walker and Company, 1993. 39 pp. ISBN 0-8027-8204-3.

Imagine knowing John James Audubon—scientist, storyteller, traveler, businessman, hunter, and writer! Many facets of Audubon's life are depicted through his journal notes and paintings. These selected passages tell his story of exploration, first in France, and then in the United States, culminating with his discussion of the publication of *Birds of America* in 1826.

22.28 Ross, Stewart. **Shakespeare and Macbeth: The Story behind the Play.** Illustrated by Tony Karpinski. Viking, 1994. 44 pp. ISBN 0-670-85629-0.

Shakespeare wrote *Macbeth* to please King James, England's new Scottish king who loved theater and witchcraft. This well-researched book is about Shakespeare, the writing of *Macbeth*, and its initial transformation to stage. Ross confesses that there are gaps in history's knowledge of Shakespeare, but he has, as accurately as possible, described the creation and the production of the play. Tony Karpinski's illustrations give the reader an image of characters, sets, and costumes authentic to Shakespeare's times.

22.29 Shakespeare, William. **Hamlet.** Abridged by Leon Garfield. Illustrated by Natalia Orlova, Peter Kotov, and Natasha Demidova. Alfred A. Knopf, 1993. 48 pp. ISBN 0-679-83871-6.

This abridged tale, with many illustrations and familiar Shakespearean language, spotlights a young man grief-stricken over his father's death. While angry about his mother's hasty marriage to Claudius and uncertain of her role in the murder, Hamlet is visited by his father's ghost. The ghost urges him to seek revenge, but Hamlet's uncertainty prevents it. This play focuses on still relevant issues of the complexities of step families, the search for identity, and peer relationships. Additional titles in the HBO Animated Tales series include *Macbeth, A Midsummer Night's Dream, Romeo and Juliet, The Tempest,* and *Twelfth Night*.

22.30 Sills, Leslie. **Visions: Stories about Women Artists.** Albert Whitman, 1993. 63 pp. ISBN 0-8075-8491-6.

The four women artists featured in this book had very different artistic styles, but they shared one commonality—a vision. This collection includes vignettes of their lives and a discussion of their art: Mary Cassatt, whose paintings depict everyday lives of women and children; Leonora Carrington, whose paintings are influenced by fairy tales, legends, and myths; Betty Saar, whose sculptures reflect tribal cultures; and Mary Frank, who sculpts visions of the human spirit and body in clay.

22.31   Stanley, Diane. **The Gentleman and the Kitchen Maid.** Illustrated by Nolan Dennis. Dial Books for Young Readers, 1994. 32 pp. ISBN 0-8037-1321-5.

This beautiful picture book gives older readers a chance to ponder the lives of characters from art. The characters in two paintings fall in love, even though they are from diverse backgrounds, one a gentleman and the other a maid. When one painting is moved to another room in the museum, a budding artist finds a way to unite them. If you love art, you'll love looking at this book with its look-alike paintings of Picasso, Monet, Jan Vermeer, Pieter de Hooch and others.

22.32   Sturgis, Alexander. **Introducing Rembrandt.** Little, Brown and Company, 1994. 32 pp. ISBN 0-316-82022-9.

Much of what we remember and interpret about Biblical and historical events has been impacted by the way Rembrandt painted them. Discussion of his inspirations and personal life are woven together in this account of the Renaissance artist's life and work. Readers will marvel at the close-up shots of specific parts of Rembrandt's paintings, specifically looking at how he painted hands and feet.

22.33   Turner, Robyn Montana. **Dorothea Lange, Illustrator/Photographer.** Little, Brown and Company, 1994. 32 pp. ISBN 0-316-85656-8.

You've probably seen one of Lange's famous photographs of migrant women and children surviving hardships during the Great Depression. Her powerful and sensitive photographs captured Americans' struggles to survive during the first half of the 20th century and helped generate significant social changes. She is also known for choosing the burnt-orange color of the famous Golden Gate Bridge in San Francisco. Other books in the Portraits of Women Artists for Children series are about Rosa Bonheur, Mary Cassatt, and Georgia O'Keeffe.

22.34   Turner, Robyn Montana. **Faith Ringgold.** Little, Brown and Company, 1993. 32 pp. ISBN 0-316-85652-5.

The author tells the remarkable story of Harlem-born artist, Faith Ringgold. There were few African American artists in 1930, when Ringgold struggled for a formal art education and the discovery of her personal style. You will enjoy reading what Ringgold says about the connections between her art and storytelling. Other books in the Portraits of Women Artists for Children series are about Rosa Bonheur, Mary Cassatt, and Georgia O'Keeffe.

22.35 Turner, Robyn Montana. **Frida Kahlo.** Little, Brown and Company, 1993. 32 pp. ISBN 0-316-85651-7.

As a child, Frida Kahlo had polio. As a young woman, she was in a near-fatal bus accident that left her in pain for the rest of her life. She learned to paint to keep her mind active while she rehabilitated her body, but her art came to express the pain and anxiety of a people. To understand her surrealistic art is to understand, in part, Mexico and the pain of its people under Aztec and Spanish rulers. Other books in the Portraits of Women Artists for Children series are about Rosa Bonheur, Mary Cassatt, and Georgia O'Keeffe.

22.36 Walker, Lou Ann. **Roy Lichtenstein: The Artist at Work.** Photographs by Michael Abramson. Dutton/Lodestar, 1994. 42 pp. ISBN 0-525-67435-7.

Well-written text and expressive photographs are provided here to show the development of artist Roy Lichtenstein's paintings. The author takes you into the pop artist's studio and displays the materials and tools he uses. The book includes many two-page photographs that help to trace the birth of his ideas to the finished pieces of art.

22.37 Waters, Elizabeth, and Annie Harris. **Painting: A Young Artist's Guide.** Photographs, reproductions, and drawings selected by art editor Karen Fielding. Dorling Kindersley, 1993. 46 pp. ISBN 1-56458-348-1.

Take out your sketch pad; dust off your paint brush. Get ready to sketch, create collage, play around with color and light, and paint all day! This book will show you how. Using reproductions by artists such as Cezanne to illustrate still life, Van Gogh to exemplify rhythm and movement, and Seurat to model pointillism, this guide book offers an up-close look at how the masters achieve their effects. Lots of hands-on projects are provided so you can practice the same techniques.

22.38 Woolf, Felicity. **Picture This Century: An Introduction to Twentieth Century Art.** Delacorte Press, 1993. 40 pp. ISBN 0-385-30852-3.

What's that blue streak across the white canvas? Is that really art? Many strange and different kinds of art have been recognized in the twentieth century. This book explains the evolution of art as color, materials, space, and subjects merged into an amalgamation known as "modern art." Picasso, Warhol, Frankenthaler, and Cristo are a few of the artists whose works are represented in this concise book, which examines style, historical influences, artists, and artistic pieces of this century.

22.39 Yenawine, Philip. **People.** Delacorte Press, 1993. 22 pp. ISBN 0-385-30901-5.

People is one volume in an inventive series designed to pique your imagination and refine your capacity for careful observation. Portraits and paintings of people are the focus of this volume. All the books in the series combine reproductions of modern art works with thoughtful questions for the reader/observer. Other titles in this series include *Stories, Colors, Lines, Shapes,* and *Places.*

23 More about Sports

23.1 Andretti, Michael, with Robert Carver and Douglas Carver. **Michael Andretti at Indianapolis.** Photographs by Douglas Carver. Simon & Schuster, 1993. 56 pp. ISBN 0-671-79674-7.

Meet Michael Andretti, family member of the famous racing dynasty headed by Mario Andretti. With his dad as his hero, Michael dreamed of winning the Indy 500. In 1991 he had his chance. Through color photographs and Michael's own words, we see him up close and personal as we watch him prepare for the race and then run it.

23.2 Brashler, William. **The Story of Negro League Baseball.** Ticknor & Fields, 1994. 166 pp. ISBN 0-397-67169-8.

Excluded from the major league baseball teams by written and unwritten Jim Crow laws, African Americans were forced to play in leagues of their own, the Negro Leagues. Interviews, anecdotes, and black-and-white photographs are interwoven to tell the story of a rough and rugged game, played by such greats as pitcher Satchel Paige, outfielder Josh Gibson, homerun king Jimmie Crutchfield, and others who were as good as any major league player of their time.

23.3 Crisman, Ruth. **Racing the Iditarod Trail.** Dillon Press, 1993. 72 pp. ISBN 0-87518-523-1.

It's the sports event of the year in Alaska: the 1,049-mile Iditarod dogsled race from Anchorage to Nome. How did this race for gold and glory begin? What goes into training a winning team? How do mushers deal with blizzard whiteouts, frostbite, and attacks by moose? As Crisman takes you along the Iditarod Trail, you will share the excitement of this race, almost feeling the stinging snow in your face and hearing the barking huskies as they mush toward the finish line.

23.4 Dunnahoo, Terry Janson, and Herma Silverstein. **The Pro Football Hall of Fame.** Crestwood House, 1994. 48 pp. ISBN 0-89686-851-6.

Canton, Ohio, home of the Pro Football Hall of Fame, is a shrine to the sport. Learn about the criteria for selection into the Hall of Fame and about the induction ceremonies. This book also gives descriptions of the displays and mementos and offers anecdotes and facts about famous football players and the events that made them famous. The Hall of Fame series also includes *The Baseball Hall of Fame* and *The Basketball Hall of Fame.*

23.5 Green, Carl R. **Troy Aikman.** Crestwood House, 1994. 48 pp. ISBN 0-89686-833-8.

This short biography of Dallas Cowboy quarterback Troy Aikman lays out the two-time Super Bowl winner's route to success from his high school football days, through the college ranks, and finally to the dazzling world of the Dallas Cowboys. Numerous color photographs emphasize Aikman's athletic achievements. If you want to read about other sports stars, some of the other books in the Sports Headliners series profile Olympic track champion Jackie Joyner Kersee, Olympic Dream Team basketball star David Robinson, and "two-sport winner" Deion Sanders.

23.6 Gutman, Bill. **The Kids' World Almanac of Football.** World Almanac Books, 1994. 274 pp. ISBN 0-88687-764-4.

Want to know more about football from A to Z, its history, records, trivia, wild and wacky facts, memorable quotes, and language of the game? This easy to read and understand almanac provides this information, as well as photographs, cartoons, and the addresses of professional football teams. An extensive index provides access to the fact or quote that you need.

23.7 Herzog, Brad. **Heads Up! Puzzles for Sports Brains.** Bantam Books, 1994. 61 pp. ISBN 0-553-48160-6.

Are you a sports nut? If so, you'll enjoy trying your hand at over thirty puzzles written by a team of sports experts. Who quarterbacked the San Francisco 49ers to four Super Bowl victories? Who has the most career rushing yards in NFL history? What was Kareem Abdul-Jabar's original name? Trivia questions such as these, as well as crossword puzzles, rebus puzzles, and scrambled puzzles are just a few of the challenges in this book.

23.8 Herzog, Brad. **Seventh Inning Stretch: Time-Out for Baseball Trivia.** Bantam, 1994. 76 pp. ISBN 0-553-48162-2.

Take "time out for baseball trivia!" Who was the last player to bat 400 in the major leagues? Which famous pitcher lost the most games in baseball history? Answers to these questions, as well as entertaining puzzles, wacky facts, amazing stories, and other trivia about baseball can be found in the *Seventh Inning Stretch.*

23.9 Knapp, Ron. **Michael Jordan: Star Guard.** Enslow, 1994. 104 pp. ISBN 0-89490-482-5.

No NBA player ever had a better points-per-game average than Michael Jordan. Why then did he retire in 1993 at the height of his career? Perhaps we will never know, but we can find out about Michael's life until retirement along with important "stats" about his career in this easy-to-read biography. Others in this Sports Reports series include books about sports heroes Jim Kelly, Chris Mullin, Cal Ripken, Jr., David Robinson, Barry Sanders, and Thurman Thomas.

23.10 Knapp, Ron. **Top Ten Basketball Scorers.** Enslow, 1994. 48 pp. ISBN 0-89490-516-3.

The ten greatest basketball scorers in the history of the game include Wilkins, Bird, Jordan, Chamberlain, Malone, Erving, Baylor, Robertson, and West. Career statistics, color photos, chapter notes, and an index add details about how each made his personal mark on the game. Other books in the Sports Top 10 series include *Top 10 Baseball Pitchers, Top 10 Basketball Centers, Top 10 Football Quarterbacks, Top 10 Football Rushers,* and *Top 10 Hockey Scorers.*

23.11 Lewin, Ted. **I Was a Teenage Professional Wrestler.** Illustrated by Ted Lewin. Orchard Books, 1993. 128 pp. ISBN 0-531-05477-2.

When Ted Lewin's father took him and his brother to wrestling matches when they were kids, he never dreamed that someday he would become a professional wrestler, much less the book illustrator he is today. He tells his own story of being a professional wrestler and introduces you to other wrestlers, from college men to huge fat men in outrageous costumes who nonetheless think like wrestlers, and "no one but a wrestler thinks like one."

23.12 Lipsyte, Robert. **Jim Thorpe: 20th-Century Jock.** HarperCollins, 1993. 103 pp. ISBN 0-06-022988-8.

Although Mr. and Mrs. Thorpe usually called him Jim, rather than his Native American name Bright Path, the old people told him tales of his great-uncle, the famous chief, Black Hawk. Jim was sent away to school to become acquainted with the ways of the white man's world. At Carlisle Indian School, coached by "Pop" Warner, Jim starred in track, football, and baseball. Later he won Olympic Gold Medals, but he was forced to give them up because he had once played for money. Also in this Superstar Lineup series is the book *Arnold Schwarzenegger: Hercules,* the story of the Austrian bodybuilder who came to America, became an actor in such movies as *Conan the Barbarian* and *The Terminator,* and served as chair of the President's Council on Physical Fitness.

23.13 Lipsyte, Robert. **Michael Jordan: A Life above the Rim.** HarperCollins, 1994. 106 pp. ISBN 0-06-024235-3.

"Michael can do things on the court that we can barely imagine," said Magic Johnson. Why then did Michael Jordan quit basketball at his peak? This brief biographical account of Michael's career, the beginning of basketball, and African Americans' entry into the game may provide the answer. This book in the Superstar Lineup series includes photographs and a useful index.

23.14 Littlefield, Bill. **Champions: Stories of Ten Remarkable Athletes.** Little, Brown and Company, 1993. 132 pp. ISBN 0-316-52805-6.

"Winning is neither everything nor the only thing. It is one of many things," says Olympic gold medalist marathon runner Joan Benoit Samuelson. *Champions* highlights ten athletes who know the truth of Samuelson's statement. They triumph over obstacles and injuries to achieve success in their sports, yet each is also a winner out of the spotlight as they break barriers of discrimination and inspire others to fulfill their potential. Athletes profiled include Muhammad Ali, Billie Jean King, Satchel Paige, and Pele.

23.15 Macy, Sue. **A Whole New Ball Game: The Story of the All-American Girls Professional Baseball League.** Henry Holt, 1993. 140 pp. ISBN 0-8050-1942-1.

When the professional ball players ran onto the field in short dresses, they certainly created a stir! It wasn't the dresses that caused a sensation, it was that the players were women. The All-American Girls Professional Baseball League, created when male players went off to fight in World War II, played from 1943 to 1954. Author Sue Macy explores the development of this era of baseball and how the AAGBL shaped and was shaped by women's roles in society.

23.16 McKissack, Patricia C., and Fredrick McKissack, Jr. **Black Diamond: The Story of the Negro Baseball Leagues.** Scholastic, 1994. 184 pp. ISBN 0-590-45809-4.

One of baseball's greatest pitchers, Satchel Paige; one of the sport's fastest runners, Cool Papa Bell; and one of the greatest hitters of all time, Josh Gibson; never played in the major leagues. These legends of the game played in the Negro Baseball Leagues until the sport was desegregated in 1947. The stories of players who crossed over into the major leagues, like Jackie Robinson, Willie Mays, and Hank Aaron, add to this extraordinary history. Photographs, a timeline, Hall-of-Fame listings, and player profiles clarify this information.

23.17 Paulsen, Gary. **Father Water, Mother Woods.** Delacorte, 1994. 159 pp. ISBN 0-385-32053-1.

"Write about what you know," is a piece of advice passed down by teachers, editors, and publishers. Gary Paulsen keeps that counsel; his books set in the outdoors draw on his own experiences. The strength of those experiences shines through in these collected essays on hunting, fishing, and camping as he shares the thrill of casting for walleyes, the comedy of a camping trip gone awry, and the drama of a first deer kill.

23.18 Rappoport, Ken. **Shaquille O'Neal.** Walker and Company, 1994. 129 pp. ISBN 0-8027-8294-9.

Shaq is a household name in basketball. Once described as an "army brat," Shaq became the first professional player to dunk a basketball hard enough to bring down the basket. Anecdotes and thrilling moments in Shaq's NBA career present a picture of a man who is more than a basketball-playing monster machine. He is also a person with a family, with likes and dislikes, fears and hopes.

23.19 Rivers, Glenn, and Bruce Brooks. **Those Who Love the Game: Glenn "Doc" Rivers on Life in the NBA and Elsewhere.** Henry Holt and Company, 1993. 159 pp. ISBN 0-8050-2822-6.

Basketball is a game of beauty and symmetry. It involves long hours of practice in order to be successful. Doc Rivers and his friends and foes, including Isaiah Thomas, Michael Jordan, and Kevin McHale, share their lessons learned "in the NBA and elsewhere." Talking with award-winning author Bruce Brooks, Rivers convinces us of his love of the game.

23.20 Sullivan, George. **In-Line Skating: A Complete Guide for Beginners.** Cobblehill/Dutton, 1993. 48 pp. ISBN 0-525-65124-1.

Whether you have already mastered the simple techniques of in-line skating, or you are trying the sport for the first time, this complete how-to guide covers all of the basics with step-by-step instructions and photographs. The book explains beginning maneuvers (skating forward and backward, swizzling and turning corners), advanced techniques (sidesurfing and performing an

More about Sports

arabesque), and competitive skating. There is a discussion of renting, purchasing, and caring for equipment. Safety equipment and procedures are emphasized throughout the book.

23.21 Sullivan, George. **Pitchers: Twenty-Seven of Baseball's Greatest.** Atheneum, 1994. 74 pp. ISBN 0-689-31825-1.

Sullivan explores the achievements, artistic abilities, and statistics of twenty-seven of baseball's most outstanding pitchers, including Roger Clemens, Nolan Ryan, and Satchel Paige. The introduction concisely explains the evolution of pitching since the 1800s and the importance of pitchers today. Action photos are included for each player.

23.22 Weidhorn, Manfred. **Jackie Robinson.** Atheneum, 1993. 207 pp. ISBN 0-689-31644-5.

In 1947, Jackie Robinson broke "the color barrier" when he became the first African American to play major-league baseball. Though he endured racial prejudice and harassment, his athletic ability and winning personality finally helped America see the benefits of integration, as he led the Brooklyn Dodgers through several successful seasons. This biography explores how one gifted athlete, with patience, hard work, skill, and determination, changed the course of baseball and affected social policy.

23.23 Weiss, Ann E. **Money Games: The Business of Sports.** Houghton Mifflin, 1993. 186 pp. ISBN 0-395-57444-7.

What percentage of high school athletes become professional players? How much does a pair of Air Jordan shoes actually cost Nike to make? Answers to such questions can be found in *Money Games*, an exploration of the complex business of sports. Issues discussed include players' salaries, contracts, and product endorsements. In addition, the book examines the impact of discrimination, drugs, and gambling problems on the players' lives and the sports profession.

23.24 Young, Ken. **Cy Young Award Winners.** Walker and Company, 1994. 152 pp. ISBN 0-8027-8300-7.

The Cy Young Award is named after the pitcher who won more games than anyone in the history of baseball. Recounted are the stories of ten of its most notable winners: Whitey Ford, Sandy Koufax, Denny McLain, Tom Seaver, Bob Gibson, Jim Palmer, Steve Carlton, Fernando Valenzuela, Dwight Gooden, and Roger Clemens. Includes a helpful appendix of all Cy Young Award Winners, and an index.

24 How, Why, and What: Fun, Facts, and Trivia

24.1 Barkin, Carol, and Elizabeth James. **The Holiday Handbook.** Illustrated by Melanie Marder Parks. Clarion Books, 1994. 240 pp. ISBN 0-395-65011-9.

Next year you may want to celebrate Dictionary Day, National Grouch Day, and National Sandwich Day, a few of the American holidays highlighted in this comprehensive resource. Divided according to seasons, the handbook focuses on well-known and obscure American secular holidays within each season, describes the origin of the holidays, and explains the ways in which they are observed. There are also fun-filled activities and suggestions for ways to get your family involved.

24.2 Busenberg, Bonnie. **Vanilla, Chocolate, & Strawberry: The Story of Your Favorite Flavors.** Lerner Publications, 1994. 112 pp. ISBN 0-8225-1573-3.

What makes mouth-watering foods such as vanilla shakes, chocolate kisses, and strawberry shortcake taste as good as they do? Learn the history behind the flavors—where they come from, how they got their names, how they are used, and how they are prepared. There are even a few recipes to try. You'll never take flavors for granted again.

24.3 Carter, Philip I., and Ken A. Russell. **Young Genius Book of Brain Teasers.** Ward Lock/Sterling, 1993. 143 pp. ISBN 0-7063-7102.

Coded words, analogies, diagrams, synonyms, and number sequences are just a few of the types of brain teasers you'll encounter in this collection of puzzles. Want to have fun while testing your intelligence? Challenge your brain with the four baffling tests in this entertaining book. For those who score well on the tests, information is provided on how to join Mensa, a society for individuals with high IQs.

24.4 **Concise Columbia Encyclopedia** 3rd Edition. Houghton Mifflin, 1994. 973 pp. ISBN 0-395-62439-8.

From Aachen (a city in West Germany) to zydeco (an American musical form), this encyclopedia offers you information on thousands of topics. Arranged like a dictionary, the concise entries give you basic facts and places to look for additional data. So if you need to find out what hassium is, want to know where Nikko is, or wonder who Henry Stimson was, look here!

24.5 Czerneda, Julie. **Great Careers for People Interested in Living Things.** UXL, 1993. 48 pp. ISBN 0-8103-9387-5.

The best way to decide on a career is to explore different options, see what appeals to you, and talk to individuals who have chosen a career that you favor. If you like to work with both plants and animals, the options range from scientific illustrator to police-dog handler. Interviews with ten professionals give an overview of what's available in this field, as well as a sense of the day-to-day activities. This same format marks other books in the Career Connections series, such as *Great Careers for People Interested in How Things Work* by Peter and Bob Richardson, . . . *in the Human Body* by Lois Edwards, . . . *in Math and Computers* by Peter and Bob Richardson, . . . *in the Environment* by Lesley Grant, and . . . *in Being Outdoors* by Helen Mason.

24.6 Dahl, Roald. **Roald Dahl's Revolting Recipes.** Viking, 1994. 61 pp. ISBN 0-670-85836-6.

Here's your chance to actually make and taste the mouth-watering foods that appear in Roald Dahl's books. This wacky cookbook with its humorous illustrations contains over thirty recipes for all occasions. You'll find step-by-step instructions for preparing Willy Wonka's Nutty Crunch Surprise and Eatable Marshmallow Pillows from *Charlie and the Chocolate Factory*. The Hot Frogs and Fresh Mudburgers may bring back fond memories of *James and the Giant Peach*.

24.7 Feinberg, Barbara Silberdick. **Words in the News: A Student's Dictionary of American Government and Politics.** Franklin Watts, 1993. 141 pp. ISBN 0-531-11164-4.

Terms such as *gerrymander, laissez-faire,* and *reapportionment* appear often in the news, but do you really know what they mean? Here's your chance to brush up on the meaning of 500 political terms and concepts that every informed citizen should know. Many of the entries go beyond the definition of the word and provide information about its origin, as well as facts, trivia, and examples that make the term more meaningful.

24.8 Fiedhoffer, Bob. **The Magic Show: A Guide for Young Magicians.** Millbrook Press, 1994. 80 pp. ISBN 1-56294-355-3.

If you are planning a magic show, this book is a must! Written by a professional magician known as "The Madman of Magic," this resource provides sound advice about how to plan and stage a good magic show. It includes step-by-step instructions for eighteen astounding tricks. The vanishing soda bottle, the cut and restored rope, and silks from an empty newspaper are just a few of the sleights of hand you'll learn to perform.

24.9 Gay, Kathlyn. **Getting Your Message Across.** New Discovery Books, 1993. 128 pp. ISBN 0-02-735815-1.

While words are an important part of communication, about eighty to ninety percent of all information is revealed in other ways. How can we be aware of indirect messages we send to others? What can we do to improve both verbal and nonverbal communication? Kathlyn Gay gives us a place to start—by examining our body language, the clothes we wear, the tone of our voices, and the words we use.

24.10 Goodman, Alan. **The Big Help Book.** Minstrel/Pocket Books, 1994. 132 pp. ISBN 0-671-51927-1.

You and your friends can make a difference in your community by getting involved in volunteer projects! The Big Help is a campaign sponsored by television cable network Nickelodeon, which urges kids to participate in community service. Filled with 365 ideas for getting involved, this guide will help you choose a project that is rewarding. Erasing graffiti, working at homeless shelters, taking an older person shopping, planting a tree, cleaning the beach, and adopting an animal are just a few of the projects here.

24.11 Graham-Barber, Lynda. **Doodle Dandy! The Complete Book of Independence Day Words.** Illustrated by Betsy Lewin. Avon/Camelot, 1994. 150 pp. ISBN 0-380-72100-7.

Let's celebrate America's birthday! Almost everything you ever wanted to know about the Fourth of July can be found in this resource. Interesting trivia about words typically associated with this holiday, such as *picnic, fireworks, hamburger,* and *watermelon* bring new meaning to Independence Day celebrations. Famous historical events and symbols, such as Revolutionary War battles, the Declaration of Independence, Old Glory, our national anthem, and Uncle Sam are also highlighted.

24.12 Granger, Neill. **Stamp Collecting.** Millbrook Press, 1994. 93 pp. ISBN 1-56294-399-5.

Here's some stamp trivia for philatelists everywhere: the rarest stamp in the world (sold for $935,000), the date of the first stamp issued (1840), the first collector (John Tomlynson), and the best forger (Juan de Sperati). Add information about Cinderellas and covers, as well as tips for beginning and maintaining an individual collection, and *Stamp Collecting* becomes more than a book. It's the basis for a fascinating and exciting hobby.

24.13 Immell, Myra H. **Automobiles: Connecting People and Places.** Lucent Books, 1994. 96 pp. ISBN 1-56006-226-6.

The invention of the automobile began over 5,000 years ago, with the invention of the wheel, and progressed beyond steam to internal combustion engines, to mass production, to electric cars, and to sophisticated computer systems. The Encyclopedia of Discovery and Invention series also includes *Guns, Radios,* and *Submarines.*

24.14 James, Elizabeth, and Carol Barkin. **Sincerely Yours: How to Write Great Letters.** Clarion Books, 1993. 166 pp. ISBN 0-395-58832-4.

If you love to receive letters but hate to write them, help is on the way! In *Sincerely Yours*, you will learn how to write many kinds of letters, from a personal note for a friend to a fan letter to your favorite sports star. Step-by-step instructions and plenty of lively examples show you that writing letters can be easy and fun. There's also information on how to find a pen pal!

24.15 Johnstone, Michael. **Cars: Look Inside Cross-Sections.** Dorling Kindersley, 1994. 32 pp. ISBN 1-56458-681-2.

Did you know that the Ford Model T sold for $825 in 1908, or that a Ferrari Testarossa can go 181 miles per hour? Packed with interesting trivia about cars, this book uses intricate cross-section diagrams to provide a detailed look inside eleven automobiles. Full-color, two-page spreads of each car highlight the design and construction of such favorites as the Ford Model T, Jeep, Cadillac, Ferrari, and the powerful Formula I racer.

24.16 Johnstone, Michael. **Planes: Look Inside Cross-Sections.** Illustrated by Hans Jenssen. Dorling Kindersley, 1994. 32 pp. ISBN 1-56458-520-4.

Colored illustrations provide aviation buffs with a detailed look inside ten aircraft, ranging from military planes to passenger airliners and light airplanes. Each double-page spread in this *Look*

Inside Cross-Sections book highlights the design and construction of a different aircraft and includes a chart with technical data. An aircraft timeline illustrates the milestones of flight, beginning with the 1903 Wright Flyer and ending with the sophisticated F-117 Stealth Fighter of the 1980s.

24.17 Levine, Michael. **The Kid's Address Book.** Berkley/Perigee, 1994. 220 pp. ISBN 0-399-51875-4.

Want to write to Arnold Schwarzenegger or Madonna? This handy resource provides the addresses of more than 2,000 movie stars, television stars, music stars, and sports stars. Addresses for clubs, organizations, businesses, magazines, publishers, museums, and federal and state agencies are also included. With access to these addresses, you can become more involved in the world and express your opinions through letter writing.

24.18 Madama, John. **Desktop Publishing: The Art of Communication.** Lerner Publications, 1993. 64 pp. ISBN 0-8225-2303-5.

Want to create slick newsletters, advertisements, or brochures? You don't have to be a professional advertising agent or design specialist to do so. What you need is a personal computer, a printer, appropriate software, and a hefty dose of creativity. Many of us still do need help. *Desktop Publishing* suggests what to look for in software packages, as well as how to write text, insert illustrations, select fonts, and lay out the final product.

24.19 Madgwick, Wendy. **Citymaze!** Millbrook Press, 1995. 40 pp. ISBN 1-56294-561-0.

Paris. Beijing. London. Moscow. Each of the great cities of the world holds a special allure, and each attracts thousands of visitors each year. Here's your chance to visit without the hassle of passports, shots, and transportation problems. Curl up in your chair, choose a city, and take a virtual trip, winding through the pictorial maps, each of which becomes a complicated maze. But plan your trip well; a wrong turn leads to dead ends and possible trouble.

24.20 Maestro, Marco, and Giulio Maestro. **Riddle City, USA! A Book of Geography Riddles.** HarperCollins, 1994. 64 pp. ISBN 0-06-023368-0.

"How scared is the forest in Arizona?" (It's petrified!) "When does a Great Lake think it's the greatest?" (When it's feeling Superior.) After solving riddles such as these, read on to learn more interesting facts about the Petrified Forest and Lake Superior. The original riddles included in this mind-stretching collection focus on famous places in each of the fifty states, including names of cities, states, parks, and rivers.

24.21 Markle, Sandra. **Exploring Autumn.** Avon, 1993. 152 pp. ISBN 0-380-719100-X.

Celebrate autumn with more than a Halloween costume and a reunion at Thanksgiving. Activities detailed here include making a corn-husk doll, peanut butter, apple carvings, plant drawings, and monster masks. Each project fits right into the season, helping you discover how the world changes and what fall really means.

24.22 Meltzer, Milton. **Gold: The True Story of Why People Search for It, Mine It, Trade It, Steal It, Mint It, Hoard It, Shape It, Wear It, Fight and Kill for It.** HarperCollins, 1993. 168 pp. ISBN 0-06-022983-7.

Gold. We've used it to create beautiful objects, as the basis for scientific discovery, and as the excuse to enslave other human beings. Gold links pirates, fortune hunters, and outlaws, but it also touches our teeth, our fingers, and our altars. Here's a twenty-four-karat study of this precious mineral that mines little known facts, filters out interesting nuggets of information, and shapes a fascinating history.

24.23 Otfinoski, Steve. **Putting It in Writing.** Scholastic, 1993. 144 pp. ISBN 0-590-49459-7.

Writing provides a permanent record of our thoughts, our compliments, our complaints, our actions, our wishes, and our status. We write letters, notes, reports, and invitations. But each format dictates a different style. These handy tips on writing all sorts of messages, from friendly letters to lengthy term papers, help determine the best form for the targeted function. Sample letters and papers provide extra guidance.

24.24 Phillips, Louis. **School Daze: Jokes Your Teacher Will Hate.** Viking, 1994. 58 pp. ISBN 0-670-84929-4.

"Did you hear about the cannibal who was expelled from school for buttering up the teacher?" Join the fun as you chuckle over teachers, classmates, report cards, homework, excuses, and recesses. This hilarious collection is filled with school jokes, riddles, and puns that your teacher will probably hate!

24.25 Rosin, Arielle. **Eclairs & Brown Bears.** Ticknor & Fields, 1994. 56 pp. ISBN 0-395-68380-7.

White-chocolate brownies with almonds and heart-shaped butter cookies are just two of the luscious bakery creations featured in this easy-to-use cookbook from the Young Gourmet series. Step-by-step recipes and colored photographs will guide you in the art of making meringues, brownies, butter cookies, tarts and pies, cream-puff pastries, and cakes. Dessert lovers will also enjoy the accompanying historical notes, such as the "history of meringue" and "how pastries get their names."

24.26 Ryan, Steve. **Test Your Math IQ.** Sterling Publishing Company, 1994. 96 pp. ISBN 0-8069-0724-X.

Ready for a real challenge? Be prepared to "stretch your brain to the limit" with more than seventy-five mathematical puzzles. There are special clues for those who run into puzzling difficulties. A difficulty rating of one-, two-, or three-penciller is assigned to each mind bender, and solutions are provided at the end of this baffling book.

24.27 Schleifer, Jay. **Jaguar.** Crestwood House, 1994. 48 pp. ISBN 0-89686-814-1.

Buckle up your seat belt, and enjoy the ride as you browse the pages of *Jaguar*! Car nuts will relish each book in this Cool Classics series focusing on the world's most popular automobiles. *Mercedes Benz, Jaguar, Thunderbird,* and *Bugatti* trace the histories of these powerful machines and the car companies that make them. The easy-to-read text, accompanied by a glossary and photographs of the classic automobiles, will put you in the driver's seat.

24.28 Schwartz, Alvin, collector. **Tomfoolery: Trickery and Foolery with Words.** Illustrated by Glen Rounds. HarperCollins, 1994 (originally published in 1973). 125 pp. ISBN 0-06-446154-8.

Playing with our language can be fun. Using American folklore, Schwartz shows that many jokes, riddles, elephant tales, and catchy ghost stories work because of plays on words, simple gestures, and tricks. See if your friends don't fall for some of these jokes or hoaxes that date back a century.

24.29 Shapiro, William, editor. **Kingfisher Young People's Encyclopedia of the United States.** Kingfisher Books, 1994. 808 pp. ISBN 1-85697-521-5.

Were you wondering why the FBI was created? Perhaps you need a list of some of the most important American inventors and their inventions. Or maybe you want information on significant Americans such as Stokely Carmichael, Kit Carson, Zebulan Pike, or Carl Sandburg. Whatever historical facts you need about the United States, you can probably find them here. For geography, people, sports, science, literature, religion, or industry, you can consult this one-volume, illustrated encyclopedia. It will provide you with the facts.

24.30 Stevens, Carla. **A Book of Your Own: Keeping a Diary or Journal.** Clarion Books, 1993. 100 pp. ISBN 0-89919-256-4.

Keeping a diary or journal can be a great way to let off steam, keep your secrets, or record exciting events in your life. *A Book of Your Own* tells you how to start a diary or journal and how to keep it going. Lots of excerpts from real diaries by other young people demonstrate how journal writing can be both enjoyable and meaningful.

24.31 Sullivan, George. **How an Airport Really Works.** Lodestar Books, 1993. 122 pp. ISBN 0-525-67378-4.

Interested in what goes on behind-the-scenes at an airport? Have you ever wondered how traveling pets are cared for in airports? What happens in the control tower? These are just a few of the questions answered in this fascinating look at "cities that never sleep."

24.32 Tchudi, Stephen. **Lock and Key.** Charles Scribner's Sons, 1993. 113 pp. ISBN 0-684-19363-9.

We lock bicycles, and we unlock diaries and the secrets of science. Legend tells us that holding a key in your hand will stop sickness, while lovers speak of finding the key to their hearts. The history of locks and keys extends from ancient seals and pins to present day computer codes and electronic safes, with each invention revealing as much about the people who lock as the devices they use.

24.33 Tennyson, Jeffrey. **The Illustrated History of the Hamburger: Hamburger Heaven.** Hyperion Books, 1993. 128 pp. ISBN 1-56282-982-3.

Can you imagine owning a hamburger lamp or a radioburger? Author/graphic designer Jeffrey Tennyson, owner of the world's largest collection of hamburger memorabilia, certainly can! In this comprehensive work, he shares not only his memorabilia, but also his vast knowledge of America's favorite food, as he traces the history of the hamburger and the various drive-ins and restaurant chains associated with the famous sandwich. He also highlights the architecture and graphic signage used to advertise burgers.

24.34 Terban, Marvin. **It Figures! Fun Figures of Speech.** Illustrated by Giulio Maestro. Clarion, 1993. 63 pp. ISBN 0-395-61584-4.

Want to have fun with language? Want to write a livelier, more colorful paper for your English class? Perhaps *It Figures* can help you get started! Learn how to use common figures of speech such as similes, metaphors, onomatopoeia, alliteration, hyperbole, and personification to create vivid, interesting stories. As you savor the suggestions and illustrative examples, you will delight in the humorous drawings used to clarify the various figures of speech.

24.35 Vecchione, Glen. **World's Best Outdoor Games.** Sterling, 1993. 128 pp. ISBN 0-8069-8436-8.

Time to go outside and play a new game! Why not try your hand at whip-ball, a version of baseball that uses a hose for a bat? Or learn to play *lapkta*, a Russian baseball game. More than a hundred challenging outdoor activities from around the world are highlighted in this entertaining resource. Ball games, relay races, Frisbee games, bowling games, tag games, running games, marble games—they are all here, just waiting to be played.

24.36 Wegman, William. **ABC.** Hyperion Books for Children, 1994. 32 pp. ISBN 1-56282-696-4.

If you love dogs, you'll delight in this witty alphabet book starring the author's four weimaraners—Battey, Fay Ray, Battina, and Chundo. Using a Polaroid camera, Wegman takes photographs of his lovable dogs as they pose in a group to illustrate each letter of the alphabet. Each letter is accompanied by a full-color photograph. For example, for the letter *E*, we read and see that "Battey has a sock on her nose. She thinks she looks like an elephant."

24.37 Wilks, Mike. **The Ultimate Noah's Ark: Perfect Puzzle for All Ages.** Henry Holt and Company, 1993. 80 pp. ISBN 0-8050-2802-1.

Mike Wilks challenges readers to solve the puzzle hidden in these extraordinary surreal paintings of animals. In keeping with the story of Noah, 355 animals are painted twice in the book, but one creature is missing its mate. Find and name this lonely creature for a $10,000 reward. Watch out! While on the surface the puzzle seems simple, Wilk says he intends to "baffle, bemuse, bedevil, befuddle, and generally drive you to distraction."

24.38 Young, Mark C., editor. **The Guinness Book of Records 1995.** Facts on File, 1994. 320 pp. ISBN 0-8160-2646-7.

The heaviest baby born to a healthy mother was a boy weighing 22 pounds and 8 ounces, in Italy in 1955. The longest sneezing fit on record lasted 978 days! The largest turtle ever measured was 9 feet, 5 1/2 inches long, from nose to tail, and weighed 2,120 pounds! Peruse the *Guinness Book of Records* to find out all kinds of fascinating facts and figures. This new edition includes interviews with many of the record holders.

Appendix A: 100 Books from 25 Years of Young Adult Literature (1967–1992)

The publication in 1967 of S. E. Hinton's *The Outsiders* marks a turning point in the history of literature for young adults. This edition of *Your Reading* starts with the twenty-sixth publication year after the appearance of Hinton's touchstone book, so we decided to put together a list of 100 notable young-adult books published in the twenty-five years from 1967 to 1992.

Obviously, no list of one hundred books in a twenty-five year period can claim to be complete. First of all, we included only one book for each author listed. That does not mean that other books by these authors are not worthy of being listed. Second, we selected books that we thought were most representative of outstanding reading for junior high school and middle school; therefore, our selections may not reflect some of the books that appear on other lists of young-adult literature aimed at a broader audience.

Our list includes fiction and nonfiction, mysteries and romances, fantasy and realism, poetry and short stories, biography and autobiography. But ultimately, our list is a subjective one. It represents our favorites and our choices. We hope it will be a helpful list for you and that it will lead to many hours of pleasurable reading. That, after all, is the major goal of *Your Reading*.

Adams, Douglas. *The Hitchhiker's Guide to the Galaxy*

Alexander, Lloyd. *Westmark*

Anonymous. *Go Ask Alice*

Armstrong, William. *Sounder*

Arrick, Fran. *Chernowitz*

Ashabranner, Brent. *Always to Remember: The Story of the Vietnam Veterans Memorial*

Avi. *Nothing But the Truth: A Documentary Novel*

Babbitt, Natalie. *Tuck Everlasting*

Banks, Lynne Reid. *The Indian in the Cupboard*

Bennett, Jay. *The Birthday Murderer: A Mystery*

Blume, Judy. *Are You There, God? It's Me, Margaret*
Brancato, Robin. *Winning*
Bridgers, Sue Ellen. *Home before Dark*
Brooks, Bruce. *The Moves Make the Man*
Byars, Betsy. *The Pinballs*
Cannon, A. E. *Amazing Gracie*
Card, Orson Scott. *Ender's Game*
Cary, Lorene. *Black Ice*
Childress, Alice. *A Hero Ain't Nothin' but a Sandwich*
Cleaver, Vera, and Bill Cleaver. *Where the Lilies Bloom*
Cole, Brock. *The Goats*
Collier, James, and Christopher Collier. *My Brother Sam Is Dead*
Conrad, Pam. *Prairie Songs*
Cooper, Susan. *The Dark Is Rising*
Cormier, Robert. *I Am the Cheese*
Crutcher, Chris. *Running Loose*
Danziger, Paula. *The Cat Ate My Gymsuit*
Davis, Jenny. *Sex Education*
Dickinson, Peter. *Eva*
Dorris, Michael. *Morning Girl*
Duncan, Lois. *Killing Mr. Griffin*
Fleischman, Paul. *Joyful Noise: Poems for Two Voices*
Fox, Paula. *The Slave Dancer*
Frank, Anne. *Diary of a Young Girl*
Freedman, Russell. *Lincoln: A Photobiography*
Fritz, Jean. *Homesick: My Own Story*
Gaines, Ernest. *The Autobiography of Miss Jane Pittman*
Gallo, Donald, ed. *Sixteen: Short Stories by Outstanding Writers for Young Adults*
George, Jean Craighead. *Julie of the Wolves*
Glenn, Mel. *Class Dismissed! High School Poems*
Greene, Bette. *Summer of My German Soldier*
Guy, Rosa. *The Friends*
Hall, Lynn. *The Leaving*
Hamilton, Virginia. *The House of Dies Drear*
Hinton, S. E. *The Outsiders*
Hobbs, Will. *Downriver*

Appendix A: 100 Books from 25 Years of Young Adult Literature (1967–1992)

Holman, Felice. *Slake's Limbo*
Holland, Isabelle. *The Man without a Face*
Hunt, Irene. *No Promises in the Wind*
Jacques, Brian. *Redwall*
Janeczko, Paul. *Pocket Poems*
Kerr, M. E. *Dinky Hocker Shoots Smack*
Klein, Norma. *Mom, the Wolfman and Me*
Korman, Gordon. *Don't Care High*
L'Engle, Madeleine. *A Wrinkle in Time*
Lasky, Kathryn. *Beyond the Divide*
Lawrence, Louise. *Children of the Dust*
Le Guin, Ursula. *A Wizard of Earthsea*
Lester, Julius. *To Be a Slave*
Lipsyte, Robert. *The Contender*
Lowry, Lois. *Number the Stars*
Macaulay, David. *The Way Things Work*
MacLachlan, Patricia. *Sarah, Plain and Tall*
Mahy, Margaret. *Memory*
Mazer, Harry. *The Last Mission*
Mazer, Norma Fox. *After the Rain*
McCaffrey, Anne. *Dragonsong*
McKinley, Robin. *The Hero and the Crown*
Meltzer, Milton. *Rescue: The Story of How Gentiles Saved Jews in the Holocaust*
Myers, Walter Dean. *Scorpions*
Nixon, Joan Lowry. *The Seance*
O'Brien, Robert C. *Z for Zachariah*
O'Dell, Scott. *Island of the Blue Dolphins*
Oneal, Zibby. *The Language of Goldfish*
Paterson, Katherine. *Bridge to Terabithia*
Paulsen, Gary. *Hatchet*
Peck, Richard. *Are You in the House Alone?*
Peck, Robert Newton. *A Day No Pigs Would Die*
Pfeffer, Susan Beth. *The Year without Michael*
Prelutsky, Jack. *Nightmares: Poems to Trouble Your Sleep*
Rawls, Wilson. *Where the Red Fern Grows*
Reiss, Johanna. *The Upstairs Room*

Rylant, Cynthia. *A Fine White Dust*

Sebestyen, Ouida. *Words by Heart*

Siegel, Aranka. *Upon the Head of a Goat*

Silverstein, Shel. *A Light in the Attic*

Sleator, William. *House of Stairs*

Soto, Gary. *Baseball in April and Other Stories*

Speare, Elizabeth George. *The Sign of the Beaver*

Spinelli, Jerry. *Maniac Magee*

Staples, Suzanne Fisher. *Shabanu: Daughter of the Wind*

Swarthout, Glendon. *Bless the Beasts and Children*

Taylor, Mildred. *Roll of Thunder, Hear My Cry*

Taylor, Theodore. *The Cay*

Voigt, Cynthia. *Dicey's Song*

White, Robb. *Deathwatch*

Wolff, Virginia Euwer. *Probably Still Nick Swansen*

Yep, Laurence. *Dragonwings*

Yolen, Jane. *Two Thousand Forty-One: Twelve Stories about the Future by Top Science Fiction Writers*

Zindel, Paul. *The Pigman*

Appendix B: Award-Winning Books in *Your Reading*

Many different reviewing sources select what they consider the "best-books" list each year. The list below is a compilation of titles annotated in this edition of *Your Reading* that have been judged outstanding by some of those reviewers.

Key to Abbreviations for Reviewing Sources

ALA Notable: American Library Association Notable Children's Books, 1994, 1995

BBYA: Best Books for Young Adults, 1994, 1995 (American Library Association)

BEC: *Booklist* Editors' Choice, 1994, 1995

RYAR: Recommended Books for the Reluctant Young Adult Reader (American Library Association, published as "Quick Picks")

SLJ BB: *School Library Journal* Best Books, 1993, 1994

TC: Teacher's Choices (International Reading Association)

VOYA: *Voya,* June 1994 (Outstanding Books of '94 for the Middle School Reader)

YAC: Young Adults' Choices (International Reading Association)

Major awards such as the **Caldecott,** Coretta Scott King (**CS King**), and Mildred Batchelder Awards (**Batchelder**) are also noted. **Newbery HB** indicates a Newbery Honor Book, and **Newbery M** indicates a Newbery Medal winner.

Recognized Books for 1993 and 1994

Alcock, Vivien. *Singer to the Sea God*. BBYA

Atkin, S. Beth. *Voices from the Fields: Children of Migrant Farm Workers Tell Their Stories*. BBYA, BEC

Avi. *The Barn*. ALA Notable, BEC

Bachrach, Susan D. *Tell Them We Remember: The Story of the Holocaust*. ALA Notable, BBYA, BEC, RYAR

Bash, Barbara. *Ancient Ones: The World of the Old-Growth Douglas Fir*. SLJ BB

Bauer, Marion Dane. *A Question of Trust*. SLJ BB

Bauer, Marion Dane. *Am I Blue? Coming Out from the Silence*. BBYA, RYAR

Bawden, Nina. *The Real Plato Jones*. SLJ BB

Beake, Lesley. *Song of Be*. ALA Notable, BBYA

Bennett, James. *Dakota Dream*. BBYA, RYAR

Blacker, Terence. *Homebird*. YAC

Block, Francesca Lia. *Missing Angel Juan*. BBYA, RYAR, SLJ BB

Blume, Judy. *Here's to You, Rachel Robinson*. BBYA

Bode, Janet. *Death is Hard to Live With: Teenagers Talk About How They Cope With Loss*. YAC

Bode, Janet, and Stan Mack. *Heartbreak and Roses: Real-Life Stories of Troubled Love*. BBYA

Bosse, Malcolm. *Deep Dream of the Rain Forest*. VOYA

Bosse, Malcolm. *The Examination*. BBYA, BEC

Brandenburg, Jim. *Sand and Fog: Adventures in Southern Africa*. RYAR

Brandenburg, Jim. *To the Top of the World: Adventures with Arctic Wolves*. BBYA, RYAR, SLJ BB, VOYA

Brooks, Martha. *Traveling on into the Light and Other Stories*. BBYA, SLJ BB, RYAR

Busenberg, Bonnie. *Vanilla, Chocolate & Strawberry: The Story of Your Favorite Flavors*. RYAR

Butterfield, Moira. *Space: Look Inside Cross Sections*. RYAR

Carmody, Isobelle. *The Gathering*. RYAR

Carrick, Carol. *Whaling Days*. ALA Notable, BEC

Casey, Maude. *Over the Water*. SLJ BB

Cohn, Amy. *From Sea to Shining Sea: A Treasury of American Folklore and Folk Songs*. ALA Notable, BEC, SLJ BB, VOYA

Colman, Penny. *Toilets, Bathtubs, Sinks, and Sewers: A History of the Bathroom*. RYAR

Coman, Carolyn. *Tell Me Everything*. ALA Notable, RYAR, SLJ BB

Conford, Ellen. *I Love You, I Hate You, Get Lost*. RYAR

Conly, Jane Leslie. *Crazy Lady!* ALA Notable, BBYA, BEC, Newbery HB, YAC

Cooney, Caroline B. *Driver's Ed*. BBYA, BEC, RYAR

Cooney, Caroline B. *Whatever Happened to Janie?* BBYA, YAC

Cooper, Susan. *The Boggart*. ALA Notable, BEC, SLJ BB

Corcoran, Barbara. *Wolf at the Door*. YAC

Coville, Bruce. *Oddly Enough*. BBYA, RYAR

Creech, Sharon. *Walk Two Moons*. ALA Notable, Newbery M, SLJ BB

Cross, Gillian. *The Great American Elephant Chase.* SLJ BB

Crutcher, Chris. *Staying Fat for Sarah Byrnes.* BBYA, SLJ BB

Cushman, Karen. *Catherine, Called Birdy.* ALA Notable, BBYA, BEC, Newbery HB, RYAR, SLJ BB

Derby, Pat. *Grams, Her Boyfriend, My Family, and Me.* SLJ BB

Deuker, Carl. *Heart of a Champion.* BBYA, RYAR, VOYA

Dewey, Jennifer Owings. *Wildlife Rescue: The Work of Dr. Kathleen Ramsay.* SLJ BB

Dickenson, Peter. *A Bone from a Dry Sea.* ALA Notable, BBYA, BEC, SLJ BB, VOYA

Dorris, Michael. *Guests.* ALA Notable

Drucker, Malka, and Michael Halperin. *Jacob's Rescue: A Holocaust Story.* TC

Durrell, Ann, et al. *The Big Book for Our Planet.* TC

Farmer, Nancy. *The Ear, the Eye and the Arm.* ALA Notable, BBYA, Newbery HB

Feelings, Tom. *Soul Looks Back in Wonder.* BBYA, RYAR

Filipovik, Zlata. *Zlata's Diary.* RYAR

Fine, Anne. *Flour Babies.* ALA Notable, RYAR, SLJ BB

Fleischman, Paul. *Bull Run.* ALA Notable, BBYA, BEC, SLJ BB, TC, VOYA

Fletcher, Ralph. *I Am Wings: Poems about Love.* RYAR, SLJ BB

Fletcher, Susan. *Flight of the Dragon Kyn.* BBYA, YAC

Ford, Michael Thomas. *100 Questions and Answers about AIDS: What You Need to Know Now.* YAC

Fox, Paula. *Western Wind.* SLJ BB

Freedman, Russell. *Eleanor Roosevelt: A Life of Discovery.* ALA Notable, BBYA, BEC, Newbery HB, SLJ BB, VOYA

Freedman, Russell. *Kids at Work: Lewis Hine and the Crusade against Child Labor.* ALA Notable, BBYA, SLJ BB

Garland, Sherry. *Shadow of the Dragon.* BBYA, BEC

George, Jean Craighead. *Julie.* BEC

Giblin, James Cross. *Be Seated: A Book about Chairs.* ALA Notable

Gorman, Carol. *Graveyard Moon.* YAC

Gowell, Elizabeth Tayntor. *Sea Jellies: Rainbows in the Sea.* SLJ BB

Granfield, Linda. *Cowboy: An Album.* RYAR

Grant, Cynthia. *Uncle Vampire.* BBYA, RYAR

Greenberg, Jan, and Sandra Jordan. *The Sculptor's Eye: Looking at Contemporary American Art.* ALA Notable

Griffin, Peni R. *Switching Well.* SLJ BB

Hahn, Mary Downing. *The Wind Blows Backward.* BBYA, YAC

Hamilton, Virginia. *Many Thousand Gone: African Americans from Slavery to Freedom*. ALA Notable, BEC, VOYA

Hamilton, Virginia. *Plain City*. ALA Notable, SLJ BB

Haynes, Betsy. *Deadly Deception*. RYAR

Hesse, Karen. *Phoenix Rising*. ALA Notable, BBYA, SLJ BB

Hobbs, Will. *Beardance*. BBYA, VOYA

Hodge, Merle. *For the Life of Laetitia*. BBYA

Hoose, Phillip. *It's Our World, Too! Stories of Young People Who Are Making a Difference*. ALA Notable

Isaacs, Anne. *Swamp Angel*. ALA Notable, Caldecott Honor Book, SLJ BB

Isaacson, Philip M. *A Short Walk around the Pyramids and through the World of Art*. ALA Notable, BBYA, SLJ BB, VOYA

Janeczko, Paul B. *Stardust otel*. BBYA, RYAR

Janeczko, Paul B., editor. *Looking for Your Name: A Collection of Contemporary Poems*. BBYA

Johnson, Angela. *Toning the Sweep*. ALA Notable, BBYA, BEC, Newbery HB, SLJ BB, VOYA

Johnson, James Weldon. *Lift Every Voice and Sing*. BEC

Johnson, James Weldon. *The Creation*. ALA Notable, CS King

Johnston, Julie. *Adam and Eve and Pinch-Me*. ALA Notable, SLJ BB

Johnston, Julie. *Hero of Lesser Causes*. ALA Notable, SLJ BB

Johnstone, Michael. *Cars: Look Inside Cross Sections*. RYAR

Jones, K. Maurice. *Say It Loud! The Story of Rap Music*. BBYA

Jordan, Sherryl. *Winter of Fire*. BBYA

Jordan, Sherryl. *Wolf-Woman*. BBYA

Kindl, Patrice. *Owl in Love*. ALA Notable, BBYA, RYAR

Klass, David. *California Blue*. RYAR, SLJ BB

Klass, Sheila Solomon. *Rhino*. RYAR

Klause, Annette Curtis. *Alien Secrets*. ALA Notable, BEC, SLJ BB, VOYA

Koertge, Ron. *Tiger, Tiger, Burning Bright*. ALA Notable, BBYA

Konigsburg, E. L. *T-Backs, T-Shirts, Coat, and Suit*. SLB BB

Krisher, Trudy. *Spite Fences*. BBYA

Krull, Kathleen. *Lives of Musicians: Good Times, Bad Times (And What the Neighbors Thought)*. ALA Notable, BEC, SLJ BB, TC

Kuklin, Susan. *Surviving Suicide: Young People Speak Up*. BBYA, RYAR

Kuklin, Susan. *Speaking Out: Teenagers Take On Race, Sex, and Identity*. BEC

Lasky, Kathryn. *Beyond the Burning Time*. BBYA

Lavies, Bianca. *Compost Critters*. SLJ BB

Lavies, Bianca. *A Gathering of Garter Snakes*. ALA Notable, RYAR

Lawrence, Jacob. *The Great Migration: An American Story*. ALA Notable, BEC, TC

LeMieux, A. C. *The TV Guidance Counselor*. BBYA

Lester, Julius. *John Henry*. ALA Notable

Lester, Julius. *The Last Tales of Uncle Remus*. BEC

Levine, Ellen. *Freedom's Children*. BBYA, BEC, SLJ BB, VOYA

Levitin, Sonia. *Escape from Egypt*. BEC, BBYA

Lewin, Ted. *I Was a Teenage Professional Wrestler*. ALA Notable, BEC, RYAR, SLJ BB

Lisle, Janet Taylor. *Forest*. SLJ BB

Littlefield, Bill. *Champions: Stories of Ten Remarkable Athletes*. BBYA, TC

Lowry, Lois. *The Giver*. ALA Notable, BBYA, BEC, Newbery M, SLJ BB, TC, VOYA

Lynch, Chris. *Gypsy Davey*. BBYA, RYAR

Lynch, Chris. *Iceman*. BBYA, BEC, RYAR

Lynch, Chris. *Shadow Boxer*. BBYA, RYAR, SLJ BB

Lyons, Mary. *Master of Mahogany: Tom Day, Free Black Cabinetmaker*. BEC

Macaulay, David. *Ship*. BEC, TC

Macy, Sue. *A Whole New Ball Game: The Story of the All-American Girls Professional Baseball League*. BBYA, SLJ BB

McCurdy, Michael. *Escape from Slavery: The Boyhood of Frederick Douglass in His Own Words*. BEC

McNaughton, Colin. *Making Friends with Frankenstein: A Book of Monstrous Poems and Pictures*. BEC

Marrin, Albert. *Unconditional Surrender: U. S. Grant and the Civil War*. BBYA, BEC, SLJ BB

Marsden, John. *Letters from the Inside*. BBYA, RYAR, SLJ BB

Mazer, Harry. *Who Is Eddie Leonard?* BBYA, VOYA

Mazer, Norma Fox. *Out of Control*. BBYA

McFann, Jane. *Nothing More, Nothing Less*. YAC

McKissack, Patricia C. and Frederick L. McKissack. *Christmas in the Big House, Christmas in the Quarters*. CS King

Meltzer, Milton. *Cheap Raw Material: How Our Youngest Workers Are Exploited and Abused*. BEC

Meltzer, Milton. *Lincoln: In His Own Words*. TC

Merrick, Monte. *Shelter*. BBYA

Meyer, Carolyn. *White Lilacs*. BBYA, VOYA, YAC

Mori, Kyoko. *Shizuko's Daughter*. BBYA

Murphy, Jim. *Fly Like an Eagle*. RYAR

Murphy, Jim. *Across America on an Emigrant Train*. ALA Notable, BEC, SLJ BB

Murphy, Jim. *Night Terrors*. YAC

Myers, Walter Dean. *Brown Angels: An Album of Pictures and Verse*. ALA Notable

Myers, Walter Dean. *The Glory Field*. BBYA

Myers, Walter Dean. *Malcolm X: By Any Means Necessary*. BBYA, TC, VOYA, YAC

Napoli, Donna Jo. *Magic Circle*. BBYA, BEC, RYAR

Orlev, Uri. *Lydia, Queen of Palestine*. BEC

Panzer, Nora. *Celebrate America in Poetry and Art*. ALA Notable, BBYA, SLJ BB

Paulsen, Gary. *Father Water, Mother Woods*. RYAR

Paulsen, Gary. *Harris and Me*. BBYA, BEC, RYAR, VOYA

Paulsen, Gary. *Nightjohn*. ALA Notable, BBYA

Paulsen, Gary. *Winterdance: The Fine Madness of Running the Iditarod*. BBYA

Peck, Richard. *Bel-Air Bambi and the Mall Rats*. SLJ BB

Philbrick, Rodman. *Freak the Mighty*. BBYA, RYAR, VOYA, YAC

Platt, Richard. *Castle*. Illustrated by Stephen Biesty. RYAR

Plowden, Martha Ward. *Famous Firsts of Black Women*. YAC

Polacco, Patricia. *Pink and Say*. ALA Notable, BEC, SLJ BB

Reaver, Chap. *Bill*. SLJ BB

Reiss, Kathryn. *Dreadful Sorry*. YAC

Reuter, Bjarne. *The Boys from St. Petri*. ALA Notable, BBYA, Batchelder

Rinaldi, Ann. *In My Father's House*. BBYA, YAC

Rivers, Glenn, and Bruce Brooks. *Those Who Love the Game: Glenn "Doc" Rivers on Life in the NBA and Elsewhere*. BBYA

Rochman, Hazel, and Darlene Z. McCampbell. *Who Do You Think You Are? Stories of Friends and Enemies*. SLJ BB

Rodowsky, Colby. *Hannah in Between*. BBYA, RYAR

Rogasky, Barbara. *Winter Poems*. ALA Notable, SLJ BB

Ross, Ramon Royal. *Harper and Moon*. ALA Notable, SLJ BB

Ross, Stewart. *Shakespeare and Macbeth: The Story behind the Play*. BBYA

Roybal, Laura. *Billy*. BBYA, RYAR

Rubin, Susan Goldman. *Emily Good as Gold*. YAC

Ruby, Lois. *Miriam's Well*. BBYA, VOYA

Rylant, Cynthia, and Walker Evans. *Something Permanent*. BBYA, BEC

Salisbury, Graham. *Under the Blood-Red Sun*. ALA Notable, BBYA, BEC

Sattler, Helen Roney. *The Earliest Americans*. SLJ BB

Scott, Michael. *October Moon*. RYAR

Sebestyen, Ouida. *Out of Nowhere*. SLJ BB

Shetterly, Will. *Nevernever*. YAC

Sills, Leslie. *Visions: Stories about Women Artists*. ALA Notable

Sleator, William. *Oddballs*. BBYA, RYAR

Sleator, William. *Others See Us*. RYAR, VOYA

Snyder, Zilpha Keatley. *Cat Running*. SLJ BB

Soto, Gary. *Local News*. VOYA

Springer, Nancy. *Toughing It*. RYAR

Stanley, Jerry. *I Am an American: A True Story of Japanese Internment*. ALA Notable, SLJ BB

Staples, Suzanne Fisher. *Haveli*. BBYA, BEC

Stefoff, Rebecca. *Herman Melville*. BEC

Steiner, Barbara. *Deathline*. YAC

Stolz, Mary. *Cezanne Pinto*. BBYA

Sullivan, George. *Pitchers: Twenty-Seven of Baseball's Greatest*. RYAR

Sutcliff, Rosemary. *Black Ships before Troy: The Story of the Iliad*. BBYA

Swanson, Diane. *Safari beneath the Sea: The Wonder World of the North Pacific Coast*. RYAR

Sweeney, Joyce. *Shadow*. BBYA, RYAR

Taylor, Theodore. *Timothy of the Cay*. BBYA, BEC, VOYA

Temple, Frances. *The Ramsay Scallop*. BBYA, BEC

Thomas, Joyce Carol. *Brown Honey in Broomwheat Tea*. TC

Tolan, Stephanie S. *Save Halloween*. BEC

van der Rol, Ruud, and Rian Verhoeven. *Anne Frank, beyond the Diary: A Photographic Remembrance*. ALA Notable, BBYA, BEC, RYAR, TC, VOYA

Visual Dictionary of the Horse. RYAR

Volavkova, Hana, editor. *I Never Saw Another Butterfly... Children's Drawings and Poems from Terezin Concentration Camp 1942–1944*. BBYA

Walker, Kate. *Peter*. ALA Notable, BBYA, RYAR

Watkins, Yoko Kawashima. *My Brother, My Sister, and I*. BBYA

Weaver, Will. *Striking Out*. BBYA

Weidhorn, Manfred. *Jackie Robinson*. YAC

Wesley, Valerie Wilson. *Where Do I Go from Here?* YAC

Williams, Vera. *Scooter*. ALA Notable, BEC

Wisler, G. Clifton. *Jericho's Journey*. YAC

Wittlinger, Ellen. *Lombardo's Law*. BBYA, RYAR

Wolff, Virginia Euwer. *Make Lemonade*. ALA Notable, BBYA, BEC, RYAR, SLJ BB, TC, VOYA

Woodson, Jacqueline. *I Hadn't Meant to Tell You This*. ALA Notable, BBYA, BEC

Yep, Laurence. *Dragon's Gate*. ALA Notable, Newbery HB, VOYA

Young, Ronder Thomas. *Learning by Heart*. ALA Notable

Zindel, Paul. *Loch*. RYAR

Directory of Publishers

ABC-CLIO Contemporary World Issues. P.O. Box 1911, Santa Barbara, CA 93116-1911. 800-422-2546.

Archway Hardcover Pocket Books. Imprint of Pocket Books. Orders to: 200 Old Tappan Road, Old Tappan, NJ 07675. 800-223-2336.

Arte Público Press. Division of University of Houston, 4800 Calhoun, Houston, TX 77204. 800-633-2783.

Atheneum. See Macmillan Publishing Company.

Avon/AvoNova. See Avon Books.

Avon Books. Orders to: P.O. Box 767, Dresden, TN 38225. 800-223-0690.

Avon/Camelot. See Avon Books.

Avon/Flare Books. See Avon Books.

Bantam Books. Division of Bantam Doubleday Dell. Orders to: 414 E. Golf Road, Des Plaines, IL 60016. 800-223-6834.

Bantam/Skylark Books. See Bantam Books.

Beacon Press. Distributed by Farrar, Straus and Giroux, 19 Union Square West, New York, NY 10003. 800-631-8571.

Beech Tree Books. See William Morrow & Company.

Berkley Books. Orders to: P.O. Box 506, East Rutherford, NJ 07073. 800-223-0510.

Berkley/Perigee. See Berkley Books.

Blue Sky/Scholastic. Orders to: P.O. Box 120, Bergenfield, NJ 07621. 800-325-6149.

Boyds Mills Press. Distributed by St. Martin's Press, Inc., 175 Fifth Ave., Room 1715, New York, NY 10010. 800-221-7945.

Bradbury Press. See Macmillan Publishing Company.

BridgeWater Books. Distributed by Penguin USA, 375 Hudson Street, New York, NY 10014-3657. 800-331-4624.

Browndeer Press/Harcourt Brace & Company. See Harcourt Brace & Company.

Candlewick Press. Division of Walker Books, London, England. Orders to: Penguin USA, P.O. Box 120, Bergenfield, NJ 07621. 800-526-0275.

Carolrhoda Books. 241 First Avenue North, Minneapolis, MN 55401. 800-328-4929.

Chelsea House. Division of Main Line Book Co., 300 Park Avenue South, No. 6, New York, NY 10010-5313. 800-848-2665.

Children's Press. Division of Grolier, Inc., 5440 N. Cumberland Avenue, Chicago, IL 60656. 800-621-1115.

Clarion Books. See Houghton Mifflin.

Cobblehill Books. See E. P. Dutton.

Cobblehill/Dutton. See E. P. Dutton.

Crabtree Publishing. P.O. Box 3451, Federal Way, WA 98063. 206-927-3777.

Crestwood House. See Macmillan Publishing Company.

Crown Publishing Group. Affiliate of Random House. Orders to: 400 Hahn Road, Westminster, MD 21157. 800-733-3000.

Delacorte Press. Division of Bantam Doubleday Dell. Orders to: 1540 Broadway, New York, NY 10036-4094. 800-223-6834.

Delacorte Press/Whitney Museum of American Art. See Delacorte Press.

Dell Publishing. Division of Bantam Doubleday Dell. Orders to: 1540 Broadway, New York, NY 10036-4094. 800-223-6834.

Dell/Laurel Leaf. See Dell Publishing.

Dell/Yearling. See Dell Publishing.

Dial Books. Division of Penguin USA. Orders to: P.O. Box 120, Bergenfield, NJ 07621. 800-387-0600.

Dial Books for Young Readers. See Dial Books.

Dillon Press. See Macmillan Publishing Company.

Dorling Kindersley Publishing. Distributed by Houghton Mifflin, Wayside Road, Burlington, MA 01803. 800-225-3362.

Doubleday Books for Young Readers. Division of Bantam Doubleday Dell. Orders to: Doubleday Consumer Services, P.O. Box 5071, Des Plaines, IL 60017-5071. 800-223-6834.

E. P. Dutton. Division of Penguin USA. Orders to: P.O. Box 120, Bergenfield, NJ 07621-0120. 800-526-0275.

Dutton Children's Books. See E. P. Dutton.

Dutton/Cobblehill Books. See E. P. Dutton.

Dutton/Lodestar. See E. P. Dutton.

William B. Eerdman's Publishing Company. 255 Jefferson Avenue, S.E., Grand Rapids, MI 49503. 800-253-7521.

Enslow Publishers, Inc. Bloy Street and Ramsey Avenue, Box 777, Hillside, NJ 07205. 800-398-2504.

Facts on File. Subsidiary of Infobase Holdings, 460 Park Avenue South, New York, NY 10016. 800-322-8755.

Farrar, Straus and Giroux. 19 Union Square West, New York, NY 10003. 800-631-8571.

Fawcett/Juniper. Imprint of Fawcett Book Group. Orders to: 400 Hahn Road, Westminster, MD 21157. 800-733-3000.

Directory of Publishers

Four Winds Press. See Macmillan Publishing Company.

Golden Books/Golden Press. Imprints of Western Publishing Co., Inc. Orders to: 5945 Erie Street, Racine, WI. 800-225-9514.

Greenhaven Press, Inc. Orders to: P.O. Box 289009, San Diego, CA 92198. 800-231-5163.

Greenwillow Books. Division of William Morrow. Orders to: 39 Plymouth Street, P.O. Box 1219, Fairfield, NJ 07007. 800-843-9389.

Grosset & Dunlap. See G. P. Putnam's Sons.

Gulliver Books/Harcourt Brace & Company. See Harcourt Brace & Company.

Gulliver Green Books/Harcourt Brace & Company. See Harcourt Brace & Company.

Harcourt Brace & Company. (Formerly Harcourt Brace Jovanovich.) Orders to: 6277 Sea Harbor Drive, Orlando, FL 32887. 800-346-8648.

Harcourt Brace Children's Books. See Harcourt Brace & Company.

Harcourt Brace Jovanovich. See Harcourt Brace & Company.

HarperCollins. (Formerly Harper & Row.) Orders to: 1000 Keystone Industrial Park, Scranton, PA 18512-4621. 800-242-7737.

HarperCollins/Museum of Modern Art. See HarperCollins.

HarperCollins/Festival. See HarperCollins.

HarperKeypoint. See HarperCollins.

HarperTrophy. See HarperCollins.

Holiday House. 425 Madison Avenue, New York, NY 10017. 212-688-0085.

Henry Holt and Company. 115 West 18th Street, New York, NY 10011. 800-488-5233.

Houghton Mifflin. Orders to: Wayside Road, Burlington, MA 01803. 800-225-3362.

Hyperion Books. Division of Disney Books. Orders to: Little, Brown and Company, 200 West Street, Waltham, MA 02254. 800-343-9204.

Hyperion Books for Children. See Hyperion Books.

Jewish Publication Society. 1930 Chestnut Street, Philadelphia, PA 19103. 800-234-3151.

Jove Books. See Berkley Books.

Joy Street Books/Little, Brown and Company. See Little, Brown and Company.

Kingfisher Books. 2150 N. Tenaya Way, No. 1052, Las Vegas, NV 89128. 702-242-9009.

Kingfisher Books in association with the United Nations. See Kingfisher Books.

Alfred A. Knopf. Subsidiary of Random House. Orders to: 400 Hahn Road, Westminster, MD 21157. 800-733-3000.

Lerner Publications. 241 First Avenue North, Minneapolis, MN 55401. 800-328-4929.

Linnet Books. Imprint of Shoe String Press, Inc., 2 Linsley Street, North Haven, CT 06473-2517. 203-239-2702.

Little, Brown and Company. Division of Time Warner. Orders to: 200 West Street, Waltham, MA 02254. 800-343-9204.

Ward Lock/Sterling. See Sterling Publishing Company.

Lodestar Books. See E. P. Dutton.

Lothrop, Lee & Shepard. Division of William Morrow. Orders to: 39 Plymouth Street, P.O. Box 1219, Fairfield, NJ 07007. 800-237-0657.

Lucent Books. Distributed by Greenhaven Press, 10911 Technology Place, San Diego, CA 92127. 619-485-7424.

Lucent Overview Books. See Lucent Books.

Macmillan Publishing Company. Orders to: 100 Front Street, Box 500, Riverside, NJ 08075. 800-257-5755.

Macmillan/Margaret K. McElderry Books. See Macmillan Publishing Company.

Macmillan/New Discovery Books. See Macmillan Publishing Company.

Julian Messner. See Simon & Schuster.

The Metropolitan Museum of Art. Orders to: Special Service Office, Middle Village, NY 11381-0001. 718-326-7050.

Millbrook Press. 2 Old New Milford Road, Brookfield, CT 06804. 203-740-2220.

Minstrel Books. See Pocket Books.

Minstrel/Pocket Books. See Pocket Books.

Morrow Junior Books. See William Morrow & Company.

William Morrow & Company. Orders to: Wilmor Warehouse, P.O. Box 1219, 39 Plymouth Street, Fairfield, NJ 07007. 800-843-9389.

New Discovery Books. See Macmillan Publishing Company.

Orchard Books. Division of Franklin Watts, 95 Madison Avenue, 11th Floor, New York, NY 10016. 800-672-6672.

Oryx Press. 4041 North Central Avenue, Suite 700, Phoenix, AZ 85012-3397. 800-279-6799.

Oxford University Press. Orders to: 2001 Evans Road, Cary, NC 27513. 800-451-7556.

Pelican Publishing Company. 1101 Monroe Street, Gretna, LA 70053. 800-843-1724 (800-843-4558 in Louisiana).

Penguin Books. Division of Penguin USA. Orders to: 120 Woodbine Street, Bergenfield, NJ 07621. 800-631-3577.

Willa Perlman Books. See HarperCollins.

Directory of Publishers

Philomel Books, See G. P. Putnam's Sons.

Piñata Books. Imprint of Arte Público Press, 4800 Calhoun, Houston, TX 77024. 800-633-2783.

Pocket Books. Orders to: Paramount Publishing, 200 Old Tappan Road, Old Tappan, NJ 07675. 201-767-5937.

Pocket Books/Minstrel. See Pocket Books.

Byron Preiss Visual Publications/Bantam Books. See Bantam Books.

Puffin Books. See Bantam Books.

G. P. Putnam's Sons. Division of Putnam. Orders to: 390 Murray Hill Parkway, East Rutherford, NJ 07073-2185. 800-631-8571.

Random House. Orders to: 400 Hahn Road, Westminster, MD 21157. 800-733-3000.

The Rosen Publishing Group, Inc. 29 East 21st Street, New York, NY 10010. 800-237-9932.

Runestone Press. Imprint of Lerner Publication Company, 241 First Avenue North, Minneapolis, MN 55401. 800-328-4929.

St. Martin's Press. 175 Fifth Avenue, New York, NY 10010. 800-221-7945.

Schocken Books. Division of Random House. Orders to: 400 Hahn Road, Westminster, MD 21157. 800-733-3000.

Scholastic. Orders to: P.O. Box 120, Bergenfield, NJ 07621. 800-325-6149.

Scholastic Madison Press. See Scholastic.

Charles Scribner's Sons. Division of Macmillan Publishing Company. Orders to: 100 Front Street, Box 500, Riverside, NJ 08075. 800-257-5755.

Seal Bantam Books. See Bantam Books.

Sierra Club Books for Children. Distributed by Little, Brown and Company. Orders to: 200 West Street, Waltham, MA 02254. 800-343-9204.

Silver Burdett Press. See Simon & Schuster.

Simon & Schuster. 1230 Avenue of the Americas, New York, NY 10023. 212-698-7000.

Simon & Schuster Books for Young Readers. See Simon & Schuster.

Skylark Books. See Bantam Books.

Sterling Publishing Company. 387 Park Avenue South, New York, NY 10016-8810. 800-367-9692.

Sterling/Lark. See Sterling Publishing.

Tambourine Books. See William Morrow & Company.

Ticknor & Fields. Affiliate of Houghton Mifflin. Orders to: Wayside Road, Burlington, MA 01803. 800-225-3362.

Ticknor & Fields Books for Young Readers. See Ticknor & Fields.

Ticknor & Fields/Houghton Mifflin. See Ticknor & Fields.

UXL. Imprint of Gale Research, Inc., 835 Penobscot Building, Detroit, MI 48226-4094. 800-877-4253.

Viking. Division of Penguin USA. Orders to: P.O. Box 120, Bergenfield, NJ 07621-0120. 800-526-0275.

Viking/Penguin. See Viking.

Walker & Company. Division of Walker Publishing Company, Inc., P.O. Box 1192, Marble Falls, TX 78654. 210-693-5113.

Franklin Watts. Orders to: 5450 North Cumberland Avenue, Chicago, IL 60656. 800-672-6672.

Albert Whitman & Company. 6340 Oakton Street, Morton Grove, IL 60053. 800-255-7675.

World Almanac Books. Distributed by St. Martin's Press, 175 Fifth Avenue, New York, NY 10010. 800-221-7945.

Jane Yolen Books/Harcourt Brace & Company. See Harcourt Brace & Company.

Author Index

Aaseng, Nathan, 15.1
Abodaher, David J., 15.2
Ackerman, Karen, 1.1
Adams, Carmen, 9.1
Adkins, Jan, 7.1
Adler, C. S., 1.2
Alcock, Vivien, 6.1, 8.1
Alcott, Louisa May, 11.1, 11.2, 11.3
Alexander, Lloyd, 6.2
Altman, Linda Jacobs, 12.1
Amoss, Berthe, 6.3
Anderson, Joan, 17.1, 22.1
Anderson, Kelly C., 13.1, 15.3
Anderson, Madelyn Klein, 13.2
Anderson, Margaret J., 13.3
Andretti, Michael, 23.1
Andronik, Catherine M., 13.4, 13.5
Andryszewski, Tricia, 12.2
Angell, Judie, 1.3
Angelou, Maya, 20.1
Antle, Nancy, 11.4
Archbold, Rick, 13.6
Archer, Jules, 13.7, 15.4
Arginteanu, Judy, 22.2
Arkin, Anthony Dana, 8.2
Arrick, Fran, 3.1
Arter, Jim, 2.1
Ashabranner, Brent, 11.21, 15.5, 15.6
Atkin, S. Beth, 15.7
Averill, Esther, 13.8
Avery, Gillian, 2.2
Avi, 1.4, 6.4, 8.3, 11.5, 11.6, 11.7
Avi-Yonah, Michael, 12.3
Avila, Alfred, 5.1
Ayoub, Abderrahman, 12.4

Babbitt, Lucy Cullyford, 6.5
Bachrach, Susan D., 12.5
Bailey, Jill, 17.2
Balanchine, George, 22.3
Baldwin, Joyce, 13.9
Bandon, Alexandra, 14.1
Banks, Jacqueline Turner, 1.5
Banks, Lynne Reid, 1.6, 6.6, 6.7
Barkin, Carol, 24.1, 24.14
Barnes-Svarey, Patricia, 16.1
Barre, Shelley A., 3.2

Barrett, Elizabeth, 1.7
Barrett, Tracy, 12.6
Barrie, Barbara, 3.3
Bash, Barbara, 17.3
Battaglia, Laura, 12.84
Bauer, Marion Dane, 1.8, 9.2, 21.1
Bawden, Nina, 1.9
Baylis-White, Mary, 11.8
Beake, Lesley, 3.4
Beatty, Patricia, 11.9, 11.10
Bechard, Margaret, 2.3
Bedard, Michael, 6.8
Bellairs, John, 9.3, 9.4, 9.5
Bellingham, David, 5.2
Bennett, James, 3.5
Bentley, Bill, 13.10
Berry, James, 11.11, 21.2
Betancourt, Jeanne, 3.6
Bial, Raymond, 12.7, 12.8, 14.2, 15.8
Binous, Jamila, 12.4
Black, Christine M., 15.9
Blacker, Terence, 1.10
Block, Francesca Lia, 3.7
Blue, Rose, 15.10
Blume, Judy, 1.11
Bode, Janet, 19.2, 19.3
Bolden, Tonya, 21.3
Bond, Nancy, 1.12
Bonvillain, Nancy, 14.3
Booth, Jerry, 18.1
Bosse, Malcolm, 10.1, 11.12
Botchway, Christine, 3.8
Bowen, Betsy, 18.2
Boyd, Candy Dawson, 1.13
Boyd, George, 19.4
Bradshaw, Gillian, 6.9
Brandenburg, Jim, 17.4, 18.3
Branley, Franklyn M., 16.2, 16.3, 16.4
Brashler, William, 23.2
Breathed, Berkeley, 6.10
Breckenridge, Judy, 16.5
Brennan, J. H., 6.11, 6.12
Bridgers, Sue Ellen, 2.4
Brimner, Larry Dane, 12.9
Brittain, Bill, 7.2
Brooke, William J., 5.3, 5.4, 6.13
Brooks, Bruce, 18.4, 23.19
Brooks, Caryl, 2.5

Brooks, Martha, 21.4
Broome, Errol, 3.9
Bruce, Harry, 13.11
Bruchac, Joseph, 5.5
Brust, Beth Wagner, 22.4
Bryan, Jenny, 19.5
Buchanan, Dawna Lisa, 1.14
Buehler, Stephanie Jona, 1.15
Bunting, Eve, 1.16, 1.17
Bunyan, John, 6.14
Burchard, Peter, 13.12
Burford, Betty, 13.13
Burgess, Barbara Hood, 8.4
Burnie, David, 17.5
Busenberg, Bonnie, 24.2
Bussell, Darcey, 22.5
Busselle, Rebecca, 2.6
Butler, Beverly, 9.6
Butterfield, Moira, 16.6
Byars, Betsy, 8.5

Cadnum, Michael, 3.10
Calvert, Patricia, 11.13
Campbell, Darlene Z., 21.23
Campbell, Eric, 10.2
Canault, Nina, 16.7
Cannon, A. E., 1.18
Carmody, Isobelle, 9.7
Carrick, Carol, 12.10
Carris, Joan, 1.19
Carroll, Lewis, 6.15
Carter, Alden R., 3.11, 3.12, 12.11, 12.12
Carter, Jimmy, 15.11
Carter, Peter, 11.14
Carter, Philip I., 24.3
Carver, Douglas, 23.1
Carver, Robert, 23.1
Casalini, Max, 12.84, 12.85
Casey, Maude, 1.20
Cash, Terry, 16.8
Cassedy, Sylvia, 6.16
Catt, Hastings, 2.7
Cavan, Seamus, 14.4
Cavanaugh, Helen, 10.3
Cerullo, Mary M., 18.5
Charnas, Suzy McKee, 6.17
Chase, Richard, 5.6
Cheetham, Ann, 9.8
Cheney, Glen Alan, 15.12
Chenoweth, Russ, 6.18
Chetwin, Grace, 6.19
Children's Task Force on Agenda 21, 17.6

Choi, Sook Nyul, 11.15, 11.16
Christopher, John, 7.3
Christopher, Matt, 4.1, 4.2
Clapp, Patricia, 9.9
Clare, John D., 12.13
Clark, Clara Gillow, 11.17
Clark, Margaret Goff, 18.6
Clarke, Judith, 2.8
Clements, Bruce, 2.9
Cobb, Josh, 16.9
Cobb, Vicki, 16.9, 16.10, 16.11
Cohen, Daniel, 9.10, 9.11, 15.13, 15.14, 21.5, 21.6
Cohen, Peter Zachary, 10.4
Cohn, Amy, 5.7
Collard, Sneed B., III, 18.7
Collier, Christopher, 11.18
Collier, James Lincoln, 11.18
Collins, James, 12.14
Colman, Penny, 12.15, 13.15
Coman, Carolyn, 3.13
Conford, Ellen, 21.7
Conly, Jane Leslie, 3.14
Cooney, Caroline B., 1.21, 3.15
Cooper, Floyd, 13.16
Cooper, Illene, 2.10, 2.11
Cooper, Kay, 12.16
Cooper, Melrose, 1.22
Cooper, Susan, 6.20
Corcoran, Barbara, 3.16
Cormier, Robert, 3.17
Cossi, Olga, 17.7
Coville, Bruce, 6.21, 21.8
Cowley, Marjorie, 10.5
Cox, Clinton, 12.17
Cozic, Charles P., 17.8
Cramer, Alexander, 21.9
Creech, Sharon, 1.23
Crew, Gary, 10.6
Crew, Linda, 1.24
Crisman, Ruth, 23.3
Crocker, Mary, 19.6
Cross, Gillian, 10.7
Crutcher, Chris, 3.18
Cullen, Lynn, 2.12
Cuneo, Mary Louise, 1.25
Cushman, Karen, 11.19
Cusick, Richie Tankersley, 9.12, 9.13
Cutler, Jane, 11.20
Cytron, Barry, 13.17
Cytron, Phyllis, 13.17
Czernecki, Stefan, 5.8
Czerneda, Julie, 24.5

Author Index

Dahl, Roald, 24.6
Danziger, Paula, 2.13
Darling, Kathy, 16.10
Davidson, Nicole, 9.14
Davidson, Rosemary, 22.6
Davies, Nancy Millichap, 15.15
Davis, Deborah, 1.26
Davis, Lloyd Spenser, 18.8
Davis, Russell G., 11.21
Davis, Terry, 2.14
Dawson, Imogen, 12.18
Day, Nancy, 15.16
de Trevino, Elizabeth Borton, 11.23
Deaver, Julie Reece, 2.15, 3.19
DeClements, Barthe, 2.16, 3.20
Deem, James M., 16.12
DeFelice, Cynthia, 8.6, 10.8, 11.22
Denenberg, Barry, 13.18
Dentemaro, Christine, 19.7
Derby, Pat, 1.27
Deuker, Carl, 4.3
DeVito, Cara, 1.28
Dewey, Jennifer Owings, 18.9
Dickens, Charles, 10.9
Dickinson, Peter, 1.29, 6.22, 10.10
Disher, Garry, 3.21, 3.22
Dixon, Dougal, 18.10
Docekal, Eileen M., 16.13
Doherty, Berlie, 3.23
Dolan, Edward, 19.8
Dolan, Ellen M., 13.19
Dorris, Michael, 11.24
Douglas, William O., 13.20
Dowden, Anne Ophelia, 17.9, 17.10, 17.11
Downer, Ann, 6.23
Drake, Jane, 17.22
Draper, Sharon M., 3.24
Drucker, Malka, 11.25
Duffey, Betsy, 1.30
Duffy, Carol Ann, 20.2
Duffy, James, 11.26
Duffy, Trent, 17.12
Duncan, Lois, 12.19
Dunlop, Eileen, 3.25
Dunnahoo, Terry Janson, 23.4
Duran, Gloria, 13.21
Durrell, Ann, 17.13
Durrett, Deanne, 13.22, 19.9
Dygard, Thomas J., 4.4
Dyjak, Elisabeth, 1.31

Echo-Hawk, Roger, 15.17

Echo-Hawk, Walter, 15.17
Egger-Bovet, Howard, 12.72
Ehrlich, Amy, 12.20
Eisaguirre, Lynn, 15.18
Emory, Jerry, 18.11
Englehart, Steve, 16.14
Eschle, Lou, 12.21
Evans, J. Edward, 13.23

Facklam, Margery, 18.12
Fakih, Kimberly Olson, 1.32
Farmer, Nancy, 7.4
Farmer, Penelope, 6.24
Favors, Jean M., 9.15
Feelings, Tom, 20.3
Feinberg, Barbara Silberdick, 24.7
Ferguson, Alane, 2.17, 8.7, 9.16
Ferris, Jean, 1.33, 3.26
Fiedhoffer, Bob, 24.8
Filipovic, Zlata, 13.24
Fine, Anne, 1.34, 3.27, 6.25
Fireside, Bryna J., 13.25
Fischer, Susan, 19.14
Fleischman, Paul, 11.27, 12.22, 22.7, 22.8
Fleming, Alice, 13.26
Fleming, Thomas, 13.27
Fletcher, Ralph, 20.4
Fletcher, Susan, 6.26
Ford, Michael Thomas, 19.10
Fox, Mary Virginia, 13.28
Fox, Paula, 1.35, 3.28
Fraser, Mary Ann, 12.23
Freedman, Russell, 12.24, 13.29
Fremon, David K., 12.25
Friesner, Esther M., 6.27
Fritz, Jean, 12.26, 13.30
Fromm, Pete, 3.29
Fry, Annette R., 12.27
Fry, Plantagenet Somerset, 12.28

Gabhart, Ann, 3.30, 10.11
Gaeddert, Louann, 11.28
Galas, Judith C., 19.11
Gale, David, 21.10
Gallo, Donald R., 13.31, 21.11, 21.12
Gardner, Robert, 16.15, 16.16
Garfunkel, Trudy, 22.9
Garland, Sherry, 1.36, 10.12
Garth, G. G., 9.17
Gatti, Anne, 5.9
Gay, Kathlyn, 15.19, 19.12, 19.13, 24.9

George, Jean Craighead, 10.13, 17.13
Geras, Adèle, 8.8
Gerstenfeld, Sheldon L., 18.13
Gherman, Beverly, 13.32
Giblin, James Cross, 22.10
Gifaldi, David, 2.18
Gilden, Mel, 7.5
Gilmore, Kate, 2.19
Gleitzman, Morris, 1.37
Godfrey, Martyn, 2.20
Goldish, Meish, 15.20
Goldman, E. M., 10.14
Goldner, Kathryn A., 17.31
Gonen, Rivka, 12.29
Gonzalez, Christina, 12.30
Goode, Diane, 5.10
Goodman, Alan, 24.10
Goodman, Joan Elizabeth, 1.38
Gordon, Ruth, 20.5
Gorman, Carol, 2.21, 9.18
Gorog, Judith, 21.13
Gottfried, Ted, 15.21
Gowell, Elizabeth Tayntor, 18.14
Grace, Eric S., 18.15
Grady, Sean M., 15.22
Graff, Nancy Price, 13.33
Gragueb, Abderrazak, 12.4
Graham-Barber, Lynda, 24.11
Granfield, Linda, 12.31
Granger, Neill, 24.12
Grant, Cynthia, 1.39
Gravelle, Karen, 19.14
Green, Carl R., 23.5
Greenberg, Jan, 22.11
Greenberg, Martin H., 21.14
Greene, Bette, 11.29
Greene, Constance C., 1.40
Greene, Jacqueline Dembar, 11.30
Greene, Patricia Baird, 3.31
Greenfeld, Howard, 12.32
Greenfield, Eloise, 13.34
Greenlaw, M. Jean, 12.33
Greenwald, Sheila, 3.32
Gregory, Kristiana, 10.15
Gribbin, John, 16.17
Gribbin, Mary, 16.17
Griffin, Peni R., 7.6
Grimm, Jacob, 5.11
Grimm, Wilhelm K., 5.11
Grollman, Earl A., 19.15
Grove, Vicki, 1.41
Grover, Wayne, 2.22
Guernsey, JoAnn Bren, 15.23, 15.24

Guerrier, Charlie, 22.12
Gustafson, John, 16.18
Guthrie, Donna, 2.23
Gutman, Bill, 10.16, 10.17, 23.6

Haas, Carol, 15.25
Hackman, Peggy, 15.26
Hafen, Lyman, 1.42
Hahn, Mary Downing, 2.24, 10.18
Hakim, Joy, 12.34
Hall, David E., 19.16
Hall, Elizabeth, 11.55
Halperin, Michael, 11.25
Halpern, Robert R., 17.14
Hamilton, Virginia, 1.43, 12.35
Handler, Andrew, 13.35
Hardy, Robin, 9.19
Harrell, Janice, 9.20
Harris, Annie, 22.37
Harris, Robie H., 19.17
Haskins, James, 12.36, 12.37, 12.38, 21.15, 22.13, 22.14
Hawks, Robert, 9.21
Hayes, Daniel, 2.25
Haynes, Betsy, 1.44, 8.9
Hecht, Jeff, 18.16
Heisel, Sharon E., 8.10
Hendry, Diana, 1.45
Heneghan, James, 3.33
Herbst, Judith, 16.19
Hermes, Patricia, 1.46, 1.47, 1.48
Herriot, James, 18.17
Herzog, Brad, 23.7, 23.8
Heslewood, Juliet, 22.15
Hesse, Karen, 7.7
Hest, Amy, 1.49
Heyes, Eileen, 12.39, 13.36
Hickman, Janet, 1.50
Hicyilmaz, Gaye, 3.34
Hildick, E. W., 11.31
Hill, David, 2.26
Hirshi, Ron, 17.15
Hite, Sid, 10.19
Hobbs, Will, 1.51, 10.20, 10.21
Hodge, Merle, 1.52
Hoffius, Stephen, 4.5
Holland, Isabelle, 11.32
Honeycutt, Natalie, 1.53
Hoose, Phillip, 15.27
Hopkins, Lee Bennett, 20.6, 20.7
Hosie-Bounar, Jane, 2.27
Houston, Gloria, 11.33

Author Index

Howarth, Lesley, 7.8
Howarth, Sara, 12.40
Hughes, Dean, 4.6
Hughes, Langston, 20.8
Hughes, Monica, 7.9
Hull, Robert, 12.41
Hunter, Mollie, 6.28
Hurwitz, Johanna, 13.37

Immell, Myra H., 24.13
Irwin, Hadley, 11.34
Isaacs, Anne, 5.12
Isaacson, Philip M., 22.16

Jacques, Brian, 6.29, 6.30, 21.16
Jaffe, Nina, 5.13, 5.14
James, Alison J., 9.22
James, Elizabeth, 24.1, 24.14
James, Mary, 1.54. *See also* Kerr, M. E.
Janeczko, Paul B., 20.9, 20.10, 20.11
Jarrow, Gail, 6.31
Jennings, Paul, 21.17
Johnson, Angela, 1.55
Johnson, James Weldon, 20.12, 20.13
Johnson, Rebecca L., 17.16
Johnson, Scott, 2.28
Johnston, Julie, 1.56, 1.57
Johnstone, Michael, 24.15, 24.16
Jones, Adrienne, 11.35
Jones, Diana Wynne, 6.32, 7.10
Jones, Hettie, 20.14
Jones, K. Maurice, 22.17
Jordan, Martin, 17.17
Jordan, Sandra, 22.11
Jordan, Sherryl, 6.33, 6.34
Jordan, Tanis, 17.17

Kalman, Bobbie, 12.42
Kalman, Maira, 22.18
Karl, Jean, 12.43
Karr, Kathleen, 10.22, 11.36
Kassem, Lou, 6.35
Kaye, M. M., 6.36
Kaye, Marilyn, 3.35
Keene, Ann T., 17.18
Keene, Carolyn, 8.11
Kehret, Peg, 3.36, 10.23
Kennedy, Barbara, 3.37
Kennedy, Dorothy M., 20.15
Kennedy, X. J., 20.16

Kent, Zachary, 12.44, 15.28
Kerr, M. E., 3.38, 8.12, 13.38. *See also* James, Mary.
Kettlekamp, Larry, 16.20
Kherdian, David, 3.39
Killingsworth, Monte, 3.40
Kimmell, Eric A., 1.58
Kincaid, Beth, 3.41
Kindl, Patrice, 6.37
Kingman, Lee, 2.29, 4.7
Klass, David, 3.42
Klass, Sheila Solomon, 1.59
Klause, Annette Curtis, 7.11
Klausner, Janet, 13.39
Kline, Suzy, 2.30
Knapp, Ron, 23.9, 23.10
Knight, Lindsay, 18.18
Knudson, R. R., 13.40
Knutson, Barbara, 5.15
Koertge, Ron, 1.60, 1.61, 1.62
Konigsburg, E. L., 3.43
Kort, Michael, 12.45
Kosser, Mike, 22.19
Kranz, Rachel, 19.7, 19.23
Kreikemeier, Gregory Scott, 14.5
Krisher, Trudy, 11.37
Krizmanic, Judy, 19.18
Kronenwetter, Michael, 15.29
Krull, Kathleen, 13.41, 14.6
Kuklin, Susan, 15.30, 19.19
Kuraoka, Hannah, 9.23

L'Engle, Madeleine, 8.13
Lancaster-Brown, Peter, 16.21
Lance, Kathryn, 1.63
Landau, Elaine, 15.31, 15.32, 18.19, 19.20, 19.21
Lang, Paul, 15.33
Lang, Susan S., 15.33, 18.20
Langone, John, 14.7
Lankford, Mary D., 14.8
Lasky, Kathryn, 1.64, 9.24, 11.38, 14.9, 18.21
Lavies, Bianca, 17.19, 18.22, 18.23, 18.24
Lawlor, Laurie, 1.65
Lawrence, Jacob, 22.20
Lazo, Caroline, 22.21
Lee, Marie G., 2.31
Lee, Tanith, 6.38
Lehne, Judith Logan, 11.39
Leigh, Stephen, 7.12
LeMieux, A. C., 3.44

Lerner, Carol, 17.20
Leroe, Ellen, 9.25
Leroux, Gaston, 9.26
Lester, Julius, 5.16, 5.17
Levine, Ellen, 12.46
Levine, Michael, 24.17
Levinson, Marilyn, 1.66, 1.67
Levinson, Nancy Smiler, 12.47
Levitin, Sonia, 1.68, 11.40
Levoy, Myron, 2.32, 2.33
Levy, Elizabeth, 2.34
Levy, Robert, 6.39, 6.40
Lewin, Ted, 23.11
Lewis, J. Patrick, 5.18
Lewis-Ferguson, Julinda, 13.43
Lindbergh, Anne, 7.13
Lindblad, Lisa, 18.25
Lindop, Edmund, 15.34
Lingard, Joan, 11.41
Linnea, Sharon, 13.42
Linton, Patricia, 22.5
Lipsyte, Robert, 3.45, 4.8, 23.12, 23.13
Liptak, Karen, 14.10, 15.35, 15.36
Lisle, Janet Taylor, 6.41
Little, Lessie Jones, 13.34
Littlefield, Bill, 23.14
Livingston, Myra Cohn, 20.17
Locke, Joseph, 9.27, 9.28
Longo, Pierluigi, 12.85
Lourie, Peter, 17.21
Love, Ann, 17.22
Love, Douglas, 17.23
Lowell, Melissa, 2.35
Lowry, Lois, 7.14
Lukas, Scott E., 19.22
Lynch, Chris, 1.69, 4.9, 4.10
Lyons, George Ella, 7.15
Lyons, Mary, 22.22

Macauley, David, 12.48
MacBride, Roger Lea, 11.42
Mack, Stan, 19.3
MacLachlan, Patricia, 11.43
Macy, Sue, 23.15
Madama, John, 24.18
Madgwick, Wendy, 24.19
Maestro, Giulio, 24.20
Maestro, Marco, 24.20
Maguire, Gregory, 1.70
Mahy, Margaret, 6.42
Makris, Kathryn, 2.36
Maloney, Michael, 19.23
Mango, Karin N., 2.37

Marino, Jan, 1.71, 3.46
Markle, Sandra, 16.22, 24.21
Marrin, Albert, 12.49, 13.44
Marsden, John, 1.72
Marshall, Mary Ann, 22.23
Martin, Ana, 12.50
Matas, Carol, 11.44, 11.45, 11.46
Maugham, W. Somerset, 9.29
Maynard, Thane, 17.24
Mayne, William, 10.24
Mayo, Margaret, 5.19
Mazer, Harry, 1.73, 3.47
Mazer, Norma Fox, 3.47, 3.48
McCann, Helen, 2.38
McClung, Robert M., 10.25, 17.25
McCullough, Frances, 20.18
McCurdy, Michael, 13.45
McDaniel, Lurlene, 3.49, 3.50
McEwan, Ian, 3.51
McFann, Jane, 2.39, 2.40
McGowen, Tom, 6.43
McGuire, Kevin, 22.24
McKean, Thomas, 7.16
McKinley, Robin, 5.20, 21.18
McKissack, Fredrick L., 11.47, 12.51, 23.16
McKissack, Patricia C., 11.47, 12.51, 23.16
McLean, Susan, 1.74
McNaughton, Colin, 20.19
McPherson, Stephanie Sammartino, 13.46
McVey, Vicki, 17.26
Mebane, Robert C., 16.26
Medearis, Angela Shelf, 13.47
Meisel, Jacqueline Drobis, 15.37
Meltzer, Milton, 13.48, 15.38, 24.22
Merino, Jose Maria, 11.48
Merrick, Monte, 1.75
Meschel, Susan V., 13.35
Mettger, Zack, 12.52, 12.53
Meyer, Carolyn, 11.49, 21.49
Mikaelsen, Ben, 10.26, 10.27
Miklowitz, Gloria, 8.14
Miller, Maryann, 15.39
Mills, Claudia, 2.41
Minters, Frances, 5.21
Monroe, Jean Guard, 12.54
Moon, Pat, 20.20
Mori, Kyoko, 1.76
Morpurgo, Michael, 10.28
Morris, Desmond, 18.26
Morris, Jeffrey, 12.55
Morris, Juddi, 12.56
Morse, Eric, 9.30
Moser, Barry, 12.57
Mtimet, Ali, 12.4

Mühlberger, Richard, 22.25
Mulford, Phillipa Greene, 1.77
Murdoch, David H., 12.58
Murphy, Barbara Beasley, 1.78
Murphy, Catherine Frey, 3.52
Murphy, Jim, 12.59, 21.20
Murphy, Pat, 16.23
Murrow, Liza Ketchum, 3.53
Myers, Anna, 11.50
Myers, Christopher A., 1.79
Myers, Edward, 10.29
Myers, Jack, 18.27
Myers, Lynne Born, 1.79
Myers, Walter Dean, 3.54, 10.30, 11.51, 13.49, 20.21, 22.20

Naden, Corrine J., 15.10
Naidoo, Beverle, 3.55
Namioka, Lensey, 1.80
Napoli, Donna Jo, 5.22
Nardo, Don, 12.60, 18.28
Nasaw, Jonathan, 3.56
Naylor, Phyllis Reynolds, 2.42, 2.43, 2.44, 3.57
Nelson, Peter, 2.45
Nelson, Theresa, 3.58
Nelson, Vaunda Micheaux, 3.59
Neumann, Peter, 2.46
Newton, David E., 16.24
Nichelason, Margery G., 15.40
Nirgiotis, Nicholas, 12.61
Nixon, Joan Lowery, 8.15, 8.16, 11.52, 11.53, 11.54
Nottridge, Rhoda, 19.24

Obbink, Laura Apol, 20.32
O'Dell, Scott, 11.55
Oldenbury, Don, 15.26
O'Neal, Michael, 9.31
Onyefulu, Obi, 5.23
Oodgeroo, 5.24
Oppel, Kenneth, 7.17
Oppenheim, Joanne, 17.27
Orgel, Doris, 5.25
Orlev, Uri, 11.56
Otfinoski, Steve, 24.23
Owen, Marna, 15.41

Pace, Sue, 7.18
Panzer, Nora, 20.22
Parker, Rev. Julie F., 15.42

Parker, Steve, 18.29
Patent, Dorothy Hinshaw, 15.43, 18.30, 18.31
Paterson, Katherine, 2.47, 17.13
Patneaude, David, 8.17
Paulsen, Gary, 1.81, 1.82, 2.48, 3.60, 10.31, 11.57, 11.58, 23.17
Pearson, Gayle, 2.49
Peck, Richard, 1.83, 2.50, 7.19, 7.20, 7.21
Peck, Robert Newton, 11.59
Peel, John, 9.32, 9.33, 9.34, 9.35, 9.36
Perham, Molly, 5.26
Perkins, Mitali, 1.84
Pevsner, Stella, 1.85
Pfeffer, Susan Beth, 2.51, 3.61
Pflaum, Rosalynd, 13.50
Pfoutz, Sally, 8.18
Philbrick, Rodman, 2.52
Phillips, Ann, 9.37
Phillips, Louis, 24.24
Piazza, Linda, 9.38
Picard, Barbara Leonie, 5.27
Pickford, Ted, 9.39
Pierce, Richard, 9.40
Pierce, Tamora, 6.44
Pike, Christopher, 9.41
Pinkwater, Jill, 7.22
Pitts, Paul, 3.62
Platt, Richard, 12.62, 12.63, 12.64
Plowden, Martha Ward, 13.51
Polacco, Patricia, 11.60
Polese, Carolyn, 3.63
Posner, Richard, 9.42
Prelutsky, Jack, 20.23
Pringle, Laurence, 17.28

Quiri, Patricia Ryan, 13.52

Rainey, Richard, 13.53
Rana, Indi, 3.64
Rappoport, Ken, 23.18
Rau, Margaret, 21.21
Ray, Karen, 11.61
Razzi, Jim, 21.22
Reaver, Chap, 1.86
Reeder, Carolyn, 11.62, 11.63
Regan, Dian Curtis, 10.32
Reid, Struan, 12.65
Reiss, Johanna, 13.54
Reiss, Kathryn, 9.43
Reuter, Bjarne, 11.64
Rhodes, Judy Carole, 3.65

Ricciuti, Edward R., 14.11
Richards, Roy, 16.25
Rinaldi, Ann, 11.65, 11.66, 11.67
Rivers, Glenn, 23.19
Roalf, Peggy, 22.26
Roberts, Willo Davis, 1.87, 8.19, 8.20
Robinet, Harriette Gillem, 11.68
Robinson, Barbara, 1.88
Rochelle, Belinda, 12.66
Rochman, Hazel, 21.23
Rodda, Emily, 7.23, 7.24
Rodgers, Mary, 14.12
Rodowsky, Colby, 1.89
Rogasky, Barbara, 20.24
Rollins, Charlemae Hill, 5.28
Roop, Connie, 22.27
Roop, Peter, 22.27
Rosen, Dorothy, 11.69
Rosen, Roger, 15.44
Rosen, Sidney, 11.69
Rosin, Arielle, 24.25
Ross, Gayle, 5.29
Ross, Ramon Royal, 3.66, 11.70
Ross, Stewart, 22.28
Roybal, Laura, 1.90
Rubin, Susan Goldman, 3.67
Ruby, Lois, 3.68, 3.69
Ruckman, Ivy, 8.21, 8.22
Rumbaut, Hendle, 1.91
Rupert, Janet E., 11.71
Russell, Ken A., 24.3
Russo, Monica, 17.29
Ryan, Cary, 13.14
Ryan, Mary C., 7.25
Ryan, Steve, 24.26
Rybolt, Thomas R., 16.26
Rylant, Cynthia, 20.25, 20.26

Sachs, Marilyn, 1.92
Salat, Christina, 1.93
Salisbury, Graham, 11.72
Salsitz, Rhondi Vilott, 6.45
Salter, Charles A., 19.25
San Souci, Robert D., 5.31, 5.32, 21.24
Sandler, Martin W., 12.67
Sanfield, Steve, 5.30
Sattler, Helen Roney, 12.68
Sauerwein, Leigh, 21.25
Savage, Deborah, 11.73
Say, Allen, 3.70
Schleifer, Jay, 24.27
Schraff, Anne, 13.55
Schur, Maxine Rose, 11.74

Schwartz, Alvin, 5.33, 5.34, 5.35, 24.28
Scieszka, Jon, 5.36
Scott, Michael, 7.26, 9.44
Seabrooke, Brenda, 1.94
Sebestyen, Ouida, 3.71
Seidler, Tor, 6.46
Senna, Carl, 12.69
Sevastiades, Patra McSharry, 15.44
Sexton, Colleen, 14.12
Seymour, Tryntje Van Ness, 14.13
Shakespeare, William, 22.29
Shapiro, William, 24.29
Sharmat, Mitchell, 1.95
Sharpe, Susan, 3.72
Sherman, Josepha, 6.47, 6.48
Sherrow, Victoria, 13.56, 15.45
Shetterly, Will, 6.49
Shreve, Susan, 1.96, 3.73
Shusterman, Neal, 1.97
Siegel, Barbara, 9.45
Siegel, Beatrice, 12.70
Siegel, Scott, 9.45
Sierra, Patricia, 11.75
Sills, Leslie, 22.30
Silverman, Jerry, 12.71
Silverstein, Alvin, 18.32, 19.26, 19.27
Silverstein, Herma, 23.4
Silverstein, Robert, 18.32, 19.26, 19.27
Silverstein, Virginia, 18.32, 19.26, 19.27
Simon, Seymour, 16.28
Sinnott, Susan, 13.57
Sinykin, Sheri Cooper, 6.50
Siroff, Harriet, 2.53, 19.28
Sita, Lisa, 14.14
Siy, Alexandra, 14.15, 14.16
Skurzynski, Gloria, 16.27
Slater, Jack, 13.58
Sleator, William, 7.27, 13.59
Slepian, Jan, 7.28
Slim, Hedi, 12.4
Slote, Alfred, 4.11
Small, Terry, 5.37
Smith, Carter, 12.73
Smith, Doris Buchanan, 1.98, 1.99
Smith, Douglas, 19.29
Smith, Jane Denitz, 1.100
Smith, L. J., 9.46
Smith-Baranzini, Marlene, 12.72
Smith, Sherwood, 6.51
Snedden, Robert, 18.33
Snodgrass, Mary Ellen, 15.46
Snyder, Zilpha Keatley, 6.52, 6.53, 10.33, 11.76
Sobol, Donald J., 7.29

Author Index

Somtow, S. P., 6.54
Soto, Gary, 21.26
Souza, D. M., 16.29
Spinelli, Jerry, 2.54
Springer, Nancy, 2.55, 3.74
St. George, Judith, 13.60, 13.61
Stacey, T. J., 13.62
Stanley, Diane, 13.63, 13.64, 22.31
Stanley, Jerry, 12.74
Staples, Donna, 1.101
Staples, Suzanne Fisher, 1.102
Stefoff, Rebecca, 13.65
Stein, R. Conrad, 12.75, 12.76, 12.77
Stein, Wendy, 16.30
Steiner, Barbara, 9.47, 9.48, 9.49
Sterman, Betsy, 6.55
Sterman, Samuel, 6.55
Stevens, Carla, 24.30
Stevenson, Robert Louis, 10.34
Stewart, Gail B., 12.78
Stine, R. L., 9.50, 9.51, 9.52
Stolz, Mary, 1.103, 11.77, 12.79
Strauch, Eileen Walsh, 2.56
Streissguth, Tom, 14.12
Strickland, Brad, 9.3, 9.4
Strom, Yale, 14.17
Strommen, Judith Bernie, 3.75
Sturgis, Alexander, 22.32
Sullivan, George, 12.80, 13.66, 23.20, 23.21, 24.31
Sutcliff, Rosemary, 5.38, 5.39, 5.40, 5.41
Swanson, Diane, 18.34
Sweeney, Joyce, 7.30
Swenson, May, 20.27

Talbert, Marc, 1.104
Tanaka, Shelley, 12.81
Tarr, Judith, 6.56
Tashlik, Phyllis, 21.27
Taylor, Barbara, 18.35
Taylor, David, 17.30, 18.36
Taylor, Richard L., 13.67
Taylor, Theodore, 8.23, 10.35, 10.36, 11.78
Tchudi, Stephen, 24.31
Temple, Frances, 11.79
Tennyson, Jeffrey, 24.33
Terban, Marvin, 24.34
Terkel, Susan Neiburg, 12.82
Thesman, Jean, 1.105, 9.53
Thomas, Catherine, 17.2
Thomas, Joyce Carol, 1.106, 20.28
Thomas, Roy Edwin, 5.42
Thompson, Joan, 2.57

Thompson, Julian F., 2.58
Thompson, Sharon Elaine, 15.47
Toffolo, Antonella, 12.84
Tolan, Stephanie S., 3.76
Toll, Nelly S., 13.68
Tomey, Ingrid, 1.107
Tomlinson, Theresa, 3.77
Turner, Glennette Tilley, 11.80
Turner, Robyn Montana, 22.33, 22.34, 22.35
Turner, Ann, 20.29

Ude, Wayne, 5.43
UNICEF, 20.30
Ure, Jean, 7.31

Vail, Rachel, 2.59, 2.60, 2.61
Valasquez, Gloria, 3.78
van der Linde, Laurel, 12.83, 18.37
van der Rol, Ruud, 13.69
Van Rose, Susanna, 16.31
Vecchione, Glen, 24.35
Vennema, Peter, 13.63, 13.64
Ventura, Maria Murgo, 12.84, 12.85
Ventura, Piero, 12.84, 12.85
Verhoeven, Rian, 13.69
Vigor, John, 8.24
Vogel, Carole G., 17.31
Vogt, Gregory L., 16.32
Voigt, Cynthia, 6.57
Volavkova, Hana, 20.31
Vornholt, John, 2.62
Vos, Ida, 11.81
Vuong, Lynette Dyer, 5.44, 5.45

Wakin, Daniel, 12.86
Wakin, Edward, 12.87
Waldherr, Kris, 5.46
Walker, Kate, 2.63
Walker, Lou Ann, 12.88, 22.36
Walker, Paul Robert, 4.12
Walker, Richard, 19.30
Wallace, Bill, 3.79, 4.13, 8.25
Wangerin, Walter, 10.37
Wardlaw, Lee, 1.108
Warkski, Maureen, 3.80
Waters, Elizabeth, 22.37
Watkins, Yoko Kawashima, 13.70
Watson, Jerry, 20.32
Waugh, Charles G., 21.14
Waugh, Sylvia, 6.58

Weaver, Will, 4.14
Wegman, William, 24.36
Weidhorn, Manfred, 23.22
Weiss, Ann E., 23.23
Wekesser, Carol, 17.32, 19.31
Welch, Sheila Kelly, 21.28
Werlin, Nancy, 2.64
Wesley, Valerie Wilson, 3.81
Westall, Robert, 8.26, 9.54, 10.38, 21.29
Westcott, Nadine Bernard, 20.33
Westheimer, Ruth, 19.32
Westwood, Chris, 1.109, 9.55
Whelan, Gloria, 1.110
Whitehead, Fred, 15.48
Whitman, Sylvia, 17.33
Wilkinson, Brenda, 2.65
Wilks, Mike, 24.37
Willey, Margaret, 3.82
Williams, Carol Lynch, 1.111
Williams, Karen Lynn, 2.66
Williams, Michael, 1.112, 3.83
Williams, Vera B., 1.113
Williamson, Ray A., 12.54
Wills, Charles A., 12.89
Wilson, Nancy Hope, 2.67
Winthrop, Elizabeth, 6.59
Wisler, G. Clifton, 11.82
Wittlinger, Ellen, 2.68
Wolff, Virginia Euwer, 1.114
Wolfson, Evelyn, 17.34
Wolitzer, Meg, 2.69
Wood, June Rae, 1.115

Wood, Marcia, 1.116
Woodruff, Elvira, 7.32, 11.83
Woods, Geraldine, 15.49
Woodson, Jacqueline, 2.70, 2.71, 2.72
Woolf, Felicity, 22.38
Wormser, Richard, 12.90, 12.91
Wosmek, Frances, 11.84
Wrede, Patricia, 6.60
Wright, Betty Ren, 9.56
Wright, Richard, 3.84
Wu, William F., 7.33, 7.34
Wyeth, Sharon Dennis, 2.73
Wyss, Thelma Hatch, 9.57

Yancey, Diane, 12.92
Yenawine, Philip, 22.39
Yep, Laurence, 5.47, 6.61, 6.62, 11.85
Yolen, Jane, 6.63, 10.39
Young, Jay, 16.33
Young, Ken, 23.24
Young, Mark C., 24.38
Young, Ronder Thomas, 1.117

Zall, P. M., 12.93
Zambreno, Mary Frances, 6.64
Zassenhaus, Hiltgunt, 13.71
Zeitlin, Steve, 5.14
Zeleza, Tiyambe, 14.18
Zevin, Jack, 12.94
Zindel, Paul, 2.74, 6.65, 13.72

Title Index

ABC, 24.36
Abortion: Understanding the Controversy, 15.23
Absolutely True Story . . . How I Visited Yellowstone Park with the Terrible Rupes, The, 8.19
Across America on an Emigrant Train, 12.59
Across the Grain, 3.26
Across the Wild River, 10.16
Adam and Eve and Pinch-Me, 1.56
Adam Zigzag, 3.3
Adolf Hitler, 13.36
Adoption Controversies, 15.35
Adventures of King Midas, The, 6.6
African Mask, The, 11.71
Against the Storm, 3.34
Ajeemah and His Son, 11.11
AK, 10.10
Al Capsella Takes a Vacation, 2.8
Al Gore: United States Vice President, 13.13
Ali and the Golden Eagle, 2.22
Alias Madame Doubtfire, 1.34
Alice Dodd and the Spirit of Truth, 3.52
Alien Prey, 9.32
Alien Secrets, 7.11
All but Alice, 2.42
Along the Dangerous Trail, 10.17
Alvin Ailey, Jr.: A Life in Dance, 13.43
Always, Julia, 1.116
Am I Blue? Coming Out from the Silence, 21.1
Amazing Gracie, 1.18
Amazing Paper Cuttings of Hans Christian Andersen, The, 22.4
America Alive: A History, 12.43
Amish Home, 14.2
Amy Dunn Quits School, 1.96
Ancient Ones: The World of the Old-Growth Douglas Fir, 17.3
Animal Experimentation: Cruelty or Science?, 15.16
Animal Rights: A Handbook for Young Adults, 15.13
Animal Rights: Yes or No?, 15.41
Anna Is Still Here, 11.81

Anne Frank, beyond the Diary: A Photographic Remembrance, 13.69
Anne Is Elegant, 1.25
Annie's Choice, 11.17
Applebaum's Garage, 2.66
Appointment, 9.29
April and the Dragon Lady, 1.80
Aquarium Take-along Book, The, 18.13
Are You Alone on Purpose?, 2.64
Arena Beach, 1.101
Ariadne, Awake!, 5.25
Around the World in a Hundred Years, 12.26
Ask Me Something Easy, 1.53
Asking the River, 3.39
Automobiles: Connecting People and Places, 24.13

Baby Alicia Is Dying, 3.49
Back to Before, 7.28
Backyard Dragon, 6.55
Backyard Ghost, The, 2.12
Bamboo Flute, The, 3.21
Band, The, 9.1
Barn, The, 11.5
Battle for the Castle, The, 6.59
Battle of the Ironclads: The Monitor and the Merrimack, 12.11
Battlefields and Burial Grounds: The Indian Struggle to Protect Ancestral Graves in the United States, 15.17
Be Kind to Your Mother (Earth) and Blame It on the Wolf, 17.23
Be Seated: A Book about Chairs, 22.10
Beardance, 10.20
Beauty Trap, The, 19.20
Beauty: A Retelling of the Story of Beauty and the Beast, 5.20
Because She's My Friend, 2.53
Becoming American: Young People in the American Revolution, 12.93
Beggars' Ride, The, 3.58
Beheaded Freshman and Other Nasty Rumors, The, 21.6
Behind the Lines, 11.32
Behind the Secret Window: A Memoir of a Hidden Childhood during World War II, 13.68

Bel-Air Bambi and the Mall Rats, 2.50
Bending Light, 16.23
Best Girl, 1.98
Best School Year Ever, The, 1.88
Bette Bao Lord: Novelist and Chinese Voice for Change, 13.28
Between Madison and Palmetto, 2.72
Between Two Worlds, 11.41
Beyond the Ancient Cities, 11.48
Beyond the Burning Time, 11.38
Beyond the Magic Sphere, 6.31
Beyond the North Wind, 6.9
Big Book for Our Planet, The, 17.13
Big Bugs, 18.1
Big Help Book, The, 24.10
Big Wander, The, 10.21
Bigger, 11.13
Bill, 1.86
Billy, 1.90
Bird Atlas, The, 18.35
Black and Blue Magic, 6.52
Black Diamond: The Story of the Negro Baseball Leagues, 23.16
Black Music in America: A History through Its People, 22.13
Black Press and the Struggle for Civil Rights, The, 12.69
Black Ships before Troy: The Story of the Iliad, 5.38
Blackwater Swamp, 8.25
Blood Wolf, 9.33
Blossom Culp and the Sleep of Death, 7.19
Blossom on the Bough, The, 17.11
Blue Heron, 1.4
Bobby's Watching, 9.39
Body Atlas, The, 19.6
Boggart, The, 6.20
Bonanza Girl, 11.9
Bone from a Dry Sea, A, 1.29
Book of the American Indians, 12.72
Book of Your Own, A: Keeping a Diary or Journal, 24.30
Book That Jack Wrote, The, 5.36
Books of the Keepers, The, 6.23
Borning Room, The, 11.27
Boy on a Black Horse, The, 2.55
Boy Who Loved Alligators, The, 3.37
Boys against Girls, 2.43
Boys from St. Petri, The, 11.64
Boys Start the War, The/The Girls Get Even, 2.44
Break a Leg, Betsy Maybe!, 2.29

Breaking Free, 11.28
Breaking Out, 3.20
Breast Implants: Making Safe Choices, 19.12
Breathing: The Respiratory System, 19.5
Bridge to Courage, 3.30
Bridges of Summer, The, 1.94
Bright Days and Stupid Nights, 3.47
Brother of Mine, 1.109
Brown Angels: An Album of Pictures and Verse, 20.21
Brown Bird Singing, A, 11.84
Brown Honey in Broomwheat Tea, 20.28
Brush with Magic, A, 6.13
Bull Run, 12.22
Burning Time, The, 11.44

Cages, 3.36
California Blue, 3.42
Call of the Deep, 9.38
Call of the Wendigo, 9.19
Calling All Monsters, 9.55
Calling Home, 3.10
Captain Grey, 11.6
Captain Hawaii, 8.2
Capturing Nature: The Writings and Art of John James Audubon, 22.27
Car, The, 2.48
Care for Your Body, 19.24
Careers for Women as Clergy, 15.42
Cars, 24.15
Cat Running, 11.76
Catherine, Called Birdy, 11.19
Cattail Moon, 9.53
Caught, 8.20
Cave, The, 11.36
Celebrate America in Poetry and Art, 20.22
Censorship, 15.33
Cezanne Pinto, 11.77
Chain of Fire, 3.55
Champ Hobarth, 3.75
Champions: Stories of Ten Remarkable Athletes, 23.14
Changes in Latitudes, 1.51
Charge! Weapons and Warfare in Ancient Times, 12.29
Charles Darwin: Naturalist, 13.3
Charles Darwin: Revolutionary Biologist, 13.23
Charles Dickens: The Man Who Had Great Expectations, 13.64

Title Index 347

Cheap Raw Material: How Our Youngest Workers Are Exploited and Abused, 15.38
Cheater, Cheater, 2.34
Chemo Kid, The, 3.45
Chernobyl: The Ongoing Story of the World's Deadliest Nuclear Disaster, 15.12
Chevrolet Saturdays, 1.13
Chicken Gave It to Me, The, 6.25
Chief, The, 4.8
Children of the Swastika: The Hitler Youth, 12.39
Children of the Wolf, 10.39
Children's Atlas of the Human Body, The, 19.30
Childtimes: A Three-Generation Memoir, 13.34
Chimes of Alyafaleyn, The, 6.19
China Past—China Future, 12.12
China under Communism, 12.45
Chinese Americans, 14.1
Chinye: A West African Folk Tale, 5.23
Chive, 3.2
Choctaw Code, The, 11.21
Christmas Gif': An Anthology of Christmas Poems, Songs, and Stories, 5.28
Christmas in the Big House, Christmas in the Quarters, 11.47
Cinder-Elly, 5.21
Circle within a Circle, 3.40
Circlemaker, The, 11.74
Circus Comes Home, The, 12.19
City of Light, City of Dark: A Comic Book Novel, 6.4
City within a City: How Kids Live in New York's Chinatown, 14.6
Citymaze!, 24.19
Clan of the Shape-Changers, 6.39
Cleopatra, 13.63
Climb or Die, 10.29
Clothing: Garments, Styles, and Uses, 12.84
Coaster, 1.30
Collage of Crafts, A, 22.12
Colonial American Medicine, 12.82
Come Go with Me: Old-Timer Stories from the Southern Mountains, 5.42
Come with Me to Africa: A Photographic Journey, 14.5
Coming About, 2.9

Coming Home: From the Life of Langston Hughes, 13.16
Coming to America: The Irish-American Experience, 14.4
Coming-of-Age: Traditions and Rituals around the World, 14.10
Complete Poems to Solve, The, 20.27
Compost Critters, 17.19
Concise Columbia Encyclopedia 3rd Edition, 24.4
Copier Creations, 22.8
Countdown to the Moon, 16.14
Cousins' Club, The: I'll Pulverize You, William, 1.48
Cowboy, 12.58
Cowboy: An Album, 12.31
Cowboys, 12.67
Cowboys, Indians, and Gunfighters: The Story of the Cattle Kingdom, 12.49
Crazy Horse, 13.60
Crazy Lady!, 3.14
Creation, The, 20.13
Criminal Justice: Opposing Viewpoints, 15.8
Crisis in Haiti, 15.20
Cross Your Fingers, Spit in Your Hat: Superstitions and Other Beliefs, 5.33
Crossroads, 3.62
Crosstown, 2.36
Crying for a Vision, The, 10.37
Crystal Drop, The, 7.9
Cults, 15.14
Culture Wars: Opposing Viewpoints, 15.48
Curse of Tutankhamen, The, 12.21
Cy Young Award Winners, 23.24

Daddy's Climbing Trees, 1.2
Dakota Dream, 3.5
Dance till You Die, 8.11
Dancing on Dark Water, 3.11
Danger, Dolphins, and Ginger Beer, 8.24
Dangerous Promise, A: The Orphan Train Adventures, 11.52
Dangerous Spaces, 6.42
Daniel's Story, 11.45
Dar and the Spear-Thrower, 10.5
Dark Silence, 3.80
Dark Stars, The: A Herculeah Jones Mystery, 8.5
Dark Visions: The Strange Power, 9.46

Darnell Rock Reporting, 3.54
David & Della, 2.74
Day the Women Got the Vote, The: A Photo History of the Women's Rights Movement, 12.80
Daydreamer, The, 3.51
Days of the Dead, 14.9
Dead Water Zone, 7.17
Deadly Deception, 8.9
Deadly Game at Stony Creek, 10.4
Dear Levi: Letters from the Overland Trail, 11.83
Dear Mr. Bell . . . Your Friend, Helen Keller, 13.61
Dear Mr. President, 15.26
Dear Mr. Sprouts, 3.9
Dear Nobody, 3.23
Death Is Hard to Live With: Teenagers Talk about How They Cope with Loss, 19.2
Deathline, 9.47
Deep Dream of the Rain Forest, 10.1
Deep-Sea Explorer: The Story of Robert Ballard, Discoverer of the Titanic, 13.6
Definitely Cool, 2.65
Democracy, 12.60
Desktop Publishing: The Art of Communication, 24.18
Devil's Bridge, 10.8
Diabetes, 19.26
Diane Goode's Book of Scary Stories and Songs, 5.10
Dictionary of Nature, 17.5
Dig This! How Archaeologists Uncover Our Past, 12.3
Dinah in Love, 2.41
Dinosaur Planet, 7.12
Dinosaurs, 18.10
Dinosaurs: Great Mysteries, 16.30
Disappearing Bike Shop, The, 7.32
Disaster of the Hindenburg, The, 12.81
DJs, Ratings, and Hook Tapes: Pop Music Broadcasting, 22.14
DNA Pioneer: James Watson and the Double Helix, 13.9
Do Cats Really Have Nine Lives?, 18.27
Do-Over, 2.61
Dogwolf, 3.12
Dolley Madison, 13.52
Don't Look Back, 1.108
Doodle Dandy! The Complete Book of Independence Day Words, 24.11

Dorling Kindersley Illustrated History of the World, The, 12.28
Dorothea Lange, Illustrator/Photographer, 22.33
Double Vision, 1.45
Dove Dream, 1.91
Dr. Ruth Talks to Kids: Where You Came From, How Your Body Changes, and What Sex Is All About, 19.32
Dragon Cauldron, 6.61
Dragon War, 6.62
Dragon's Gate, 11.85
Dragons Are Singing Tonight, The, 20.23
Drat These Brats, 20.16
Dreadful Future of Blossom Culp, The, 7.21
Dreadful Sorry, 9.43
Dream Keeper and Other Poems, The, 20.8
Dreamtime: Aboriginal Stories, 5.24
Driver's Ed, 3.15
Drug Abuse in Society: A Reference Handbook, 15.49
Drugs and Sex, 19.4
Druid Curse, The, 6.35
Drum, the Doll, and the Zombie, The, 9.4
Dusk of Demons, A, 7.3
Dust Bowl, The: Disaster on the Plains, 12.2

E. B. White: Some Writer!, 13.32
Ear, the Eye and the Arm, The, 7.4
Earliest Americans, The, 12.68
Earth, 16.31
Earth Keepers, 17.1
Earth Lines: Poems for the Green Age, 20.20
Earthkeepers: Observers and Protectors of Nature, 17.18
Echoes in the Grove, 11.75
Echoes of the White Giraffe, 11.15
Eclairs & Brown Bears, 24.25
Edgar Allan Poe: A Mystery, 13.2
Eeyou, The: People of Eastern James Bay, 14.15
Eight Mules from Monterey, 11.10
18th Century Clothing, 12.42
Eleanor Roosevelt: A Life of Discovery, 13.29
Emily Good as Gold, 3.67
Empty Summer, The, 2.5
End of the Race, 4.6

Title Index

Endangered Animal Babies, 17.24
Endangered Florida Panther, The, 18.6
Endangered Ocean Animals, 17.30
Endangered Peoples, 15.36
Engel vs. Vitale: Separation of Church and State, 15.25
Environmental Experiments about Renewable Energy, 16.26
Erie Canal: Gateway to the West, 12.61
Escape from Egypt, 11.40
Escape from Exile, 6.40
Escape from Slavery: The Boyhood of Frederick Douglass in His Own Words, 13.45
Ever After, 2.59
Everglades: Buffalo Tiger and the River of Grass, 17.21
Examination, The, 11.12
Experimenting with Science in Sports, 16.15
Exploration by Land, 12.79
Exploration by Sea, 12.65
Exploring Autumn, 24.21
Extinction of the Dinosaurs, The, 18.28
Extra Innings: Baseball Poems, 20.7
Extraordinary Asian Pacific Americans, 13.57
Eye of the Beholder, 2.25

Faith Ringgold, 22.34
Falcon's Wing, The, 1.14
Famous Firsts of Black Women, 13.51
Fatal Magic, 9.20
Father Water, Mother Woods, 23.17
Fear Place, The, 3.57
Fear Street Saga: The Betrayal, 9.50
Feather Merchants and Other Tales of the Fools of Chelm, The, 5.30
Fell Down, 8.12
Fifth of March, The: A Story of the Boston Massacre, 11.67
Final Frenzy, 9.45
Find Buck McHenry, 4.11
Finders Keepers, 7.23
Finn's Search, 3.25
First Houses: Native American Homes and Sacred Structures, 12.54
First Solo Flight around the World, The: The Story of Wiley Post and His Airplane, 13.67
First Wedding, Once Removed, 2.15
Flight of the Dragon Kyn, 6.26
Fling, The, 2.58

Flip-Flop Girl, 2.47
Floratorium, 17.27
Flour Babies, 3.27
Fly! A Brief History of Flight Illustrated, 12.57
Fly Like an Eagle, 1.78
Fog Doggies and Me, The, 2.49
Food & Feasts in the Middle Ages, 12.18
Food Risks and Controversies: Minimizing the Dangers in Your Diet, 19.25
Fool's Gold, 10.33
For the Life of Laetitia, 1.52
For the Love of Pete, 1.71
Forest, 6.41
Forest of the Clouded Leopard, 1.79
Forgotten Heroes, The: The Story of the Buffalo Soldiers, 12.17
Foster Care, 15.15
Fourteenth-Century Towns, 12.13
Frankenlouse, 1.54
Frankenstein's Children: Book One—The Creation, 9.40
Freak the Mighty, 2.52
Fred Field, The, 8.4
Free Fall, 1.7
Free the Conroy Seven, 2.40
Freedom's Children, 12.46
Frida Kahlo, 22.35
Frog Prince, The, 5.18
Frog's Eye View, A, 2.6
Frogs and Toads, 18.29
From Flower to Fruit, 17.9
From Sea to Shining Sea: A Treasury of American Folklore and Folk Songs, 5.7
From the Earth to beyond the Sky, 17.34
Frontier Home, 12.7
Funny You Should Ask, 21.10
Future-Telling Lady and Other Stories, 21.2

Game Over, 9.28
Game Plan, 4.4
Gathering of Garter Snakes, A, 18.22
Gathering of Pearls, 11.16
Gathering, The, 9.7
Gemini Game, 7.26
Gentleman and the Kitchen Maid, The, 22.31
Genuine Half-Moon Kid, The, 1.112
Get on Board: The Story of the Underground Railroad, 12.38
Get the Message, 16.27

Getting Your Message Across, 24.9
Ghost in the Mirror, The, 9.5
Ghost of Elvis and Other Celebrity Spirits, The, 9.10
Ghost Stories, 21.29
Ghosts I Have Been, 7.20
Ghosts of Mercy Manor, The, 9.56
Gideon and the Mummy Professor, 10.22
Gift of the Changing Woman, The, 14.13
Gift of the Girl Who Couldn't Hear, The, 3.73
Giver, The, 7.14
Gleaming Bright, 6.47
Glory Field, The, 11.51
Goddesses, Heroes, and Shamans: The Young People's Guide to World Mythology, 5.2
Going to See Grassy Ella, 1.63
Gold and Silver, Silver and Gold: Tales of Hidden Treasure, 5.34
Gold Unicorn, 6.38
Gold: The True Story of Why People Search for It, Mine It, Trade It, Steal It, Mint It, Hoard It, Shape It, Wear It, Fight and Kill for It, 24.22
Golden Carp and Other Tales from Vietnam, The, 5.44
Golem & the Dragon Girl, The, 1.68
Goodnight Opus, 6.10
Grams, Her Boyfriend, My Family, and Me, 1.27
Grandpa's Mountain, 11.62
Grass Songs, 20.29
Graveyard Moon, 9.18
Great American Elephant Chase, The, 10.7
Great Ball Game, The: A Muskogee Story, 5.5
Great Careers for People Interested in Living Things, 24.5
Great Dad Disaster, The, 1.44
Great Migration, The: An American Story, 22.20
Great Yellowstone Fire, The, 17.31
Green Planet Rescue: Saving the Earth's Endangered Plants, 17.14
Gruel and Unusual Punishment, 2.1
Guests, 11.24
Guinness Book of Records 1995, The, 24.38
Gypsy Davey, 1.69

H.O.W.L. High Goes Bats, 9.25
Haidas, The: People of the Northwest Coast, 14.3
Hamlet, 22.29
Hand, Heart, & Mind: The Story of the Education of America's Deaf People, 12.88
Hand in Hand: An American History through Poetry, 20.6
Hannah in Between, 1.89
Harmony Arms, The, 1.62
Harper & Moon, 3.66, 11.70
Harper's Ferry: The Story of John Brown's Raid, 12.6
Harriet Beecher Stowe and the Beecher Preachers, 13.30
Harris and Me, 1.81
Harry S Truman, President, 13.27
Harvey Girls, The: The Women Who Civilized the West, 12.56
Hate Groups, 15.47
Haunted Circus, The, 7.16
Haunted Houses, 9.31
Haunted Year, A, 9.37
Haveli, 1.102
Haymeadow, The, 1.82
Headless Haunt and Other African-American Ghost Stories, The, 21.15
Heads Up! Puzzles for Sports Brains, 23.7
Health Care in America: Opposing Viewpoints, 19.31
Heart of a Champion, 4.3
Heartbreak and Roses, 19.3
Hello . . . This Is My Father Speaking, 1.95
Here and Then, 7.15
Here There Be Unicorns, 6.63
Here's to You, Rachel Robinson, 1.11
Herman Melville, 13.65
Hero of Lesser Causes, 1.57
Hester Bidgood: Investigatrix of Evill Deedes, 11.31
Hexwood, 7.10
Hey You, Sister Rose, 2.56
Hidden Children, The, 12.32
High on the Hog, 1.32
Hillary Rodham Clinton: Activist First Lady, 13.62
His Majesty's Elephant, 6.56
Hispanic, Female and Young: An Anthology, 21.27

Title Index

Historical Album of California, A, 12.89
History of US, A: The First Americans, 12.34
Holiday Five: Trick or Trouble?, 2.11
Holiday Handbook, The, 24.1
Hollywood Wars: Seeing Red, 2.10
Homebird, 1.10
Homeless or Hopeless?, 15.40
Horse for All Seasons, A, 21.28
Horses: Understanding Animals, 18.30
Hot Country, 22.19
Houses: Structures, Methods, and Ways of Living, 12.85
How an Airport Really Works, 24.31
How Rabbit Tricked Otter and Other Cherokee Trickster Stories, 5.29
How to Catch a Flying Saucer, 16.12
How to Sneak into the Girls' Locker Room, 2.62
Hugh Glass, Mountain Man: Left for Dead, 10.25
Hummingbirds' Gift, The, 5.8
Hunted, The, 11.14
Hunter's Heart, The, 3.65

I Am an American: A True Story of Japanese Internment, 12.74
I Dream of Peace: Images of War by Children of Former Yugoslavia, 20.30
I Hadn't Meant to Tell You This, 2.70
I Love You, I Hate You, Get Lost, 21.7
I Never Saw Another Butterfly, 20.31
I Should Have Listened to Moon, 1.31
I Thought I'd Take My Rat to School, 20.15
I Was a Teenage Professional Wrestler, 23.11
I Wouldn't Thank You for a Valentine, 20.2
I'm Emma: I'm a Quint, 1.85
Iceman, 4.9
If It Hadn't Been for Yoon Jun, 2.31
If Rock and Roll Were a Machine, 2.14
Illiteracy, 15.22
Illustrated History of the Hamburger, The: Hamburger Heaven, 24.33
Immigration, 15.3
In My Father's House, 11.66
In the Shogun's Shadow: Understanding a Changing Japan, 14.7
In-Between Days, The, 1.17

In-Line Skating: A Complete Guide for Beginners, 23.20
Inca Civilization, 12.30
Incredibly Small, 16.7
Initiation, The, 10.32
Ink-Keeper's Apprentice, The, 3.70
Into the Land of the Unicorns, 6.21
Into the Valley, 3.83
Introducing Picasso, 22.15
Introducing Rembrandt, 22.32
Investigating the Ozone Hole, 17.16
Invisible Bugs and Other Creepy Creatures That Live with You, 18.20
Iron Hans, 5.11
Iron Horse, The, 12.90
Is There a Woman in the House . . . or Senate?, 13.25
It Figures! Fun Figures of Speech, 24.34
It Happened to Nancy, 19.1
It's Nothing to a Mountain, 10.19
It's Our World, Too! Stories of Young People Who Are Making a Difference, 15.27
It's Perfectly Normal: A Book about Changing Bodies, Growing Up, Sex, and Sexual Health, 19.17
It's Raining Cats and Dogs: All Kinds of Weather and Why We Have It, 16.2

Jack Tales, The, 5.6
Jackie Robinson, 23.22
Jacob's Rescue: A Holocaust Story, 11.25
Jaguar, 24.27
James Herriot's Cat Stories, 18.17
Jane-Emily, 9.9
Japan and the United States: Economic Competitors, 15.46
Jasmine Candle, The, 3.8
Jason and Marceline, 2.54
Jason and the Bard, 2.19
Jefferson Way, The, 12.55
Jericho, 1.50
Jericho's Journey, 11.82
Jim Henson, 13.22
Jim Thorpe: 20th-Century Jock, 23.12
Jim-Dandy, 11.34
Jimmy Spoon and the Pony Express, 10.15
Jo's Boys, 11.1
Jobs vs. the Environment: Can We Save Both?, 15.1

John Henry, 5.17
Join In: Multiethnic Short Stories, 21.11
Journey Back, The, 13.54
Journeyman Wizard: A Magical Mystery, 6.64
Juanita Fights the School Board, 3.78
Julie, 10.13
Jungle Days, Jungle Nights, 17.17
Just a Little Ham, 1.19

Kazakhstan, 14.12
Keeping Christina, 2.4
Keeping Time: From the Beginning and into the 21st Century, 16.3
Kelly and Me, 1.111
Kid's Address Book, The, 24.17
Kids at Work: Lewis Hine and the Crusade against Child Labor, 12.24
Kids' World Almanac of Football, The, 23.6
Killer Bees, 18.23
Killing Boy, The, 8.14
Kind of Thief, A, 8.1
Kindred Spirit: A Biography of L. M. Montgomery, Creator of Anne of Green Gables, 13.5
King Arthur & the Legends of Camelot, 5.26
King Philip: The Indian Chief, 13.8
Kingdom by the Sea, The, 10.38
Kingdom of Kevin Malone, The, 6.17
Kingfisher Illustrated History of the World, The: 40,000 B.C. to Present Day, 12.94
Kingfisher Young People's Encyclopedia of the United States, 24.29
Kiss List, 2.23
Knot in the Grain and Other Stories, A, 21.18

Land of Dreams, 11.53
Land of Promise, 11.54
Last Oasis, The, 7.18
Last Tales of Uncle Remus, The, 5.16
Last Vampire 2, The, 9.41
Last Victim, The, 9.23
Learning by Heart, 1.117
Learning to Live in the World: Earth Poems by William Stafford, 20.32
Leaves in October, The, 1.1
Legacy, The: Making Wishes Come True, 3.50
Legend of John Henry, The, 5.37

Leona: A Love Story, 11.23
Leonard Bernstein: A Passion for Music, 13.37
Letters from the Inside, 1.72
Life Belts, 2.27
Life Riddles, 1.22
Lift Every Voice and Sing, 20.12
Light Action, 16.9
Light beyond the Forest, The, 5.39
Light on Hogback Hill, The, 8.6
Like Some Kind of Hero, 3.46
Lincoln: In His Own Words, 13.48
Linger, 3.38
Little House on Rocky Ridge, 11.42
Little Louis and the Jazz Band: The Story of Louis "Satchmo" Armstrong, 13.47
Little Men, 11.2
Little Women, 11.3
Little Women: A Novel Based on the Motion Picture Screen Play by Robin Swicord from the Novel by Louisa May Alcott, 1.65
Lives of Musicians: Good Times, Bad Times (And What the Neighbors Thought), 13.41
Living in Secret, 1.93
Living in Space, 16.20
Living with Learning Disabilities: A Guide for Students, 19.16
Lobsters: Gangsters of the Sea, 18.5
Local News, 21.26
Loch, 6.65
Lock and Key, 24.32
Lombardo's Law, 2.68
Long Time Passing, 11.35
Looking at Paintings: Musicians, 22.26
Looking for Your Name, 20.10
Lost Magic, 6.3
Lost Wild America: The Story of Our Extinct and Vanishing Wildlife, 17.25
Lostman's River, 11.22
Louisa May Alcott: Her Girlhood Diary, 13.14
Love Is Like the Lion's Tooth, 20.18
Low Tide, 10.24
Lucie Babbidge's House, 6.16
Luck of the Miss L, The, 4.7
Lydia, Queen of Palestine, 11.56

Maasai, 14.18
Magic Circle, 5.22
Magic Show, The: A Guide for Young Magicians, 24.8

Magical Tales from Many Lands, 5.19
Magician's Apprentice, The, 11.69
Maizon at Blue Hill, 2.71
Make Believe, 2.51
Make Lemonade, 1.114
Making and Using Scientific Equipment, 16.24
Making Friends with Frankenstein, 20.19
Making Room for Katherine, 1.77
Making Sense: Animal Perception and Communication, 18.4
Malcolm X, 13.58
Malcolm X: By Any Means Necessary, 13.49
Malinche: Slave Princess of Cortez, 13.21
Many Thousand Gone: African Americans from Slavery to Freedom, 12.35
Maphead, 7.8
Marauder, 7.34
March on Washington, The, 12.36
Maria's Italian Spring, 2.2
Marie Curie and Her Daughter Irene, 13.50
Mariposa Blues, 1.60
Martin the Warrior, 6.29
Mary by Myself, 1.100
Master of Mahogany: Tom Day, Free Black Cabinetmaker, 22.22
Master Violinmaker, The, 22.7
Mathew Brady: His Life and Photographs, 13.66
Maud: The Life of L. M. Montgomery, 13.11
Maybe I Will Do Something, 5.43
Mayfield Crossing, 3.59
Me Me Me Me Me: Not a Novel, 13.38
Me Two, 7.25
Melinda Zone, The, 3.82
Memoirs of a Bookbat, 1.64
Mennyms, The, 6.58
Mermaid Summer, The, 6.28
Mexican Ghost Tales of the Southwest, 5.1
Mexican Revolution 1910-1920, The, 12.75
Michael Andretti at Indianapolis, 23.1
Michael Jordan: Star Guard, 23.9
Michael Jordan: A Life above the Rim, 23.13
Middle Ages, The, 12.40
Mind Reader, The, 9.52
Miraculous Makeover of Lizard Flanagan, The, 2.21
Miriam's Well, 3.69

Misery Guts, 1.37
Missing Angel Juan, 3.7
Missing Person, 8.18
Missing Sisters, 1.70
Mississippi Chariot, 11.68
Mister Fred, 7.22
Mohandas Gandhi: The Power of the Spirit, 13.56
Monarchs, 18.21
Money Games: The Business of Sports, 23.23
Money to Burn, 10.14
Monkey Tag, 3.29
Mononucleosis, 19.27
Monster Factory, The, 13.53
Montgomery Bus Boycott, The, 12.76
Monument, The, 3.60
Moonshiner's Son, 11.63
More Short & Shivery, 21.24
Most Amazing Science Pop-up Book, The, 16.33
Mountain Valor, 11.33
Movies of Alfred Hitchcock, The, 22.2
Mr. Tucket, 11.57
Mudpack and Me, The, 2.57
Muir of the Mountains, 13.20
Mummy's Curse, The: 101 of the World's Strangest Mysteries, 9.11
Murder on the Highway: The Viola Liuzzo Story, 12.70
My Brother Has AIDS, 1.26
My Brother, My Sister, and I, 13.70
My Fabulous New Life, 3.32
"My Name Is Amelia," 7.29
My Name is ~~Brain~~ Brian, 3.6
My Soul to Keep, 9.15
My Wartime Summers, 11.20
Myriam Mendilow: Mother of Jerusalem, 13.17
Mystery of the Cupboard, The, 6.7

Name of the Game Was Murder, The, 8.16
Nature's Creatures of the Dark, 18.36
Nekomah Creek Christmas, 1.24
Never Say Quit, 4.13
Never Take a Pig to Lunch, 20.33
Nevernever, 6.49
New Deal, The, 12.78
New Frontier, A: The Peace Corps in Eastern Europe, 15.5
New One, The, 1.5

New Power of Women in Politics, The, 15.19
Newbery Halloween, A: A Dozen Scary Stories by Newbery Award–Winning Authors, 21.14
Nick of Time, 7.13
Night Cries, 9.48
Night in Moonbeam County, A, 21.9
Night of Fear, 10.23
Night Prowlers: Everyday Creatures under Every Night Sky, 18.11
Night Terrors (Davidson), 9.14
Night Terrors (Murphy), 21.20
Night Wings, 9.34
Nightjohn, 11.58
Nightmare Matinee, 9.17
No Boys Allowed, 1.66
No Such Country, 10.6
Nora: Maybe a Ghost Story, 1.40
Northern Lights, 16.29
Not for a Billion Gazillion Dollars, 2.13
Nothing but Trouble, Trouble, Trouble, 1.46
Nothing More, Nothing Less, 2.39
Now Hiring: Music, 22.23
Nutcracker, The, 22.3

October Moon, 9.44
Oddballs, 13.59
Oddly Enough, 21.8
Oil Spills: Damage, Recovery, and Prevention, 17.28
Oliver Twist, 10.9
On Heroes and the Heroic: In Search of Good Deeds, 15.44
On the Pulse of Morning, 20.1
On Wings of Joy: The Story of Ballet from the 16th Century to Today, 22.9
One Foot Ashore, 11.30
One Good Tern Deserves Another, 1.58
100 Questions and Answers about AIDS: What You Need to Know Now, 19.10
101 Physics Tricks: Fun Experiments with Everyday Materials, 16.8
101 Science Surprises, 16.25
One More River, 1.6
1-900-Killer, 9.27
Operation: Save the Teacher: Wednesday Night Match, 2.69
Ordinary Princess, The, 6.36
Organ Transplants, 19.9
Orphan Trains, The, 12.27
Others See Us, 7.27
Out of Control, 3.48
Out of Nowhere, 3.71
Over the Joshua Slope, 1.42
Over the Water, 1.20
Overkill, 9.16
Overnight Sensation, 2.28
Owl in Love, 6.37

P. T. Barnum: The World's Greatest Showman, 13.26
Painted Devil, The, 6.8
Painting: A Young Artist's Guide, 22.37
Panther Glade, 10.3
Part of the Sky, A, 11.59
Patakin: World Tales of Drums and Drummers, 5.13
Peace and Bread: The Story of Jane Addams, 13.46
Peace Commandos, The: Nonviolent Heroes in the Struggle against War and Injustice, 15.29
Peeling the Onion, 20.5
Penguin: A Season in the Life of the Adélie Penguin, 18.8
Pennies for the Piper, 1.74
People, 22.39
Persephone and the Pomegranate: A Myth from Greece, 5.46
Persian Gulf War, The: "The Mother of All Battles," 15.28
Pete and Lily, 1.49
Peter, 2.63
Phantom Animals, 21.5
Phantom of the Opera, The, 9.26
Phoenix Rising, 7.7
Photographer II, The: The Dark Room, 9.49
Photos That Made U.S. History: Volume 1, From the Civil War Era to the Atomic Age, 12.87
Picture This Century: An Introduction to Twentieth Century Art, 22.38
Pictures of Adam, 2.33
Pictures of the Night, 8.8
Pigman & Me, The, 13.72
Pilgrim's Progress, 6.14
Pink and Say, 11.60
Pit, The, 9.8
Pitchers: Twenty-Seven of Baseball's Greatest, 23.21
Place Apart, A, 3.28
Place to Hide, A, 8.26
Plague, 7.31

Title Index

Plain City, 1.43
Planes, 24.16
Planet Earth, 17.2
Plants That Make You Sniffle and Sneeze, 17.20
Playing a Virginia Moon, 2.46
Please Do Not Touch: A Collection of Stories, 21.13
Please Remove Your Elbow from My Ear, 2.20
Poems about Love, 20.4
Poetry from A to Z: A Guide for Young Writers, 20.11
Poison, 8.7
Poisons in Our Path, 17.10
Pollution, 17.8
Pony Express, The, 12.83
Portrait of Miranda, 2.37
Predator, 7.33
Prehistoric Stone Monuments, 12.50
Prelude to War, 12.73
Presenting Richard Peck, 13.31
Presidents versus Congress: Conflict and Compromise, 15.34
Prince of Humbugs: A Life of P. T. Barnum, 13.4
Privacy: Individual Right v. Social Needs, 15.21
Pro Football Hall of Fame, The, 23.4
Promise Not to Tell, 3.63
Pronounce It Dead, 8.21
Prose Anthology of the First World War, A, 12.41
Puerto Rico: America's 51st State?, 15.2
Pullman Strike of 1894, The, 12.1
Pumpkins of Time, The, 7.5
Punch with Judy, 11.7
Purple Heart, The, 1.104
Pursuit of the Presidency '92 and Beyond, The, 15.9
Putting It in Writing, 24.23

Question of Magic, A, 6.43
Question of Trust, A, 1.8
Quinceañera: A Latina's Journey to Womanhood, 14.8

Rabies, 18.19
Racing the Iditarod Trail, 23.3
Radical Red, 11.26

Rage in the Streets: Mob Violence in America, 15.4
Ramsay Scallop, The, 11.79
Ranch Dressing: The Story of Western Wear, 12.33
Raoul Wallenberg: The Man Who Stopped Death, 13.42
Ratface, 3.22
Rattle and the Drum, The, 14.14
Real Friends, 3.72
Real Heroes, 3.35
Real Plato Jones, The, 1.9
Really No Big Deal, 2.3
Reason for Janey, The, 2.67
Reconstruction: America after the Civil War, 12.53
Red Wolf, The, 18.32
Relative Strangers, 1.33
Remarkable Journey of Prince Jen, The, 6.2
Remember the Red-Shouldered Hawk, 1.99
Rescue Josh McGuire, 10.26
Rescue Mission—Planet Earth: A Global Handbook for the 21st Century, 17.6
Restless Dead, The: More Strange Real-Life Mysteries, 21.22
Return of the Home Run Kid, 4.1
Reunification of Germany, The, 12.92
Rhino, 1.59
Riddle City, USA! A Book of Geography Riddles, 24.20
Riding the Waves, 3.77
Right to Die, The, 15.31
Right to Die, The: Public Controversy, Private Matter, 19.13
Righteous Revenge of Artemis Bonner, The, 10.30
Rimwalkers, 1.41
Ring of Truth, The, 3.61
Rio Grande Stories, 21.19
Rite of Passage, 3.84
Rites of Passage, 21.3
Road Back, The: Living with a Physical Disability, 19.28
Road to Camlann, The, 5.40
Road Trip (Friday the 13th), 9.30
Roald Dahl's Revolting Recipes, 24.6
Roarr: Calder's Circus, 22.18
Roll Along: Poems on Wheels, 20.17
Roller Birds of Rampur, The, 3.64
Rosie's Tiger, 11.50

Roy Lichtenstein: The Artist at Work, 22.36
Royal Kingdoms of Ghana, Mali, and Songhay, The: Life in Medieval Africa, 12.51
Runa, 9.22
Running for Our Lives, 11.80

Sabbath Garden, The, 3.31
Safari beneath the Sea: The Wonder World of the North Pacific Coast, 18.34
Salamandastron, 6.30
Sand and Fog: Adventures in Southern Africa, 17.4
Savage Carrot, 1.107
Save Halloween, 3.76
Save Our Oceans and Coasts, 17.15
Say It Loud! The Story of Rap Music, 22.17
Schizophrenia, 19.29
School Daze: Jokes Your Teacher Will Hate, 24.24
Science Dictionary, 16.28
Science Experiments You Can Eat, 16.10
Science Projects about Electricity and Magnets, 16.16
Science to the Rescue, 16.22
Scooter, 1.113
Scottsboro Boys, The, 12.37
Sculptor's Eye, The, 22.11
Sea Jellies: Rainbows in the Sea, 18.14
Sea Snakes, 18.7
Search for the Killer Asteroid, The, 16.32
Secrets to Tell, 10.11
See Ya, Simon, 2.26
Sequoyah's Gift: A Portrait of the Cherokee Leader, 13.39
Serengeti Migration, The: Africa's Animals on the Move, 18.25
Settling the American West, 12.14
Seven Strange & Ghostly Tales, 21.16
Seventeen and In-Between, 2.16
Seventh Inning Stretch: Time-Out for Baseball Trivia, 23.8
Sexual Harassment, 15.32
Sexual Harassment: A Reference Handbook, 15.18
Shadow Boxer, 4.10
Shadow Like a Leopard, A, 2.32
Shadow of the Dragon, 1.36
Shadow Walkers, 6.18
Shadow, 7.30
Shadowmaker, 8.15
Shakedown Street, 3.56
Shaker Home, 12.8
Shakespeare and Macbeth: The Story behind the Play, 22.28
Shape-Changer, 7.2
Shaquille O'Neal, 23.18
Share of Freedom, A, 1.115
Sharing Susan, 1.16
Shark Callers, 10.2
Shattered, 9.35
Shell Woman and the King, The, 5.47
Shelter, 1.75
Sheltering Rebecca, 11.8
Ship, 12.48
Shiva Accused, 6.11
Shiva's Challenge: An Adventure of the Ice Age, 6.12
Shizuko's Daughter, 1.76
Short Walk around the Pyramids and through the World of Art, A, 22.16
Should We Have Capital Punishment?, 15.24
Sierra Club Book of Small Mammals, The, 18.18
Sierra Club Kid's Guide to Planet Care and Repair, The, 17.26
Silent Night 2, 9.51
Silent Stalker, 9.12
Silent Storm, The, 10.12
Silver Blades: In the Spotlight, 2.35
Silver Creek Riders: Back in the Saddle, 3.41
Simple Physics Experiments with Everyday Materials, 16.5
Sincerely Yours: How to Write Great Letters, 24.14
Singer to the Sea God, 6.1
Sirens, 6.50
Skin Deep, 3.68
Sky Detective: Investigating the Mysteries of Space, 16.13
Sky Legends of Vietnam, 5.45
Skylark, 11.43
Skywatch: Eyes-On Activities for Getting to Know the Stars, Planets, and Galaxies, 16.21
Sluggers Club, The: A Sports Mystery, 4.12
Smithsonian Visual Timeline of Inventions, The, 12.62
Snakes, 18.15
Snow Wife, The, 5.32
Soda Jerk, 20.25

Someone at the Door, 9.13
Someone to Count On, 1.47
Someone Was Watching, 8.17
Something Permanent, 20.26
Song of Be, 3.4
Song of Sedna, 5.31
Song of the Gargoyle, 6.53
Songs and Stories from the American Revolution, 12.71
Songs from Home, 1.38
Soul Looks Back in Wonder, 20.3
South Africa at the Crossroads, 15.37
Space, 16.6
Spanish Kidnapping Disaster, The, 10.18
Sparrow Hawk Red, 10.27
Speaking Out: Teenagers Take On Race, Sex, and Identity, 15.30
Spell It Murder, 8.22
Spite Fences, 11.37
Stamp Collecting, 24.12
Star Crossing: How to Get around in the Universe, 16.19
Stardust otel, 20.9
Stardust, 2.17
Staying Fat for Sarah Byrnes, 3.18
Stephen Biesty's Cross-Sections: Castle, 12.64
Stephen Biesty's Cross-Sections: Man-of-War, 12.63
Steroids, 19.22
Still a Nation of Immigrants, 15.6
Stitch in Time, A, 11.65
Stones of Muncaster Cathedral, The, 9.54
Storm without Rain, A, 7.1
Story of Negro League Baseball, The, 23.2
Straight Talk about Death for Teenagers: How to Cope with Losing Someone You Love, 19.15
Straight Talk about Eating Disorders, 19.23
Straight Talk about Student Life, 19.7
Stranger Here, A, 9.57
Striking Out, 4.14
Summer of My German Soldier, 11.29
Summer's End, 9.21
Sungura and Leopard: A Swahili Trickster Tale, 5.15
Sunita Experiment, The, 1.84
Surviving Suicide: Young People Speak Up, 19.19
Susan Butcher and the Iditarod Trail, 13.19
Swamp Angel, 5.12
Sweet Dreams: Romance on the Run, 2.7

Sweet Friday Island, 10.35
Sweet Notes, Sour Notes, 1.67
Sweet Sixteen and Never Been Killed, 9.42
Switching Well, 7.6
Sword and the Circle, The, 5.41
Sworn Enemies, 11.46
Sylvia Smith-Smith, 2.45

T-Backs, T-Shirts, Coat, and Suit, 3.43
Tackle without a Team, 4.2
Take a Look: An Introduction to the Experience of Art, 22.6
Take Action: An Environmental Book for Kids, 17.22
Tales from the African Plains, 5.9
Tales of Ancient Persia: Retold from the Shah-Nama of Fidausi, 5.27
Talking Peace: A Vision for the Next Generation, 15.11
Talking to Dragons, 6.60
Talons, 9.36
Taste of Smoke, A, 9.2
Tears of a Tiger, 3.24
Teen Suicide, 19.11
Teen's Guide to Going Vegetarian, A, 19.18
Teenage Drinking, 19.21
Teenagers and Compulsive Gambling, 19.8
Tell Me Everything, 3.13
Tell Them We Remember: The Story of the Holocaust, 12.5
Teller of Tales, 5.4
Telling of the Tales, A, 5.3
Ten Mile Day and the Building of the Transcontinental Railroad, 12.23
Terra Cotta Army of Emperor Qin, The, 22.21
Test Your Math IQ, 24.26
There's No Surf in Cleveland, 1.15
They Had a Dream: The Civil Rights Struggle from Frederick Douglass to Marcus Garvey to Martin Luther King to Malcolm X, 13.7
Thicker than Water, 6.24
Thirteen Going On Seven, 1.92
This Land Is Your Land, 17.33
Thomas Edison, 13.1
Those Who Love the Game: Glenn "Doc" Rivers on Life in the NBA and Elsewhere, 23.19
Three Faces of Vietnam, 12.91

Through the Looking Glass and What Alice Found There, 6.15
Thunder Rolling in the Mountains, 11.55
Tiger, Tiger, Burning Bright, 1.61
Till Victory is Won: Black Soldiers in the Civil War, 12.52
Time and Space, 16.17
Time and the Clockmice Etcetera, 6.22
Time to Keep Silent, A, 1.110
Timekeeper, The, 7.24
Timothy of the Cay, 10.36
To Cross a Line, 11.61
To Race a Dream, 11.73
To the Top of the World, 18.3
Toby Scudder, Ultimate Warrior, 2.18
Toilets, Bathtubs, Sinks, and Sewers: A History of the Bathroom, 12.15
Tomfoolery: Trickery and Foolery with Words, 24.28
Toning the Sweep, 1.55
Top Ten Basketball Scorers, 23.10
Torn Away, 3.33
Tough Choices: A Story of the Vietnam War, 11.4
Toughing It, 3.74
Tracks in the Wild, 18.2
Trail of Tears, The, 12.25
Traveler's Guide to the Solar System, 16.1
Traveling on into the Light and Other Stories, 21.4
Treasure Island, 10.34
Tree Almanac: A Year-round Activity Guide, 17.29
Trees Stand Shining, The, 20.14
Troubling a Star, 8.13
Troy Aikman, 23.5
True Friends, 3.79
True Story of J. Edgar Hoover and the FBI, The, 13.18
Truth to Tell, 1.12
Tundra Swans, 18.24
Tunes for Bears to Dance To, 3.17
Turn of the Century, 12.47
TV Guidance Counselor, The, 3.44
Twelve Days in August, 3.53
Twilight Gate, The, 6.45
Twins on Toes: A Ballet Debut, 22.1
Twist of Gold, 10.28

U.S. Health Care Crisis, The: The Fight over Access, Quality, and Cost, 15.45

Ultimate Noah's Ark, The: Perfect Puzzle for All Ages, 24.37
Ulysses S. Grant, 13.10
Umm El Madayan: An Islamic City through the Ages, 12.4
Uncertain Roads, 14.17
Uncle Vampire, 1.39
Unconditional Surrender: U. S. Grant and the Civil War, 13.44
Under the Blood-Red Sun, 11.72
Unfinished Portrait of Jessica, 1.83
Unmentionable! More Amazing Stories, 21.17

Vanilla, Chocolate, & Strawberry: The Story of Your Favorite Flavors, 24.2
Vanishing Feast, The: How Dwindling Genetic Diversity Threatens the World's Food Supply, 15.43
Vanishing Life: The Mystery of Mass Extinctions, 18.16
Vanishing Wetlands, The, 17.12
Vengeance of the Witch-Finder, The, 9.3
Venus, 16.4
Visions: Stories about Women Artists, 22.30
Visual Dictionary of Ancient Civilizations, 12.86
Visual Dictionary of the Horse, 18.38
Voice in the Wind, A, 9.24
Voices from the Camps, 12.9
Voices from the Fields: Children of Migrant Farm Workers Tell Their Stories, 15.7

Wainscott Weasel, 6.46
Walk Two Moons, 1.23
Walking up a Rainbow, 11.78
Walls: Resisting the Third Reich—One Woman's Story, 13.71
Wanna Bet? Science Challenges to Fool You, 16.11
Waorani, The: People of the Ecuadoran Rain Forest, 14.16
War in Yugoslavia: The Breakup of a Nation, 14.11
Water, 17.32
Water Wars, 17.7
Way Home, The, 21.25
"We'll Stand by the Union": Robert Gould Shaw and the Black 54th Massachusetts Regiment, 13.12

Title Index

Weirdo, The, 8.23
Western Wind, 1.35
Whaling Days, 12.10
What Are We Going to Do about David?, 1.87
What Daddy Did, 1.97
What Does the Crow Know? The Mysteries of Animal Intelligence, 18.12
What Good Is a Tail?, 18.31
What Is a Bird?, 18.33
What Makes a Degas a Degas?, 22.25
What Time of Night Is It?, 1.103
What You Don't Know Can Kill You, 3.1
What's French for HELP, George?, 2.38
Whatever Happened to Janie?, 1.21
When the Nightingale Sings, 1.106
When the Ragman Sings, 11.39
When the Road Ends, 1.105
Where Are My Birth Parents?, 19.14
Where Do I Go from Here?, 3.81
Where I Want to Be, 1.28
Where the River Runs: A Portrait of a Refugee Family, 13.33
Where the Truth Lies, 6.5
While Standing on One Foot: Puzzle Stories and Wisdom Tales from the Jewish Traditions, 5.14
White Lilacs, 11.49
White Stallions, The: The Story of the Dancing Horses of Lipizza, 18.37
Who Do You Think You Are?, 21.23
Who Is Eddie Leonard?, 1.73
Who Put the Cannon in the Courthouse Square?, 12.16
"Who Was That Masked Man, Anyway?", 8.3
Who's Orp's Girlfriend?, 2.30
Whole New Ball Game, A: The Story of the All-American Girls Professional Baseball League, 23.15
Wildlife Rescue: The Work of Dr. Kathleen Ramsay, 18.9
Wind Blows Backward, The, 2.24
Windleaf, 6.48
Wings of a Falcon, The, 6.57
Winners and Losers, 4.5
Winter of Fire, 6.33
Winter Poems, 20.24
Winterdance: The Fine Madness of Running the Iditarod, 10.31
Wishing Season, 6.27
Witch Week, 6.32

Witch's Fire, 9.6
Witcracks: Jokes and Jests from Folklore, American, 5.35
With Every Drop of Blood, 11.18
Within Reach, 21.12
Witnesses to Freedom: Young People Who Fought for Civil Rights, 12.66
Wizard's Apprentice, The, 6.54
Wolf at the Door, 3.16
Wolf-Speaker, 6.44
Wolf-Woman, 6.34
Woman Unafraid, A: The Achievements of Frances Perkins, 13.15
Women of Peace: Nobel Peace Prize Winners, 13.55
Wonder, 2.60
Wonderful Pen of May Swenson, The, 13.40
Woodworking for Kids: 40 Fabulous, Fun, & Useful Things for Kids to Make, 22.24
Words in the News: A Student's Dictionary of American Government and Politics, 24.7
Working Together against Gun Violence, 15.39
Working Together against Hate Groups, 15.10
World of Animals, The, 18.26
World of Daughter McGuire, The, 2.73
World War I: The War to End Wars, 12.44
World War II: America Goes to War, 12.77
World's Best Outdoor Games, 24.35
World's Scariest "True" Ghost Stories, 21.21
Wounded Knee: An Indian History of the American West, 12.20
Wrapped in a Riddle, 8.10
Wren's Quest, 6.51

You Bet Your Life, 3.19
Young Dancer, The, 22.5
Young Genius Book of Brain Teasers, 24.3
Young People Speak: Surviving the Holocaust in Hungary, 13.35
Young Stargazer's Guide to the Galaxy, The: Stars, Clusters, and Galaxies, 16.18
Yours Truly, 1.3

Zlata's Diary, 13.24

Subject Index

Abandonment, 1.53, 1.71, 1.87, 1.103, 1.112, 3.71
Abolitionists, 12.69, 13.12, 13.45
Aborigines, 5.24, 10.6
Abortion, 15.23, 19.31
Acid rain, 17.32, 17.33
Actors, 2.10, 2.17, 2.19, 9.48, 13.57, 23.12. *See also* Theater.
Addams, Jane, 13.46, 13.55
Addresses, 23.6, 24.17
Adoption, 1.70, 2.31, 3.77, 15.35, 19.14
Adventure and survival, 1.74, 1.105, 5.31, 6.4, 6.5, 6.10, 6.18, 6.40, 6.43, 6.57, 6.60, 6.61, 7.3–7.5, 7.7, 7.9, 7.11, 7.31, 8.13, 10.1–10.39, 11.16, 11.22, 11.25, 11.43, 11.46, 12.79, 21.25
Africa, 3.4, 3.8, 10.10, 11.71, 12.51, 14.5, 14.18, 17.4, 18.25
African Americans, 1.13, 1.55, 1.94, 1.114, 2.65, 2.71–2.73, 3.31, 3.54, 3.81, 5.28, 11.49, 11.51, 11.77, 12.6, 12.17, 12.35, 12.36, 12.37, 12.46, 12.52, 12.66, 12.69, 12.76, 13.7, 13.12, 13.16, 13.34, 13.43, 13.47, 13.49, 13.51, 13.58, 20.3, 20.8, 20.12, 20.13, 20.21, 20.28, 21.15, 22.13, 22.20, 22.22, 22.34, 23.2, 23.9, 23.16, 23.18, 23.22
Aging, 19.31
Agriculture, 15.43
AIDS, 1.26, 3.1, 3.35, 3.49, 19.1, 19.4, 19.31, 19.32, 20.10
Aikman, Troy, 23.5
Ailey, Alvin, Jr., 13.43
Airplanes, 12.57, 13.67, 24.16
Airports, 24.31
Alaska, 10.13, 10.31, 13.19, 18.3, 23.3
Alcohol abuse, 4.3, 19.21
Alcoholics, 1.86, 1.89, 1.110, 1.115, 2.74, 3.14
Alcoholism, 3.10, 8.18, 11.54, 19.21, 21.4
Alcott, Louisa May, 13.14
Ali, Muhammad, 23.14
Aliens, 6.25, 6.43, 7.11, 9.32
Allegory, 6.14, 6.15
Allergies, 17.20
Alligators, 3.37
Almanacs, 17.29, 23.6
Alphabet, 24.36

Alzheimer's disease, 10.23
Amazon, 17.17
America, colonial, 11.31, 11.38, 11.67, 12.42, 12.82, 13.8, 20.6
American Revolution, 12.71, 12.93, 24.11
Amish, 14.2
Amphibians, 18.29
Amsterdam, 11.30, 13.69
Anatomy, 19.30
Ancestors, 20.3
Ancient civilizations, 12.30, 12.86
Andersen, Hans Christian, 22.4
Andes Mountains, 12.30
Angelou, Maya, 20.2, 20.22
Angels, 21.8
Animals, 3.16, 15.13, 15.41, 17.2, 17.13, 17.14, 17.24, 18.4, 18.9, 18.11, 18.12, 18.18, 18.19, 18.26, 18.27, 18.31, 21.5, 24.5. *See also* specific animals.
   endangered, 3.42, 15.1, 17.24, 17.25, 17.30, 18.6, 18.24
   experimentation, 15.16
   extinct, 17.25
   migration, 18.21, 18.23, 18.24, 18.25
   nocturnal, 18.11, 18.36
   perception and intelligence, 18.4, 18.12
   rights, 15.13, 15.16, 15.41
   sea, 1.58, 18.13, 18.14, 18.34
   tracks, 18.2
Anne of Green Gables, 13.11
Anorexia nervosa, 19.23
Antarctica, 8.13, 18.8
Anthony, Susan B., 11.26
Anti-Semitism, 2.28, 3.17, 11.61, 11.74, 12.5, 12.39, 13.35, 13.54. *See also* Holocaust, Prejudice.
Apaches, 14.3, 14.13
Apartheid, 3.55, 15.37
Apollo (Greek god), 6.9
Appomattox, 11.66
Aquariums, 18.13
Arabs, 2.22
Archeology, 1.29, 9.36, 10.3, 10.6, 12.3, 12.29, 12.48, 12.68, 12.86, 15.17, 22.21
Architecture, 12.40, 12.86, 22.16
Aristide, Jean-Bertrand, 15.20
Armenian Americans, 3.39
Armstrong, Louis, 13.2, 13.22, 13.47
Arson, 10.23

Art, 6.13, 6.50, 20.3, 20.22, 22.4, 22.6, 22.11, 22.20, 22.25, 22.26, 22.31, 22.32, 22.38, 22.39. *See also* Painting, Sculpture.
  folk, 5.44
  history, 22.16, 22.26
  projects, 22.8, 22.12, 22.37, 24.21
Artists, 3.60, 3.70, 13.22, 13.57, 20.13, 22.11, 22.15, 22.22, 22.25, 22.27, 22.30, 22.31, 22.33, 22.34, 22.36, 22.37
Asia, 14.12
Asian Pacific Americans, 13.57
Asteroids, 16.32
Astronauts, 16.14
Astronomy, 16.1, 16.4, 16.13, 16.18, 16.19, 16.21
Athletes. *See* Sports, figures.
Athletes and drug use, 19.22
Attention deficit disorder, 19.16
Audubon, J. J., 22.27
Aurora borealis, 16.29
Australia, 1.37, 2.8, 10.6, 3.21
Authors, 13.2, 13.5, 13.11, 13.14, 13.16, 13.28, 13.30–13.32, 13.38, 13.53, 13.57, 13.59, 13.64, 13.65, 13.72, 21.10, 21.12
  classic, 21.29
  Newbery Award–winning, 21.14
  student, 21.19, 21.27
Autism, 2.64
Autobiography, 13.24, 13.34, 13.35, 13.38, 13.54, 13.59, 13.68, 13.71, 13.72, 23.11
Automobiles, 2.48, 20.17, 24.13, 24.15, 24.27
  racing, 23.1
Aviation, 12.57, 24.16
Aztec empire, 13.21

Babysitting, 1.46
Bacon, Roger, 11.69
Badgers, 6.30
Baghdad, 9.29
Ballet, 22.1, 22.3, 22.5, 22.9
  schools, 22.5
Barnum, P. T., 13.4, 13.26
Bartram, William, 17.18
Baseball, 4.1, 4.3, 4.11, 4.12, 4.14, 20.7, 23.2, 23.4, 23.8, 23.15, 23.16, 23.21, 23.22, 23.23, 23.24
Basketball, 23.4, 23.9, 23.10, 23.13, 23.18, 23.19, 23.23
Bathrooms, history of, 12.15

Battle of Bull Run, 12.22. *See also* Civil War.
Battle of the Little Big Horn, 13.60
Bears, 10.20, 10.26
Beasts, 5.20
Beauty, 19.20
Bees, Africanized, 18.23
Beethoven, Ludwig van, 7.29
Bell, Alexander Graham, 13.61
Berlin Wall, 12.92
Bernstein, Leonard, 13.37
Betrayal, 9.50
Betting, 2.23
Bible stories, 20.13
Biography, 12.33, 13.1–13.23, 13.25–13.33, 13.36, 13.37, 13.39–13.53, 13.55–13.58, 13.60, 13.62–13.67, 13.69, 15.27, 22.1, 22.22, 22.34, 23.1, 23.5, 23.9, 23.12–23.14, 23.18, 23.22
Biological diversity, 15.43, 17.3, 17.21
Biologists, 17.5
Biology, 17.2, 24.5
Bioluminescence, 18.36
Bird-watching, 1.58
Birds, 6.26, 17.24, 18.24, 18.27, 18.33, 18.35, 22.27
Black holes, 16.17
Blackmail, 8.16
Blue Ridge Mountains, 11.62, 11.63
Blues music, 22.13
Boarding schools, 11.1, 11.2
Boating, 4.7
Body language, 24.9
Bodybuilding, 23.12
Bonheur, Rosa, 22.33–22.35
Book banning. *See* Censorship.
Bootlegging, 1.86
Borneo, 1.79, 10.1
Bosnia-Herzegovina, 14.11
Boston Massacre, 11.67
Botany, 17.9–17.11, 17.29, 17.34, 24.5. *See also* Plants.
Boxing, 4.8, 4.10
Brady, Mathew, 13.66
Brain damage, 3.11
Breast implants, 19.12
Broadway shows, 9.26
Brothers, 1.109, 2.46, 3.28, 3.29, 3.74, 4.9, 4.10, 10.21, 11.12
Brothers and sisters, 1.11, 1.21, 1.26–1.28, 1.35, 1.41, 1.51, 1.57, 1.75, 1.77, 1.85, 1.103, 2.15, 2.43, 3.1, 3.17, 3.22, 3.26, 6.1, 6.18, 6.20, 6.41, 7.4, 7.9, 7.17,

7.30, 8.17, 8.24, 10.28, 10.29, 10.32, 11.4, 11.6, 13.59
Bruegel, Pieter, 22.25
Bulimia, 2.72, 19.23
Bullies, 2.62, 3.25
Bureau of Land Management, 18.30
Burial customs, 15.17
Burial grounds, 10.3, 15.17
Bussing, 3.59
Butcher, Susan, 13.19
Butterflies, 3.42, 18.21

California, history of, 12.89
Cambodian Americans, 13.33
Camelot, 5.26, 5.39, 5.40, 5.41
Camp, summer, 1.100, 2.11, 3.41, 8.22
Camping, 10.11, 10.35, 23.17
Canada, 14.3, 14.15
Cancer, 1.63, 3.45, 3.50, 3.69, 6.45
Capital punishment, 15.24, 15.25
Careers, 15.42, 22.14, 22.23, 24.5
Caribbean region, 1.52, 10.36
    history of, 11.11
Carpentry projects, 22.24
Carrington, Leonora, 22.30
Cartooning, 1.54
Cartoonists, 3.70
Cassatt, Mary, 22.30, 22.33, 22.34, 22.35
Castles, 6.20, 12.64, 12.85
Cats, 1.8, 7.30, 18.17
Cattle, 1.42, 12.49, 21.28
Cattlemen, 12.14
Cave dwellers, 6.11, 6.12, 10.5
Caves, 11.36
Celebrities, 9.10, 24.17
Censorship, 1.64, 15.25, 15.33
Chants, Native American, 20.14
Charlemagne, 6.56
Charms, 10.28
Cheating, 2.34
Chemistry, 16.16
Chemotherapy, 3.45
Chernobyl, 15.12
Cherokee, 5.29, 12.25, 13.39
Chickasaw, 1.91
Child abuse, 1.112, 2.55, 2.70, 3.11, 3.18, 3.63, 3.66, 3.80, 6.17, 6.57
Child labor laws, 12.24, 15.38
Children, 12.32, 12.66, 15.26, 20.16, 20.30, 20.31
    feral, 6.34, 10.39
China, 6.13, 11.12, 12.12, 12.45, 22.21
    history of, 12.12, 12.45

Chinese Americans, 1.68, 1.80, 13.28, 14.1, 14.6
Chinook, 3.40
Chippewa, 3.12, 11.84
Choctaw, 11.21
Choreographers, 13.43
Choreography, 22.3
Christianity, 6.14
Christmas, 1.24, 5.28, 11.47, 22.3
Circulatory system, 19.5
Circus, 11.7, 12.19, 13.4, 13.26, 22.18, 24.19
Citizen action, 17.26
Civil rights, 12.36, 12.37, 12.46, 12.47, 12.66, 12.69, 12.70, 12.76, 13.7, 13.58
Civil War, 7.15, 11.13, 11.18, 11.27, 11.32, 11.33, 11.34, 11.47, 11.52, 11.58, 11.60, 11.66, 12.11, 12.22, 12.52, 12.53, 12.73, 13.10, 13.12, 13.44, 13.66, 20.6
Clans, 6.34, 10.5
Classics, 1.65, 6.14, 6.15, 9.26, 10.9, 10.34, 11.1–11.3
Claustrophobia, 10.33
Cleopatra, 13.63
Clergy, 15.42
Clinton, Bill (William Jefferson), 15.20, 15.26, 20.1
Clinton, Hillary Rodham, 13.62
Cliques, 2.60
Clocks, 6.22, 16.3
Cloning, 7.25
Clothing, 12.33
    history of, 12.42, 12.84
Coaching, 4.4
Coasts, 17.15
Colds, 19.27
Color, 16.9, 16.29
Comic books, 6.4
Comic strips, 6.10
Coming-of-age, 1.65, 1.101, 14.8, 14.10, 14.13
Communes, 12.8
Communication, 16.27, 18.4, 24.9, 24.14, 24.18, 24.23
Communism, 12.45
Community service, 24.10
Composers, 13.22, 13.37, 13.41
Compulsive behavior, 19.8, 19.23
Computer games, 7.23, 7.24, 7.26
Computers, 24.18
Concentration camps, Nazi, 11.45, 20.31
Congress, U.S., 13.25, 15.34
Conquistadors, 13.21
Conservation, 17.18, 17.25, 17.33
Constitution, U.S., 15.21, 15.33

Contraception, 19.32
Convicts, 2.52
Cooper, Floyd, 20.28
Costumes, 12.84
Country music, 22.19
Courage, 15.44
Cousins, 1.41, 1.77, 8.21
Cowboys, 12.31, 12.49, 12.58, 12.67
Crafts, 14.14, 22.8, 22.10, 22.12, 22.24, 24.21
   Native American, 12.72
Crazy Horse, 13.60
Creativity, 20.3, 22.8, 22.12
Cree, 14.15
Creek, 14.14
Crime, 7.2, 7.17, 13.18, 15.24
Criminal justice system, 15.8
Criminals, 15.8
Cross-sections, 12.63, 12.64, 16.6, 24.15, 24.16
Crow, 12.72
Crusades, 11.79
Cults, 3.22, 15.14
Cultural differences, 2.31, 3.64, 14.7, 15.30, 21.11
Cultures, 21.19, 21.26
Curie, Marie, 13.3, 13.50
Curses, 9.12, 12.21
Custer, George Armstrong, 11.34
Custody battles, 1.16
Cy Young Award, 23.24

Dancers, 13.22, 13.43
Darwin, Charles, 13.3, 13.23
Dating, 1.44, 2.3, 2.7, 2.30, 19.3
Day, Tom, 22.22
Daydreaming, 3.51
Days of the Dead, 14.9
Deafness, 3.73, 12.88
Death, 1.2, 1.14, 1.23, 1.25, 1.26, 1.38, 1.51, 1.55, 1.74, 1.100, 1.107, 1.110, 1.111, 1.112, 2.26, 2.27, 2.47, 3.10, 3.13, 3.14, 3.15, 3.17, 3.24, 3.28, 3.33, 3.42, 3.50, 3.74, 4.14, 6.24, 7.28, 8.12, 9.29, 10.2, 10.6, 10.8, 10.19, 10.27, 11.4, 11.39, 11.50, 11.75, 15.32, 19.2, 19.13, 19.15, 19.31
Death penalty, 15.25
Decision making, 7.14
Degas, Edgar, 22.25
Delaware (Native Americans), 12.54
Democracy, 15.20, 15.34
   history of, 12.60

Demons, 7.3
Denmark, 11.64
Depression, mental, 1.15, 1.18, 2.24, 19.11, 19.23
Design, 22.24, 22.39
Desktop publishing, 24.18
Detectives, 8.2, 8.5, 8.11
Devil, 9.5, 21.24
   worship, 9.15
Diabetes, 19.26
Diaries and memoirs, 1.64, 11.77, 12.41, 12.48, 12.59, 12.93, 13.14, 13.24, 13.34, 13.38, 13.48, 13.59, 13.68, 13.69, 19.1, 24.30
Diaz, Porfirio, 12.75
Dickens, Charles, 13.64
Dickinson, Emily, 20.22
Dictionaries, 12.86, 16.28, 18.38, 24.7
   science, 17.5
Dieting, 2.57
Digestive system, 19.5, 19.6
Dinosaurs, 7.12, 16.30, 16.32, 18.10, 18.16, 18.28
Disabilities, 2.64, 19.28, 22.35
   learning, 2.52, 3.3, 3.6, 3.14, 3.67, 6.35
   mental, 2.67
   physical, 1.57, 1.70, 2.32, 2.52, 3.29, 3.73, 3.79, 8.6, 12.88, 13.61
Disappearances, 8.18
Disasters, 12.81
Discrimination. *See also* Civil rights.
   ethnic, 3.78
   gender, 12.80, 13.25, 13.62, 15.18, 15.31
Diseases, 7.27, 7.31, 18.19, 19.26, 19.27. *See also* specific diseases.
Divers, 12.48
Divorce, 1.3, 1.4, 1.7, 1.8, 1.10, 1.13, 1.15, 1.30, 1.34, 1.66, 1.75, 1.83, 1.93, 1.108, 1.113, 2.36, 2.45, 2.51, 2.61, 2.67, 3.35, 3.44, 3.82, 8.7, 8.20, 9.53, 11.56
Dogs, 3.71, 10.4, 11.13, 23.3, 24.36
Dogsled racing, 10.31, 23.3
Dolls, 6.16, 6.58
Dolphins, 8.24, 18.29, 20.20
Douglass, Frederick, 13.45
Dracula, 9.25, 13.53
Dragons, 6.26, 6.55, 6.60, 6.61, 6.62, 20.23
Drama, 9.48, 17.23, 22.29. *See also* Theater.
Dreams, 6.42, 9.16, 18.27, 20.3, 20.8, 20.25
Droughts, 11.43
Drowning, 2.27
Drug smugglers, 8.13, 10.27
Drugs and drug abuse, 1.3, 4.2, 8.4, 8.9, 10.14, 15.49, 19.4, 19.22, 19.31

Druids, 6.35
Drums, 5.13, 9.4
Dust Bowl, 11.36, 11.76, 12.2
Dust mites, 18.20
Dwellings, 12.54, 12.85
Dyslexia, 3.3, 3.6

Eagles, 2.22
Earhart, Amelia, 7.29
Earth, 20.20
Earth science, 17.2
Earth Summit, 17.6
Eating disorders, 19.23
Ecology, 7.9, 8.15, 8.23, 10.13, 17.1, 17.6, 17.7, 17.12, 17.14, 17.18, 17.19, 17.22, 17.23, 17.24, 17.25, 17.26, 20.20, 20.32
Economy, international, 15.46
Ecuador, 14.16
Edison, Thomas, 13.1
Education, 19.16
Eeyou, 14.15
Egypt and Egyptians, 7.19, 11.40, 12.21, 13.63
Einstein, Albert, 16.17
Elections, 15.9
Electricity, 16.16
Elephants, 6.56, 10.7
Ellis Island, 11.53, 11.54
Emotional problems, 1.103, 2.33
Emperors, 12.12, 22.21
Encyclopedias, 24.4, 24.13, 24.29
Endangered peoples, 15.36
Energy, 16.26, 17.28
    alternative, 17.8
    solar, 16.26
England, 1.45, 6.58, 10.38, 22.28
Environment, 8.15, 20.32, 22.26
Environmental issues, 3.25, 2.42, 2.45, 7.4, 7.17, 14.16, 15.1, 15.12, 15.36, 16.22, 17.1, 17.2, 17.6, 17.7, 17.13, 17.14, 17.15, 17.16, 17.19, 17.22, 17.23, 17.26, 17.28, 17.30, 17.32, 17.33, 18.1, 18.32, 20.20
Environmental Protection Agency (EPA), 17.8
Epidemics, 11.75
Erie Canal, 12.61
Eskimos, 10.13
Essays, 17.13
Ethnology, 15.36
Europe, 14.17
    Eastern, 15.2

Evans, Walker, 20.26
Everglades, 10.3, 17.21
Evolution, 12.28, 18.16
Excalibur, 5.41
Experiments, scientific, 16.5, 16.8, 16.9, 16.10, 16.11, 16.15, 16.22, 16.25, 16.26, 16.33
Explorers, 12.26, 13.6
Extinct species, 18.16, 18.28
Extrasensory perception (ESP), 6.40, 6.42, 7.27, 7.30, 9.24
Extraterrestrial beings, 6.25, 7.10, 7.22

Fairies, 6.48
Fairy tales, 5.3, 5.4, 5.11, 5.18, 5.20, 5.21, 5.22, 5.23, 5.44
Faith healers, 1.63
Family, 1.1–1.117, 6.34, 15.15, 20.5, 20.28, 22.26
    extended, 1.43, 1.117
    foster, 1.56, 1.81, 1.105, 1.106, 3.40
    history, 1.50, 9.3, 11.51
    problems, 1.11, 1.14, 1.19, 1.22, 1.52, 1.98, 2.1, 2.49, 3.7, 3.21, 3.75, 3.76, 11.4 11.17, 11.27, 11.33, 11.41, 11.59, 11.65, 20.9
    relationships, 7.1, 7.8, 7.13, 7.28, 7.30, 9.53
    single-parent, 1.49, 1.53, 1.69, 1.114, 2.3, 2.42
    step-, 1.4, 1.18, 1.33, 3.80, 9.6, 11.50
    violence, 11.26
Fantasy, 6.1–6.65, 7.10, 7.23, 7.24, 7.32
Farm life, 1.20, 1.81, 3.65, 4.14, 11.17, 11.28, 11.59
Farmers, 12.14
Fashion, 12.42
Fast-food restaurants, 24.33
Fathers, 1.34, 1.44, 1.86, 1.107
    and daughters, 1.1, 1.2, 1.4, 1.14, 1.33, 1.38, 1.71, 1.83, 1.101, 1.108, 1.110, 2.70, 3.11, 5.20, 6.41, 8.1, 8.26, 10.35, 11.84
    and sons, 1.17, 1.42, 1.60, 1.62, 1.78, 1.79, 1.82, 1.90, 1.95, 1.97, 1.104, 3.30, 3.35, 4.5, 4.6, 4.7, 10.22, 11.5, 11.13, 11.35, 11.63
    step-, 1.12, 1.13, 3.20, 11.34
Fear, 3.57, 9.50
Federal Bureau of Investigation (FBI), 13.18

Feelings, 21.25
Feminist movement, 11.26, 15.19
Figures of speech, 24.34
Fire ecology, 17.31
First-person narratives, 12.53, 12.91, 21.12, 23.17
Fish, 18.33
Fishing, 10.8, 23.17
Fishing industry, 18.5
Fitzgerald, Ella, 13.2
Flavors, 24.2
Flight history, 12.57, 12.81, 13.67, 24.16
Floor hockey, 2.20
Florida, 11.22
Florida, history of, 12.89
Florida panther, 18.6
Flowers, 17.9, 17.27
Flu (influenza), 19.27
Flying saucers, 16.12
Folklore, 5.13, 5.16, 5.36, 5.43, 21.5, 21.15, 21.24, 24.28. *See also* Legends.
   African, 5.9, 5.15, 5.23
   American, 5.7, 5.33, 5.35, 5.42
   African American, 5.16, 5.28
   Appalachian, 5.6
   Native American, 5.29, 5.43
   Chinese, 5.47
   international, 5.19
   Japanese, 5.32
   Jewish, 5.14, 5.30
   Mexican, 5.1, 5.8
   Persian/Iranian, 5.27
   Russian, 5.18
   Vietnamese, 5.44, 5.45
Fong, Hiram, 13.57
Food, 12.18, 16.11, 19.25, 20.33, 24.2, 24.6, 24.25, 24.33
   additives, 19.25
   chain, 17.22
   supply, 15.43, 17.12
Football, 4.2, 4.4, 23.4, 23.5, 23.6, 23.23
Foreign policy, 15.46
Forest ecology, 17.3
Fossil fuels, 17.28
Fossil record, 18.10
Foster care, 1.115, 3.5, 3.84, 15.15, 15.35
France, 2.38, 11.44
Frank, Anne, 13.69
Frank, Mary, 22.30
Frankenstein, 9.40, 13.53
Freedom of speech, 15.33

Friendship, 1.5, 1.49, 1.100, 2.1–2.74, 3.2, 3.9, 3.18, 3.26, 3.28, 3.31, 3.34, 3.36, 3.41, 3.46, 3.47, 3.50, 3.66, 3.69, 3.71, 3.72, 3.77, 3.79, 3.80, 4.3, 4.5–4.8, 6.17–6.19, 6.31, 6.35, 6.42, 6.59, 7.2, 8.23, 9.1, 9.16, 10.33, 11.8, 11.9, 11.15, 11.21, 11.29, 11.52, 11.60, 11.67, 11.70, 11.76, 13.61, 20.8, 20.9, 20.21, 21.1, 21.3, 21.7, 21.11, 21.23
   interracial, 1.70, 1.72, 4.6, 10.36, 11.68
Frogs, 18.29
Fruits, 17.9
Furniture, 12.85, 22.10

Galveston, 10.12
Gambling, 19.8
Games, 12.13, 24.35
Gandhi, Mahatma, 13.56
Gangs, 1.36, 2.32, 2.50, 2.73, 3.58, 3.84
Gardening, 17.19, 18.1
Gargoyles, 6.53, 9.25, 9.54
Gay and lesbian issues, 1.93, 2.63, 3.53, 21.1
Gender, 2.44
Genesis, 20.13
Genetic research, 15.43, 19.31
Genetics, 13.9
Genies, 6.27
Geography, 17.2, 18.35, 24.20
Geology, 16.31, 17.2
Geometry, 16.25
Germ warfare, 7.31
Germany, history of, 12.92, 13.36
   Nazi, 11.61, 12.39
Ghana, 12.51
Ghost stories, 5.1, 5.10, 21.15
Ghosts, 1.68, 2.12, 6.24, 7.16, 8.4, 9.2, 9.6, 9.8, 9.9, 9.10, 9.24, 9.31, 9.37, 9.38, 9.43, 9.45, 9.53, 9.56, 9.57, 21.2, 21.5, 21.6, 21.8, 21.9, 21.16, 21.21, 21.22, 21.24, 21.29, 22.29
Giants, 6.9
Gifted students, 1.11, 1.13, 2.71
Ginsburg, Ruth Bader, 15.19
Glass, Hugh, 10.25
Global warming, 17.33
Goddard, Robert, 16.19
Gold, 24.22
Gold Rush, 11.9, 12.89, 14.1
Gore, Al (Albert, Jr.), 13.13

Government, 12.60, 24.7
Graham, Martha, 13.22
Grandfathers, 1.9, 1.47, 1.61, 1.92, 1.111, 6.28, 7.1, 10.12
Grandmothers, 1.25, 1.27, 1.31, 1.35, 1.50, 1.55, 1.71, 1.94, 1.99, 1.103, 1.117, 8.10, 10.23
Grandparents, 1.32, 1.80, 1.87, 1.97, 10.19, 11.62
Grant, Ulysses S., 13.10, 13.44
Graves, 9.3
Great Depression, 11.36, 11.59, 11.62, 11.76, 12.2, 12.78, 20.26, 22.33
Great Plains, 12.49, 12.67
Greece, 1.9
Greed, 6.6
Grief, 2.47, 3.24, 19.2, 19.15, 19.19
Griots, 12.51
Growing up, 2.51, 2.61, 2.63, 3.26, 3.65, 3.67, 3.83, 13.72, 21.1, 21.2, 21.3, 21.26
Gun control, 15.39
Guns, 10.10
Gypsies. *See* Roma.

Haidas, 14.3
Haiti, politics, 15.20
Haley, Alex, 13.62
Halloween, 3.76, 9.15, 9.25, 21.13, 21.14, 21.15
Hamburgers, 24.33
Harlem, 3.84, 13.16, 21.27, 22.34
Harper's Ferry, Virginia, 12.6
Harvey girls, 12.56
Harvey, William, 13.3
Haslam, Bob, 12.83
Hate groups, 15.10, 15.47
Hauntings, 9.10
Hawaii, 8.2
Hay fever, 17.20
Headhunters, 10.1
Healers, 6.19
Health, 19.5, 19.10, 19.12, 19.21, 19.23, 19.24, 19.26, 19.27, 19.29
  care, 15.45, 19.31
    hazards, 19.25
    insurance, 19.31
    mental, 19.11
Henson, Jim, 13.22
Hepatitis, 19.27
Heritage, 20.21

Heroes, 5.7, 5.17, 5.44, 15.29, 15.44
Hindenburg, 12.81
Hispanic Americans, 21.27
Historians, 12.16
Historical fiction, 21.12
History
  local, 12.16
  medieval, 12.40
  U.S., 5.7, 12.1, 12.2, 12.6. 12.7, 12.17, 12.20, 12.22, 12.23, 12.24, 12.25, 12.27, 12.31, 12.34, 12.35, 12.36, 12.38, 12.41, 12.42, 12.43, 12.46, 12.47, 12.52, 12.58, 12.60, 12.61, 12.66, 12.67, 12.71, 12.72, 12.73, 12.80, 12.83, 12.87, 12.90, 13.7, 13.51, 15.5, 24.11, 24.29
  world, 12.26, 12.28, 12.50, 12.62, 12.65, 12.77, 12.79, 12.94
Hitchcock, Alfred, 22.2
Hitler, Adolf, 13.36
Hitler Youth, 12.39
HIV, 19.10. *See also* AIDS.
Hoban, Russell, 20.15
Hobbies, 22.8, 22.24, 24.12, 24.14
Hoboes, 21.9
Hockey, 4.9
Holidays, 12.82, 14.9, 24.1, 24.11. *See also* specific holidays.
Holland, 13.54
Holocaust, 3.17, 11.25, 11.45, 12.5, 12.32, 13.42, 13.54, 13.68, 13.69. *See also* Anti-Semitism.
Homelessness, 1.1, 1.43, 3.2, 3.32, 3.54, 3.56, 3.58, 3.62, 13.70, 15.27, 15.40, 21.4. *See also* Poverty.
Homesteading, 11.5
Homework, 20.15
Homophobia, 21.1
Honesty, 3.52
Hoover, J. Edgar, 13.18
Hopi, 12.72, 14.14
Horror, 6.8, 9.13, 9.17, 9.18, 9.22, 9.25, 9.28, 9.37, 9.39, 9.47, 9.55, 21.13
Horse racing, 1.60
Horses, 2.55, 3.63, 9.44, 12.49, 18.30, 18.37, 18.38, 21.28
  race, 11.73
Houses. *See* Dwellings.
Hubble telescope, 16.6
Hudson River Valley, 17.1
Hughes, Langston, 13.16
Human body, 19.5, 19.30

Subject Index

Human rights, 15.11, 15.37
Humane society, 3.36, 3.75, 15.13
Humor, 1.88, 2.3, 2.8, 2.23, 2.26, 2.30, 2.38, 2.50, 3.19, 5.3, 5.4, 5.21, 5.36, 5.42, 6.10, 6.32, 7.13, 7.22, 10.30, 17.23, 20.15, 20.16, 20.17, 20.19, 20.33, 21.10, 21.17, 24.6, 24.24, 24.28, 24.36
Humorous poems, 20.15, 20.19, 20.33
Hungary, 13.35
Hunting, 10.4, 23.17
Hurricanes, 10.12
Hussein, Saddam, 15.28
Hygiene, 19.24

Ice skating, 2.35
Identity, 1.9, 1.16, 1.21, 1.31, 1.49, 1.79, 1.90, 1.91, 2.63, 2.66, 3.12, 3.20, 3.82, 6.36, 7.1, 8.26, 22.29
Iditarod, 10.31, 13.19, 23.3
Iliad, The, 5.38
Illinois, history of, 12.89
Illiteracy, 15.22
Imagination, 3.51, 6.16
Immigrants, 1.6, 3.39, 11.41, 11.53, 11.54, 12.59, 13.33
Immigration, 3.70, 12.43, 12.47, 14.1, 14.4, 15.4, 15.6
Incas, 12.30
Independence, 1.60, 2.16, 3.82, 11.35, 20.5
Independence Day, 24.11
India, 1.84, 3.64, 10.39, 13.56
Indianapolis 500, 23.1
Indigenous peoples, 3.8, 15.36
Individual rights, 15.21
Individuality, 7.14
Inheritance, 3.65
Initiation and initiation rites, 9.18, 10.5
Injuries, 19.28, 20.9
Inquisition, 11.69
Insects, 18.1, 18.21, 18.33
Inventions, 7.32, 12.8, 12.62, 24.13, 24.29, 24.32
Inventors, 13.1, 13.20, 13.61
Investments, 1.95
IQ tests, 24.3
Iraq, 15.28
Ireland, 1.20, 3.33, 9.44, 10.28, 11.54
Irish Americans, 14.4
Iroquois, 12.54
Irving, Washington, 13.53
Islamic history, 12.4

Isolation, 3.18
Israel, 1.6
Israelites, 11.40
Italy, 2.2

Jamaica, 7.34, 11.11, 21.2
Japan, 1.76, 3.70, 13.70, 14.7
  economic relations, 15.46
Japanese Americans, 11.72, 12.9, 12.75
  internment camps, 12.9, 12.74
Jazz, 13.47, 22.13
Jealousy, 1.109, 2.6, 2.10, 2.53, 3.1
Jefferson, Thomas, 12.55
Jellyfish, 18.13, 18.14
Jerusalem, 13.17
Jews and Judaism, 1.6, 1.67, 1.68, 2.28, 2.64, 3.31, 5.14, 5.30, 11.8, 11.14, 11.25, 11.29, 11.45, 11.56, 11.61, 11.81, 12.5, 12.32, 13.17, 13.35, 13.42, 13.68, 13.69, 20.31, 21.19
  Russian, 11.46, 11.74
Jim Crow laws, 12.76, 23.2
Johnson, Lyndon Baines, 13.2
Jokes, 5.35, 24.24
  practical, 1.43, 20.16
Jordan, Michael, 23.9, 23.13
Journalism, 3.47, 15.9
Journalism, history of, 12.69
Journals, 11.19, 12.93, 19.15, 22.27, 24.30
Journeys, 7.9, 7.18, 10.28, 11.12, 11.48, 11.79, 12.35
Jungle ecology, 17.17
Justin, Enid, 12.33

Kahlo, Frida, 22.35
Kazakhstan, 14.12
Keller, Helen, 13.52, 13.61
Kelly, Jim, 23.9
Kennedy, John F., 15.2
Kenya, 18.25
Kerr, M. E., 13.38
Kersee, Jackie Joyner, 23.5
Keys, 24.32
Kibbutz life, 1.6, 11.56
Kidnapping, 1.21, 1.90, 7.4, 8.17, 8.24, 9.4, 9.51, 10.18, 11.30
King Arthur, 5.26, 5.39, 5.40, 5.41
King, Billie Jean, 23.14
King, Dr. Martin Luther, 12.36
King Philip's War, 13.8

Kingdoms, 6.3
Knights, 6.53, 11.19
Korea and Koreans, 11.15, 11.16, 11.50, 13.70
Korean Americans, 2.31
Korean War, 12.77
Kraits, 18.7
Ku Klux Klan, 12.70
Kuwait, 15.28

Lab equipment, 16.24, 16.33
Labor
   laws, 12.24, 13.15, 15.38
   movement, 15.1
   unions, 12.1
Lakota, 10.37
Lange, Dorothea, 22.33
Language, 13.39, 24.7, 24.9, 24.28, 24.34, 24.36
Latino Americans, 14.6, 14.8
Latvia, 11.41
Law, 13.18, 15.5, 15.8, 15.18, 15.21, 15.24, 15.25
Learning disabilities, 19.16
Lee, Robert E., 13.52
Legends, 5.26, 5.45, 9.11, 9.19, 13.63, 15.44. *See also* Folklore.
   African American, 5.17, 5.37
   Eskimo, 5.31
Lenses, 16.23
Lesbians. *See* Gay and lesbian issues.
Letters, 1.72, 1.116, 3.9, 8.10, 11.20, 11.83, 12.41, 12.72, 12.93, 15.26, 24.14, 24.17, 24.23
Lewin, Ted, 23.11
Libraries, 11.10
Lichtenstein, Roy, 22.36
Lifeguarding, 3.46
Light, 16.9, 16.16, 16.23, 16.29, 16.33
Lincoln, Abraham, 7.29, 12.55, 13.48, 20.12
Lipizza, 18.37
Literacy, 11.58
Livingston, Myra Cohn, 20.6
Lobsters, 18.5
Loch Ness monster, 6.65
Locks, 24.32
London, 1.10, 7.31, 9.8, 10.9
Loneliness, 3.9
Lord, Bette Bao, 13.28, 13.57
Louganis, Greg, 13.57
Louisiana, 8.25

Love, 20.18
Love poetry, 20.4, 20.18
Lusitania, The, 12.44

Maasai, 14.18
Macbeth, 22.28
Madison, Dolley, 13.52
Magellan space craft, 16.4
Magic, 6.3, 6.7–6.9, 6.12, 6.13, 6.19–6.21, 6.26, 6.27, 6.31, 6.33, 6.38, 6.39, 6.44, 6.47, 6.50–6.56, 6.59, 6.60, 6.62, 6.64, 7.16, 9.5, 9.33, 21.2, 21.18
Magic tricks, 16.10, 24.8
Magicians, 6.52, 8.21, 9.5, 9.20, 24.8
Maine, 9.36
Makeup, 22.5
Malcolm X, 13.49, 13.58
Mali, 12.51
Mammals, 18.18
Manassas (Virginia), 11.66
Mandela, Nelson, 15.37
Manzanar, 12.74
Maps, 5.34, 24.19
Marriage, 1.102
   arranged, 11.19, 11.71
Mars, 16.20
Martha's Vineyard (Massachusetts), 10.8
Massachusetts, history of, 13.45
Match making, 2.69
Math, 24.26
Mazes, 16.25, 24.19
Media, 15.33
Medical ethics, 15.32, 19.9, 19.31
Medical research, 19.26, 19.27
Medicine, 17.34, 19.9
   history of, 12.82
Melville, Herman, 13.65
Mendilow, Myriam, 13.17
Mensa, 24.3
Mental illness, 1.43, 19.29
Mermaids, 6.28
Merrimack, The, 12.11
Meteorology, 16.2
Mexican Americans, 3.78, 15.7, 21.26
Mexico, 5.1, 5.8, 11.48, 14.9, 22.35
   art, 22.35
   Revolution, 12.75
   War of Independence, 11.23
Miccosukee, 17.21
Mice, 6.22, 6.29
Michelangelo, 13.22
Microbiology, 17.19, 18.20, 18.34

Microscopes, 16.24
Midas, 6.6
Middle Ages, 5.39, 5.40, 5.41, 6.59, 11.12, 11.19, 11.69, 11.79, 12.13, 12.18, 12.40, 12.64
Migrant workers, 11.76, 15.7
Military, 1.54
Mime, 22.5
Mind control, 7.14, 7.27, 9.7, 9.17, 9.19
Miners and mining, 12.14, 24.22
Minnesota, 17.1, 18.2
Missing children, 1.73
Mississippi, 11.68
Missouri, 11.42
Moby Dick, 13.65
Mohave, 12.54
Monarch butterflies, 18.21
Monet, Claude, 22.25
Money, 2.13, 10.14
Monitor, The, 12.11
Mononucleosis, 19.27
Monsters, 5.27, 9.55, 13.53, 20.19
Montgomery, L. M., 13.5, 13.11
Monuments, 3.60
  prehistoric, 12.50
Moon, 16.14
Mother Teresa, 13.55
Mothers, 1.23
  and daughters, 1.20, 1.28, 1.40, 1.47, 1.76, 1.83, 1.89, 1.93, 1.96, 1.98, 1.101, 1.113, 3.13, 3.49, 8.18, 11.37, 11.39, 13.50, 20.28
  step-, 1.76, 8.1, 8.7, 8.8, 11.43
Mountain climbing, 3.57, 10.29
Movies, 22.2
Moving, 1.15, 1.32, 1.47, 1.68, 1.71, 1.77, 1.113, 2.36, 2.50, 3.32, 3.34, 11.42, 11.82
Mozart, Wolfgang Amadeus, 13.22
Muir, John, 13.20
Mule trains, 11.10
Mullin, Chris, 23.9
Multiple personalities, 1.39
Mummies, 9.11, 10.22, 21.13, 21.20
Murder, 1.97, 3.74, 6.49, 8.4, 8.7, 8.9, 8.11, 8.14, 8.22, 8.23, 9.14, 9.16, 9.18, 9.23, 9.27, 9.30, 9.33, 9.35, 9.47, 9.49, 9.51, 9.52, 11.22, 11.85, 12.7
Muscular and skeletal system, 19.5, 19.6
Muscular dystrophy, 2.26
Museums, 12.5
Music, 1.106, 3.21, 5.13, 5.21, 9.53, 13.47, 22.7, 22.13, 22.17, 22.19, 22.23
  history of, 22.13
  instruments, 22.7
  musicians, 1.67, 8.8, 13.2, 13.22, 13.37, 13.41, 13.47, 13.57, 22.26
Muskogee, 5.5
Mussolini, 11.14
Myers, Walter Dean, 20.3, 22.20
Myrdal, Alva, 13.55
Mysteries, 2.40, 4.2, 4.12, 6.7, 6.24, 6.32, 6.35, 6.46, 6.64, 8.1–8.26, 9.1, 9.11, 9.22, 9.23, 9.26, 9.27, 9.32, 9.44, 9.48, 9.49, 9.54, 9.57, 10.22, 10.35, 11.70, 13.2, 21.18, 21.22
  scientific, 16.30
Myths, 5.2, 6.65
  Australian, 5.24
  Greek, 5.25, 5.38, 5.46, 6.1
  Norse, 9.22

Namib Desert, 17.4
Namibia, 3.4
Napoleonic era, 12.63
Nation of Islam, 13.49, 13.58
National Museum of American Art, 20.22
National parks, 11.62, 13.20, 17.31
Native Americans, 1.23, 1.78, 1.91, 3.5, 3.12, 3.40, 3.62, 4.8, 5.5, 6.7, 9.24, 10.15, 10.16, 10.20, 10.37, 11.21, 11.24, 11.55, 11.57, 11.84, 12.20, 12.25, 12.43, 12.54, 12.68, 12.72, 13.8, 13.21, 13.39, 13.60, 14.3, 14.6, 14.13–14.15, 15.17, 17.34, 18.2, 20.14. *See also* specific peoples.
Naturalists, 13.3, 13.20, 13.23, 17.18, 22.27
Nature, 17.5
Nature poems, 20.14, 20.20, 20.24, 20.32
Navaho, 3.62, 12.54, 21.19
Naval battles, 12.11
Navy, Royal British, 12.63
Navy vessels, 12.11
Nazi Germany, 11.61, 12.39
NBA, 23.19
Near-Earth objects, 16.32
Negro Leagues, 4.11, 23.2, 23.16
Neo-Nazis, 3.68
Neolithic Age, 12.50
Nervous system, 19.6
New Deal, 12.78
New England, 1.65
New Mexico, 18.9, 21.19
New York, 13.72
New York City, 1.63, 14.6, 17.1

New York City Ballet, 22.3
New Zealand, 1.12, 10.24
Newspapers, 3.54
Nez Perce, 11.55
Nickelodeon, 24.10
Nigeria, 15.2
Nightmares, 7.3, 9.14, 9.55, 10.11
Noah's Ark, 24.37
Nobel Prize winners, 13.9, 13.46, 13.50, 13.55, 13.71
Nonsense, 6.15
Nonverbal communication, 24.9
Nonviolence, 15.29
North Africa, 12.4
North Carolina, 13.34
Northern Ireland, 13.55
Nuclear accidents, 7.7, 15.12
Nurses, 7.15
Nursing homes, 1.61
Nutrition, 19.18, 19.25

O'Keeffe, Georgia, 22.33, 22.34, 22.35
O'Neal, Shaquille, 23.18
Occupational therapy, 19.28
Oceanography, 18.13, 18.34
Oceans, 17.15, 17.27
Oil spills, 17.28
Olympic athletes, 23.12, 23.14
Oral history, 5.42, 12.16
Oregon, 11.5
Oregon Territory, 11.83
Oregon Trail, 10.16, 10.17, 11.57
Organ donation and transplants, 19.9
Orphan trains, 12.27
Orphans, 1.73, 1.105, 2.2, 3.66, 6.16, 6.24, 6.51, 7.6, 9.56, 10.9, 10.12, 10.19, 10.37, 10.39, 11.7, 11.28, 11.70, 11.78, 12.27, 13.29
Ospreys, 6.46
Outdoor activities, 23.17, 24.35
Owls, 6.37, 18.32
Ozone layer, 17.16

Pacifist movement, 15.29
Paige, Satchel, 23.14
Painting, 13.68, 22.6, 22.15, 22.35, 22.37, 22.38. See also Art.
Paintings, 20.22, 22.25, 22.26, 22.27, 22.30, 22.31, 22.32, 22.34, 22.36, 22.39, 24.37
Paiute, 12.72
Pakistan, 1.102, 13.56

Pancho Villa, 12.75
Paper cuttings, 22.4
Parallel worlds, 6.45, 7.8, 7.23, 7.24
Paralysis, 3.29
Parapsychology, 9.31
Parenthood, 3.27, 15.35, 21.4
  teenage, 1.114, 3.23
Parents, 1.37, 1.58, 7.8, 19.4, 21.11
  step-, 22.29
Parks, Rosa, 12.76
Parody, 5.36
Patriotism, 12.71, 20.22
Pawnee, 12.54
Peace, 13.46, 13.55, 15.11, 20.1, 20.30
Peace Corps, 15.2
Pearl Harbor, 11.72
Peck, Richard, 13.31
Peer pressure, 1.45, 1.84, 1.96, 2.5, 2.18, 2.21, 2.27, 2.35, 2.42, 2.59, 2.65, 2.66, 3.6, 3.25, 3.30, 3.46, 3.48, 3.54, 3.72, 10.32
Pele, 23.14
Pen pals, 1.72
Penguins, 18.8
Pennsylvania, 14.2
Perkins, Frances, 13.15
Persian Gulf War, 3.38, 15.28
Pesticides, 17.22, 19.25
Pets, 1.19, 1.46, 1.48, 3.75, 18.19
Phobias, 3.30, 10.33
Photography, 2.33, 3.44, 12.24, 12.87, 13.66, 14.2, 14.5, 16.7, 17.4, 18.3, 20.21, 20.26, 22.33
Photojournalism, 14.5
Physical science, 16.16
Physical therapy, 19.28
Physicists, 13.50
Physics, 16.5, 16.8–16.10, 16.15, 16.16, 16.23, 16.26, 16.29
Picasso, Pablo, 22.15
Picture books for older readers, 5.5, 5.8, 5.11, 5.12, 5.15, 5.17, 5.18, 5.21, 5.23, 5.47, 6.10, 11.60, 12.10, 13.63, 13.64, 22.31
Pigs, 1.19
Pilots, 13.67
Pioneers, 11.6, 11.27, 11.34, 11.42, 11.43, 11.57, 11.78, 11.82, 12.7, 12.27, 12.67, 20.29
Pippin, Horace, 22.22
Pirates, 7.34, 10.34, 11.6, 11.48
Plains Indians, 12.54. See also specific peoples.

Planets, 16.1, 16.4, 16.13, 17.14, 17.20, 17.27
Plants, 17.2, 17.10, 17.20. *See also* Botany.
Poe, Edgar Allan, 13.2
Poetry, 6.63, 15.7, 17.13, 20.1–20.33, 22.20
Poets, 13.40, 20.11
Pokot, 14.18
Police state, 7.18
Polio, 1.57
Politics, 3.4, 3.61, 13.13, 13.15, 13.25, 13.62, 15.9, 15.19, 15.34, 24.7
Pollution, 7.17, 7.18, 17.8, 17.12, 17.21, 17.32
Polygamy, 14.18
Pony Express, 10.15, 12.83
Pop culture, 15.48, 22.17, 22.36, 24.33
Popularity, 1.41, 2.12, 2.34, 2.42, 2.45, 2.60, 3.57, 3.79
Potato Famine, 14.4
Pottery, 11.71
Poverty, 1.114, 3.21, 11.32, 13.64, 15.7, 15.11
Powers, Harriet, 22.22
Pranks, 2.1, 2.25, 3.15
Prayers, 20.14
   in public schools, 15.25
Pregnancy, 3.23, 19.17, 19.24
   teenage, 15.35
Prehistoric era, 1.29, 6.11, 6.12, 7.33, 10.5, 12.68
Prejudice, 1.20, 1.99, 2.28, 2.61, 2.65, 3.14, 3.35, 3.53, 3.59, 3.64, 3.78, 4.6, 6.39, 11.40, 12.9, 12.17, 12.88, 14.17, 15.10, 15.30, 15.47, 21.1, 23.22
Prelutsky, Jack, 20.15
Presidential inauguration, 20.1
Presidents, U.S., 12.55, 12.78, 13.2, 13.10, 13.27, 13.44, 13.48, 15.6, 15.9, 15.34
Princesses, 6.36, 6.61
Prison, 3.20, 8.1
Privacy, 15.21
Pro Football Hall of Fame, 23.4
Problem solving, 5.14, 19.7
Prohibition, 11.63
Psychic powers, 7.19, 7.20, 7.21, 9.42, 9.46
Pueblo, 12.54
Puerto Rico, 15.3
Puppets, 6.8
Puzzles, 23.7, 23.8, 24.3, 24.26, 24.37
Pyramids, 22.16

Qin Shih-huan, 22.21

Quests, 1.78, 3.5, 5.39, 6.2, 6.4, 6.5, 6.23, 6.51, 6.53, 6.57, 7.12, 7.16, 7.19, 7.20, 7.21, 11.24
Quilting, 11.65
Quintuplets, 1.85

Rabbits, 6.30
Rabies, 18.19, 19.27
Race relations, 1.117, 2.70, 2.72, 3.55, 3.59, 3.83, 4.6, 11.18, 11.32, 11.37, 11.49, 11.68, 12.8, 12.53, 15.30, 20.1, 20.5
Racism, 1.5, 1.99, 12.37, 12.46, 12.52, 12.70, 15.10, 15.47. *See also* Prejudice.
Radio broadcasting, 22.14
Railroads, 5.17, 5.37, 11.85, 12.14, 12.23, 12.59, 12.90, 21.9
   Transcontinental, 11.85, 12.23, 14.1
Rain forests, 10.1, 17.17, 17.27, 18.35, 20.20
Ransome, James E., 20.13
Rap music, 5.21, 22.17
Raphael, 22.25
Reagan, Ronald, 12.55
Recipes, 12.18, 12.31, 14.14, 16.11, 19.18, 24.2, 24.6, 24.21, 24.25
Reconstruction era, 12.53
Recycling, 17.8
Reference books, 12.28, 12.43, 12.94, 15.18, 15.49, 17.2, 17.5, 18.27, 18.38, 19.30, 23.6, 24.1, 24.4, 24.7, 24.29, 24.38
Refugees, 1.36, 11.8, 11.14, 11.16, 11.20, 11.41, 11.61, 13.33, 13.70
Relationships, 1.75, 2.41, 2.67, 3.7, 3.47, 11.79, 20.4, 20.18, 21.1, 21.3, 21.11, 21.23
Religion, 3.69, 3.76, 6.5
Remarriage, 1.5, 1.40
Rembrandt, 11.30, 22.15, 22.25, 22.32
Renaissance, 12.40, 22.32
Reno, Janet, 15.19
Reproduction and the reproductive system, 19.6, 19.17
Reptiles, 18.15, 18.22
Respiratory system, 19.5
Responsibility, 3.15, 10.32
Revenge, 2.44, 3.33, 9.20, 9.30, 9.39, 10.30
Rhymes, 20.27
Richards, Ann, 15.19
Riddles, 5.30, 5.35, 6.23, 20.27, 21.16, 24.20, 24.24, 24.28
Right to die, 15.32, 19.13

Ringgold, Faith, 22.34
Rio Grande Middle School, 21.19
Riots, 15.5
Ripken, Cal, Jr., 23.9
Rituals, 3.8, 14.10, 14.13, 14.14
Rivers, 17.21
Rivers, Glenn "Doc," 23.19
Robinson, David, 23.5, 23.9
Robinson, Jackie, 23.22
Robots, 7.33, 7.34, 16.22
Rock-and-roll music, 22.13
Roller coasters, 1.30
Roma, 14.17
Romance, 1.7, 1.58, 1.108, 2.6, 2.7, 2.16, 2.19, 2.20, 2.29, 2.34, 2.37, 2.39, 2.45, 2.46, 2.54, 2.59, 2.61, 2.68, 2.69, 2.74, 3.19, 3.47, 6.48, 9.2, 9.9, 11.23, 11.35, 20.4, 20.10, 21.11, 21.18, 21.23
Rome, ancient, 12.13, 12.18
Roosevelt, Eleanor, 13.29
Roosevelt, Franklin Delano, 12.55, 12.78
Runaways, 1.10, 3.40, 3.58, 3.84, 7.18, 10.7, 10.26
Running, 4.5

Saar, Betty, 22.30
Sanders, Barry, 23.9
Sanders, Deion, 23.5
Sarajevo, 13.24
Schizophrenia, 19.29
School, 1.54, 1.88, 1.96, 2.1, 2.4, 2.12, 2.17, 2.23, 2.30, 2.36, 2.40, 2.41, 2.56, 2.60, 2.62, 3.3, 3.27, 3.48, 3.78, 7.13, 7.22, 7.25, 8.8, 15.30, 19.7, 20.15, 21.7, 24.24
School, boarding, 2.71
School of American Ballet, 22.1
School, prep, 3.81
Schools, medical, 12.82
Schwarzenegger, Arnold, 23.12
Science, 16.7, 16.24, 17.2, 18.27
    projects, 16.16
Science fiction, 21.12
Scientific terms, 16.28
Scientists, 13.1, 13.3, 13.9, 13.23, 13.57, 16.28, 16.31
Sculpture, 22.6, 22.11, 22.21, 22.30, 22.38
    mobile, 22.18. *See also* Art.
Sea lions, 17.30
Sea snakes, 18.7
Sea turtles, 1.51
Seals, 18.15
Seasons, 20.24, 24.21

Secret identities, 1.93
Secrets, 1.12, 1.32, 1.55
Segregation, 11.37, 15.25
Segregation, racial, 23.2
Self-esteem, 1.41, 1.82, 1.85, 1.87, 1.92, 1.98, 1.102, 2.5, 2.14, 2.17, 2.18, 2.20, 2.29, 2.37, 2.39, 2.42, 2.49, 2.52, 2.57, 2.59, 3.3, 3.6, 3.12, 3.19, 3.20, 3.37, 3.39, 3.52, 3.61, 3.67, 3.73, 3.75, 6.16, 15.30
Self-reliance, 10.21
Separation of church and state, 15.25
Sequoyah, 13.39
Serengeti National Park, 18.25
Sex discrimination, 12.80, 13.25, 13.62, 15.18, 15.31. *See also* Prejudice.
Sexual abuse, 1.39, 3.63, 19.17
Sexual harassment, 3.43, 3.48, 3.61, 15.18, 15.31, 20.2
Sexuality, 2.63, 19.4, 19.24, 19.32, 21.1
    and health, 19.17, 19.32
    and relationships, 19.1, 19.3
    and responsibility, 19.17
Sexually transmitted diseases, 19.4, 19.17
Shakers, 12.8
Shakespeare, William, 2.19, 22.28, 22.29
Shape-changers, 6.37, 6.39
Share croppers, 11.68
Sharks, 10.2
Shaw, Robert Gould, 13.12
Sheep ranching, 1.82
Shelley, Mary, 13.53
Ships, 13.6
Shipwrecks, 12.48
Shoplifting, 3.36
Shopping malls, 2.50
Short stories, 6.63, 17.13, 21.1–21.29
Shoshoni, 10.15
Siblings, 21.7
Sign language, 12.88
Silk, 12.79
Sioux, 3.5, 13.60
Sirens, 6.50
Sisters, 1.40, 1.45, 1.53, 1.63, 1.65, 1.92, 1.111, 1.116, 2.49, 6.38, 8.20, 9.2, 9.13, 10.18, 11.1, 11.17, 20.28, 22.1
Skateboarding, 3.2
Skating, 6.17, 23.20
Skeletal system, 19.6
Skinheads, 3.68
Slavery, 5.28, 6.33, 10.36, 11.11, 11.27, 11.28, 11.30, 11.40, 11.47, 11.51, 11.58, 11.75, 11.77, 11.80, 12.6, 12.35, 12.38, 13.21, 13.30, 13.45

Subject Index

Sleator, William, 13.59
Small towns, 20.25
Snakes, 6.40, 18.7, 18.15
Snakes, garter, 18.22
Soccer, 3.53, 4.13
Social activism, 15.27
Social issues, 15.5, 15.11, 15.15, 15.22, 15.23, 15.24, 15.25, 15.27, 15.31, 15.32, 15.38, 15.39, 15.40, 15.41, 15.45, 15.48, 15.49, 19.13, 24.10
Socialist societies, 7.14
Solar System, 16.1
Songhay, 12.51
Songs, 5.7, 5.10, 5.28, 12.31, 12.71, 12.72, 20.12, 20.14
South Africa, 3.55, 3.83, 13.56, 15.37
South America, 12.30, 14.16, 17.17
South Carolina, 1.94, 11.51
South Dakota, 11.36
Soviet Union, 14.12
Space, 16.14, 16.17, 16.30
    exploration, 16.6, 16.19, 19.20
    shuttle, 16.6
    stations, 16.20
    travel, 7.2, 7.11
Spain, 10.18
Speeches, 12.72, 13.48
Spells, 6.49, 6.54, 6.56, 6.64
Spice routes, 12.65
Spies, 8.3
Sports, 2.20, 2.35, 2.46, 13.19, 20.7, 20.10, 23.7, 24.35. *See also* specific sports.
    business, 23.23
    figures, 13.57, 23.4, 23.5, 23.9, 23.12, 23.13, 23.14, 23.16, 23.21, 23.24
    poems, 20.7
    science, 16.15
    statistics, 23.10, 23.21
    women in, 23.15
Squirrels, 6.30, 6.41
St. Petri, 11.64
Stafford, William, 20.32
Stalking, 9.39
Stamp collecting, 24.12
Stars and stargazing, 16.13, 16.18, 16.21
Statehood, 15.3
States, 12.89
Statistics, 23.6, 24.38
Stereotyping, 11.73
Steroids, 19.22
Stetson, John B., 12.33
Stevenson, Robert Louis, 12.59, 13.53
Stock market, 1.95
Stoker, Bram, 13.53

Stone Age tribes, 12.34
Storytelling, 5.1, 5.3–5.7, 5.9, 5.10, 5.12, 5.13, 5.15, 5.16, 5.18, 5.19, 5.21, 5.28, 5.29, 5.32, 5.42, 21.6, 21.9
Stowe, Harriet Beecher, 13.30
Strauss, Levi, 12.33
Student life, 19.7
Stuttering, 3.9
Suicide, 1.18, 1.76, 1.97, 2.24, 2.58, 3.18, 3.19, 3.44, 9.40, 19.11, 19.19, 19.31, 20.10, 21.4
    assisted, 19.13
Super heroes, 8.3
Supernatural, 21.5, 21.6, 21.8, 21.16, 21.17, 21.20
Superstitions, 5.33
Supreme Court, 15.25
Survivors, 11.81, 21.22
Suspense, 9.30, 9.35, 22.2
Sweden, 11.53
Swenson, May, 13.40

Tails, animal, 18.31
Tall tales, 5.12, 5.17, 5.37
Tanzania, 18.25
Teachers, 2.14, 2.56, 2.69, 7.22
Technology, 16.22, 16.24, 16.33, 17.2
Teenagers, 20.25
Telecommunication, 16.27
Telephones, 16.27
Telescopes, 16.21
Television programs, 2.10
Temperature, 16.16
Term papers, 24.23
Terrorism, 3.33
Texas, 11.49
Thanksgiving, 20.6
Theater, 2.19, 2.29, 22.28. *See also* Actors, Drama.
Thorpe, Jim, 23.12
Tiananmen Square, 12.12, 12.45
Tidal waves, 10.24
Time, 16.3, 16.17, 16.31
Time travel, 6.59, 7.1, 7.5, 7.6, 7.12, 7.13, 7.15, 7.16, 7.19, 7.20, 7.21, 7.23, 7.24, 7.28, 7.29, 7.32–7.34, 9.5, 9.8, 9.43
Timelines, 12.62
Titanic, The, 7.20, 13.6
Toads, 18.29
Tombs, 12.21, 21.20, 22.21
Toxic waste, 3.45, 7.27, 8.15
Track and field, 2.46, 4.5, 4.6
Trade routes, 12.79

Traditions, multicultural, 11.47, 14.10
Tragedies, 3.38
Trail of Tears, 12.25
Trains. *See* Railroads.
Transportation, 12.61, 20.17
Travel, 14.5, 24.19, 24.20, 24.31
Treasure, 5.34, 6.30, 10.30, 10.34, 12.3
Trees, 17.11, 17.29
Trials, 12.37, 15.25
Tribal life, 3.8, 15.36
Trickster tales, 5.15, 5.16, 5.29, 5.43
Trivia, 23.7, 23.8, 24.38
Trojan War, 5.38
Truman, Harry S, 12.55, 13.27
Tuberculosis, 19.27
Tundra swans, 18.24
Turkey, 3.34
Tutankhamen, 12.21
Twins, 1.70, 1.92, 1.109, 2.21, 2.64, 3.29, 8.19, 9.12, 9.24, 22.1

Ukraine, 15.12
Ultraviolet radiation, 17.16
Uncle Remus, 5.16
Uncles, 1.66, 11.20
Undead, 9.1
Underground Railroad, 11.80, 12.38
Unexplained phenomena, 9.29
UNICEF, 17.6
Unicorns, 6.21, 6.38, 6.45, 6.63, 21.8
Unidentified Flying Objects (UFOs), 16.12
United States
    frontier, 10.15, 10.16, 10.17, 10.30, 11.10, 11.65, 11.75, 11.83, 12.7, 12.56
    history, 20.6, 20.26, 20.29
Urban problems, 3.31
Utes, 10.20

Vacations, 2.8
Vampires, 9.21, 9.34, 9.41
Van Gogh, Vincent, 22.25
Vegetarianism, 19.18
Vehicles, 20.17
Ventriloquism, 8.12
Venus (planet), 16.4
Veterans, 1.104
    Vietnam, 2.48, 20.9
Veterinarians, 18.9, 18.17
Vice Presidents, U.S., 13.13

Victims' rights, 15.8
Victorian era, 11.1, 11.2, 11.3, 13.14
Video games, 9.28
Vietnam, 5.44, 20.6
Vietnam War, 1.104, 11.4, 11.35, 12.91, 13.13
Vietnamese Americans, 1.36
Vikings, 9.22
Violence, 15.5, 15.10, 15.39, 15.47, 20.10
Violins, 1.67, 22.7
Virginia, 11.77
Virtual reality, 7.26
Visions, 9.52, 9.56
Volcanoes, 10.2
Volunteering, 24.10
Voodoo, 9.4

Wagon trains, 10.17
Walker, Margaret, 20.3
Wallenberg, Raoul, 13.42
Waorani, 14.16
War, 10.10, 12.77, 13.24, 13.55, 14.11, 15.11, 15.29, 20.10, 20.30
Warships, 12.63
Washington, George, 12.55
Washington, Martha, 13.52
Water, 17.32
    conservation, 17.7
Watson, James, 13.9
Weapons, 12.29
Weasels, 6.46
Weather, 16.2, 16.16
Wendigo, 9.19
Werewolves, 6.49, 9.33
West Indian Americans, 14.1
West Indies, 21.2
Westward expansion, 11.21
Westward movement, 10.17, 11.9, 11.82, 12.7, 12.14, 12.17, 12.47, 12.56
Wetlands, 17.12, 17.27
Whales, 12.10, 18.29
White, E. B., 13.32
Whitman, Walt, 20.22
Whitney Museum of American Art, 22.18
Wilder, Laura, 11.42
Wilderness, 13.20, 17.21
Wildlife, 3.16, 17.1, 17.4, 17.30, 17.31, 18.25, 18.9
    photography, 18.3
Winter, 20.24
Wishes, 6.27, 7.6, 11.44

Witches, 5.22, 6.3, 6.32, 6.47, 6.48, 6.51, 6.54, 6.55, 6.60, 6.64, 7.10, 8.25, 9.6, 11.31
  trials, 11.38
Wolves, 3.16, 6.34, 6.44, 10.13, 18.3, 18.15, 18.32
Women, 3.43, 7.6, 11.26, 11.73, 12.56, 12.80, 13.15, 13.17, 13.25, 13.29, 13.34, 13.46, 13.51, 13.62, 14.8, 14.13, 15.19, 15.23, 15.42, 19.12, 19.20, 20.2, 20.29, 21.27
  in sports, 23.15
Women's rights movement, 11.26, 12.80
Woodcuts, 12.10
Woodworkers and woodworking, 22.22, 22.24
World records, 24.38
World War I, 12.41, 12.44
World War II, 8.3, 10.38, 11.8, 11.14, 11.20, 11.25, 11.29, 11.45, 11.56, 11.64, 11.72, 11.81, 12.9, 12.32, 12.39, 12.74, 12.77, 13.35, 13.42, 13.54, 13.68, 13.71, 18.37, 20.31, 23.15
Wounded Knee, 12.20
Wrestling, 23.11
Writers, 2.32, 2.74, 8.16
Writing, 1.22, 2.58, 13.11, 24.14, 24.23, 24.30, 24.34
  poetry, 20.11

Yamaguchi, Kristi, 13.57
Yellowstone National Park, 8.19, 17.31
Yoruba, 11.71
Yugoslavia, 14.11, 20.30

Zapata, Emiliano, 12.75
Zassenhaus, Hiltgunt, 13.71
Zeppelins, 12.81
Zimbabwe, 7.4
Zindel, Paul, 13.72
Zombies, 9.4

Editors

Barbara G. Samuels is associate professor of language arts and reading and director of the Greater Houston Area Writing Project at the University of Houston–Clear Lake. She is past president of the Assembly on Adolescent Literature of NCTE (ALAN) and is a frequent contributor of articles about young adult literature to books and journals.

G. Kylene Beers is a former middle school language arts teacher who has a doctorate with a specialization in juvenile literature. She teaches adolescent literature, children's literature, and reading courses at several universities and is a regular presenter at ALAN workshops and NCTE and IRA conventions. She is currently co-editing a book on middle school readers with Barbara Samuels.

About the Committee

Richard F. Abrahamson is professor of literature for children and young adults at the University of Houston. A past president of ALAN and a former member of NCTE's editorial board, Abrahamson co-edited the 1988 edition of *Books for You.*

Steven D. Bauer is a published short story writer who came to teaching late, but started reading early. Born in Pensacola, Florida, he has lived in Africa and Asia and currently teaches fifth grade. Good books, he believes, are essential to life.

Lois Buckman is the librarian for Moorhead Junior High. She is a regular contributor to the Young Adult Review column for *The Journal of Adolescent and Adult Literacy* (formerly the *Journal of Reading*). She has served on the ALAN Board of Directors.

Betty Carter teaches young adult literature in the School of Library and Information Studies at Texas Woman's University. Along with Richard Abrahamson, she co-edited the 1988 edition of *Books for You* and is a past president of ALAN.

Claudia H. DeShay, formerly a children's librarian for the city of Dallas, Texas, is a full-time doctoral student in the School of Library and Information Studies at Texas Woman's University.

Margaret H. Hill is assistant professor of reading and language arts at the University of Houston–Clear Lake. A former middle school teacher, Peggy's early work in biology has led to her current strong interest in environmental concerns.

Mary Beth Hines teaches courses in English education at Indiana University. She is co-author of (forthcoming) *Feminisms for Teachers.* Her research focuses on the development of new pedagogical frameworks for the teaching and learning of literature.

Marvin Hoffman, clinical professor of education at Rice University, is a high school English teacher in the Houston Independent School District. He is also director of the Rice University/HISD Writing Project.

Be Be Hood is educational specialist for the Region IV Education Service Center in Houston, Texas. Previously, she was reading department chair for a large middle school in the Alief Independent School District. She is currently pursuing a doctoral degree in literature, language arts, and reading at the University of Houston.

Rosemary Oliphant Ingham is professor of education at Belmont University in Nashville, Tennessee, where she teaches courses in children's and adolescent literature. She is a former member of the ALAN Board of Directors.

Lee Kobayashi, a former school librarian, teaches children's literature at the University of Houston.

Karen S. Kutiper is associate professor of curriculum and instruction at Southwest State University, where she teaches reading and language arts methods courses.

Teri S. Lesesne, a former middle school teacher, teaches children's and young adult literature classes at Sam Houston State University. Her book reviews appear regularly in *The Journal of Adolescent and Adult Literacy* (formerly the *Journal of Reading*) and the *ALAN Review*. She has served on the ALAN Board of Directors.

Hollis Lowery-Moore currently teaches reading courses for students seeking middle school and secondary certification. She has taught middle school and junior high English and reading and is involved in literacy staff development at those levels. Hollis presents at local, state, and national conferences and has published in state and national journals.

Karen Ferris Morgan teaches courses in storytelling and children's literature at Texas Woman's University. She has taught or worked as a school librarian in Arizona, New York, California, and Brazil. She also manages STORYTELL, a bulletin board on the Internet, is on the National Storytelling Association's Research Committee, and is associate director of the Texas Storytelling Festival.

Steven J. Rakow is associate professor of science education at the University of Houston–Clear Lake, where he specializes in middle school education. He is also president of the Science Teachers Association of Texas.

Judith Romo is an eighth-grade reading teacher at Southmore Intermediate School in Pasadena, Texas.

Rosemary Smith has spent fourteen years teaching seventh- and eighth-grade language arts and fourteen years as a librarian in the Alief Independent School District.

Mary Snyder is a librarian and teacher specializing in health-related issues for children and young adults. Her particular areas of interest are in sex education and AIDS education for young people.

Marti Turner is head librarian at River Oaks Baptist School in Houston, Texas.

Eleanore S. Tyson teaches courses in language arts, children's literature, and reading at the University of Houston.

Judy Mayne Wallis, a former elementary teacher, is language arts and social studies coordinator for Alief Independent School District. She teaches courses in reading and children's literature at several area universities.

About the Committee

Maureen White is assistant professor of education at the University of Houston–Clear Lake. She teaches young adult and children's literature classes and has served on the Caldecott and Batchelder Award Committees for the American Library Association.

Patricia Potter Wilson is associate professor in the School of Education at the University of Houston–Clear Lake, where she teaches courses in school librarianship. She is co-author of *Happenings: Developing Successful Programs for School Libraries.*

Other Booklists from NCTE

BOOKS FOR YOU
An Annotated Booklist for Senior High Students
1995 Edition
Leila Christenbury, editor
With a foreword by
Jerry Spinelli

Whether your students are interested in space exploration or civil rights, love stories or mysteries, they are sure to find something in the 1995 edition of *Books for You* that will appeal to them. With over 1,000 titles included, there's something for every reader—and plenty for high school teachers and librarians to select from. The twenty-one reviewers—a diverse group of public and private school teachers, administrators, and librarians—selected these titles from some 5,000 received during the creation of *Books for You*. The books are grouped by subject into thirty-five thematic chapters, including "Adventure and Survival," "Dating and Sexual Awareness," "The Holocaust," and "Self-Help: Your Health and Your Body." More than 150 titles with a multicultural focus—each of which also appears in one of the topical chapters—are highlighted in an additional chapter called "Multicultural Themes." Every booklist entry includes full bibliographic information, a concise summary of the book's contents, and a notation about any awards the book has won. Author, title, and subject indexes will help readers locate a favorite author or find more books on a particular topic. An appendix that lists winners of major book awards and a directory of publishers are also included. 432 pp. 1995. Grades 9–12. ISBN 0-8141-0367-7.
No. 03677-4019 $21.95 ($15.95)

KALEIDOSCOPE
A Multicultural Booklist for Grades K–8
First Edition
Rudine Sims Bishop,
editor

This inaugural edition of *Kaleidoscope* celebrates cultural diversity with annotations of nearly 400 books published between 1990 and 1992. The booklist focuses on people of color, especially African Americans, Asian Americans, Hispanic Americans/Latinos, and Native Americans. Some books set in countries outside the United States are also included. Whenever possible, annotations identify the particular country, nationality, or ethnic group of the characters or setting. To highlight both commonalities and differences among cultures, chapters group nonfiction books by genre or theme rather than by cultural group. Fiction entries are divided primarily by age level, with books for the very young, picture books, fiction for middle readers, and novels for older readers. A detailed subject index will prove invaluable to teachers and librarians in developing teaching units or in locating specific books. Also included are a list of resources pertaining to multicultural literature, a listing of award-winning books, a directory of publishers, and indexes of authors, illustrators, and titles. 170 pp. 1994. Grades K–8. ISBN 0-8141-2543-3.
No. 25433-4019 $14.95 ($10.95)

To order these and other
NCTE publications
or for membership information,
please call 1-800-369-6283.

National Council of Teachers of English
1111 W. Kenyon Road, Urbana, Illinois 61801-1096